HISTORY OF RUSSIA

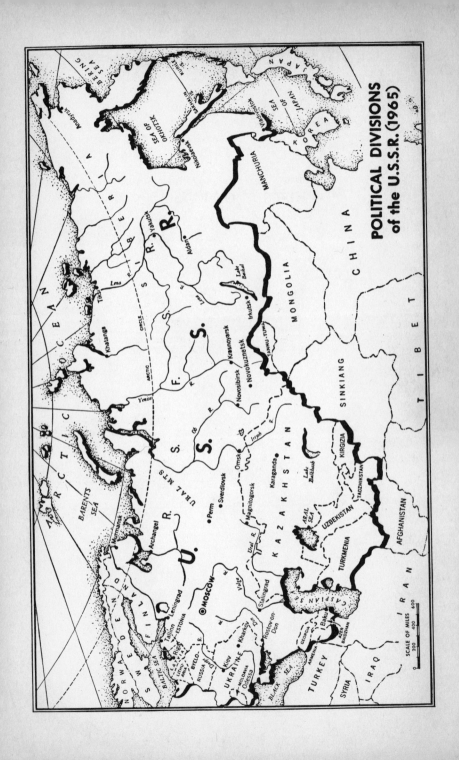

POLITICAL DIVISIONS of the U.S.S.R. (1965)

A
HISTORY OF
RUSSIA

SIXTH EDITION

BY

WALTHER KIRCHNER

BARNES & NOBLE BOOKS
A DIVISION OF HARPER & ROW, PUBLISHERS
New York, Cambridge, Philadelphia, San Francisco
London, Mexico City, São Paulo, Sydney

LIBRARY OF CONGRESS CATALOG CARD NUMBER: 76–21169

STANDARD BOOK NUMBER: 06–460169–2

84 85 86   10 9 8 7 6 5

PREFACE

In his *Geschichte Russlands,* Professor Valentin Gitermann of Zurich, Switzerland, refers to the "special charm and attraction of the broadly flowing stream of Russian history." It has been my endeavor to preserve this very attraction in a book that by its nature must limit space and must treat only the factual information essential for an understanding and for a balanced judgment of past and present-day events in our great neighbor country, Russia.

In order to assure brevity and clarity without missing the spirit of Russia or losing a sense of the complexities of life (ever-present complexities which can be unraveled only in retrospect by historians), particular care has been taken to supplement the text with appropriate appendices. The chronological table, for instance, divulges by the very sequence of events the logical—and sometimes illogical—course of history and its influence on our lives. The maps reveal better than any description the causes and results of major trends. The index provides a biographical dictionary and a glossary of foreign terms, particularly useful, the writer hopes, in a book which cannot afford to identify persons or explain terms more than once. The bibliography directs attention to easily accessible material for more bibliographical information and for further study.

The book owes much to the untiring help of my friend Dr. Harold Bierck, of the Carnegie Institute of Technology, and of my wife. Neither of them being a Russian scholar, both have perused the manuscript from the point of view of the reader, leaving the responsibility for accuracy of information and fairness of emphasis to the author, but criticizing unsparingly and improving fundamentally the presentation of the material, its organization, and its comprehensibility. Thanks of the author are due also to Dr. W. O. Sypherd, University Professor of the University of Delaware, and to Dr. Raymond Lindgren of Vanderbilt University, who have offered many helpful suggestions. The assistance of Mr. Laurin Johnson, a graduate student at the University of Pennsylvania, who has contributed much research in the compilation of a number of historical maps, is herewith gratefully acknowledged.

The book does not intend either "to promote friendship" or "to voice warnings." It has no ulterior motive, good or bad. By a presentation of facts, it does hope to reduce ignorance and thereby prejudices of all shadings, and to enable the student of Russian affairs to arrive at conclusions and judgments of his own, based not on propaganda but upon investigation.

W.K.

ABOUT THE AUTHOR

Walther Kirchner is H. Rodney Sharp Professor of
History at the University of Delaware. He received his
B.A., M.A., and Ph.D. degrees from the University of
California at Los Angeles. He has held teaching posi-
tions at the University of California at Los Angeles,
the University of Pennsylvania, and Lehigh University.
Dr. Kirchner, a research specialist in Russian history,
has written *Rise of the Baltic Question* and *Jacob
Fries' Journey through Siberia*. He has also contributed numerous articles to leading historical peri-
odicals. In 1955 he was appointed as Member of the
Institute for Advanced Study at Princeton. Professor
Kirchner has spent a Fulbright year in Denmark, has
traveled extensively in Europe where he has lectured
at numerous universities, and has visited Russia. He is
the American editor of *Jahrbücher für Geschichte
Osteuropas*.

TABLE OF CONTENTS

MAPS AND CHARTS

1

BEGINNINGS AND FOUNDATIONS OF RUSSIAN HISTORY

Significant Dates

Prehistoric Civilization . . . . 8th–6th Cent. B.C.
Invasions of Cimmerians,
    Scythians, Alans . . . 5th Cent. B.C.–1st Cent. A.D.
Invasion of Goths . . . . 2nd–4th Cent. A.D.
Invasions of Huns, Avars,
    Magyars . . . . 4th–7th Cent. A.D.
Slavs in Possession . . . . 8th Cent. A.D.

On the steps of the National Archives in Washington are engraved these words: WHAT IS PAST IS PROLOGUE. Taking such a premise very literally, historians have investigated the remotest past, delving back ten, twenty, or thirty thousand years into periods which witnessed climatic and geographic conditions very different from those prevailing in historical times. True, the strata formed in early ages have exercised an economic influence; but the "history" of a people begins properly with the appearance of man, and still more properly with his activities as known by us.

EARLIEST INHABITANTS

Primitive Man. The oldest traces of human life found in present-day European Russia date from the early Stone Age—from a

1

time after the violent heat and cold of the Tertiary period and the
ice ages had given way to equable weather. Such traces occur in
the regions of Kiev, in the Crimea, and on the banks of the Don
River. In the later Stone Age, man, accompanied by his friend the
dog, existed also farther north—on the Oka River, on the shores of
Lake Ladoga, and even as far north as present-day Archangel.
Instruments indicating his cultural level have been found, and they
reveal about the same accomplishments that prevailed in other
northern European regions during the same era. But tools of the
two succeeding periods, the Bronze and the Copper Ages, are inferior in design to those discovered in Western Europe. Findings
from the Iron Age, from the seventh century B.C. on, likewise do
not indicate a particularly developed sense of inventiveness in the
man then living in Eastern Europe. On the other hand, trading
ability seems to have supplemented what he lacked in art and craftsmanship, and intercourse with other parts of the world is known
to have developed. The distribution of objects uncovered in Eastern
Europe invites speculation as to trade connections which must have
existed between its peoples and those in the Danube region, in the
Mediterranean area, and in Persia, Babylon, and Egypt. Furs, horses,
and perhaps some agricultural products from the northern shores of
the Black Sea were exchanged for wine, vases, textiles, and other
manufactured goods produced by the higher civilizations encircling
the Mediterranean.

The First Known Peoples. Historical accounts are more precise from the Iron Age on. Names have been given to the peoples
inhabiting the regions north of the Black Sea, and we encounter
successively Cimmerians, Scythians, Sarmatians (who are difficult
to distinguish from their predecessors, the Scythians), and Alans,
who were living at the beginning of the Christian era. Although
these peoples seem to have supplemented their means of life by
plowing the earth and cultivating the land, almost all were nomads
occupied with hunting, fishing, and warring; and although the
Scythians produced interesting artistic weapons and utensils, all of
them were cruel "barbarians" in the eyes of the Greeks and Romans.
Their customs were primitive, their lives unstable. Asiatic influences
on them proved stronger than is generally surmised, despite the
infiltration of Greek ideas through Greek settlements on the northern shore of the Black Sea.

MIGRATIONS. The peoples moved back and forth, east as well as west. No general direction of their movement can be established. A real change occurred with the arrival of Germanic tribes in the first and second centuries A.D. These tribes, led by the Goths, brought more settled ways. They introduced a regional administration of their own and stimulated military reorganization and improvements. It is probable that the later capital of Kiev began its rise under them in the fourth century. They were also the first tribes on what was later Russian soil to accept the Christian faith, having been converted to it by Bishop Ulfilas. But their achievements were destroyed in the fourth century with the arrival of the Huns, who expelled them. The Huns were replaced by Avars in the sixth century, and these in turn by Magyars. Finally, in the eighth century, Turkish tribes—the Khazars—arrived, settling about the mouth of the Volga and farther west. Generally speaking, their upper class adopted the Jewish faith, their lower the Mohammedan; but some became Christians.

THE SLAVS. The movement of the Khazars came to a halt when they encountered Slavic peoples, speaking an Aryan language, who were spreading eastward and northward. Near the Baltic Sea, the Slavs came upon indigenous Lithuanians and, farther east, upon infiltrating Finns. Where the first settlement of these Slavs was made, it is impossible to say. Some students place it in the present-day Ukraine; others say it was in the region of the Carpathian Mountains; still others ascribe it to the region of the lower Danube. Certainly, like all tribes, they were rovers, and very likely they wandered eastward again after recurring Asiatic invasions had pushed them west. Eventually the Slavs, whose descendants now inhabit Russia, split into three distinguishable groups: the Great Russians (in the north and center of present-day European Russia), the Little Russians (in the Ukraine), and the White Russians (in the region north of the Ukrainians and east of the Poles). Other Slavic tribes—Wends, Czechs, Poles, and Slovaks—occupied westerly regions. Still others settled in Serbia, Bulgaria, and Rumania.

The Eastern Slavs comprised numerous tribes, such as the Severyane, Polyane, Krivichi, Drevlyane, and Dregovichi. They established themselves around three great centers—Kiev in the southwest, Novgorod in the north, and Tmutorokan in the southeast—and mingled freely with the peoples living in these sections, particularly with the Finns, the Germans, and the Turks.

GEOGRAPHIC INFLUENCES ON RUSSIAN HISTORY

The Land.

PLAINS. In spreading over the southern and western parts of present-day European Russia, the Slavs met with few natural obstacles; vast level plains, which extend from the North Sea to the Pacific Ocean, lay before them and account, in great part, for the continuous "surging" back and forth of so many different races. These plains are generally divided into four belts: (1) the tundras in the arctic region, frozen much of the year and having scant vegetation in the summer; (2) the forests and marshes south of them down to about 50 to 54 degrees north latitude, with pine and birch trees and some cultivable soil; (3) the steppe, with extensive areas of fertile agricultural "black-earth" layers; and (4) a dry alkaline or saline desert zone from the Caspian Sea into the Asiatic highlands.

MOUNTAINS. No mountains interrupt the vast plains. An elevation, not more than a thousand feet high, between Moscow and Novgorod—the Valdai Hills—and the surrounding uplands, marks the source of a mighty river system. A higher range, the Urals (the average elevation being only 1,500 feet and the highest mountains hardly more than 5,000 feet), connects rather than divides European and Asiatic Russia. Only on the southern borders of Russia do we find real mountains: the Carpathians and a range of majestic proportions, the Caucasus. Such paucity of mountains accounts for the perpetual sweep of strong winds; and, especially in southern Russia, rainfall is often scanty. Despite the remarkable fertility of the soil in some regions, cultivation in general is difficult, and before the introduction of modern methods, crops were often small—an insufficient reward for the work invested by the peasant.

Other Geographic Factors. Aside from the lack of natural boundaries which results from the unbroken extent of the plains, three geographical factors have given direction to the growth of the Russian nation: the forests, the rivers, and the sea.

FORESTS. Although Russia abounds in mineral wealth—including gold, oil, coal, and iron—the greatest wealth has consisted in the timber, which, during certain periods in Russian history, has been a bargaining point in political alliances and has dominated Russia's economic welfare.

RIVERS. The rivers have stimulated the Russian trading activities. Having few natural obstructions and being interconnected by nature and by human ingenuity, they have formed the backbone of a superior communication system. In ancient times, the two chief watercourses were explored and used. Trade flowed from the north of Europe through the Baltic to the Neva River, then to Lake Ladoga and further to Lake Ilmen, where the route divided. One course led by portage (where boats and cargoes were put on wheels) a short distance overland to the Volga River and down into the Caspian Sea—terminus of routes from Persia, India, and the Far East. The other led by portage to the Duena River, which was followed by a second portage connecting with the Dnieper; this river carried the ships to the Dnieper rapids, where a third portage became necessary to reach the Black Sea. From the Black Sea, ships made contact with the East Roman empire and the rich Mediterranean lands.

THE SEA. The third factor, the sea, was equally important in furthering the growth of Russia, though in a negative way. In relation to maritime access, Russia is the most disadvantageously situated of all large powers. The grand duchy of Muscovy, which was to give rise eventually to modern Russia, had no access whatever to the sea. In the nineteenth century, Russia, after having expanded for six hundred years, had a seacoast extending thousands of miles in the Arctic which was almost useless for transport purposes. She also secured ports on the Baltic and Black seas which were suitable for peaceful trade but which lacked free exit. The straits connecting the Baltic with the open sea were dominated by Denmark, those of the Black Sea by Turkey; and Europe saw to it that neither of these two countries would fall under Russian rule. Thus, strategically, the ports formed a liability rather than an asset. Finally, Russia in the nineteenth century had access to the northern Pacific Ocean in the east, but her ports there were icebound much of the year, and the Sea of Japan was dominated by the Japanese empire. The quest for open ports was thus first an economic, and later a strategic, driving force in Russian history.

THE RUSSIAN PEOPLE

The geography, climate, and landscape constitute a starting point for an interpretation of the "Russian character" upon which eloquent and clever essays have been written—essays that are often cited by historians. The vastness of the country has been brought into relationship with the broad outlook of Russian peoples; the climate, with such character traits as patience and humility; the nature of the soil and forests, with depth and peacefulness; the variety of regions and climates, with openness of mind and innate adaptability. But because of their vagueness and arbitrariness, the truth of such generalizations must be seriously challenged; all that we can discern is that specific political, economic, and social factors, which were in part perhaps the consequence of the geography of the country, have helped to stamp Russian man and the fate of the Russian people.

Political Factors. Among the political factors evinced early was the lack of cohesion which marked the life of the Russians. While in some regions fortified places were built and towns grew up, a well-organized state was not created. The Russian people were divided into many tribes, clans, or families; and although the clans occasionally combined into federations, "ruled" by princes, much warfare raged among them, and little state-building force was shown by any of them.

Economic Factors. At the time Russia "entered history," economic organization seems to have been more primitive than in many contemporary Germanic and Roman lands. A system of communal ownership and work prevailed. In the villages, some crafts were practiced and a measure of private property existed; but private possession of land was little known.

The cultivation of the soil was, of course, widespread. Chief crops were rye, wheat, barley, hemp, and flax. But to a large extent, the country's economy was based on the products of the forests—furs, honey, wax, and timber. Fishing, too, played an important role. Fish and forest products were sufficient to provide for lively foreign trade and were exchanged for salt, metals, armor, and a few luxury articles.

Social Factors. As in many primitive societies in early periods, matriarchal influence seems to have predominated in various regions of Russia. The institution of marriage sometimes did not exist, and incestuous relationships were not uncommon. Only gradually, with Greek, Germanic, Byzantine, and ultimately Christian influences, did fundamental changes occur. The maternal position was undermined, and eventually the women of the upper classes were confined to seclusion, much as in Asiatic lands, in a *terem* (separate quarters for the wife and her servants). Byzantine culture, itself a mixture of many diverse influences, suggested to the Russian peoples additional social changes. Among these was a system of government, often patterned along Asiatic lines and bringing despotism, bureaucracy, and centralization.

Russia in the eighth century A.D. thus appears as neither a geographical expression, nor a people, nor a civilization. It is in the ninth century that her historical growth begins to become "one of the most remarkable features in modern history." Her lack of uniformity—geographic, racial, economic, and climatic—became an overruling factor for the future, accounting largely for her reverses and failures, yet ever constituting her greatest asset and strength.*

PROBLEMS

1. Discuss the significance of migrations in Russia's historical development.
2. Discuss the significance of the river system in Russia's economic life.
3. Discuss the position of Russia with regard to access to the sea.

* Careful examination of the map on p. 19 will serve to explain and supplement the discussion in this chapter of geopolitical features and the description of land, tribes, and trade routes.

2

FORMATION OF THE RUSSIAN STATE

Significant Dates

St. Cyril and St. Methodius . . . . . *ca.* 855–885
Rurik, Ruler of Novgorod 862
Oleg, Ruler of Kiev 882
Expeditions against Byzantium 860–1043
Reign of Vladimir I 980–1015

Two events mark the importance of the ninth century in Russian history: the work of Cyril and Methodius, and the beginning of the rule of the Northmen, or Varangians.

CYRIL AND METHODIUS

The Slavic Alphabet. Cyril and Methodius were Christian missionaries from Byzantium sent out to preach the gospel to the heathen. At the time, the Christian church in Constantinople (with a patriarch at its head) still formed a part of one united Catholic church. To accomplish their task, the two missionaries worked out an alphabet for the West Slavic tongues. Cyril, who died in 869, labored among the various Slavic tribes, penetrating as far east as the Crimea and Tmutorokan, where he apparently succeeded in firmly implanting the Christian faith. Methodius devoted most of his energy to the western regions. His main field of activity was

8

Moravia, whither he was sent by the Pope to compete with the missionary work previously begun by Bavarian priests dispatched by the German kings. Ultimately neither Methodius, who died in 885, nor the Bavarians achieved anything permanent, for invading Magyars put an end to Christianity in Moravia. The significance of the work of the two clericals Methodius and Cyril consists in their having forged a link for Slavic peoples by introducing an alphabet and composing in the vernacular a text of the gospel.

THE NORTHMEN

Disunity of Slavs. The second great event—the rule of the Northmen or Varangians in Russia—is reported by the old chroniclers to have been the outcome of disunity among the Slavic tribes and of their voluntary submission to a strong foreigner who was to lead them to peace, order, and prosperity. This description of events (given in its oldest form in the so-called *Nestor Chronicle*) cannot be accepted in its totality. It may be true that the Slavic tribes in Russia were disunited, that their very existence was threatened by foreign enemies and by adverse geographic and economic conditions, and that trade requirements did not permit the independence of small groups but necessitated wider contacts. It is also correct that the open plains and long waterways suggested unification for the sake of carrying on trade in safety. Yet, archeological finds reveal that as early as the seventh and eighth centuries the Slavs possessed not only towns with fortifications, well-advanced crafts, and considerable trade, but also in various areas, political organizations which could possibly form the basis of a developing state. Considering these facts, the establishment of Northmen rule, at first only in some parts and later in the whole of the "first" Russian state, appears less as a complete departure from past experiences than as a logical continuation of existing trends.

Rurik. Northmen had long been in contact with the peoples living on the Russian plains. Following natural waterways to Lake Ladoga, they had entered Slavic territory in the eighth century, had penetrated it along the Volga River to the Caspian Sea and along the Don and Dnieper rivers to the Black Sea, and had established peaceful connections as well as military alliances. As in other parts of Europe, the Northmen proved to be not only good warriors and accomplished navigators, but clever traders and able organizers and administrators. It is therefore possible that one of their leaders, a rather obscure figure named Rurik, was asked (or perhaps succeeded by force) to assume the rulership.

Oleg. Rurik established himself in Novgorod on Lake Ilmen and placed relatives in charge of Pskov, Rostov, and other centers in the north. Two of his (perhaps legendary) companions, Askold and Dir, took possession of Kiev, which was strategically located on the border of the forest and steppe zone in the center of the waterways flowing north and south, and which was within easy reach of the great civilized metropolis Constantinople. Supposedly, they were treacherously murdered in 882 by Rurik's successor Oleg, who recognized the importance of the region and took their place in Kiev. By combining his own dominions in the north with the southern center, Oleg—through this crime—accomplished the task expected of the Northmen and benefited the country. He is regarded as the founder of "Russia." *

ORGANIZATION OF RUSSIA

Influence of the Northmen. The Scandinavian newcomers were soon assimilated. As did the Normans in England after 1066, they formed an upper class which, because of its smallness, had to fit itself into the general structure. The Scandinavians left few distinct traces.

Kiev. Oleg's transfer of central authority to Kiev shifted the political balance from Novgorod, with its dependence upon the Baltic Sea, to the south, with its Black Sea connections. Although the steppe country on the Black Sea could not be retained or recovered from invading Asiatic tribes, the mouth of the Dnieper was secured and the whole course of the river brought into "Russian" hands. From Kiev, trade routes were kept open, not only with Constantinople but also with the Volga region.

* The origin of the word "Russia" is obscure. The root may be derived from the Greek, from the name of a tribe which lived in southern Russia, from a Germanic town, from the Finnish word *ruotsi,* or from the German word *Ruderer.* Meaning originally the law of "Kievan Rus," it was eventually used to designate the entire country. The term "Rus," referring to the people, was applied not only to Russians of Slavic descent, but also to the Northmen living or ruling in Russia.

At this time, the course Russia would take for the next three centuries became evident; the main tasks ahead consisted of internal consolidation and expansion of trade and territory.

Political Consolidation. Consolidation was threatened by the lack of cohesion among the various Slavic tribes spreading from the Baltic to the Black Sea. It was also endangered by the inroads of foreigners (particularly of the Pechenegs, a tribe living in an adjoining territory to the east), although the very existence of the menace contributed indirectly to a rallying of forces. Furthermore, the changes in the relationship with Constantinople, with which wars and treaties alternated, offered serious problems. Oleg had dealt successfully with all these questions; to preserve his work thus became the first important objective.

Trade. Expansion of trade was the next task, congenial to Slavs and Northmen alike. To be sure, internal trade seems to have remained comparatively insignificant, although, with the growth of towns, there was an increasing exchange of produce of the countryside with manufactured articles made by the artisans in town and an exchange of goods between the agricultural south and the north with its predominately forest products. But foreign trade, both import-export and transit, came to be of special significance. Notwithstanding the good prospects it offered in both west and north, trade tended essentially southward, toward Constantinople, and southeastward, toward the Caspian region.

Expansion. Territorial expansion followed the direction of trade, but with little success. Numerous military campaigns were undertaken, leading as far as the Caspian coast, but most frequently directed against the East Roman emperor ruling in Constantinople. In 860 and 907, when thousands of troops were employed, and in 940, when a naval attack was attempted, Constantinople itself was endangered. After each war a trade treaty was concluded—a particularly favorable one for Russia being negotiated in 911. In consequence, very lively intercourse between Russia and the Byzantine Empire developed, and just as contact with the Arabian world in the Caucasus region had led to an infiltration of Mohammedan ideas, so the trade with Constantinople led now to considerable knowledge and appreciation of Christian life. The Christian creed, with its appeal to the lowly, was adopted by many of the poor classes, yet spread also among the highborn. Olga, regent for Oleg's grandson Sviatoslav, was the first in the ruling house and perhaps the first in the entire noble class to profess it.

Sviatoslav. During Olga's regency the thirst for territorial expansion was suppressed, but when Sviatoslav came to the throne in 960 it was revived. His military expeditions took him to the northeast as well as to the southeast, where he subdued Tmutorokan and annexed the Volga mouth. His ambition also led him southwest toward the Danube, to the banks of which he planned to move his capital. His expedition, interrupted by a new invasion of the Pechenegs, who were probably incited by the frightened Byzantine Empire, led to disaster and had to be given up. On his return to Kiev, Sviatoslav was killed. His lands were divided among his sons; but they could not agree on the share of each, and internal war broke out which ended with the triumph of an illegitimate son, Vladimir. About 980, Vladimir established himself as sole ruler in Kiev.

Vladimir I. Like his predecessor, Vladimir engaged in ceaseless warfare. He even conquered the Crimea, which, however, he returned to Constantinople after his conversion to Christianity. He built frontier fortifications and improved the internal administration, to which he devoted himself during the later part of his reign. But his fame rests less with these deeds than with the introduction of the Christian faith into Russia. Common faith and resulting common culture belonged to the most important factors which ultimately succeeded in knitting the empire together, and which gave it homogeneity and a clearly defined national identity.

PROBLEMS

1. Discuss the significance of the work of the first Slavic apostles.
2. Discuss the importance of Kiev for the new united Russian Empire.
3. Discuss the relationship of Kiev-Russia with Byzantium.

3

INTRODUCTION OF CHRISTIANITY

Significant Dates

Introduction of Christianity . . . . . . *ca.* 988
Metropolitan See at Kiev 1037
Catholic-Orthodox Schism 1054
Fourth Crusade 1202–1204

THE FAITH

Choice of Faith. Vladimir officially introduced Christianity into Russia about 988, and approximately twenty years later he issued the first "Church Statute." According to the *Nestor Chronicle,* he examined the faiths of the Jews, of the Roman Catholics, and of the Mohammedans, dispatching ambassadors to study the religious practices of these peoples before he finally accepted the Christian Orthodox faith as practiced in Constantinople. By choosing the Eastern ritual, he not only served the spiritual requirements of his country, but likewise served its political needs through closer contact with the eastern parts of the Christian world. For centuries to come, Constantinople's culture and politics were to influence Russian life. It was from Byzantium that Vladimir chose his wife, sister of the emperor, who in turn hoped to profit in his political schemes by this marriage alliance. From Byzantium, Vladimir inherited the concepts underlying the political status of the church. Like the emperors of the East, he was to claim supreme authority over the

13

church; and with this end in mind he promoted the autonomy of the Russian church, which was to be as independent as possible of external influences, including that of the Patriarch at Constantinople.

Acceptance of the Faith. Christianity was readily accepted in Russia. No prior faith or culture had existed which filled or could fill the spiritual needs of the people. In the veneration of Dashbog, god of heaven and light, of Perun, god of thunder, and of Stribog, god of winds, adoration of nature had been combined with ancestor cults. No temples and no priests, except Finnish seers and sorcerers, had inspired the people. Slavophil historians have always insisted that Christianity therefore had especial depth and meaning for the Russians, that it found virgin soil unspoiled by any pre-existing culture and was received with particular sincerity. Many historians, however, do not accept this view: They believe that because of the absence of a cultural basis among the people, Christianity failed to be truly understood, that it remained superficial, was wasted in displays and rituals, and left the converts as essentially pagan as before. In any case, many heathen customs were preserved for centuries or infiltrated the new faith which tolerated them.

By order of the grand duke, the inhabitants of Kiev were baptized in 990. Many had been converted to Christianity before this, and a Christian church is said to have existed in Kiev for more than a hundred years. Inhabitants of other regions, particularly those living on the great trade routes and engaged in business, had been in close contact with Christians from other countries; and most of them willingly followed Vladimir's orders. Only in a few regions, chiefly around Novgorod, was resistance offered. There it was overcome by force, though some seem to have taken to the woods rather than submit. On the whole, Vladimir's work was successful; but except in occasional instances, Christianity's true meaning and its demands on the conduct of daily life went unrealized at first and could only gradually become an active force in Russia.

CATHOLIC-ORTHODOX SCHISM

Despite connections with the Pope in Rome, the Orthodox church derived its tradition from the early Christian church in the East —that region which claimed, through close contact with the origins of the faith, to preserve Christianity in its purest form. All the great church councils of early times had been held there. The West, led by Rome, had gone its own way, emancipating itself in more than material aspects from Eastern domination. Indeed, a definite break between Eastern and Western Christianity occurred less than fifty years after Vladimir's death when, in 1054, ambassadors of Pope Leo IX pronounced the excommunication of the Patriarch of Constantinople. From that time on, the Roman Catholic church seemed no less heretical to the Orthodox than the Waldenses, Albigenses, and Protestants later seemed to the Catholics.

Political Differences. The main differences between Catholicism and Orthodoxy lie in the political, theological, and sociological fields. Political issues had arisen before the schism of 1054, but steadily increased thereafter. Jealousies existed between the church at Rome, which enjoyed considerable independence under the Pope, and that at Constantinople, which was under the supervision of an emperor residing close at hand. The position of the Pope or any head of the Roman church was challenged in the East, and the Patriarch at Constantinople or later at Moscow never enjoyed dominating power. Jurisdiction over various dioceses was claimed by Rome as well as by Constantinople. In the eleventh and twelfth centuries, rival claims were brought forward by the crusaders from East and West. The outrage of the Fourth Crusade, which instead of regaining the Holy Land attacked Constantinople and forced the Eastern church to submit to the rule of the Roman popes, aroused the indignation of the Orthodox. In the sixteenth, seventeenth, and nineteenth centuries, invasions and oppression by Poles and French —both Catholic powers—contributed to the old antagonism in Russia.

Theological Differences. Theological issues were likewise irreconcilable. Disputes marking different concepts in East and West had arisen long before the separation. In the third century, the date and celebration of Easter were disputed; in the fourth, the divinity of Christ was an issue; in the seventh, the question of the double or single nature of Christ led to a split; and in the eighth and ninth centuries, the use of images was debated. Other points of difference were: celibacy, which was not prescribed (indeed, not even allowed) to the lower clergy of the Eastern church; the use of milk in the first week of Lent; the use of leavened or unleavened bread for communion; indulgences; the teaching of the immaculate conception and of salvation; and the ceremony of baptism. In the question of the double procession of the Holy Ghost, the Eastern church maintained that the Holy Ghost proceeded from God alone and that the inclusion of Christ, the Son, by the Western church was the result of a falsification—of the interpolation of the word *filioque* ("and of the Son") in the creed that had been accepted at Constantinople in 381.

Sociological Differences. A contrast is said to exist between the speculative, philosophical attitude of the Eastern mind and the practical, legalistic attitude of the Western; between the Eastern "stationary tendency" and Western progressivism; between the "intellectual repose and apathy of Asia" and the "savage energy and freedom of Europe."

CHURCH ORGANIZATION

The Orthodox church started and proceeded on a road different from that taken by the Western church and helped to isolate Russia from the rest of Europe. Despite repeated earnest endeavors by Rome during the thirteenth century and during the times of Ivan the Great, Ivan the Terrible, Peter the Great, and Alexander I, no reunion was effected. The Orthodox church fused more thoroughly with the nation, and its ambitions were closely linked with those of the people. Unlike the Roman church, the Orthodox church had few desires incompatible with those of Russia's rulers or of the nation; and it was the Orthodox church which at many critical points in Russian history proved the rallying force for the people and which guided the nation.

Clergy. With the introduction of Christianity, the statues of the old gods were destroyed. Churches were built in Kiev, Suzdal, and other centers, and a new clerical class arose, which soon gained secular wealth, lands, and other privileges, including jurisdiction in its own courts.

The earliest Orthodox priests in Russia seem to have come from the shores of the Black Sea and Tmutorokan, where Cyril had introduced Christianity. It is even possible that the first bishops were drawn from there after Vladimir's conversion. But eventually the majority of the clergy came from Bulgaria and Constantinople. They preached in the vernacular—an advantage inasmuch as many difficulties resulting from the impossibility of translating specific Greek terms into Latin could be avoided, but a disadvantage in that a lack of knowledge of Greek and Latin prevented the Orthodox clergy from participating in the intellectual work of the Catholic world.

In 992 the first bishopric was established, and in 1037 a Greek bishop was consecrated as the first acknowledged metropolitan of Kiev. The appointment of a Greek, brought about by political circumstances and internal Russian feuds, had untoward consequences on the autonomy of the see at Kiev. When in 1051 Hilarion, a Russian, was created metropolitan without the assent of the Patriarch in Constantinople, he was forced out of office within two years.

Monasticism. Monasticism entered Russia in the time of Vladimir's son, Yaroslav, around 1015. The first famous monk was Anthony, a hermit, who lived in a subterranean cave not far from Kiev. After his death a monastery was built around his cave, the *Pechersky* (Cave), which in time came to play a prominent role in the national and cultural life of early Russia. The ascetic ideal, a main feature of Oriental monasticism, although strong at the beginning, was early supplemented, however, by practical aims. In times of national disaster the monasteries, being strongly built and well-provided, constituted important centers of defense.

Worldliness soon entered monastic life. Laymen were admitted and whole families—men, wives, and children—retired with their servants and dogs into cloisters to escape the dangers of the outside world. Through them, all kinds of temptations began to besiege the monks. Poverty, humility, and chastity were seldom found. Vast riches were amassed, so that in later centuries several monasteries controlled estates with tens of thousands, and even a hundred thousand serfs.

Influence of the Christian Church. The impact of the Christian church on the social and cultural life of the nation was, at first, limited. The efforts of the clergy were initially concentrated on the development of outward forms, including a colorful ritual, with services in the "Church Slavonic" idiom. These services were impressive—though perhaps chiefly in a general mystical way. Progress in penetrating the country with a Christian spirit, however, was slow. Individuals may have devoted themselves to seeking salvation through a purified life and rulers may have sought to better the conditions of slaves and improve family morals, but a change in the mores of the population was hardly noticeable. Learned works comparable to contemporary ones of the Western Catholic world were seldom forthcoming, and even the monks, devoted as they were to mysticism and contemplation, possessed little knowledge and brought forth few outstanding works. They lived in a world of their own, trying to avoid the worldly temptations to which, in the Russian mind, all ordinary men succumb. To a certain extent the monks promoted writing. A few pieces of religious literature, including *Lives* of the Saints, were produced, and some schools were founded. In church art, a few noble basilicas, following Byzantine models, were erected, and wooden churches, prevalent particularly in northern Russia, were built. Frescoes, icons, and book illustrations, likewise along Byzantine lines, were also created, and craftsmanship was improved. But few works contributing to the general intellectual development of European civilization, as did contemporary Latin, Greek, and Arab writings, have come down to present times. Dialectical controversies and discussions of questions of form and scriptural interpretation overshadowed the arts and sciences, and illiteracy among the clergy and lack of training actually remained problems well into the eighteenth century.

PROBLEMS

1. Discuss the introduction of Christianity into Kiev-Russia.
2. Discuss the main differences between Catholicism and Orthodoxy.
3. Discuss the early Christian organization in Russia.

MAP OF EARLY RUSSIA

4

DECLINE OF KIEV-RUSSIA

Significant Dates

Reign of Yaroslav	1019–1054
Reign of Vladimir II	1113–1125
Founding of Moscow	ca. 1147
Establishment of Capital at Suzdal	1157

PROBLEMS

Vladimir died in 1015, and Sviatopluk "the Accursed" succeeded him as grand prince of Kiev. With Sviatopluk began two centuries or more of grim struggle for power among the various members of the reigning family—a long and evil story interrupted by very few years of comparative quiet. The same question which Sir Bernard Pares in his *History of Russia* asked regarding the intrigues during the times of the successors of Peter the Great—"Who would take this miserable record as the history of a people?"—may be applied to the period of Vladimir's successors. However, the dynastic wars were but a small segment of the general picture; and, owing perhaps to the exclusive interest in it evinced by early chroniclers, the conflict of the princes is still overemphasized today. Behind the struggle loomed more important issues which account for the rivalries and for the ultimate disruption of Kiev-Russia: (1) divergent regional interests dividing the inhabitants of the Baltic area (which includes Novgorod), the Black Sea area (which includes Kiev), the western regions (which include Galicia), and the slowly emerging north-eastern region (which includes the upper Volga basin); (2) extraneous influences exercised from the south by Byzantium, from the

20

west by the Poles, and from the north by Scandinavians; (3) religious questions intensified by the struggle of Constantinople to secure and maintain supremacy over the Orthodox church in Russia; and (4) economic and social issues resulting from rivalry between, on the one hand, the trade interests of towns with oligarchic municipal governments, and, on the other, the feudal interests and autocratic ideas of the princes and the agricultural interests of the landowners and peasants.

GOVERNMENT

In the face of the grave problems menacing the Russian lands, centralization of power and adjustment to new needs were necessary. These were, however, not forthcoming. Instead, the administration of the country deteriorated owing to rivalries among the members of the ruling house. The struggles among the princes were aggravated by the absence of the concept of primogeniture and by a custom which provided for the dividing of the land of a deceased ruling prince among all his brothers and their children. Each generation and each line of the ruling house laid claim to its own territory. Upon the death of any one member, patrimonies of all the various princes had to be exchanged in a definite order of precedence, and this created instability and disorder. Ceaseless divisions and subdivisions among the numerous princely offspring rendered impossible fair and efficient government. Breaches of treaties, fratricidal wars, and civil disruption mark the political history of Russia from the eleventh to the thirteenth century. No more than two rulers of Kiev stand out as the builders of the empire during the first century after Vladimir's death, but these two personify the growth of the country —Yaroslav the Wise and Vladimir II Monomach.

Yaroslav the Wise. Yaroslav (1019–54) was a statesman as well as a scholar. In 1036, after the death of his brother Mstislav, he reunited Novgorod, Kiev, and Tmutorokan. He founded schools and libraries, had Greek books translated, and was a patron of art and music. He beautified Kiev by building a palace and churches, such as St. George, St. Catherine, and the magnificent St. Sophia. The church found him a loyal protector anxious to promote its prestige. Yaroslav's name is generally connected with the codification of Russian law (*Russkaya Pravda*), although some parts of the old Russian law code had originated earlier and others were added later. The code, based on customary law, included rules regarding slavery, theft, murder, inheritance, usury, and judicial procedure.

With his external policies Yaroslav was successful only in some respects. In the south, his expedition against the Greek emperor in Constantinople failed, but it put an end at least to Russia's constant warfare against Byzantium. In the east, the Pechenegs, persistent disturbers of trade and peace, were routed; but they were replaced by other eastern tribes, among whom the Polovtzy, who conquered Tmutorokan around 1100, were to prove no less dangerous than the Pechenegs. In the west, Yaroslav engaged in numerous campaigns in Galicia and Volhynia, and he waged war against the aggressive Poles. Nevertheless, so great was Yaroslav's eventual prestige that he was able to conclude marriage alliances for his relatives with a number of ruling families of Western Europe, namely those of Norway, Sweden, France, various German duchies, and Hungary, and even with the Byzantine emperor.

Vladimir II. Vladimir II Monomach (1113–25), who more than half a century later—after a period of brutal, gruesome feuds and disrupting civil wars—succeeded in reuniting the country, followed Yaroslav's example. He reduced interest rates, furthered trade, and kept peace, except for a number of "crusades" against pagan eastern neighbors. He proved himself a humane ruler, promoting justice and the Christian faith.

DISSOLUTION AND MIGRATION

Renewal of Disorder. After the rule of Vladimir II's insignificant peaceful son Mstislav I, internal strife among the various princely lines revived and again the country was pulled to pieces, each sector gaining a vast amount of independence to the detriment of the whole. A precarious and unstable system of "balance of power" resulted, by no means serving the cause of peace and order. Byzantium, watching events carefully, furthered the dissolution of the potential enemy to the north and, through such acts as the establishment of a separate archbishopric in Novgorod by the Patriarch of Constantinople, frequently exercised a powerful adverse influence in internal Russian affairs. The tasks for which the Slavic tribes had once "called in" Rurik, namely defence of the trade routes, negotiations of trade treaties with foreign powers, and composition of internal discord, were thus no longer fulfilled by the later rulers. Disunion prevailed and every section was compelled to seek its own protection and advantage.

Formation of Classes. Changes in Russian society paralleled the decline of political consolidation. A more pronounced class stratification developed. An entire caste was formed of the numerous descendants of the ruling houses; another consisted of their companions who, first employed as bodyguards, were to become eventually the formidable "boyar" class. A lesser nobility was recruited from small landowners, and a fourth stratum was formed by the burghers of the towns. The peasants themselves divided into classes, some free, some half free or indentured, and many slaves—the last in steadily increasing numbers. Small farms disappeared, giving room to princely estates.

RULING CLASS. In the course of the eleventh and twelfth centuries, the house of Rurik, divided though it was, maintained itself on the thrones of the various Russian lands, but the position of the ruling princes quickly deteriorated. The strength they had derived from their leadership of the armed forces, from the support of their companions and bodyguards (called *druzhina*), from their right to levy taxes, and from their wealth gained through trading was sapped by their bitter struggles for power and by the decline of Kiev's economic situation. As a result, the growingly autonomous boyar class assumed through their councils (*dumas*) privileges formerly enjoyed by the princes and secured vast landholdings, military command posts, and independent jurisdictional rights.

LANDED POPULATION. Increased power fell also into the hands of the smaller landed nobility, most of whom were of Slavic descent (unlike many boyars who were of Northern background). They, too, gained in independence. Earlier they had held their lands either in exchange for administrative and military services due to the prince, or like the high nobility by heredity. These latter lands, known as *ochina* or *vochina,* were not burdened with specific service duties. But later, as the princes lost authority, the small nobility freed itself of many of its service obligations; more and more land was turned into vochina holdings free of duties, and jurisdictional rights over the peasants were assumed by the individual nobleman. The influence he thus gained was further increased by his role in mercantile affairs; for the Russian nobility indulged not only in the administration of their lands but in all kinds of other economic pursuits, such as trading and banking activities, which the Western European nobility considered inferior and unworthy of a nobleman.

Under such circumstances, the peasant steadily lost his former status. Lacking the protection of a strong central government, he found his right to private or communal property infringed upon. The mere right of *usus fructus* replaced increasingly that of full ownership; and debts often led to the loss of personal freedom.

TOWN POPULATIONS. Some changes occurred also in the status of the town citizens, the burghers or freemen. Kievan Russia had for a long time been more than a wide territory of many towns adjoining Slavic and Finnish areas. Its burghers had benefited from wealth derived from craftsmanship and industries. For not only did trade —domestic, foreign and transit—and agriculture and livestock farming constitute the basis of Kievan Russia's prosperity, but, as recent researchers have demonstrated, mining, metal and woodworking, and textile industries were likewise well-developed. A monetary system existed in which silver coins (foreign and domestic) and furs (*kuna*) were used. Such advanced types of economy contributed to the importance of the town populations. Disruption after the death of Vladimir Monomach impinged, however, on the role of the towns.

In regard to town government, the burghers often still succeeded in preserving within their walls a measure of order which was superior to that in the countryside. Through general assemblies of all freemen, the *vieche,* they exercised a decisive influence on local affairs. Eventually they imposed their will even upon the princes. Pereslavl, Novgorod, Polotsk, Pskov, Smolensk, Rostov, and Suzdal became important trading and cultural centers. The city of Kiev, however, was gradually reduced to the position of but one of many important places, and after three hundred years of predominance even this position was lost in the thirteenth century.

Decline of Kiev. The decline of Kiev, and with it of the Russian empire which had centered around it, became a determining issue in Russian history. A new empire had to be built far from the fertile southern Russian region and the Dnieper basin. It was the advantageous location of Kiev at the crossroads of the waterways and on the fringe of the black-soil district which had brought her wealth and position; these same factors, inciting the jealousy of others, also brought about her ruin. The causes for Kiev's fall may be summarized as follows: (1) the inroads of covetous foreigners on this richest region of Russia, mainly of the Polovtzy, who preyed upon the Kiev traders; (2) internal warfare involving Kiev as the disputed object of rival princes, which led to destruction, famine, and in two instances the sack of the city; (3) depopulation as a result of war and lowered prosperity; (4) deforestation, depriving Kiev of protection as well as of wealth; and (5) reorientation of trade as a result of the decline of Kiev's principal trade partner and cultural support, Constantinople, and the rise of Western trade centers.

Emigration. In view of these circumstances, emigration took place, partly in a westward direction (toward Galicia) and partly in a northeastward direction (toward the region of the upper course of the Volga and its tributaries). It was in this latter area that the foundation for a new commonwealth was laid; it was there that the towns of Suzdal, Vladimir, and finally Moscow (first mentioned in 1147) were to assume the role once played by Kiev.

Suzdal was the first capital after the grand princes moved from Kiev. Vladimir near the Volga was the second, when energetic and autocratic Andrew Bogolubsky, resenting the tutelage of Suzdal's powerful and ambitious vieche, moved the political capital there in 1157.

EFFECTS OF NORTHEASTWARD MIGRATION

Territorial Losses. Both Suzdal and Vladimir were less favorably located than Kiev had been. The princes here were far from the center of Russian realms and were unable to circumvent the secession of various provinces. Within two centuries, almost all the western parts of Russia were lost. Galicia gained autonomy only to be divided in due time, in the period from 1339 to 1352, between neighboring Poland and Hungary. Chernigov and Pereslavl were also lost; and finally Volhynia was incorporated by its neighbor, Lithuania. About 1400, "Russia" comprised no more than the land within a radius of roughly two hundred and fifty miles around

Suzdal. This Russia, which thus did not even comprise the old cultural centers of the Ukraine that had formed the basis of the original "Rus" or "Kievan Russia," was then composed of a number of loosely connected principalities. Chief among them was Muscovy, so called after Moscow, residence of the grand duke. Yet, cohesion was slight, and each individual territory or appanage enjoyed far-reaching independence.

Economic Disadvantages. Loss of territory and of cohesion was but one result of the shift northeastward. The country suffered also economically, because the forest-belted upper course of the Volga offered no economic opportunities equal to those on the lower Dnieper. The soil yielded less, and the people lived more primitively. They were poorer and consequently unable to help create by taxes a strong, progressive community. With the exception of Novgorod and Pskov, hardly any town of importance could be supported in a region where trade was reduced and where difficulties in agriculture caused scarcity of foodstuffs. But Novgorod and Pskov were difficult for the rulers of Suzdal or of Vladimir and Moscow to control. Their pride in their oligarchic republican constitutions, combined with their spirit of independence and their relations with the Swedes and Germans, removed them from effective Muscovite government. Their vieche, well-suited to a progressive urban society, formed a bulwark against the autocratic tendencies of Muscovite princes.

Cultural Decline. Culturally, the change was accentuated by the severance of the direct lines of communication with Constantinople and the rich Mediterranean basin. The long routes thither were cut by nomadic tribes roaming over southern Russia, and connections with the Baltic countries by way of Novgorod were insufficient and could not compensate for the loss in the south. Artisanship, highly developed in jewelry, carving, needlework, and many other trades, began to deteriorate, as the long winters in the northern regions afforded the peasants enough time to manufacture their simple household goods and so deprived the skilled artisans in the towns of their markets. The "land of the towns," harboring science, arts, and crafts, was transformed into a primitive "land of villages."

Racial and Social Changes. The Russian people themselves were transformed. Moving northeastward, they invaded territory largely settled by Finns, with whom they intermixed, forming the "Great Russian" type as opposed to the "Little Russian" in the Ukraine. Later, immigrants arrived from Germany, Hungary, and Poland, erected villages of their own, and brought fresh blood and different ideas and institutions. Though feudalism in its Western sense was never fully developed in Russia and though the feudal concepts of personal relationship and honor were nowhere introduced, many feudal institutions evolved, and the church and landowning aristocracy increased their independence. A first and a second estate came clearly into being; but in Russia they were to pave the way for autocracy rather than for Western diets or popular representations.

External Dangers.   Andrew Bogolubsky, grand duke of Suzdal and Vladimir, who profited from the new trends and established an autocratic government, was murdered in 1174. He had accomplished little, but his reign stood out as an indication of a different development that was to take shape in the northeast. His successors devoted themselves once more to feuds and rivalries, heedless of the growing menace from without. Indeed, in the west, new enemies, in addition to Poles and Lithuanians, were rising in the persons of Swedes, Danes, and Teutonic Knights, who began to settle the Baltic seashore, and—far more ominous—in the east the Tartar empire of Genghis Khan emerged as a new and rapidly expanding power.

PROBLEMS

1. Discuss the importance of Yaroslav the Wise and the *Russkaya Pravda*.
2. Discuss the causes and effects of the decline of Kiev.
3. Compare the upper Volga basin and Kiev-Russia with respect to their geographical and political advantages.

5

RUSSIA UNDER TARTAR
DOMINATION

Significant Dates

COMING OF THE TARTARS

Tartar Invasion. In 1223 the Tartars, who had extended their rule over much of Asia, began to expand farther westward, entering what is called Europe but what in reality is only a part of the Eurasian plains. They menaced first the Polovtzy, who, despite their own frequent penetrations into Russia, had formed a valuable buffer state against Asiatic nomads and who therefore received Russian support against the Tartars. In the Battle of the River Kalka, north of the Sea of Azov, the combined armies were routed (1223 or 1224). Although the Tartars retreated in spite of their victory, the peril for Russia remained ever-present, and in vain did the church plead for preparedness and internal unity.

Tartar Conquest. The feared resumption of Tartar invasions occurred about twelve years later when, after the death of Genghis Khan, the Russian lands were granted by his successor to Batu

Khan, a grandson of Genghis. Vladimir, Pereslavl, and Chernigov were captured in 1238, and Kiev in 1240. Galicia was taken, and the Tartars entered Poland and ultimately invaded Germany by way of Silesia.

Of all the important centers, Novgorod alone was temporarily spared, for the vast forests and swamps in the north hindered the advance of the equestrian invader. But, inasmuch as Novgorod was being simultaneously menaced from the west, she could not long escape Tartar domination. In 1240 the Swedes attacked from the west and were barely turned back on the Neva by the hard-won victory of Alexander, duke of Novgorod, who thereafter was surnamed "Nevsky." Two years later an army of Teutonic Knights (who had settled in Livonia and wished to extend their rule) attacked and was beaten back on the ice of Lake Peipus by the same Alexander. Again, from 1243 to 1245 the Lithuanians relentlessly sent invading armies into Novgorod's territory. Consequently, the resources of the city were so exhausted that, to avoid further warfare, sovereignty of the Tartars had to be recognized.

TARTAR RULE

Tartar Administration. Batu established himself on the steppes between the Aral and the Black Seas. In the name of the Khan in Central Asia, yet in reality semi-independently, he, as ruler of the "Golden Horde," exercised sovereign rights over Russia. Sarai on the lower part of the Volga later became the Tartar capital. All Russians were compelled to register in order to fulfill the two chief Tartar demands: (1) to pay a heavy poll tax as tribute, and (2) to provide recruits for the Tartar army. In addition, the Tartars reserved for themselves the right to confirm the various Russian rulers, particularly the grand prince. As a rule, Russian princes were made to appear in person before the Khan to receive their appointments. To show their power, the Tartars from time to time marched troops through the country, allowing them to commit every kind of atrocity.

Significance of Tartar Invasion. The Tartars maintained sovereignty in Russia for almost two hundred and fifty years. Their hold was based on the efficiency of their financial administration, and their system of assessment and finance was hard. Themselves

influenced by Chinese civilization, they introduced Eastern bureaucratic methods, with Armenians, Jews, and Chinese monopolizing
the offices of tax collectors. The political, cultural, and economic
history of this period is full of complexities. It does not break with
the past, nor does it consist of elements wholly alien to Russian
needs; yet it accentuates certain trends in Russian history which
otherwise might have been submerged. From a present-day point
of view, the significance of Tartar domination may be considered
as sixfold:

INCREASED CONTACT WITH THE EAST. Influences from the East
increased. Tartar words and ideology found entrance into the Russian language. Asiatic customs were imitated—as, for example, regarding the position of women. Cruelty towards slaves and the
conquered increased. Bureaucratic ideas and the Eastern financial
system were eagerly and permanently adopted, and trends toward
despotism and autocracy were accentuated.

WEAKENING OF WESTERN CONNECTIONS. The decline of Kiev had,
even before the Tartar invasion, caused the Western world to become increasingly removed from the Russian horizon; and the
Orthodox-Catholic schism of 1054 and the conquest of Constantinople in 1204 by the crusaders, as well as their excesses there, had
led to further ruptures between East and West. The Tartar invasion
deepened the existing gap, which was widened by the gradual absorption by western neighbors of those parts of Russia which constituted the chief links with the West. Some acquisitions of Russian
territory were made by Poles and Lithuanians. The Poles expanded
further into Galicia and Volhynia, where their aristocracy and clergy
seized land, uprooted existing Russian customs and religion, and
enserfed the population. The Lithuanians spread their rule southeastward, conquering (during the fourteenth century) Polotsk and
Kiev. In 1395 even Smolensk fell. Under their capable ruler Olgerd
they penetrated along the Dnieper to the Black Sea, which they
reached in 1363, thus overpowering much of Little Russia. Again,
their roving expeditions brought them almost to the gates of Novgorod and Moscow. Their conquest might have led (since they were
heathen) to their adoption of the Orthodox faith, to the Russianiz-
ing of Lithuania, and to a union of the two countries. However, the
extinction of the royal line in Poland led in 1386 to a different
merger—that of Lithuania and Catholic Poland. Thus, the Russian

parts of Lithuania were combined with Poland and shared the fate of Galicia and Volhynia.

A further weakening of the connection with the West came as a result of inroads from the side of Swedes, Danes, and Germans. Under Birger Jarl the Swedes not only undertook the crusade against schismatic Novgorod, which ended in their defeat on the Neva, but also completed the subjection of Finland and Karelia. In the meantime, the Danes had conquered Estonia, and the Germans under the leadership of merchants, priests, and knights had established themselves in Livonia on the shores of the Baltic. They had founded Riga, one of the great medieval ports, and had extended their power along the Duena River, which was one of the two great waterways that connected northern Europe with the Black and Caspian seas. In 1348 the Teutonic Knights bought Estonia from the Danes. All these events meant that for centuries to come most of Russia's direct outlets to the sea and most of the overland tradeways connecting Russia and the West came under the control of Swedes, Germans, and especially Poles and Lithuanians, whose dominions cut off Russia, as by a barrier, from direct access to Central and Western Europe; Russian communications with the West therefore became subjected to their will. Essentially, only one important meeting place remained: the town of Novgorod.

ADVANCEMENT OF NOVGOROD. Novgorod was a large port located not on the sea but at an advantageous spot inland; it could be reached by ships via Lake Ladoga and the Volkhov River. The city possessed a vast hinterland which extended to the shores of the Arctic Ocean and to Siberia and provided it with some of the most important trading commodities, especially furs, timber, wax and honey. In the thirteenth and fourteenth centuries, Novgorod, which was never occupied by the Tartars, developed to its height. Its wealthy and, subsequently, powerful merchants secured the political control of the city and made it almost independent of princely domination. A constitution established equality of all freemen before the law, guaranteed fundamental rights within the hierarchy of classes, maintained the vieche, and raised standards through merchant and artisan guilds. Extensive and mutually profitable trade relations were built up, especially with Germans from Lübeck and other Hanseatic towns; these Hanseatic merchants established a "factory" or staple and exchange place in the city and concluded important commercial treaties with its leading citizens. Owing to the presence of the German merchants, Novgorod became one of the greatest commercial centers of medieval Europe, and the town's wealth, power, and prosperity were unequaled in all Russia.

DECLINE OF THE ECONOMY. The flourishing of Novgorod consti-tuted an exception in Russia under Tartar rule. Though some for-eign commerce was maintained with the help of Venetian and Genoese merchants by way of Kaffa on the Black Sea, trade as a whole suffered gravely. Tartar exactions led to a decline of living standards; production often served only the conquerors; and the landed population in particular encountered severe hardships. Crops were often ruined and impoverishment brought steadily increasing loss of liberty to the peasant.

ASCENDANCY OF THE CHURCH. Significantly, in Tartar times the church was not only maintained, but its national prestige increased immensely. The Orthodox Christian faith remained the strongest uniting tie among the Russian people. Despite its initial opposition to the Tartars, the church soon submitted and began to co-operate with them, taking advantage of their religious tolerance. The Tartars in turn recognized the usefulness of the church and granted it ex-emption from taxes. The metropolitan see was removed from Kiev in 1299; Galicia—then independent—formed a separate diocese; and the metropolitan moved to Tartar-dominated Russia, choosing Mos-cow as his permanent abode in 1325. Although the schism resulting from Galicia's separation weakened the Orthodox church and neces-sitated internal reforms, the church proved an effective influence in holding the country together and in nurturing the hope for inde-pendence. New cloisters were founded, among them the Trinity (*Troitsa*) Monastery north of Moscow, which fell heir to the Pechersky tradition and prestige.

The position of the Orthodox church was threatened during the later part of Tartar domination, not by the victors, but rather from within. In 1439 a council convened at Florence at the direction of the Roman Pope and was attended by the Patriarch of Constanti-nople and other Orthodox bishops, including the Russian metropol-itan, Isidore. The leading Greeks and, without special authorization, Isidore consented to the re-establishment of Christian unity; they accepted Cardinal's hats and acknowledged the supremacy of the

Pope. Their action was disavowed by the majority of the Orthodox; and when Isidore returned to Russia and tried to introduce the union and celebrate mass according to the Latin version, he was banned and punished. The cause of Christianity thus suffered, but the national aspirations of the Russians were furthered through the maintenance of the national character of their church. Soon thereafter, in 1453, the fall of Constantinople isolated the Russian church almost completely. Subsequently, it was to play a prime role in the liberation of Russia from the Tartar yoke.

RISE OF MOSCOW.   Under Tartar rule, Moscow gradually increased its prestige as Russia's leading city. With the loss of the western provinces, the eastern regions and their trade routes—for which Moscow was the natural terminus—assumed greater importance, and a unification process took shape around Moscow. The city, besides gaining economic position, strengthened itself as a strategic center through the construction of the Kremlin, Russia's strongest fortress of the period. Moscow's dominance was consolidated at the expense of the West, which was left to itself. Authority over Russia's political institutions—which the people of Kiev had once controlled but which, oppressed and dissatisfied, they no longer had an interest in maintaining—passed into the hands of Moscow. The transfer of the metropolitan see to Moscow added immensely to the prestige of the city. Surrounding territories were absorbed: first Pereslavl, then Nizhnii Novgorod, temporarily Tver, in 1368.

Not only Moscow itself, but also its ruling house, emerged as a potent force. Alexander Nevsky (grand duke since 1252) had recognized the necessity of co-operating with the Tartars and had gone to the Golden Horde and offered his submission. His successors imitated him and gained vast concessions in exchange, the most important of which was the right to collect in their own realms the taxes for themselves and for the Golden Horde. They also contrived to avoid Tartar interference in their political schemes. In particular they succeeded in largely suppressing, for the sake of greater unity, the system of appanages, whereby each younger member of a princely house would claim a vast amount of autonomy for himself in his personal domains, and after his death every one of his heirs would claim the same autonomy over his share of the inheritance. Furthermore, the grand dukes of Moscow, imitating the example of other provinces, subdued the minor nobility and then annexed the surrounding territories, securing for themselves a place more firmly entrenched than any Kievan grand prince had ever enjoyed. Although the Tartars, who cherished the principle of *divide et impera,* were not interested in this unification process, they did not dare oppose it owing to the diligence and punctuality of the grand dukes in collecting and paying taxes.

DECLINE OF THE TARTARS

Role of the Muscovite Rulers. Two rulers of Muscovy stand out for their achievements: Ivan I (Ivan Kalita, 1325–41), thrifty, industrious, just, and peaceful, whose diplomacy and wealth stimulated the willingness of other Russian princes to submit to him; and Dimitri (1359–89), who successfully defended the country against the Lithuanians and increased Moscow's prestige. It was Dimitri who made the first effective attempt to throw off the Tartar yoke—after a series of earlier attempts had failed between 1262 and 1327—and secured a politically promising (though militarily useless) victory over the Tartars on the Don in 1380. Tartar dominance was not broken, because of the rise of another great conqueror, the famous Tamerlane; nevertheless, Tartar prestige suffered materially, for Russia acquired practical advantages through reduction of the tribute. Dimitri, called "Donskoy" for his victory on the Don, further promoted the growth of Muscovy by abandoning the system of dividing the country among the heirs and by introducing for his dynasty the system of primogeniture.

Role of the City of Moscow. The personal shrewdness of Moscow's rulers furnishes only an incomplete explanation of that city's persistent rise to power. The true and fundamental causes were economic and political, resulting from the position of Moscow on the Moskva River which forms part of the important Volga waterway; from the collection of dues for use of the river; from trade in corn, honey, and wax; from the increase of a taxable population; from the support of the Khans; and from her strategic location in the heart of a region yet to be cultivated and organized. Even independent Novgorod could eventually be dominated to a certain extent as a consequence of Moscow's influence on the city's hinterland and sources of supply. Finally, an accidental element should be mentioned—longevity in the house of the princes of Muscovy.

From 1389 on, a rare stability of government was achieved; and the bane of earlier times, devastating feuds among the princes, was almost entirely eliminated. Over a period of about two hundred years, until 1584, Moscow was ruled by only five princes, who gave a previously unknown continuity to governmental affairs.

Twilight of Tartar Rule. In the meantime, owing to disorders and disunion, the Tartars' might waned. The Battle of the Don was but one evidence of their weakened state. By the middle of the fifteenth century, Moscow, which had been besieged several times but only once taken and sacked, could look forward to the moment when she might hopefully defy Tartar rule. The introduction of the latest type of artillery (and artillery has ever since been considered a weapon of prime importance to the Russian army) did much to move the balance in Moscow's favor. Had it not been for Tamerlane, the Tartar yoke might have been shaken off in the fourteenth century. As it happened, final victory was delayed until the time of Ivan III, later called "the Great," who ascended the grand ducal throne in 1462.

Evaluation of Tartar Rule. Historians have variously assessed the role of the Tartars in Russia. In general, it is conceded now that far from having been only destructive, they made valuable contributions in administrative knowledge and through some of their skills. Though they may have diverted the "broadly flowing stream of Russian history," they did not stop it. But as the time of their rule coincided with the age of the Renaissance when modern European concepts were formed and humanistic trends, naturalistic and scientific attitudes, representative forms of government, individualistic principles, and capitalistic organization were spreading in Western Europe, the presence of the Tartars helped somewhat to check the influx of such Western characteristics into Russia. Traditional ways were reemphasized in Russia, and feudal rather than modern patterns were intensified.

PROBLEMS

1. Discuss Tartar influences in Russia.
2. Trace the territorial changes of Russia under Tartar rule.
3. Discuss the rise of Moscow as the leading Russian center.

6

THE ERA OF IVAN THE GREAT

Significant Dates

Reign of Ivan the Great 1462–1505
"Battle" of the Oka; End of Tartar Rule . . . 1480
Conquest of Novgorod 1471–1496
Reign of Basil III 1505–1533

SIGNIFICANCE OF IVAN'S RULE

Breakdown of Medieval System. The reign of Ivan the Great (1462–1505) was a period of fulfillment rather than of inception or transition. In time the independence of the many small principalities under the appanage system was terminated, and local self-government, as exemplified by the vieche system, was reduced to complete submission. In his reign towns and trade, the pride of old Russia, barely maintained the significance they had possessed earlier, while landed lords, ruling a primitive agricultural society, tended to increase their hold. This led to a social revolution in reverse: The peasant, free in early Russia, now moved in the direction of serfdom. A peasant who wished to be free often had to abandon cultivation of the soil and make his way to frontier regions; there, like Tartars from their disintegrating empire, he might form "Cossack" groups, serve Tartar or Russian princes, and act as a free warrior or as a guide through the steppe. Muscovy emerged triumphant from her long and relentless struggle for leadership among the Russian people. Tartar rule collapsed, but recovery of the western parts of the country had to be renounced, at least temporarily. The history of these parts was not to merge with that of the rest of the country until the seventeenth century. And so, a development extending over more than a century closed with Ivan III.

Personal Influence of Ivan. The grand duke Ivan of Muscovy was an able tool of the times. Son of Basil II, who had emerged victorious—though with the loss of his eyesight—from the last vicious family struggle over the throne, Ivan had learned patience and prudence. Slow in his decisions to the extent of inviting suspicion of cowardice, he moved stealthily and doggedly, while his thriftiness provided him with the necessary means to attain his ends. Nevertheless, in the face of the contemporary economic, social, and political forces, his personal influence on internal affairs of Russia was limited. His role in external affairs, however, was substantial, and in some respects unfortunate.

INTERNAL CHANGES

Reduction of Nobility. Domestically the most important issue consisted in a metamorphosis of the upper class. Ivan succeeded in establishing his hegemony by depriving the various princely families within his realms of most of their independence. By threat of his armed might, by legal measures, and by economic pressure, he forced them to recognize his leadership and to obey him, eliminating thereby the distinction that had existed between their class and that of the ordinary boyars and those Tartar nobles who had come to serve him. Moreover, he deprived many of the princes of their administrative functions. He transferred them to a group within the lower nobility whose origins can be traced to the preceding century. This group, comprised partly of descendants of the same group of independent nobility and partly of men raised by Ivan from other levels of society, was in turn granted land by the grand duke either out of his own domains or out of expropriations and conquests; but in exchange, they had to render military and administrative service (*pomestie* system). Their rights to their lands did not imply full property rights, nor did they include that of inheritance, except when coupled with the heir's obligation of continued service to the grand duke. This combination of ownership and service, which in contrast to the vochina type of property was to constitute the chief pattern of landholding in Russia for centuries to come, had a great advantage for Ivan in that he could establish his authority over the nobility; but it also brought dangers. Care of the land suffered because of the service duties connected with its possession. Jurisdictional and administrative functions passed from the hands of ruling princes into those of exploiting landowners. Finally, constant need for additional land with which to remunerate former appanage princes, nobles, warriors, and administrators forced the grand duke onto the road of war and conquest.

New Law Code. These changes in the class structure found their reflection in a revised law code, the *Sudebnik,* which was based on Yaroslav the Wise's *Russkaya Pravda.* It embodied the principles of recently developed customary law and embraced both criminal and civil codes. It provided the foundation for an administrative organization which was adapted to the newly erected centralized state system. Within this system, a bureaucracy staffed by *diaks* (secretaries and other officials chosen, on the basis of ability, by the Tsar and responsible to him alone) played a steadily increasing role.

Growth of Serfdom. As a result of the decline of the independent princes, the reorganization of the boyar class, and the growth of the pomestie system, the position of the free peasant was undermined. Though he had never "owned" his lands, he did have generally the *usus fructus*; but now this right was constantly curtailed. Part of the crops and part of the labor were claimed by the new landowning class. If a peasant wanted to escape the new burden, he had no other alternative than to move away into uninhabited regions. Legally, he still had the right to do so; but the exercise of his right became difficult. Colonization of the northeastern region, which had attracted people from the Ukraine and had offered them a haven of freedom, was over, and land had become scarce. Furthermore, landowners, alleging neglect of their estates, could put every obstacle into the way of a peasant's departure; and eventually the peasant was forbidden to move altogether except during two weeks in autumn. In addition, financial burdens began to impede his movements. Many peasants were burdened with debts, and these had first to be repaid; moreover, in order to settle in the few fertile regions left unclaimed, he needed funds which he had to borrow at the risk of debt servitude.

Other factors, too, hindered his movements. In many parts, the peasants had organized village communities (the mir or volost) with officials of their own, and they cultivated the land in common. These communities, in imitation of a precedent set by the Tartars with their efficient system of collecting taxes, were now held jointly liable by Ivan for the tax payments of each individual member. The community, therefore, was interested in keeping the labor of each member. The taxes, imposed according to the productivity of the soil, were heavy; in lean years they surpassed the peasant's ability to pay and necessitated seasonal loans which endangered freedom. Moreover, peasants were obliged to provide a specified number of recruits for the army. All these burdens were doubly heavy because of the lack of legal machinery to protect the individual against excessive requirements.

Thus, at a time when in Western Europe towns were multiplying, a modern financial system was taking shape, and serfdom was waning, bondage—intended primarily to make the peasant repay voluntarily or involuntarily contracted debts and to guarantee the value of land grants to the new pomestie landowners—was gaining a hold in Russia. Sometimes the burdens imposed by one landowner were so unbearable that the peasant resorted to selling himself in bondage to another from whom he expected better treatment. In each case he began to work for his creditor under one of two plans: the *obrok* system, which implied the payment of a fixed sum in kind or money, or the *barchina* system, which meant the rendering of services (*corvée*) as demanded by the landowner. In this manner serfdom grew, although the final step, compulsory return and punishment of fugitives, was not taken until almost a century later and although other forms of agricultural labor—free ownership, sharecropping, hired labor, and even slavery—continued to exist side by side with it.

Reform of Clergy. Simultaneously with the changes affecting the nobility and the peasants, a serious crisis confronted the clergy. Having resisted attempts at reunion with the Catholics made at the Council of Florence, the church was threatened by new dangers over the matter of secularization of church lands. Secularization would have meant a loss to the high clergy which was the chief beneficiary of the wealth of the lands; it would have weakened the position of the grand duke who would have lost the support of the high clergy and the control he could indirectly exercise through it on the administration of the lands; and it would have strengthened the boyars into whose hands the secularized lands might ultimately have fallen. Yet, it was proposed by reformers within the church. Among them were the so-called trans-Volga Saints—mystics who feared the evil influence of worldly .possessions upon the spiritual life of the institution. The most famous of their leaders was Nils Sorsky. They may have been influenced by a "heresy," known as that of the "Judaizers," which came from the West and apparently derived some of its tenets from the reform proposals of the Hussites in Bohemia. They were opposed by men like Archbishop Gennadius of Novgorod and Josip of Volokolamsk and his followers, who rejected all reform movements and endeavored to tighten the links between church and state by subjecting the former to the will of the grand duke. The bitterly debated question affected political matters, as it was tied up with Ivan's succession plans; but eventually the party of Josip succeeded in having the solution postponed, and secularization was thereby avoided.

Establishment of Sovereignty.

END OF TARTAR RULE.   The formal sovereignty of the Tartars was ended in 1480. Through negotiations with unruly elements within the Golden Horde and with neighbors surrounding the Tartar state, Ivan had long since undermined their power; in 1480 armies of the Muscovites and the Tartars confronted each other on the Ugra River, but no real battle was fought. Winter benefited the Russians and the Tartars retreated, many of them deserting to the Russian side. No longer was tribute paid to the Golden Horde. The Turks seized the opportunity and subjected the Crimea. Within less than twenty years, the Golden Horde disappeared. Tartar people, however, retained parts of the country, such as the principalities of Kazan and Astrakhan, and constituted a danger and an annoyance for a long time to come.

RISE OF TSARISM.   In his work and ambitions, Ivan III was supported by his second wife, Sophia, niece of the last Byzantine emperor. She was married to him by the Pope in Rome—where, after the fall of Constantinople in 1453, she had spent her youth. The Pope hoped, though in vain, that her marriage would contribute to a reunion of the Catholic and Orthodox churches. As a descendant of the great East Roman imperial family, Sophia was a driving power behind Ivan's rise to supremacy and behind Muscovy's claim to Constantinople's heritage. It was she who most violently opposed recognition of suzerainty and the payment of tribute to barbarians. Likewise, it was she who enticed her husband to shake off the tutelage of the haughty nobility. Since Constantinople had fallen to the Turks, she also led him to lay claim to the title of "Tsar" (believed to be derived from Caesar), which implied supreme worldly and spiritual power. In addition she made him assert supreme rights over the Russian church, already independent from Byzantium and separated from Kiev (which in 1458 had received a metropolitan of its own). Sophia also sought to add to the prestige of the Tsar by inviting Italian artists to Russia where they would spread the glory of the Italian Renaissance which she had witnessed in Rome; but in this she failed, largely because of the different civilization of Russia and the lack of an educated nobility and middle class which in other countries proved the chief benefactors of artists and appreciators of their work.

EXTERNAL POLICIES

In his external policies, Ivan centered his attention on the "collecting of the Russian lands." In the pursuit of this policy, he was most successful.

Perm, Kazan, Tver.   In the east, Ivan put an end to the independence of Perm, situated on the road to the Urals; he also established a vague suzerainty over the Tartar state of Kazan; and further, he incorporated the valuable and strategically important province of Tver. The administration of all parts was centralized; and independent policies of any Russian prince were made impossible.

Poland-Lithuania.   Looking beyond "Russian lands," Ivan recognized in Poland-Lithuania the implacable foe of Russia. He realized that this country, seeking to expand her rule over the lost western Orthodox territories, constituted Russia's chief obstacle to a reunion of the former Kievan provinces with the Muscovite lands; she blocked a durable peace, and by her ambitions forced a series of wars upon the Tsar, involving at the same time Swedes and Teutonic Knights. This multilateral struggle against Poland-Lithuania became the key to Ivan's foreign relations as well as to those of his successors. It was also Poland which caused Russia in 1471 to attack her neighbor, wealthy and powerful Novgorod —an attack that was to lead to the acquisition of this most important Russian outlet to the Baltic Sea and the unwise destruction of its Hanseatic trade center.

Novgorod. Novgorod had not shared in the Russian trend toward an agricultural society, neofeudalism, and serfdom. Because of her advantageous location, the town had developed a special character somewhat influenced by the West. Her urban inhabitants remained free, and her class structure evolved aspects different from those of the rest of the country. The rich merchant, the middle class of merchants with their guilds, and the small tradesman played a role unknown in Muscovy and other Russian principalities. The great Hanseatic factory with its manifold monopolies and privileges for the German merchant still flourished in the midst of the Russian town. The government continued to be in the hands of the vieche which, however, was dominated increasingly by boyars and the wealthy.

Naturally, there was considerable disunity within the town. The Orthodox opposed the Catholics; the moneyed aristocracy were at odds with the artisans; various parties of the nobility were pitted against one another; and the class struggle between rich and poor was pronounced. An additional element of discord was introduced by the rise of Muscovy. There were those who wished to preserve the town's traditional independence, but also those who, in fear of the growing neighbor, advocated closer ties with Muscovy. Actually, Moscow's ascendancy had been noticeable for several decades. Governors sent by the grand dukes to Novgorod had exercised increasing control, and through Moscow's dominance over the city's hinterland Novgorod had sunk economically into considerable dependence. In this situation, those in favor of independence looked toward Catholic Poland-Lithuania for support.

It was therefore not only economic issues or desire for aggrandizement but strategic necessity which prompted Ivan's decision to incorporate the town. The true significance of Novgorod was unfortunately misunderstood by him, as he failed to see the commercial advantages which he could derive from it as a flourishing city with an exit to the Baltic Sea.

In view of the political split within the city, the conquest itself involved no great military feat. Following an attack in 1471, the city submitted to jurisdiction, taxation, payment of a war contribution, and recognition of tsarist sovereignty. Between 1476 and 1477, the assault on the city was renewed and complete subjection took place. The people were evacuated by the thousands, deported to central Russia, and replaced by settlers from Muscovy. Trade was ruined to the extent that fifteen years later, in 1492, a new trading place had to be founded at Ivangorod, opposite Narva. In 1494, Ivan made his crowning mistake when he treacherously had the Hansa merchants seized in Novgorod; their factory was closed and their commerce ruined. Thus, much to the detriment of the whole country, its finest outlet to the sea was wrecked.

BASIL III

War with Poland, which had brought about the fall of Novgorod, was continued after Ivan's death by his son Basil III (1505–33). Basil's reign was less spectacular than that of his father; but as he followed the same policies, his rule proved just as important. In 1510, without resorting to military measures, he put an end to Pskov's independence. In 1514, despite setbacks such as a grave defeat on the Orsha River, he regained Smolensk from the Poles, and three years later he incorporated Ryazan. In the south he protected his lands by strengthening the frontier fortifications against pressure from the remaining Tartars. Thus he consolidated the work of his father, adding new territory to Moscow. It was in his time that a monk, Filofei, sent him a letter in which the theory of the "Third Rome" was stated. It meant that after two Romes (ancient Rome and Byzantium) had fallen into heresy and had perished, Moscow was to be the third, and last, Rome and the capital of the world. The presumptions underlying this statement were to serve nationalist propagandists then and later. Internally, Basil III continued the centralizing policy of Ivan the Great and the reduction of the power of princes and boyars, a task which under his son Ivan IV led to the establishment of complete autocracy.

PROBLEMS

1. Discuss the changes in Russian social structure during Ivan the Great's rule.
2. Discuss the expansion of Russia under Ivan the Great and Basil III.

7

EMERGENCE OF MODERN RUSSIA

Significant Dates

Reign of Ivan IV 1533–1584
Discovery of North Cape Route 1553
Conquest of Kazan and Astrakhan . . . 1552–1556
Livonian War 1558–1582

IVAN THE TERRIBLE

Personal Character. The evaluation of Ivan IV's importance and of his place in history has undergone many changes. At the present time, historians, particularly those of Russia, seem inclined to assign him a most prominent role in Russia's past. In view of the multiplicity of his achievements and of the directions of his endeavors, which anticipated future Russian development, research confirms such an interpretation.

Ivan's personality is intriguing, and could have been a challenge to the dramatic powers of a Shakespeare or Schiller. As with other great Russian rulers, particularly Peter I and Alexander I, two natures struggled in him for dominance. The resulting contradictions made his own life as miserable as that of his subjects. Ivan was a curious combination of arrogance and humility, of brutality and mercy, of ignorance and scholarship. Lack of discipline or self-control (a result of neglect during his youth) and an animal spirit and craftiness on the one hand, coupled with great intellect and tenderness on the other, made him a barbarian, but a barbarian with admirable qualities. Throughout his life, one or the other of his natures ruled him; and his duality characterizes his personal development as well as his political career.

Opening of Reign. In 1533, at the age of three, Ivan succeeded his father on the throne. The regency was first in the hands of his mother, then alternatingly in those of the two princely families, Shuisky and Belsky. Unloved, Ivan spent an unhappy youth until he reached the age of thirteen; finally the Shuisky regency was overthrown. At sixteen Ivan had himself crowned "Tsar," thus laying claim to all the myth, glory, and privileges which that title implied but which neither his grandfather nor his father had been successful in maintaining. Ivan, "the Terrible," was to succeed. At seventeen, he married and took the government into his own hands. During the sixteenth century, when youth ruled everywhere, opened all doors, and was recognized by all, Ivan's youthfulness implied neither lack of maturity nor lack of respect from others.

As his chief advisers, Ivan appointed two men of comparatively humble origin: Daniel Sylvester, a priest and confessor of the Tsar, and Alexis Adashev, a diak. Their influence, though overweening, was fortunate for Ivan and the country. The period of their admin-istration—i.e., until about 1560—was the most fruitful of Ivan's reign.

INTERNAL ACCOMPLISHMENTS

Establishment of Autocracy. Ivan accomplished the reduction of the power of the nobility and boyars, bringing them under the law as represented by the will of the sovereign. His autocracy meant protection of the weak against the nobles. It gained popular support and found expression through popular assemblies, the *Zemsky Sobor*. A Zemsky Sobor was not a constitutional assembly but an advisory body composed of churchmen, boyars, landlords, officials, and traders nominated by the government, and of delegates chosen at random from the provinces and from Moscow and its vicinity. The Zemsky Sobor was not a democratic assembly in the modern sense, and since there was no recognized Third Estate it could not develop into one; nevertheless it somehow reflected the will of the people, provided support of the autocrat, and shared in the responsibility for the execution of orders.

Formation of Service-Nobility. The nobility was increasingly made part of the new autocratic system by the pomestie method of land grants which Ivan's grandfather had already used for this purpose. Private landholdings (vochina) whose possession was not coupled to service but constituted outright property of the holder became steadily rarer, and likewise the remnants of the petty princes with their small independent domains lost what political influence they still possessed. Several times—once during an illness of the Tsar, another time when one of the highest noblemen, Prince Kurbsky, deserted to Poland-Lithuania—the princes and boyars tried to escape their fate. But Ivan outplayed them. In 1564, in a daring counter-move, he quit his palace in Moscow and retired to the monastery of Alexandrovsk, which he had founded and which he loved as a special place of refuge from his daily tasks. The people promptly clamored for their "indispensable" Tsar and recalled him—a summons not obeyed until his conditions were fulfilled and the subjection of the nobility could proceed without further hindrance.

Extension of Serfdom. In line with the compulsion of the nobility under a service system, the status of the peasant was also reduced to one of service only. It is true that land was given him at the expense of the aristocracy, but at the same time his attachment to the soil was tightened, and his movements were further restricted by new regulations. As a result of this policy his apathy increased, his initiative was stifled, few improvements in the productive methods of agriculture were introduced, and productivity as a whole remained low.

New Law Code. In 1550 a revision of the law code was ordered. The work was entrusted to the supervision of Alexis Adashev, who was also made director of a "Ministry for Receiving Petitions." In the code, provisions were made to check corruption, particularly in the law courts, by introducing a jury system. Although the work was not wholly satisfactory, a sounder basis for administrative duties was laid through modernizing the laws and providing the people with a voice against injustice.

A number of other ministries and departments were created, but because of their overlapping functions, their dilatory work, and the unreliability of their officials, they proved to be of little service to the people.

New Church System. At the same time, the work on revision of church practices was continued. In an attempt at reform parallel to that in the rest of Europe, church councils were convened between 1547 and 1554. These dealt with questions of ritual, morals, jurisdiction, and social institutions; but in the religious field no more was accomplished than the establishment of a printing shop for clerical books—the first of its kind in Russia. The needed moral and spiritual change was not achieved. Emphasis was placed on the national duties of the church. New measures were taken against further accumulation of wealth by the church and particularly by the monasteries. Ivan's personal reverence for the church, which led him to public confession of his sins, days devoted to prayer, self-flagellation, and other acts of devotion, probably interfered with the work of thoroughgoing reform.

In Ivan's time one of the few martyrdoms in the Russian church occurred when the metropolitan Philip was deposed and starved to death. Like Sylvester before him, but with less success, he had asked the Tsar to mend his ways and to show his people greater mercy. Philip's death increased the dependence of the church on the Tsar. It was also in Ivan's time that the Roman Catholic church made renewed efforts to bring about a reunion of the two Christian worlds. When, in 1582, Muscovy was exhausted by war and needed the political good offices of the Pope, Gregory XIII used the opportunity to send his legate Possevino to Moscow; but his efforts to win over Russia for Catholicism came to naught.

Reform of Local Administration. Local administration was reformed and expanded. Each district elected members for its own administration, who supplemented those who had governed by right of heredity. Responsible as they were to the central government, they strengthened the authority of the Tsar. Their task was to collect taxes and to administer justice. This local administration, which proved effective and promising and which might have led ultimately to a national assembly, was unfortunately discontinued under later regents.

Establishment of the Oprichnina. An important institution was created in the 1560's: the *Oprichnina*. This was a separate, parallel administrative body, existing "apart" from that of the state itself. The country was divided into two parts—one remained under the traditional administration, the other was reserved for that of the

Oprichnina. Although at first small, the Oprichnina lands included many areas strategically chosen from an economic as well as a military point of view. The new system, which actually followed some precedents, had great advantages for the Tsar. It accepted orders only from the Tsar; it combined the functions of a special private police force with those of a superior political authority; it undertook punishments ordered by Ivan and could be used to deprive the old nobility of much of its power, land, and executive functions; and it checked on the activities of the regular administration, and supplanted or duplicated the latter whenever so desired.

The Oprichnina thus became the chief tool of autocracy; its illegality, ruthlessness, and irresponsibility caused it to be feared and hated by the people as well as by the regular administration. It exercised its main influence in the central regions, where its brutality and inhuman ways of tax collection led to the flight of the inhabitants and to depopulation. It was discontinued within a decade, but by then it had accomplished its task and transformed society and state.

EXTERNAL ACCOMPLISHMENTS

In external affairs, the second half of the sixteenth century likewise witnessed great developments.

Northern Trade Route. In 1553 English seamen opened up a trade route from Scotland around the North Cape to the mouth of the Dvina River. For centuries Russian rulers had struggled for a connection with the rest of the world which was not dependent upon the good will of neighbors. Such a route was not only to serve unhindered import of needed goods, but to make intercourse with other nations possible without permission from surrounding princes. In 1548 Ivan had again been made to feel the disadvantage of Russia's geographical position when he had tried to secure doctors, scientists, and artisans from Germany and when the ill will of his neighbors on the Baltic had prevented their coming. The route around the North Cape constituted an alternative to the Baltic route and a free lane to the West.

It is true that, because of navigational dangers, trade in the north with England as well as with other countries did not develop as had been anticipated. The English, who had hoped to reach China and Japan when they found Russia, were slow in recognizing the value of Russian trade and still persisted in searching for trade routes to the Far East. The Danish king, fearing the loss of dues which he collected in the Sound from all ships entering or leaving the Baltic, did his utmost to hinder the trade in the north unless the same dues were paid him for permission to traverse the sea lanes situated between his two possessions of Norway and Iceland. Yet, the possibility of reaching Europe directly meant an enormous advantage for Russia. Treaties were promptly negotiated, particularly with Denmark and England, monopolies were granted to traders of important commodities, foreign merchants were invited to establish themselves in Russia, artisans were imported without consent from neighbors, and personal relationships with rulers in the West were entered into.

The opportunities thus offered were made use of in order to strengthen autocracy. With no one class in Russia devoting itself to trade, but all sharing as they could, the Tsar appropriated trade monopolies for himself and strengthened his financial position through these and through the duties he imposed.

Southward Expansion. In the south, Ivan secured even greater advantages. Three remnants of the Tartar empire still existed in Russia: the Crimea, Astrakhan, and Kazan—all practically independent powers ruled by Tartar princes. They constituted a permanent menace to Russia, which they repeatedly invaded. After unsuccessful negotiations, Ivan's armies entered Kazan in 1552 and Astrakhan in 1554. Both countries were completely defeated and their territories incorporated into Russia. Ivan's empire was thus vastly increased, and a perpetual threat was eliminated. Only the Crimean Tartars remained outside the reach of the Russians. Supported by the Turks, they continued to make inroads into Russian territory and to block the way to the Black Sea. In vain did Adashev and Sylvester advocate their elimination. Ivan, with sound judgment, anticipated Turkish opposition if he tried to take the Crimea, and he preferred to seek access to the Baltic Sea. While he was engaged there in 1571, the Tartars burned Moscow and led away uncounted numbers of prisoners. However, they did not consolidate their conquest but, satisfied with vast booty, retreated.

Westward Advance. As Ivan through his southward expansion prepared the way for Catherine the Great's policies, so he anticipated those of Peter the Great in his attempt to reach the Baltic Sea in the west. Realizing the inadequacy of the newly opened northern route, the Tsar endeavored to gain the great harbors of Livonia on the Baltic Sea. Unlike his grandfather Ivan III, Ivan the Terrible was to recognize the economic importance of Livonia. Textiles, wines, metal objects, armor, and salt were exchanged there for Russian wheat, rye, timber, flax, hemp, pitch, and tar. Political reasons likewise compelled the Tsar to interfere in Livonia, inasmuch as the rule of the Germans, exercised through the Teutonic Knights and the Hansa merchants, was collapsing. Poland and Sweden, both traditional enemies of Russia, were likely to seize the Baltic ports.

Ivan's campaign to gain Livonia extended over a period of twenty-five years. During the first three years, from 1558 to 1560, military measures were taken. Most of the flat land was conquered, but the two important harbors of Riga and Reval could not be gained. Another ten years were spent in diplomatic negotiations. Then a Danish prince, Magnus of Holstein, was appointed puppet king of Livonia by Ivan; but he was as incapable a ruler as a general, and he failed to secure the desired ports. In the fourth and last stage, Ivan once more used military might, but his troops were repelled by the now combined forces of Poland and Sweden. The Peace of Yam Zapolie, concluded with Poland in 1582, deprived the Tsar not only of his conquests in Livonia, but also of many Russian possessions formerly gained in the Polish-Lithuanian realms. The peace with Sweden, a year later, cost Ivan the small yet growing port of Narva, his last anchor in Livonia; this was a devastating blow for the Tsar, inasmuch as the final destruction of Novgorod, which he had ordered in 1570, had left him with no outlet on the Baltic except Narva. Yet, although Russia had thus temporarily to abandon her plans in the Baltic provinces, the direction of her growth was clearly conceived and definitely indicated as a future aim of Russian rulers.

Eastward Movement.   Finally, the momentous movement eastward into Siberia was begun under Ivan's rule.

PROBLEMS

1. Discuss the position of the nobility and the peasantry under Ivan the Terrible.
2. Discuss the significance of the discovery of a sea route around the North Cape.
3. Discuss the importance of Ivan's attempt to conquer Livonia.

8

SIBERIA

Significant Dates

Stroganov's Grant 1558
Yermak's First Expedition 1581
Russians Reach Pacific 1645
Treaty of Nerchinsk 1689

GEOGRAPHICAL FACTORS

The vast plains of Siberia bear significant resemblance to those of European Russia. The same four belts are to be found: an arctic tundra, a forest, steppe, and desert zone. Except in the south, mountains are altogether lacking; and the climate, though more extreme, parallels that of European Russia. Again, and more important, Siberia's rivers form as excellent a network of communication lines as do those of Russia proper. Although a casual look at the map reveals no more than three great rivers, the Ob, Yenisei, and Lena (all flowing far apart from south to north into the Arctic Ocean), closer scrutiny shows that their tributaries form a highway from west to east for thousands upon thousands of miles. The Cossacks who crossed Siberia, being as proficient inland navigators as horsemen, found a route from the Urals to the farthest of the great rivers, the Lena. This route, entirely by water with the exception of two short portages (one of five miles from the Ob to the Yenisei basin, the other of ten miles from the Yenisei to Lake Baikal and the Lena basin), proved of utmost importance for the occupation of the land.

EXPLORATION OF SIBERIA

Opening of Siberia. In the sixteenth century, Siberia was by no means unknown to the Russians. Traders from Novgorod had traversed it from the eleventh century on; missionaries to China had entered and reported about it; in 1499 an attempt to conquer the Ob region had been made, and tributes were paid by Tartar chieftains there. Therefore, no "discovery" was needed, nor any "conquest" necessary. What happened may be called a "settlement" of Siberia; but as Russia at the end of the sixteenth century numbered fewer than fifteen million inhabitants, the occupation was slow. Essentially, the settlement was a "penetration" for future political and economic use, and this penetration was carried on by incredibly small forces. Indeed, half a continent with five million square miles was brought under Russian suzerainty by bands made up at the largest of eight hundred and fifty men, and sometimes of as few as twenty-five. Adventurers, mainly Cossacks, opened the way. They were strong in body, were of Orthodox faith, belonged to the unsettled elements of the population in quest of freedom, and followed the age-old call of "gospel, gold, and glory."

STROGANOV. The expansion into Siberia began with Grigory Stroganov, a rich merchant from Novgorod who, in 1558, secured a land concession on the Kama River east of Moscow. The grant, unlike those in the United States during the nineteenth century, was secured only under strictest conditions: Stroganov was exempted from taxes for twenty years, but in return he was pledged to build and operate salt works, to break the soil for agriculture, to equip a small army for protection, and to renounce claims to any mines which his agents might discover.

EXPLORATION. Stroganov found his concession profitable and his family secured additional grants which extended beyond the Urals. For the protection of their possessions they hired Cossacks, among whom was a former robber and pirate, Yermak (Ermak Timofeyev). Yermak, an energetic man who had proved his abilities, though in an unlawful way, was charged, in 1581, with leading an expedition into the region east of the Urals. Accompanied by priests and interpreters, he sailed up the rivers as far as possible toward the Urals, dragged his boats across the crest, and sailed down in the direction of the Ob. Being equipped with firearms, he readily defeated opposing Tartar armies and took the city of Sibir, which was later to give its name to the country. He was pardoned for his misdeeds, and for his exploits he received rich gifts from the Tsar. With undiminished energy, he proceeded to establish trade connections not only with the tribes in western Siberia, but also with the more civilized people in central Asia around Samarkand and Bokhara; and by having *ostrogs* or forts built and equipped with small guns, he provided for the defense of the newly acquired region.

SUCCEEDING EXPLORERS. In 1584 Yermak lost his life by drowning in a river during a battle. After a temporary halt, his work was continued by a succession of Cossacks and explorers. Outstanding among them were: Poiarkov, who reached the Amur River in 1644 and who also undertook to travel down the Lena; Khabarov—an able explorer but lacking in all understanding of the value of his explorations—whose misdeeds around 1650 in the region of the Amur and among the Chinese did untold damage to the Russian cause; Stepanov, who likewise devoted his attention to the Amur region and who died in 1658; and Atlasov—a colorful personality, corrupt in many instances but not entirely devoid of intelligence and feeling—who discovered Kamchatka in 1697.

Penetration. Progress through Siberia, considering its expanse, was remarkably fast. In 1587 Tobolsk on the Ob was founded. From there, the Russians always strove to push southward and eastward into more habitable regions but were persistently forced off their course by hostile native tribes into an undesirable northeasterly direction. This fact is of far-reaching importance: Had the Russians used their small forces against the resistance of the southern tribes, they might never have had the strength to continue the penetration of Asia to the Pacific. On the other hand, had they succeeded in pushing southward, their later difficulties there and their rivalry with England might have been avoided; and the fate of India would certainly have been different.

In 1618 the Russians reached the upper course of the Yenisei and, ten years later, were at the Lena, where in 1632 they founded Yakutsk. Upon reaching the Amur River in 1644, they beheld a great and uniquely different civilization—that of the Chinese. It was also there that for the first time they encountered good conditions for agricultural work. But again their attention was diverted to the barren northern parts. In 1644 they reached the mouth of the Kolima River on the Arctic Ocean, and in 1648 founded Okhotsk on the Pacific Ocean.

In the following year, a voyage was undertaken by a man called Dezhnev, who probably rounded the northeastern corner of Asia, finding the seaway from the Arctic Ocean to the Pacific Ocean—an event anticipating Bering's and Nordenskjöld's later expeditions.

In 1651 Irkutsk on Lake Baikal was founded and, finally, in 1697 Kamchatka was explored and the extreme Far East taken into possession.

GOVERNMENT IN SIBERIA

Administration. The Russian government viewed these explorations mainly from a strategic angle, considering them important above all as security measures against nomad invasions. Thus, the initiative for expanding the acquisitions in Asia remained in the hands of the conquering lawless bands who had little sense of honor, no love of country, and no respect for promises. Their exactions from the natives were generally excessive; and whenever one of their leaders, such as Atlasov, endeavored to safeguard the elementary rights of the inhabitants, he faced charges of conspiracy and heresy. The farther the conquerors were away from Europe, the greater their lawlessness. Torture, abduction, murder, and cannibalism were among their crimes; and at the cry "The Cossacks are coming," the natives were stricken with terror. However, as with contemporary Spanish explorers, so it was with the Russians: Not only the soldiers were to be feared, but so also were the traders who arrived in their wake and who, through speculation in land, provisions, transportation, and mines (particularly salt works), contributed to the hardship of the natives.

SIBERIAN DEPARTMENT. The government reacted feebly. In 1637 a Siberian Department was founded in Moscow, and various administrative units were established in Siberia. These were centralized in 1670 in Tobolsk. The officials were often corrupt, robbing not only the people but also the government they represented; and their harshness resulted in the flight of many natives to China. Their chief occupation and task consisted in collecting taxes, their main support being their superior arms. Thus, in many respects Russian aims and administration in Siberia at the beginning resembled Tartar rule in Russia two centuries earlier. If taxes were paid, the people were left alone; if they had adopted the Christian faith, they were allowed to intermix with the newcomers and to enter government service.

Commerce. Trade developed slowly, for the climate in some regions offered too great an obstacle to normal life, and silver was not found in quantities as expected. Furs alone could reward the exertions of the settlers. Only when contact was established with the mighty Chinese empire, at that time enjoying a period of great prosperity, did trade begin to show some promise. Textiles, silk, gold, and silverware from China were exchanged for hides, furs, and foodstuffs—the type of commodities offered by either side giving a significant picture of its respective civilization and living standards.

Relations with China. Attempts were also made to establish diplomatic relations, but the overbearing attitude of the Chinese rendered impossible any normal intercourse. It was only after the Russians began to penetrate along the Amur River and into Manchuria that a real necessity for diplomatic relations arose. The Chinese were not directly interested in the Amur region, particularly not along the lower course of the river; and had the Cossacks settled quietly, they probably would have been left alone. But the disturbances resulting from their activities and the reports of fleeing Chinese made it impossible for the government in Peking to remain unconcerned. Several armies were therefore sent to drive away the intruders, and, though not always successful, they made the Russian position most precarious.

TREATY OF NERCHINSK. Finally, embassies were exchanged, and on August 27, 1689, after two weeks of negotiations, a treaty was signed at Nerchinsk. It was drafted in Latin by Jesuits living at the Chinese court, and the Jesuits were of course more proficient in Latin than their treaty partners. Not only this, but their knowledge of Russia was far greater than the Russian ambassador Golovine's knowledge of China. As a result, the treaty turned out to be very satisfactory for the Chinese. Both sides of the Amur River remained China's, and Mongolia was kept within her sphere. Russia was confined to the northern, less habitable regions; but these were vast enough to provide a task for colonization which strained all the resources in matériel and manpower at the disposal of the Russians, so that there was little interest in additional territory. The peace concluded at Nerchinsk was to endure for more than one hundred and fifty years.

TREATY OF KYAKHTA. In 1727 the political treaty was supplemented, at Kyakhta, by a convention which regulated Russo-Chinese trade relations and diplomatic intercourse.

PROBLEMS

1. Explain the geographical and geopolitical structure of Siberia.
2. Compare the settling of Siberia with the Western movement in America.
3. Discuss the early political activities of Russia in Siberia.

9

TIME OF TROUBLES

Significant Dates

Law Against Fugitive Peasants 1597
Time of Troubles 1604–1613
Romanov Family Ascends Throne 1613

THE COMING OF THE "TROUBLES"

Estimate of Ivan's Reign. Ivan the Terrible died in 1584. Owing chiefly to the Livonian war and the Oprichnina, his reign had seen political insecurity, loss of agricultural production, forfeiture of taxes, further human degradation, devastation of the western and northwestern parts of the empire, and an accelerated trend toward serfdom. On the other hand, it had checked the license of the nobility, brought improvements in the church and in the legislative process, accomplished consolidation of the realm, opened new trade prospects, and fostered territorial expansion outlining the future destiny of Russia. His was the first modern government in Russia, and it is said that it constituted an early part of the great revolution known as the "Time of Troubles." It must not be inferred that Ivan himself was the sole impetus for the revolution; the work of one man can hardly carry such weight. But his policies contributed to the evolution of a new trend. Though not recognizable at first, a new concept of state emerged, influencing the attitudes of the Russian people, and this new concept determined the course of the subsequent upheavals. Once this is understood, the Time of Troubles (*Smuta*) loses its confused picture, the roles of the political figures—

57

of the Godunovs, false Dimitris, Shuiskys, and Romanovs—fall into place, and the classical pattern of revolution is revealed.

The revolution, then, began with Ivan's reign, that is, with a period of stated grievances and attempted reforms; its one remarkable feature was that the ruler allied himself with the dissatisfied classes against the privileged and the nobility.

Boris Godunov. The second stage was again a typical revolutionary step, a time of hesitation and deliberate delay in an effort to avoid otherwise inevitable destruction, terror, and later reaction. It is marked by the rule of Boris Godunov, dominant figure behind Ivan's son, Tsar Feodor I (1584–98), who succeeded his father. Feodor played no role; he was a pious, incompetent, perhaps even weak-minded man—"a sacristan, not a tsarevitch," as his father said. His demise in 1598 was of importance only inasmuch as with him the family died out; and since autocracy had stifled the people's ability to govern themselves, it cleared the way for full assumption of power by Boris Godunov (1598–1605). A boyar, Godunov was proclaimed Tsar by a Zemsky Sobor which was convoked and cleverly manipulated by him for the purpose. Able, shrewd, rich, and also vain and insecure in his actions, he accomplished a by no means negligible job, continuing Ivan's struggle against the privileged nobility and ruthlessly suppressing their attempts to overthrow him and regain power. It was he who began to use Siberia as a place of banishment for political adversaries. The period of his rule brought comparative peace and order. Moscow gained enormously by the raising of the metropolitan see to a patriarchate, trade was encouraged, exports increased, building activities were revived, and fortifications against the Poles, Tartars, and Swedes were erected.

Agriculture and Serfdom. But all this could not stem the tide of revolution. Towards the end of Feodor's reign, signs of the coming upheaval had become unmistakable. Unrest had grown when attacks from the outside necessitated military expansion and led to wider recruiting and the imposition of higher taxes. In consequence, more peasant flights occurred and many joined the ranks of the free Cossacks on the frontiers. To halt the exodus of peasants, a law of grave consequences was passed in 1597 that permitted the landowners a five-year interval in which to reclaim fugitive peasants. It also forbade the kidnaping of peasants from one estate to another. This law, whereby free mobility suffered further, meant another step on the road to serfdom. After Godunov ascended the throne, the roused lower classes found an additional cause for discontent when a terrible famine occurred in 1601–03. This famine was closely connected with the flight of peasants from the cultivated central regions and led to starvation and death for tens or perhaps hundreds of thousands. The superstitious populace blamed the new Tsar—upon whom, because of his numerous misdeeds, they saw God's wrath descend. They also accused him—and justly, in the opinion of modern investigators—of having killed Ivan the Terrible's youngest son Dimitri in 1591, in order to secure the power for himself. The dissatisfaction was turned to use by the boyars, who hoped to settle accounts with the hated "usurper" risen from their own midst. Their party was joined by merchants and people of the middle class, who were losing by the disorder and whose trade and travel were being disrupted by roving brigands. The situation worsened for Godunov when, in 1604, the crops improved and the landowners, on the basis of the law of 1597, began to ask for the return of their serfs after having willingly let them go free during the times of starvation.

CIVIL WAR

Appearance of False Dimitri. At this point, the next revolutionary step was taken—that of violence and civil war. In the Russia of 1604, it took the form of the emergence of a pretender to Godunov's throne, who naturally found support among the dissatisfied elements comprising more or less the whole population. He appeared as a "false Dimitri," impersonating Ivan's son, whose murderers were said to have taken by mistake the life of a substitute. Although historians generally concur nowadays that "Dimitri" was an impostor, he may have acted in good faith, as he is said to have been carefully trained for his role from earliest youth. He secured military help from the Poles, who took pleasure in the opportunity to disturb the peace of Russia and who extorted vast territorial, religious, and political promises in exchange for their unofficial support. "Dimitri" invaded Russia and was joined by thousands, including the Cossack legions, whereas Godunov was confined to fighting him with weak forces and with propaganda accusing him of fraud and subservience to the Catholic church. In the midst of war (1605) Godunov died, leaving his claims to the throne to a well-educated and able son, Feodor II. Shortly thereafter, "Dimitri" took Moscow and induced the real Dimitri's mother, Ivan's widow, to "recognize" him; then disposing of Feodor II, the last of the Godunov family (Feodor's sister Irene was sent to a nunnery), he established himself on the throne.

Reaction. During his brief reign in 1605–06, "Dimitri" (Demetrius I) proved a capable administrator, conscientiously working on affairs of state, easing the status of the serfs, lowering taxes, and raising wages. But the boyars had no desire merely to exchange one usurper for another. Taking advantage of "Dimitri's" foreign leanings, his disdain for uncouth Russian customs and manners, and his insulting behavior towards the Patriarch (whom he had the poor judgment to replace by a man of doubtful orthodoxy), the boyars raised from their midst a Prince Shuisky and with the help of a handsomely bribed Zemsky Sobor set him on the throne. Shuisky (Basil IV, 1606–10) was weak and unreliable; and though "Dimitri" was eliminated by murder in 1606, he failed to bring back the conditions for which his backers had hoped. His incompetence led to the final and bloodiest stage of the revolution—foreign war and civil terror.

Polish Invasion. After the death of "Dimitri" the Cossacks and underprivileged endeavored to produce another pretender as standard-bearer—either a false Peter or a second false Dimitri; and it is significant that they spoke of their "legitimate" ruler before he even existed. Several men vied for the position, and in 1608 a "second false Dimitri" succeeded in establishing his claims and gaining the support of the Cossacks. He invaded Russia with another Polish army and was received by the "first false Dimitri's" wife (the adventurous Polish noblewoman Marina Mniszek) as her legal husband, although secretly, after sharing his bed, she had herself married to him by a Jesuit priest. The Polish danger prompted Shuisky to call in the Swedes, and as a result war and civil strife ravaged the unhappy country. Shuisky boyars fought anti-Shuisky boyars, one group of Cossacks stood against another group of Cossacks, pomestie landlords were aligned against the peasants, and the merchants were opposed to the boyars. Finally, all were fighting one another.

Realignment in Russia. The new pretender failed to turn the situation to his own advantage, for his abilities did not match those of his predecessor. He was unsuccessful in his attempt to take Moscow, and his troops pillaged the country and discredited the revolution. In 1610 he was murdered in a private feud. Although worse suffering was still to come, this year brought a clarification of the issues at stake and the emergence of definite parties. On the one side were the Poles, who quickly ruined their chances by their destructive actions. Their king, Sigismund, who wanted the Russian crown for his family, pursued the customary policy of territorial aggrandizement at Russia's expense; but he insisted also on reunion with Catholicism. In Russia he was supported first by the lower nobility and merchant class, later only by the high boyars, who expected to secure the same extravagant privileges which their Polish brethren had won. On the other side were two groups: (1) a national movement rallying around the Orthodox church under the valiant leadership of the Patriarch, stout defender of independence, and (2) a social movement supported by the Cossacks, who struggled for economic improvements. Shuisky had nothing to offer to either and therefore was deposed early in 1610 and banished to a cloister. The throne was left vacant.

Climax and End of "Troubles." During the ensuing interim, the Poles penetrated to Moscow, burned the suburbs, and established themselves in the Kremlin. They also besieged the famous Trinity Monastery which, under the direction of the dauntless Patriarch, withstood their assault for a year and a half. The fearsome peril to the nation and to the Orthodox faith brought a fusion of the Russian forces through which, it is true, the social revolutionary aims were defeated; but the national cause was saved.

First a triumvirate was instituted, consisting of a boyar, a nobleman, and a Cossack hetman (the latter being also the third husband of Marina Mniszek, who had not yet given up her hopes for the throne). This triumvirate failed to rally all national forces, for it lost the support of the radical elements by publishing a number of decrees which benefited essentially the service-nobility and which neglected the interests of those in favor of free land. It also was unable to stem the tide of foreign interventionists—the Poles, who reconquered Smolensk, and the Swedes, who captured Novgorod. A new organization had to be created, and this was done in 1611 by leaders of the church and by volunteers from the more conservative strata of the population, among whom were such outstanding men

as the Novgorod merchant, Kuzma Minin. With their help, a
national army was called into being and organized in the unoccu-
pied northeastern provinces. Then this army, more homogeneous
than that of the triumvirate, marched against Moscow. It succeeded
in engaging the support of the moderate elements among the triumvirate's forces, and the thereby-strengthened national army started
the siege of the Kremlin. The Poles, who had committed the crime
of starving the Russian Patriarch to death, now suffered a like fate
themselves, and at the end of 1612 Moscow and the Kremlin were
retaken. In the meantime, the revolutionary Cossacks and their
friends, weakened through defection, had to retire into Astrakhan,
where their forces gradually dissolved. As the capture of Moscow
and the expulsion of the Poles marked the end of the national
struggle, so did the disintegration of the revolutionary Cossack
forces terminate the civil war.

RECONSTRUCTION

Michael Romanov. The next pressing task was the choice of a
new head of state, for the desire for order, which usually follows
revolution, was paramount. The service-nobility, which had es-
poused the national cause and had shown its preponderance toward
the end of the Time of Troubles, represented the class best fitted to
fulfill this desire. It was under their influence that a Zemsky Sobor,
which was convened in 1613 in order to appoint a new Tsar, chose
a compromise candidate, sixteen-year-old Michael Romanov. He was
a member of the high nobility and a relative of the first wife of Ivan
the Terrible, yet he was also acceptable to the service-nobility and
the peasants. With him, in 1613, began the reign of the dynasty
which was to last until 1917, and with him order was re-established.

As a revolution, the "Troubles" had failed. Few social gains had
been achieved, inasmuch as autocracy and the service-nobility, as
founded by Ivan the Terrible, triumphed. The gains which were
achieved had all been anticipated by Ivan the Terrible, and the
behavior of the Cossacks themselves was to a large extent responsible for the failure of further reforms. Yet Russia survived. Poland,
momentarily within grasp of uniting the Slavic world, had bungled
the task; if Poland had succeeded, Siberian and eastern interests
would certainly have been sacrificed to European schemes. As it was,

Russia entered a new and definitely separate stage of her history, a period of enormous outward expansion and painful inner tension.

Summary. The century and a quarter following the end of Tartar rule saw Russian developments channeled in a new, and in many respects tragic, direction. Only those technological and utilitarian features of Renaissance Europe which seemed fit for immediate practical application had been adopted; otherwise, little interest had been shown in becoming part of Europe. On the contrary, the urge to preserve their identity had made the Russians maintain barriers against the West and had given particular fervor to the struggle against Catholic Poland. It perhaps had also directed attention eastward toward the Urals and Siberia. Russia gained nothing from Europe's gradual emancipation from feudal patterns; not even the members of the Russian middle class became carriers of the ideas of revolutionary capitalism, since the few important merchants (*gosti*) acted less often as independent merchants than as agents of the autocrat. Contradictions within the political structure of the country increased and found expression in the actions of such colorful but discordant personalities as Ivan the Terrible, Prince Kurbsky, Boris Godunov, the first False Dimitri—personalities at once attractive, repulsive, and fascinating. Yet Russia had overcome, largely intact, the nadir of her development since Kievan times and, though continuing to be beset by tremendous problems, could start on the road toward greatness.

PROBLEMS

1. Discuss the social significance of the Time of Troubles.
2. Discuss the role of a "popular voice" (Zemsky Sobor) at the turn of the sixteenth century.
3. Discuss Russia's international position during the Time of Troubles.

10

CONSOLIDATION UNDER ROMANOV DYNASTY

Significant Dates

Reign of Michael 1613–1645
Reign of Alexis I 1645–1676
New Law Code 1649
Cossack Revolt of Stenka Razin 1667–1671

CONDITIONS AT THE END OF THE "TROUBLES"

Social and Economic Conditions. The revolution encompassing the reign of Ivan the Terrible and the *Smuta* or "Troubles" consolidated the triumph of the service-nobility over the great hereditary nobility. It also confirmed the failure both of the peasantry, which had risen against the landholding classes, and of the middle class, which had been unsuccessful in gaining a political voice. Thus, the times ushering in the house of Romanov brought no social improvement.

Economically, Russia was largely ruined: The material damage, aggravated by the foreign wars which had accompanied the *Smuta,* called for extensive repair; money was needed for the treasury; foodstuffs were necessary for the stores; manpower—through exchange of prisoners—was required for work on the land. Trade revival was exigent and had to be bought at the price of vast privileges and monopolies in foreign commerce, which were accorded to the English and the Dutch, adversely affecting the future of the Russian merchant. Politically, peace had yet to be concluded with Poland and Sweden. With the former, no final settlement was possible; the latter, under its great king Gustavus Adolphus, agreed in the Peace of Stolbovo (1617) to the evacuation of Novgorod but held fast to the Baltic harbors in Livonia and Ingria.

The Tsars. The government itself needed reorganization. Michael (1613–45), the first Romanov, was a weakling Tsar, whose reign acquired color only through his father, Patriarch Philaret, who took the title of *"Veliki Gosudar"* and thus, as a second "Great Lord" or sovereign, exercised until his death in 1633 equal power with the Tsar in state and church. Michael was succeeded by Alexis (1645–76), a man of high principles, humanity, and ability, but likewise possessed of insufficient resolution. After the period of Alexis came the short reign of Feodor III (1676–82).

The rule of these first three Romanovs witnessed the gradual consolidation of the empire, the settlement with Poland, and widespread social changes.

REORGANIZATION

Finances. Consolidation of the country was carried out through centralization under autocracy. For the purpose of strengthening central authority, the taxation system was revised. Burdens on the taxpayers, having increased because of the revolution, were further aggravated through direct and indirect impositions. To a high sales tax were added scores of internal duties, salt taxes, and especially regular capital taxes which sometimes amounted to as much as 20 per cent. Strict edicts were issued against selling oneself into bondage in order to escape payment, and against various other stratagems resorted to for the same purpose. But despite all government laws, the inefficiency and corruption of the administration were too great to guarantee the correct use of taxes. As everywhere in Europe, a large share of these never reached the treasury; and, likewise as in other countries, good use was seldom made of those amounts which did come in. Instead of being applied to financing productive improvements, gold and jewels were stored and wealth was hoarded; in France or Spain these would have served at least to increase the credit of the nation, but in Russia they lay unused in palaces and churches, while the currency depreciated.

Army. The autocracy naturally paid close attention to the army, and vast sums were expended for improving it. All the gentry were required to serve in the wars, and specific contingents of common soldiers were recruited forcibly from each estate—a measure hindering the rebuilding of the land. A nucleus was formed of *Streltsi* (archers) who furnished the professional part of the army and at the same time formed a praetorian guard for the ruler; many among them were mercenaries from France, Switzerland, Germany, Scotland, and other countries.

Trade. Foreigners also formed the backbone of the revived trade. Not only did the Dutch and English profit, but artisans were attracted from various other countries. They opened shops and imported and exported. Their importance grew as they introduced not only their skills but also their ways and customs. Their contributions were numerous, their cleanliness, order, and thrift were commonly appreciated, and the "German suburb" of Moscow, which housed Germans and other foreigners, became the most progressive part of the capital. Yet, the foreigners caused also certain disadvantages insofar as no strong Russian merchant class developed and not enough native artisans were trained. Most of the trade that existed among the Russians was not handled by established merchants but was shared by a motley crowd of boyars, soldiers, peasants, and artisans, every one of whom tried to gain some additional income through trade in the most varied commodities. The disadvantages of the situation were reflected in stagnation and emphasized by want of markets, as the rich would not buy Russian products and the poor—particularly the peasants—because of poverty produced their own most primitive tools.

Industry. During the seventeenth century, Russian industry grew rapidly. Farsighted statesmen devoted their attention to its improvement and liberally used foreign experts to help them. Dutch, German, and English engineers and entrepreneurs came and directed the building of a more advanced economy. Among them was Vinius who founded iron works, Marselis who established armament and tool factories and a postal service, and others who helped establish glass, textile, and machine industries. In addition, printers, scientists, teachers, and army officers came and spread Western knowledge. Many of the industries were government-owned or government-supervised.

Government. Through its ownership of industry and through centralization, taxation, and reliance on services by foreigners, the administration succeeded in reducing self-government and in emancipating itself from the Zemsky Sobors and other former popular institutions of the country. The first Romanov had owed his crown to a Zemsky Sobor, and at the beginning of his reign the assembly retained no inconsiderable amount of power. It sat virtually continuously from 1613 to 1622 and during this time not only enacted a number of important measures, such as those concerning taxation, but also showed its independence by boldly assuming questionable prerogatives—for example, in confirming the Patriarch in 1619. But because of the general trends, the Zemsky Sobor began to recruit its members more and more exclusively from the service-nobility and no longer represented the Russian people as a whole. It thus forfeited the support of other classes, and ultimately relinquished all power to the growing autocracy. Until 1642, the Zemsky Sobor continued to influence domestic issues; and it was active on several foreign questions—one being that regarding the fortress of Azov conquered by Don Cossacks. As a matter of fact, the assembly advocated its return to the Turks lest war with them result. In 1649 the Zemsky Sobor was consulted in connection with the new law code of that year, but by then no peasant representative could be found among its members and its role had become entirely passive. After 1653 it convened no more.

Law. The reorganization of the country was confirmed through the law code of 1649. The code was in many respects a retrogressive one and marked an important step in the development of the Russian nation. It constituted a revision of the code of 1550 adopted in Ivan the Terrible's time. But it went further in that it collected customary procedures or codified existing legal concepts and introduced new precepts and methods derived from the study of the laws of Byzantium as well as those of the Lithuanian grand duchy. However, despite all endeavors, the code represented no truly scientific approach to the establishment of principles of justice, but remained a superficial work. Its adoption led to an intolerable chain of misdeeds.

PURPOSE OF THE CODE. The primary purpose of the new laws, as of most of the measures taken during the seventeenth century, consisted in the strengthening of central authority. All over Europe the trend was toward centralization and theories of the "divine right of kings," and Russia was no exception. In the code of 1649, not only was the taxing power of the state secured, but commerce was made dependent upon the state. The trading privileges of the foreigners were greatly restricted. The jurisdiction of the church was limited and so were its rights to the acquisition of property. Moreover, stipulations were made providing for a certain amount of state control over all private property.

DEFECT OF THE CODE. The chief shortcoming of the code consisted in its failure to define the legal position of the peasants, who actually found themselves outside the law. In 1646 they had been compelled to register at the places where they lived and worked, and, once this was done, they had been forced to remain there. In practically every respect the peasants became subjected to the landowners, who were made responsible for their work and taxes and who, from now on, could reclaim them, if fugitive, without time limit. Wider jurisdiction over them was granted the landowner, and thus the last stone was laid in the structure for enslaving the agricultural workers. A peasant became largely a piece of property, attached not only to the soil but, in some respects, also—as a personal belonging —to a master.

EXTERNAL AFFAIRS

Throughout Russian history there have existed connections— economic, religious, and political—between Russia and the West. In the sixteenth century, these had increased in intensity, and in the seventeenth century they showed further progress. Not only were closer cultural ties established, under Michael and then under Alexis, through the introduction of secular Western literature, of Western theater and the ballet, but also, politically, continental Europe came to play a greater role in Russia.

Poland and Sweden. Of course, Russia's neighbors, Poland and Sweden, continued to hold the special attention of the Russians. The relationship with both countries changed to the advantage of Russia. Possessing few men and institutions fit for modern times, Poland disintegrated internally and had to abandon ambitions for external greatness. Eight wars between 1615 and 1667 confirmed the rise of Russia, brought the return of the town of Smolensk, guaranteed greater future security, and established Russian supremacy even in the internal affairs of Poland.

The disintegration of Poland had far-reaching consequences. It led not only to a settlement between Russia and Poland, but also to a decision of the territorial issues between Russia and Sweden. Since the time of Ivan the Terrible, Sweden had increased her hold on the southern shores of the Baltic Sea. With the collapse of Poland, she tried to expand further her marine possessions and was brought once more into conflict with the Tsars. A long war (1656–61) was fought, which for the first time did not result in encroachments on the Russian sphere. Because of general exhaustion, peace was concluded at Cardis (1661) without gain to either side, thus bringing a stalemate which was to be followed in Peter the Great's time, less than half a century later, by a full reversal of previous power relationships.

Germany and Western Europe. In the course of the seventeenth century, Russia was beginning to be considered a factor in the European balance of power. She did not participate in the Thirty Years' War (1618–1648), but indirectly through her policies toward Sweden affected the course of events. Regularly, she exchanged representatives with Western countries and negotiated on a common policy toward Turkey. Russian statesmen emerged, such as Ordyn Nashchokin and Artamon Matveyev, who distinguished themselves as capable diplomats well-informed about European affairs.

PEASANT RISINGS

The direction of reconstruction and consolidation in the middle seventeenth century was challenged by the peasants, at whose expense it took place. However, the development of internal conditions in Russia can not be traced to the whim of any lawmaker, but stems directly from the rapid succession of social upheavals in the sixteenth and early seventeenth centuries. Chaos had led to a reduction of cultivated land, to depopulation, to appalling accumulations of private debt, to dangerously reduced armed strength, and to a vast decrease of state income. Even after the *Smuta* was over, famines continued to occur. Recovery necessitated resettlement of free or abandoned land and the insertion of the individual into the whole for the benefit of the state. In its essence, the development may therefore be described as a natural and compulsory result of prevailing circumstances; but at the same time, it was destined to lead not only to graver complications in the future, but to violent opposition while in progress.

Revolts.   The period of the first three Romanovs, and particularly that of the benevolent Alexis, is indeed marked by an almost uninterrupted chain of revolutionary outbreaks. Freedom prevailed only on the fringes of the empire, in the north, in Siberia, and in the territories of the Cossacks to the south. There the independent elements assembled, the fugitive peasants found haven, and from thence issued the spirit of liberty. Hundreds of small-scale revolts are traceable. By 1648 and 1650 the disturbances commenced to increase in violence. In 1662 a serious uprising occurred in connection with the depreciation of money, when the minting of valueless copper pieces in lieu of silver resulted in inflation and impoverishment.

Stenka Razin.   These sporadic outbreaks finally touched off a revolt of great magnitude. It began in 1667 and reached its climax in 1670. Led by a Cossack, Stenka Razin, who promised liberation of the peasants, forces of from seven to ten thousand men succeeded in seizing thousands of square miles of Russian territory, and fleets of the revolutionaries sailed up and down the Volga River and on the Caspian Sea, plundering even the great harbor of Derbent. Important cities like Tsaritsyn and Astrakhan were seized. Razin's actions were directed against the rich landowners, and his fidelity to the Tsar, or at least to the institution of tsarism, was frequently reiterated. However, as it generally happened, the behavior of the Cossacks themselves, their outrages and brutality, cost them the fruits of victory and alienated the sympathies even of those for whom they were said to be fighting. By 1671 the government had the situation in hand. Stenka Razin was betrayed, captured, and executed. More than one hundred years were to elapse before the forces for a new great uprising could be collected.

The suppression of the Cossack revolt of Stenka Razin was of fundamental importance for the success of one of the greatest tasks accomplished during the reign of the first three Romanovs—the reabsorption of the long-lost southern parts of the country, the Ukraine.

PROBLEMS

1. Discuss the rise of the service-nobility and the decline of popular representation.
2. Discuss the change of the balance of power in eastern Europe.
3. Summarize the causes of the discontent of peasants and Cossacks.

11

THE UKRAINE

Significant Dates

Capture of Kiev by Lithuania 1320
Union of Lithuania and Poland 1386
Cossack Risings against Poland in Ukraine 1604–1649
Peace of Andrusovo 1667

CONDITIONS UNDER LITHUANIAN RULE

Separation from Russia. The reabsorption of the southern parts of Russia into the Muscovite dominions during the seventeenth century marked the end of a period which had brought misfortune to both sections. In 1320, after continuous wars during which Lithuania and Poland had carved off vast regions of the Ukraine, the capital Kiev, fell under the rule of Lithuania. Thus, in the midst of the Tartar period, the center of Old "Rus" had become severed from the political body of "Russia." Autonomous local Russian princes remained nominally under Tartar suzerainty but in reality were dependent upon Lithuania.

Toward the end of the fourteenth century, three political events altered the situation: Around 1375 Tartar rule in western Russia ceased to function; in 1380 the last Ukrainian prince of Russian blood was deposed; and in 1386 a personal union was established between Lithuania and Poland, and the Poles established their supremacy in the united countries. Separation of the Ukraine from Muscovy was emphasized when, following rivalries within the Russian Orthodox church during the fifteenth century, the bishops of Kiev, with Polish support, succeeded in making their see a metropolitan area, independent of Moscow.

Desolation. The consequences of these changes soon became evident. Externally, the Ukraine was exposed anew to invasions. The Tartars tried to reconquer their former possessions there and, together with Turkish tribes, sent expeditions into the country. The eastern parts were laid waste, settlers fled, and what once had been one of the most prosperous regions of Russia was largely abandoned to wild beasts. Internally, the Polish-Lithuanian union caused calamities. As long as the Lithuanians were dominant, the Ukrainians had peacefully practiced their Orthodox religion, hoping to spread it among their conquerors. The union with Poland, however, drove a wedge between Lithuanians and Ukrainians, for the Poles were Catholic and introduced their own faith into Lithuania. The Orthodox creed thus lost any opportunity to amalgamate Lithuanians and Ukrainians, and those who followed it were exposed to persecution. The Orthodox clergy was assailed, and public offices were filled by converts to Catholicism.

Uprisings. Against these injustices, revolts soon broke out; and, finding no other support in their struggle, the Ukrainians sought help from their Orthodox brethren in Muscovy. From that time on, a constant struggle between Poland and Russia raged over the possession of the Ukrainian lands with the religious issues emphasizing the irreconcilable national aspirations of both sides. In 1500 Tsar Ivan the Great seized the opportunity and proclaimed a protectorate over the Kievan region. To counter the blow, the Poles found themselves forced into concessions which culminated in 1539 in the establishment of an Orthodox bishopric in Lvov.

Flights and Resettlement. Caught between Russia and Poland, many Ukrainians decided to leave their homes. In their search for freedom and relative security, their attention was attracted by the deserted eastern parts of their country. The first to re-enter this region were typical frontiersmen. Hardy, brave, and adventurous, they organized themselves into armed bands and made the steppe their permanent home. Attracted by the plenitude of fish, buffalo, duck, and other game, they may have intended to live peaceably by hunting and trading; however, they undertook military tasks as well. Recognizing Polish suzerainty, they defended the land for

Poland and in exchange received a guarantee of personal and religious freedom and political autonomy.

ZAPOROZHE COSSACKS. Below the Dnieper rapids the frontiersmen erected forts and established themselves as a Cossack Union, famed under the name of "Zaporozhe Cossacks." Profiting by their power and independence, they soon began to attack and plunder Tartars, Turks, and Muscovites alike. As long as their military services were needed, they were able to preserve the privileges granted them. During the times of King Stephen Báthory of Poland, they even secured the concession of a special governor for their region, whereby they were removed from the jurisdiction and supervision of the central authority. They elected their own officials, and among their commanders (hetmans) were such able leaders as Vishnevetsky (*ca.* 1550), Kishka (*ca.* 1600), Sahaidachny (*ca.* 1620), Khmelnitsky (*ca.* 1640), Doroshenko (*ca.* 1665), and finally Ivan Mazepa (*ca.* 1700).

SETTLERS. The frontiersmen were followed by settlers, and an enormous increase in population resulted. Peasants, attracted by the fertility of the soil, arrived to complete resettlement and to reclaim the soil. They hoped to find in the eastern Ukraine "a land without a landlord," and to be free from exorbitant taxation and from toil for the nobles. At first they found what they sought; and, living among lowly and freedom-loving Cossacks, they enjoyed unaccustomed freedom. But their position was inconsistent with the trends of the time and became untenable in the face of a steady influx of additional peasants. The vicious cycle of political encroachment and economic oppression started anew.

INCORPORATION OF EASTERN UKRAINE

Toward the end of the sixteenth century, the final stage of Polish domination in the eastern Ukraine began. It was introduced by measures pertaining to the enserfment of the peasant, the subjection of the Cossacks, and the extirpation of the Orthodox creed. The end of Ukrainian autonomy was thereby envisaged.

Serfdom. The first steps toward the enserfment of the peasants were undertaken by Stephan Bathory, who granted estates in the eastern Ukraine to Polish noblemen as compensation for their services during the war against Russia. The recipients promptly introduced the oppressive conditions of serfdom prevailing in Poland. During subsequent decades, they steadily increased their demands on the labor and production of the peasants; for now that many wars had destroyed crops in other regions, the high prices paid for wheat and other agricultural products and the growing role which Poland played in the European grain market offered opportunities for great profit.

Subjection of the Cossacks. Simultaneously, measures were taken to weaken the position of the Cossacks. The Cossacks derived their main strength and importance from their position as defenders of the realm. But after the wars with Russia were over, their services were no longer needed and consequently their influence was reduced. The Poles saw a chance not only to deprive them of the privileges granted under pressure of war but to punish them for pillaging and creating disturbances in times of peace. In 1596 a punitive expedition was sent against them which subdued the unruly elements and reduced their liberties.

Religious Oppression. Furthermore, the Poles undertook to settle the religious isues. Because of the inadequate support which Muscovy could offer its coreligionists at the end of the sixteenth century, the moment seemed favorable for severing the remaining religious bonds which tied the Ukrainians with tsarist Russia and which constituted a threat to Poland's national unity. On Christmas Day, 1595, the Orthodox faithful in the Ukraine and in White Russia were compelled to submit to a Polish decree: Although they were allowed to maintain their own discipline, they were enjoined, in line with the decisions of the Council of Florence (1439), to recognize the Pope and to obey the Catholic church. The bishops acknowledging the new order were henceforth known as "Uniate" bishops.

This arrangement, however, did not turn out to Poland's advantage, for thousands of Orthodox refused to recognize the "union." Those who did were held in low esteem by the majority which did not, and what had been intended to lead to a strengthening of the Polish state led in reality to a further split which, in due time, was to culminate in the disruption of the entire nation.

Resurgence of Independence Movement. Enserfment and political and religious oppression revived the national spirit in the eastern Ukraine. The Cossacks, taking advantage of Polish embarrassments in new external and civil wars, assumed the lead. They succeeded in strengthening their own ranks and soon their fellow-ship numbered no fewer than twenty thousand men. They increased their financial resources through successful expeditions against Moscow (1604–12), the Turks (1606), and the Tartars (1608), which brought them rich booty. They furthered their own Ukrainian culture, which was preserved through excellent and growing educational centers at Kiev. Strong and independent, they also began to interest themselves anew in the fate of the peasants, many of whom were related to their own lower ranks. And most of all, they rebuilt among their people the Orthodox church. In 1620, against the stipulations of the "union," they secretly chose a new metropolitan, ordained five Orthodox bishops, and in this way strengthened their links with Moscow, toward which the new clergy necessarily looked for support and inspiration.

Polish Countermeasures.   The Poles watched these trends with grave premonition. In 1625, choosing a moment when no external enemy threatened them, they suddenly attacked the Cossacks, sub-dued them, and forced them to reduce their forces from 20,000 to 6,000 men. They also required all members to register so as to prevent secret restoration of Cossack strength. Such measures proved ineffectual, for several years later, the Cossacks got help from their brothers of the Don region and took revenge; and from then on a bitter struggle raged, bringing alternating successes. In 1639 the Poles believed they had gained the final victory, but a new Cossack uprising in 1647 reversed the situation. The Cossack forces were raised to 40,000, the Uniate church was abolished in the eastern Ukraine, and autonomous Cossack administration was re-established. In 1649 the Poles guaranteed the new status.

Transformation of Independence Struggle.   However, with the passage of time, the social background of the Cossack state on the Dnieper had changed—a circumstance which directed the whole struggle into different channels. The interests of Cossacks and peasants began to drift apart. The land became densely settled by peasants, but Cossack officers seized large estates. Thus a caste of landed Cossack proprietors was built up, no less interested than the Polish gentry in attachment of the peasant to the soil and in com-pulsory labor. Serfdom as it existed in Poland and Russia became an integral part also of Ukrainian life. Hence, the "independence struggle" of the Dnieper Cossacks and the Ukraine, which had become a struggle of survival for Poland as well as for the Cossacks, could no longer be hailed by the peasant as a means for his own liberation. In the final analysis, it assumed the form of warfare between two governments or ruling classes in which the common man had scarcely a share.

Submission to Russia. It is in the light of these facts that we must view the step which, after the Poles defaulted in their promises of 1649, was undertaken by the Cossack hetman Khmelnitsky, a gifted national leader but also a rich and greedy landowner. In 1654 he determined to transfer the allegiance of the Cossack state from Poland to Russia. His action, undertaken for selfish reasons, reflected the redistribution of power between Russia and Poland; and the Tsar, after consulting a Zemsky Sobor (the last one, convened in 1653), did not hesitate to accept Khmelnitsky's submission and to declare war on Poland.

The transition of the Ukraine from Polish to Russian suzerainty, accompanied by renewed warfare, failed, of course, to benefit the peasantry; but neither did it bring the expected fruits for the Cossacks. Although the Tsar at first treated them with consideration, he refused to make promises regarding the Ukrainian autonomy. Moreover, he demanded the subordination of the metropolitan at Kiev to Moscow's Patriarch. Fearing his policy might prove unworkable, Khmelnitsky began to look for allies and to conspire with Sweden. His death prevented the completion of his plans, but his actions served as a warning to the Russians. They profited by the existing rift betwen Cossack and peasant interests and by the resulting discord and weakness and, accusing the Cossacks of perfidy, tightened their hold. In vain did Khmelnitsky's successors try to gain the assistance first of Poland and later of Turkey and to play these two against Russia. The balance of power inclined toward Moscow's side, and in 1667, during the Peace of Andrusovo between Poland and Russia, the fate of the Ukraine was settled. While nominally some sort of joint administration was provided and Ukrainian self-government established, actually the country was divided—the eastern parts being annexed by Muscovy and the western ones remaining Polish. Kiev itself was temporarily handed over to the Tsar, and permanently incorporated in 1680.

Effects on Russia. Thus, after centuries of foreign domination, at least a part of the Ukraine, including the old capital of Kiev, was again joined to the other Russian lands. Politically, this was a great Russian success, for it so weakened Poland that she no longer could challenge Russian predominance. Economically, too, it was a gain for Russia. Renewed migration from the right bank of the Dnieper to the left helped to re-establish the productivity of the region after the wars were over, and the wealth of the nation was proportionately increased. Strategically it strengthened the position of Russia, particularly in relation to the Turks, and further increased Russian manpower. Socially, however, the acquisition brought no advantage. The freedom formerly allowed in the Ukraine was not extended to the Russian people in the rest of the country, but the exact reverse: The concepts of serfdom and the policy of oppression, as existent in Muscovy, were spread in the Ukraine. They strengthened the conditions introduced in the Ukraine under hetman autocracy and precluded the social rejuvenation which a free Cossack state might have brought to the whole of Russia.

PROBLEMS

1. Discuss the growth of Cossack might in the Ukraine.
2. Trace the causes of tension between the Ukraine and Poland.
3. Discuss the effects of the reincorporation of the Ukraine into Russia.

12

THE SCHISM

Significant Dates

Nikon's Patriarchate 1652–1666
Beginning of Schism 1656
Death of Nikon and Avvakum 1681

CHURCH AND STATE

During the reign of the first Romanov, Michael, the Patriarch Philaret had played a dominant role. The spectacle of father and son ruling together ended with the death of Philaret; but there was to emerge in the times of Michael's son, Alexis, another Patriarch, Nikon, who was destined to exercise still greater influence upon Russia's history.

Position of Church. Nikon followed Philaret in his advocation of reform, just as Philaret had followed his predecessors. The desire for change in the church can be traced from the times of the controversies between Nils Sorsky and Josip of Volokolamsk—a desire which increased as attempts at carrying out reforms were thwarted. Chiefly because of its role during the "Troubles," the church had gained enormously in prestige during the hundred years from 1550 to 1650; it had augmented its material wealth, the administration had been reorganized and extended to Siberia, and the clergy had successfully defended such privileges as exemption from taxes and from state jurisdiction. The church had also succeeded in maintaining satisfactory relations with the state without aspiring to dominate it, since not only religious but also political and economic factors linked the two institutions and made each an indispensable partner of the other.

Weaknesses. In the spiritual field, no healthy growth had been witnessed. Attempts at moral reform had miscarried; formalism remained a characteristic preoccupation of the clergy; and national piety was still coupled with forms and ceremonies. A deep social gap separated the village priest—married, poor, and ill-educated as he generally was—from the higher clergy, which was recruited from the ranks of the monks. These vowed celibacy, often possessed some learning, and played a leading role in the administration and economy of the country.

NIKON'S PATRIARCHATE

Nikon. Nikon's patriarchate, beginning in 1652, marked a change. Yet it would be as incorrect to infer that he endeavored to carry out a thoroughgoing internal moral reform as it would be to assert that he wanted to lay claim to leadership in the state and to raise the church above the Tsar. Arrogant and arbitrary, but courageous, noble, and devoted, he pursued no such remote aims. His work was confined to a realignment of the Russian church and to the adoption of the slightly different principles embodied in the contemporary Greek branch of the Orthodox church. Politically, such a change was necessary after the incorporation of the Ukraine to allow for the reabsorption of the Ukrainian church and the Academy of Kiev, which showed definite leanings toward Greek teachings. Without such concessions to the Ukrainians a split might have resulted, endangering the authority of the Moscow Patriarch over the whole of the Russian church.

The Proposed Reforms. Theologically, a reform of the church according to Greek precepts meant the introduction of some new ceremonial details, which, to be sure, were closely connected with the very dogma of the church. It involved the making of the sign of the cross with three fingers instead of two, an eastward direction of processional marches, a ban on beard shaving, a correction in the Russian spelling of the name "Jesus," and the singing of the word "Hallelujah." It also included correction of the theological books and eradication of errors which had slipped into them in the course of the centuries. However, unlike the reforms of the humanists of western Europe during the sixteenth century, these corrections were based not on the original texts but on the traditions of the Greek patriarchate. There were also certain changes proposed in connection with reforms of the church choirs and the introduction of sermons, for which most of the ignorant clergy were unqualified. But in a practical sense what caused the greatest stir and most furious opposition was the fact that Nikon chose to surround himself with Greeks who favored his ideas, and to appoint them to church offices coveted by the indigenous clergy.

Opposition. The result of the innovations was the formation of several factions animated by the most contradictory considerations: by religious traditionalism and mysticism as opposed to the intellectual, scholarly trends of the reformers; by nationalism and fear of the introduction of Western heresies as against interest in, and imitation of, Western habits; by devotion on the one side and selfish motives on the other; and by economic or political advantages confronted by purely religious views. Avvakum—a man in many ways similar in character to Nikon—was outstanding among the opposition. Alexis backed the Patriarch, for whom he had love and respect; but exacerbated by Nikon's arrogance, he eventually withheld his support and in 1658 the angry Patriarch laid down the insignia, confessed his sins, and retired to a monastery from which he continued the struggle. No new patriarch was named. After a number of years, Nikon tried to resume his functions, but he was condemned by the church hierarchy and ignored by his former friend, Tsar Alexis. In a moving scene he thereupon resigned his office and, refusing all proffered gifts, went into exile, one of the most dramatic figures in Russian history. Only when near death was he permitted to return, but on the way to Moscow, he died. As to Nikon's adversary, Avvakum, he persisted in the fight for his cause, although he had been condemned and exiled. With moving devotion, his wife supported him until the cruel end, when he was burned at the stake.

THE SPLIT

The Raskolniki. Although Nikon himself was deposed, his reforms were essentially upheld by the church council of 1666 to 1667. Unfortunately, the innovations, being confined largely to forms, represented no great contributions; nevertheless, they led to most serious consequences. A schism arose within the church and promptly engulfed the state, endangering its existence. The separating party, known as *Raskolniki* (schismatics, "Old Believers," or "Old Ritualists"), clung to time-honored Russian traditions. They not only denounced Nikon as the Antichrist, but also broke out in open rebellion against the government which had accepted Nikon's reforms. They transferred their hatred from the dead Patriarch to the Tsar; from the Tsar to his daughter Sophia, who followed her father's policies; and from her to her successor Peter the Great.

The Fate of the Raskolniki. As a result of their stand, the Old Believers found themselves exposed to persecutions, to discrimination, and to special taxation. Thousands of them, believing that with the Antichrist the end of the world had come, committed suicide. Other thousands, likewise refusing any compromise, departed and, relinquishing all worldly possessions, became wanderers, having no home, recognizing no legal marriage, and assuming no status within society. Many of them found refuge in the inhospitable north with the monks of the Solovetsky Monastery; from this almost impregnable place they defended themselves successfully for seven years against persecuting armies of the Tsar. There were also those who settled in small communities in various parts of the country and, incidentally, came to form a rather useful and important economic force in the colonization of those regions. One group arose which later made concessions to the government and, in exchange for an unmolested life, paid a double poll tax. All Raskolniki had to find a solution for the problem of legitimate succession of their priesthood, which had been shattered by the reformers. Considering the adherents of Nikon unqualified to duly appoint and anoint new priests, some dispensed entirely with priests (the "priestless" or *Bispopovtsi*); others preserved precariously the system of priesthood. They had new priests (the "priestists" or *Popovtsi*) consecrated only by those who had themselves been anointed according to the "true" faith before the acceptance of the Nikonian innovations.

Eventually, considerable groups of Raskolniki emigrated and for a hundred years lived abroad in the Danube region, in the Hapsburg empire, and even beyond the seas. Under Catherine the Great they were invited to return and were promised an undisturbed life. Scores did return and settled in regions east of the Volga; but in the nineteenth century they were exposed to new persecutions and gave rise to new sects—the Beguni, the Khlysti, the Dukhobors, and others. Of these many were alternatingly persecuted, reconciled, accepted, or expelled. A considerable number of Dukhobors eventually migrated to Canada, where, from time to time, they likewise came in conflict with the authorities.

Significance of Schism. Perhaps the only advantage of Nikon's innovations and of the resulting schism was an increased religious consciousness among those within the official church as well as those outside it; but this was by far outweighed by the evil consequences of religious persecution. A considerable part of the population found itself excluded from the life of the nation; evil instincts were evoked in the "righteous"; through emigration, able and devoted workers were lost for the country's economy; and regard for law and internal unity was endangered.

The total number of Old Believers during the second half of the nineteenth century has been estimated at five to ten million—perhaps even more. Such an enormous part of the population could not indefinitely remain under special laws. In the revolutionary years of 1903 to 1905, the schismatics were granted many rights; but full equality was not restored to them until the advent of the Provisional Government in 1917.

PROBLEMS

1. Discuss the significance of Nikon's attempts at reform.
2. Discuss the results of the schism.
3. Discuss the relationship of church and state.

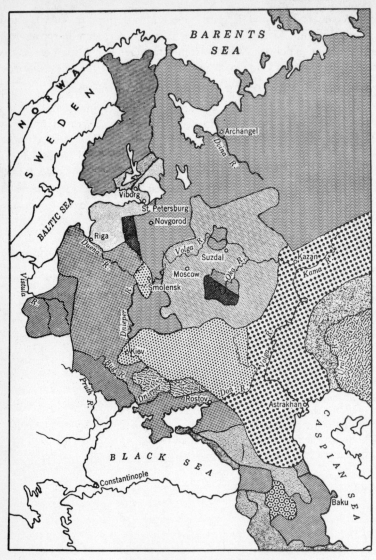

EXPANSION IN EUROPE

MUSCOVY 1462	ALEXIS d. 1676	PAUL d. 1801
IVAN III d. 1505	PETER I d. 1725	ALEXANDER I d. 1825
VASILY III d. 1533	ANNA d. 1740	NICHOLAS I d. 1855
IVAN IV d. 1584	ELIZABETH d. 1761	ALEXANDER II d. 1881
MICHAEL d. 1645	CATHERINE II d. 1796	

13

EMERGENCE OF RUSSIA AS A EUROPEAN POWER

Significant Dates

Reign of Peter I 1682–1725
The Great Northern War 1700–1721
Battle of Poltava 1709
Loss of Azov 1711
Peace of Nystad 1721

The rule of the first three Romanovs had brought few social improvements. The well-being of the people had been neglected, whereas the needs of the army and the accumulation of gold in the Tsar's treasury had found paramount attention. Even so, the basis for future advancement had been laid; for the country was led along the road to reunion with the West through contact with Poland, through the reincorporation of parts of the Ukraine, through the coming of foreign scientists and merchants, through greater endeavors to build seagoing ships, and through a sporadic struggle with Sweden for the possession of Livonia. The greatest step in this direction was, however, left to Peter I (1682–1725), later called "the Great."

EARLY PART OF PETER'S REIGN

Accession of Peter. At the instigation of the Patriarch, Peter became Tsar, at the age of ten, upon the death of his stepbrother,

Tsar Feodor III. The actual rule, however, was exercised by his older sister, Sophia, who had usurped the regency with the help of the archer guards, the Streltsi, and of her lover, Prince Golitsyn. Golitsyn was a well-meaning and enlightened administrator, but utopian in his aims with regard to emancipation of serfs, rapid introduction of Western standards, and the creation of a powerful army. The over-all effect of his work was slight. An unsuccessful war in alliance with Poland against Turkey put an end to his plans and to the rule of Sophia. Under the sponsorship of his mother and with the support of the Streltsi, whom Sophia had tried to suppress even though she owed them her regency, Peter was made ruling Tsar in 1689. A weak-minded older brother, Ivan V, who had formally shared the throne from 1682 on, continued as co-Tsar until he died in 1696.

Peter I. Peter's education had been neglected; but he was alert and thirsted for knowledge. In the "German suburb" of Moscow, he learned a variety of arts and skills and also a deep respect for foreign customs and accomplishments. He possessed inborn genius, intellectual curiosity, and an uncommon capacity for work; and it was his good luck subsequently to find capable tutors and advisers, such as Patrick Gordon, a Scotsman, and especially François Lefort, a Swiss. From early youth Peter's attention to military affairs was keen, and regiments formed of his playmates were later to become the famed Preobrazhensky and Semenovsky guards. Though he himself never lost his uncouth manners, he learned to appreciate Western culture, which he ardently hoped Russian accomplishments would one day "put to shame."

Conquest of Azov. In 1694 Peter visited Archangel, where acquaintance with the sea stimulated his childhood interest in shipbuilding and a navy. Whether or not it was because of an understanding of the influence of sea power or because of love for military affairs in general, this preoccupation remained with the Tsar for the rest of his life. The need for a strong navy was soon to be demonstrated to him. To fulfill treaty obligations and to prevent recurrent invasions by Crimean Tartars, Peter was forced to declare war on Turkey in 1695, and a siege of the fortress of Azov was started. Despite all efforts, no gain could be made until after a navy had been hurriedly built during the winter. In the following year it proved its value; for by cutting off Azov's sea lanes to Constantinople, Peter forced the garrison of Azov to surrender.

Journey through Europe. However, Turkey could not be induced to withdraw from the war, and in an effort to strengthen the coalition against her, Peter sent a "great embassy" composed of his principal advisers to various European powers. He himself joined them incognito as a minor official for the purpose of studying European ways and methods. During the journey he hired artisans and doctors whose services and knowledge were to be drawn upon to further Russia's progress along European lines. He negotiated with the Elector of Brandenburg, the Hanover family, the Dutch government, the English king, and the German emperor; he established contacts with one of the great thinkers of the century, Leibnitz, and with the Dutch scientists Leeuwenhoek and Boerhaave; and he spent much of his time in manual work as a shipwright in Holland and England. He also intended to visit Turkey's most persistent enemy, the great commercial and maritime center of Venice, but his journey was interrupted by news of a rising of the Streltsi at home.

Suppression of the Streltsi. The rebellion of the Streltsi was due partly to mistreatment by their officers; but more important, the Streltsi disliked the Tsar's foreign leanings and were antagonized by his harsh policies toward dissenters, many of whom they counted among their own ranks. They also felt their position, influence, and privileges threatened by the creation of new military contingents, who were equipped with advanced weapons and trained according to modern methods. Although the rising had been suppressed even before Peter reached home, the Tsar proceeded to destroy the whole organization brutally and mercilessly, thus abolishing in time a potentially dangerous praetorian guard and strengthening the freedom of action of the autocrat.

NORTHERN WAR

Baltic Plans. Having failed to bring about the desired anti-Turkish coalition, and faced with an English and Dutch conspiracy against Russia in Constantinople, Peter was compelled to abandon his plans for gaining a firm hold on the Black Sea coast and to content himself with the acquisition of the fortress of Azov. Peace on this basis was concluded with Turkey in 1700. To make up for the failure to reach the sea, it was planned to annex the Baltic Sea coast instead. Following ideas proposed by Ordyn Nashchokin three decades earlier, an alliance was made with Poland—and also with Denmark—in order to detach some of the Baltic ports from Sweden. But the Swedish king, Charles XII, anticipated the attack. He resolutely invaded Denmark and in a lightning war crushed her completely. Then, in November, 1700, he turned quickly against Russia, and, despite numerical inferiority, won a smashing victory at Narva.

War with Sweden. Historians have speculated as to the possible course of events had Charles pursued the victory and marched on Moscow instead of turning, as he did, against Poland and reducing that country. Perhaps he could have taken Russia's capital; but it is unthinkable that little Sweden could have dominated Peter's growing empire for any length of time or that Charles could have changed the course of history. In any case, while Charles was occupied in Poland, Peter had time to reorganize his forces, and from 1701 on his armies were generally successful against Sweden. Slowly all of Livonia and Ingria were conquered and successfully defended, even after Poland had been forced to withdraw from the war in 1706, leaving Russia alone to face Charles's might. In 1709 the decisive battle was fought at Poltava in southern Russia. The Swedish king was enticed there by strategic and economic considerations as well as by the hope of finding a powerful ally in the Cossack hetman Ivan Mazepa, famous not only for his philanthropic work (the remodeling of the Pechersky Monastery and the protection of the Kiev Academy of Sciences) but also for his autocratic character and his vacillations. The expected support was only partially forthcoming. The Swedish army was beaten, that country's power broken, and Charles XII was obliged to flee to Turkey.

Significance of Victory at Poltava. The Russian victory had significant consequences. Not only did it raise the international prestige of Russia as the first nation able to cope with the famous conqueror, but also it strengthened the Tsar's position at home.

RUSSIAN REALMS. The victory at Poltava enabled Peter to hold on to the Swedish possessions in Livonia and thus to accomplish an old Russian ambition by gaining free access to the sea. It also precipitated the full incorporation of the eastern Ukraine. Although most of the Ukrainians had remained faithful to Moscow, the Cossack state was dissolved and the hetmanship abolished—never, except nominally, to be revived. Tsarist commanders and judges as well as tax collectors were imposed on the Ukraine; Cossack detachments were made to serve in Peter's wars regardless of the regions in which they were fought; laborers were drafted for the building of canals and roads or any other task, wherever it might arise. Great areas of Cossack land were granted to Russian noblemen who replaced Cossack officers; forced labor, existing *de facto* since the middle seventeenth century and legalized by the Cossacks themselves during Mazepa's hetmanship in 1701, was expanded. Serfdom proper, however, was not recognized by law until the second half of the eighteenth century.

EUROPEAN RELATIONS. Another important result of Peter's victory was the new role of Russia in European affairs and her participation in Continental diplomacy. After the Battle of Poltava, the seat of war did not long remain in the south. A short new struggle with Turkey, brought about by the fugitive Charles's intrigues, ensued; it led to disastrous results for Peter. The war had to be concluded in 1711 at the price of the recently won fortress of Azov, which was returned to the Sultan. From then on attention was once more focused on the Baltic region. Not only did Peter gain there the provinces adjoining Russia, but by forming marriage alliances with other Baltic countries, by moving his capital to St. Petersburg in 1713, and by building and maintaining a navy on the Baltic Sea, he soon came to exercise dominating influence on the entire sea and began to formulate plans for securing its outlet. It was even rumored that while starting an invasion of southern Sweden Peter went so far as to consider also the conquest of Denmark. Such ambitions were viewed with great alarm by most European powers, notably England, which now had to allow for Russia's place in the European balance-of-power system. To underscore his new position and to conclude trade treaties and further his Swedish invasion plans, Peter undertook a second trip to the Continent in 1716 and 1717, and this time included France in his itinerary. Together with Prussia, France was induced to acknowledge the changes in northern Europe and to guarantee their permanence.

Peace of Nystad. With Russia thus strengthened against English ambitions, negotiations were started to bring an end to the Northern War. Begun in 1718, they were concluded at Nystad in

1721. Russia's incorporation of Livonia, Ingria, and parts of Finnish Karelia were confirmed.

War against Persia. Despite English misgivings, another triumph was secured during the following two years when an expedition against declining Persia led to the acquisition of a large part of the west coast of the Caspian Sea, including the towns of Derbent and Baku with their petroleum resources.

SUMMARY

Viewed as a whole, Peter's times witnessed an enormous strengthening of Russia. Excellent ports were acquired on the Baltic and in the Caspian area, though not on the Black Sea; close intercourse with the West was established; Poland and Sweden were both definitely eliminated as powerful enemies; and, entering the political scene of Europe as an important factor, Russia secured contact with progressive nations—an event which was to stimulate the political and intellectual life within the empire.

Russia's international progress during Peter's reign thus proved to be spectacular, though it was matched by important changes introduced in the interior. These were hailed and criticized by one of the first great publicists of Russia, Ivan Pososhkov (d.1726). A defender of autocracy, serfdom, and orthodoxy, Pososhkov yet advocated reforms to stamp out corruption, improve judicial institutions, reorganize the military, better the conditions of the peasant, and strengthen the economy by increasing trade, building new industries, and raising fiscal revenues.

PROBLEMS

1. Discuss the training of Peter the Great.
2. Explain the issues of the Great Northern War.
3. Compare the international position of Russia at the beginning and at the end of Peter's reign.

14

DOMESTIC REFORM WORK

BASIC FACTORS

The list of Peter's achievements in domestic affairs is truly impressive. A concerted program of reform, however, cannot be traced, for the work of Peter was dominated by needs of the moment. Mercantilist ideas prevailed regarding the exploitation of mineral wealth, reforestation policies, and establishment of an active trade balance. Their exponents demanded restrictions on raw-material exports. Protection through tariffs was granted domestic industries, monopolies were accorded for the trade of tobacco (which up to Peter's time had been forbidden in Russia) and of many minor commodities, and subsidies were freely given to weak industries. Socially, corruption of judges and administrative officers, criminality, lethargy, and lack of cleanliness were fought; but little was done about such evils as tyranny, flogging, serfdom, and the prevailing disregard for human dignity. Essentially, military and fiscal considerations rather than humanitarian ideals dictated Peter's actions.

SOCIAL REORGANIZATION

Nobility. The council of the boyars was abolished. All the nobility became subject to service, a *noblesse de robe* was put on equal footing with the heredity nobility, and the noble service class became the leading element within the state. It was rewarded by land grants, and land possession was made hereditary.

Military Class. The army, navy, and entire military class were reformed. The Streltsi were abolished, and recruits were drawn from all classes and all regions of the empire. Promotion was based on ability. Because Prince Golitsyn had, in 1682, abolished the old tables of rank based on birth, new ranks were now introduced. These were based on military or administrative office and contributed to the streamlining of the entire system. In addition to their regular duties soldiers acted also as policemen.

Clergy. The church and clergy were completely identified with the state. This arrangement was accomplished with little difficulty because of the pre-existing close relationship. In 1721 the patriarchate, unfilled for twenty-one years, was entirely abolished and replaced by a council, the "Synod," which was less likely ever to gain the political influence Philaret or Nikon had possessed. The administration of church wealth and especially of monastic lands was put under state supervision, the training of the clergy was improved, and the growth of monasteries was restricted and discipline restored. Jurisdictional rights of the church were also more closely circumscribed, and tolerance was extended to several non-Orthodox religious groups, but not to Jews or dissenters.

Merchant Class. The growth of a merchant and artisan class was encouraged. The social status of the commercial class was raised and merchants were given ranks like the military in order to equalize them with the other classes of free men. Guilds with a measure of self-government were re-established to give the merchant standing, to control his activities, and to form a link between him and the state, which he was to serve in his field of endeavor. Foreigners were invited into the country for the purpose of increasing production and developing material resources.

Peasantry. As the noble service class worked for the state, so was the peasantry made accountable to this service class. The landlord's jurisdictional rights over peasants were expanded; bondage was extended to hitherto free territories; strict fugitive serf laws were enforced; and all proposals for the abolition of serfdom were categorically rejected by Peter. Additional burdens were imposed on the peasant by a new recruiting system for the army and by a poll tax levied on every male peasant ("soul") regardless of age or ability to work. Despite the fact that tens of thousands of peasants were thereby forced to flee into unsettled regions or Cossack territories, the area under cultivation was vastly increased, and while cattle raising, except for sheep, continued to be neglected, the production of cereals, flax, and hemp made rapid progress.

Factory Workers. The laboring class was expanded. Factory owners received the right to buy bonded peasants and put them to work in mines and other industries, and peasants were assigned by state law to factory work. Indeed, many peasants turned voluntarily to factory work, where they could earn their quit rent or obrok and thereby free themselves from labor service obligations under the barchina system. Idle sons of priests, vagabonds, and criminals were recruited for useful service in state and private enterprise.

Women. Special attention was paid to a change in the status of women. On his trips through Europe, Peter had witnessed the freedom and activities of women abroad; and despite his own shameful relationships with women and his promiscuity, he contributed to a thorough improvement. The terem was abolished. Women were partially emancipated and were now invited to court functions, receptions, and balls, thus setting an example for social life in all spheres.

ADMINISTRATIVE CHANGES

Government. The country was divided into provinces and districts and, notwithstanding the principle of absolutism and autocracy, a certain amount of decentralization was brought about. Through a very complicated administrative system, eight (later eleven) districts were created, each with a governor and a judicial and financial officer; and a number of "colleges" (departments) for finance, commerce, justice, manufacturing, and the like were organized. Owing to overlapping functions of central and local authorities, no uniformity in administrative procedures was actually achieved, and the new system never worked satisfactorily. A special order for townships was instituted also; this, however, proved equally unsuccessful. Above the districts and municipalities, a Senate, whose members were appointed by the Tsar to advise the Tsar and to govern the country in his absence, was created which was also invested with judicial functions.

FOUNDING OF ST. PETERSBURG. A new capital, St. Petersburg, was founded near the Baltic shores and designed to serve as both a fortress against invasion and as a connecting link with the West. It helped to emphasize Russia's international position and to strengthen the European character of Russian court life and manners. Because of its location in unhealthful and unfavorable surroundings, the city has been called "an outrage to common sense"; its construction alone cost the lives of more than twenty thousand workmen. Eventually, however, it was to serve well the purpose for which it was developed. Peter invited foreign architects and sculptors to come and adorn it with their works, and men such as Trezzini, LeBlond, Rastrelli, and others gave it a distinctly Western (Dutch, German, French) character through their creation of Baroque palaces, churches, bridges, and statues.

Educational Measures. Schools were founded, and attendance was made compulsory for the children of the noble service class. Yet many of these schools gave only the rudiments of learning and necessitated supplementary training of the students abroad.

THE ACADEMY OF SCIENCES. A new calendar was introduced, which began the year on January 1 instead of in September, counted the years from the birth of Christ rather than from the Creation, and eliminated a difference of eight years between Russian and Western chronology; on the whole, however, this innovation was unsatisfactory inasmuch as the Julian calendar was adopted instead of the Gregorian one used in most European countries. A simplified alphabet likewise was worked out and put into practice. Moreover, an Academy (founded by Peter the Great, but not established until after his death) was created after European models. It greatly promoted the study of geography and exploration. Although all these activities have been termed "a lisping of barbarians striving to spell out European civilization," the Academy of Sciences was to become in due time an important cultural factor.

MANNERS. For the improvement of manners, special institutions were founded, and various enactments put into effect. The long dresses of the peasants, despite their obvious advantage during the rigors of the winter, were forbidden so that the peasants would be unencumbered while at work. The beards of men, except of clergy and peasants, were ordered shaved as a sanitary measure—although some hold that this decree was a result of the Tsar's drunkenness and the shortcomings of his own beard. This decree was a challenge to the church, which demanded unshaven faces, and it led to grave new difficulties with the Old Believers. Eventually beards were allowed provided that a special tax was paid.

Economic Measures. The enormous burdens shouldered by the state in carrying out reforms could not be met without a parallel increase in the budget. Expenditures rose sharply, and in consequence all means had to be strained to provide the necessary income.

FINANCES. By far the greatest costs were, in Peter's time, caused by the military, for which heretofore unheard of sums were expended, absorbing from one half to three-quarters of the total revenue. Large amounts were also needed to provide for the shipping trade which Peter, in line with mercantilist theory, tried to build up to save costs for the Russian economy and gain independence from foreign carriers. Likewise, the complicated new administration made great demands upon the financial resources of the country. In order to meet the needs, church lands were confiscated whenever possible, trade monopolies were sold to the highest bidder, state industries were endowed with special rights which would make them profitable, and the customary and worst expedient of all was also resorted to: adulteration of coin.

TAXATION. In addition, greatly augmented taxes were levied and import duties were raised sharply. A census was held in 1718, which served as an inventory of bonded peasants, and on the basis of this numerous new taxes were imposed. Among these, the most important was the poll tax. It was collected from the peasant by his landlord, who in turn had to pay it to the state. Unfortunately, this system brought terrible injustices, for, since only male persons were counted as taxable "souls," a wealthy peasant with, for example, three daughters capable of work had to pay less than any poor peasant with two male babies and an aged father to support. Furthermore, owing to corruption and the system of farming out taxes (in use also in contemporary France and elsewhere), not more than one third or one half of the collected sums reached the treasury.

INDUSTRIES. Factories were built. Many remained in government hands, particularly those in the Ural mining district. Others, which were allowed to pass into private hands, were subjected to state supervision. State assistance was granted if needed, although this policy often served to increase corruption and waste. Fiscal needs and military considerations essentially governed decisions concerning the foundation of new factories. All plants suffered from a scant labor supply and from want of competent directors. The century-long neglected bourgeoisie were unable to provide the necessary men for the organization of efficient industries, and considerable numbers of foreign managers had to be invited. With their help, industries were developed; some of them—for example, the Russian iron industry—came to be among the most important of Europe.

Building. Roads, bridges, and canals were constructed. Inspired by the Dutch example and following the old Russian tradition, the Tsar exerted his utmost energy in the direction of increasing and bettering existing waterways. Many important constructions were undertaken, and plans were laid for the Don-Volga and Ladoga canals, both of which were completed after Peter's death.

SIGNIFICANCE OF PETER'S REFORM WORK

Criticism. The list of Peter's personal activities is imposing; his unflagging energy and detailed advice stand behind many of the achievements of the time. But historians, and foremost those of Russia, do not agree as to his usefulness. Peter has been given credit for raising agricultural and industrial production, improving the military establishment, gaining for Russia access to the sea, and for introducing some Western standards and accomplishments. But he has also been accused of destroying the Russian way of life and of contributing to laxity of morals through the example of his own dissolute living, his coarseness, and the vulgarity of his amusements —jesters, dwarfs, and their kind. Furthermore, his reforms are said to have been too speedily adopted, and thus to have been lacking in depth. Yet, he encouraged activity, and "finding little, he left much." The charge that his influence sufficed to lead Russia on a road not in line with the country's natural development is untenable, because such is beyond the power of one human being. But it may be true that the abruptness and speed of his reforms and the autocratic form of his government damaged the promise of existing institutions, and exercised an unwholesome influence on the civilization of the people. Much of the initiative sprang not from Peter's mind but from that of his advisors; in addition, pressure of circumstances and the climate of opinion of his times contributed their share to the undertaking of the reform work. The writings of the Croat Krizhanic, who had come to Russia in 1659 but was later banished to Siberia and who had written a perspicacious criticism of existing conditions, influenced the thinking of the reformers. Likewise, the ideas of Ivan Pososhkov, great admirer of Peter, advocating the need for absolutism, mercantilistic economic policies, and a reform of church, army, and fiscal administration, bear witness to the widespread realization of the urgency of fundamental changes.

Reaction. Reaction against Peter's work was strong. A long series of Cossack and peasant uprisings occurred which could be suppressed only with great brutality. As so often happened in Russian history, reaction was supported peculiarly enough not only by the older but also by the younger generation. This characteristic trait was mirrored in the opposition of Peter's son Alexis to his father. The drunkard weakling Alexis, devoted to narrow ideas and conspicuous for bad manners, is no attractive personality; but his struggle against his father, his flight to Italy, return, and gruesome end by torture (consumption would have ended his life soon enough) do not lack the elements of great tragedy. Had Alexis succeeded his father on the throne, opposition to the innovations might have retarded the Westernization of Russia. But lack of decision in the actual successors made impossible the formation of an influential opposition, and Peter's death left the way free for his most trusted ministers, Menshikov and Ostermann, to consolidate, if not carry further, the work of their master.

PROBLEMS

1. Discuss the main causes for Peter's reform work.
2. Discuss the social changes brought about by the "Westernization" efforts.
3. Discuss the justification for criticisms of Peter's reform work.

15

POLITICAL TRENDS AND CULTURAL PROGRESS IN THE MIDDLE EIGHTEENTH CENTURY

Significant Dates

Reign of Catherine I	1725–1727
Reign of Elizabeth	1741–1762
Incorporation of Transcaspia	1740
Discovery of Bering Sea and Straits	1741
Founding of Moscow University	1755

The period between the death of Peter the Great in 1725 and the accession of Catherine the Great in 1762 has been considered by some historians as an era of shallowness, confusion, and decay, whereas others attribute to it much of Russia's spiritual growth and political advancement. The truth seems to lie on both sides. Rapid and violent changes, as under Peter, were discontinued, but slowly the process of Westernization went on, gaining in depth and leading to a better proportion between the ambitions and the actual potentialities of the country.

POLITICAL CONDITIONS

Peter's Successors. During the middle of the eighteenth century few contributions to the rise of Russia were made by her rulers.

Most of Peter's successors owed their thrones to usurpation and to the support of court cliques and factions which they dared not antagonize even after gaining autocratic power. Peter himself had laid the basis for these conditions when he altered the succession law and left to each ruling prince the choice of his successor; however, he had died before so appointing his own successor and straightway the intrigues had begun. They led first to the accession of Peter's wife, Catherine I (1725–27). Her elevation, a "triumph over prejudice," for she was a woman and came besides from the lowest stratum of society, she owed to her former lover, Menshikov. At the time of her death, two years later, the succession law was again altered, and she was followed by a boy, Peter II (1727–30); after his short reign came another woman, Anna I (1730–40); then an infant, Ivan VI (1740–41), who was promptly dethroned; then a third woman, Elizabeth (1741–62); and finally, for a few months, Peter III (1762). None of these rulers possessed sufficient character and ability to give direction to Russian growth; by sheer inertia, the work of Peter the Great was followed through and his ideas, unchallenged, gradually entrenched themselves as a part of Russian life. The next self-willed ruler, Catherine II, was not to mount the throne until almost forty years after his death.

STATESMEN. The main agent directing the continued Westernization and integration of the country according to Peter's aims was Menshikov, who was dismissed and banished in 1727 because of his arrogance, vanity, and ruthlessness. Thereafter, power was exercised for a short while by a Privy Council under the influence of a Prince Dolgoruki, a member of the high nobility; but under Anna it fell to the so-called German party. Its strongest exponent was Baron Ostermann, an excellent and honest administrator and a capable foreign minister, to whom the Russia of Peter's immediate three successors owes much for its stability. Men like Münnich, builder of the Ladoga Canal and successful general, contributed their share; but the ambitions of the Germans, perhaps in combination with their efficiency, antagonized the Russians—the more so as Tsarina Anna's favorite, Biron, likewise a German, pursued primarily the aim of personal aggrandizement. Political mistakes, combined with the fact that they were of foreign origin and that their positions were coveted by native Russians, accounted for the small favor their party found with the service-nobility. Their domination was ended in 1740. Succeeding them were less progressive men, mostly Russians, and of less than mediocre stature with the possible exception of the brothers Shuvalov and Alexis Bestuzhev-Ryumin, the latter the foreign minister under Elizabeth.

THE OPPOSITION. All statesmen during this period had to fight the conservative opposition which, under the leadership of the old noble families, repeatedly came to the fore. Upon the accession of Anna in 1730, the aristocracy saw themselves within reach of their aims. They succeeded in returning the court and the "colleges" from St. Petersburg to Moscow; they renounced Peter's maritime plans; and they managed to impose on the new ruler, Anna, a constitution modeled after Sweden's, which restored their lost privileges and freed them of compulsory service. But Anna, once secure on the throne, recognized that in a struggle with the court aristocracy she would be able to enlist sufficient support from their opponents, and she subsequently abrogated all prior concessions.

Anna. As a matter of fact, Anna became the most autocratic of Peter's successors. Not only did she put an end to the Privy Council and the Dolgoruki faction, but she reduced the powers of the Senate and subordinated the whole body to a "cabinet" which, however, was not to remain long in existence. She and the German party sought to halt the decay of the administration; order was reintroduced; and rebellious elements were punished with torture, death, and exile. While giving little attention to the navy, Anna saw to the rejuvenation of the army and the establishment of a cadet corps.

Elizabeth. Elizabeth, who succeeded Anna except for the brief intermezzo of the accession of the baby Ivan VI, is generally credited with having restored "Russian" ways. Indeed, Biron had been removed in 1740; and the capable and devoted Ostermann together with General Münnich were tortured and exiled. But the overthrow of the German court officials only increased other alien influences and intrigues, particularly French ones, and strengthened the hands of favorites and of selfish Russian nobles. The landholding nobility was freed of many service obligations and received special rights to army posts. The nobles also gained a monopoly on ownership of serfs and so extended jurisdiction over them that the position of the peasants became almost indistinguishable from that of slaves. As was to be expected, Elizabeth, ignorant, dissolute, bigoted, and lazy, was incapable of improving the state of the country; and, though she sometimes showed a kindly disposition and a flair for meeting popular needs and demands, the vaunted "Russification" meant no essential improvement in the administration.

Peter III. In 1762 Elizabeth died, leaving the throne to her nephew Peter III. It is not easy to speculate as to which road Russia would have taken had he kept the throne for a number of years. In the memory of the people, particularly the lower classes, he lived on as a reformer, sympathetic to their desires. Their hopes were derived from Peter's various edicts regarding a general amnesty, dissolution of the secret police, toleration of sects, secularization of church property, reduction of salt prices, and release of the gentry from obligatory service (an edict believed to promise parallel action for enserfed peasants). Yet, despite the remarkable and numerous liberal edicts of the few months of his reign, Peter's character was not such as to warrant the expectation of a steadily progressive course. His injudicial, blind imitation of foreign manners and alien spirit, his extraneous interests, his insistence on Prussian military drill, his arrogance and recurrent seizures of insanity made him unfit to rule, and he was forthwith overthrown by the court nobility in a *coup d'état* supported by his wife Catherine, who thereupon seized the throne (1762–96). A few days thereafter, Peter was murdered by one of the accomplices.

CULTURAL DEVELOPMENTS

Culturally, little was accomplished during the period from 1725 to 1762 that may properly be called Russian. French ideas continued to find entrance, and the manners and customs as well as the philosophy of France began to exercise a powerful influence at least among part of the ruling caste. The French language came to be widely used by the educated classes, and French style dominated the arts.

Education. Some new schools were founded, yet education remained confined to a limited number of fields and benefited only the privileged few. The Academy of Sciences was enlarged, and scholars, especially German ones, were attracted—the mathematician Euler, the historian Müller, the naturalist Gmelin and the brothers Bernoulli. They helped to build the Academy of Sciences into a foremost center of scholarship and to train young Russians. The first great native scholar was Lomonosov, who, like thousands of other Russians, had studied in Germany, had worked under Leibnitz's disciple, the polyhistor Wolff, and had attended the School of Mines at Freiberg. In 1755 the first Russian university, that of Moscow, was founded. The cultural centers in the Ukraine, however, continued to decline; Kiev lost its long-held reputation for scholarship, and Great Russian dialect and customs supplanted the indigenous civilization there.

Discoveries. Exploration was carried on under the auspices of the Academy of Sciences. The trans-Caspian region was explored, the direct way to India opened, and extensive scientific expeditions were conducted to investigate the natural history of Siberia and its peoples. A major part of the operations, however, centered around the task of studying the geography of Siberia and charting its confines. Five separate expeditions were charged with circumnavigating and mapping the north coast, each being assigned to a different sector. Because of a mild season, they achieved the objective in the summer of 1737. The rounding of the corner farthest east remained unaccomplished, but a land expedition did manage to reach the limits of Asia in the northeast. Finally, in 1741, Vitus Bering, a cautious and conscientious Danish explorer, and the Russian Chirikov, who commanded a second ship of Bering's expedition, succeeded in reaching the American shore, sighting the southern coast of Alaska and landing on an island. With the help of the German botanist Steller, the fact was established that the two continents were separated by water. Thus, after having tried for thirteen years, during which he had traveled as far as 67° 15′ north latitude and, without realizing it, had actually sighted America in 1732, Bering solved (through his dramatic expedition, which neither he nor many of his companions survived) the long-perplexing question whether or not a land bridge connected the old and the new world.

PROBLEMS

1. Discuss the persistence of Western influences in Russia after the death of Peter I.
2. Discuss the exploration and expansion in Asia in the middle of the eighteenth century.

16

LIFE AND ACTIVITIES IN THE EIGHTEENTH CENTURY

Significant Dates
Nobility Freed from Obligation of Service . . 1762
Secularization of Church Lands 1764

Military undertakings, foreign policies, personalities of rulers, and court intrigues hold a rather outstanding place in the history of eighteenth-century civilization. More than in other ages, they provide a key for an understanding of the growth of nations in that particular period of history. But too much accent on them has at times led to the neglect of a study of the contemporary social and economic currents. Yet, these possessed a dynamic seldom paralleled in earlier ages. This was true not only for Western Europe, where industrialization was growing, but also for Russia.

COURT AND TOWN LIFE

The Court Nobility. In eighteenth-century Russia, the governing class was still composed of the court nobility, many of whom were, despite Peter's reforms, descendants of the old hereditary princely families. Even more than elsewhere, this nobility was separated, as by an abyss, from the mass of the people whose labor—and to a large extent, slave labor—supported it. Enjoying wealth and comfort, the nobility made court life in St. Petersburg one of the most luxurious and extravagant of all of Europe. It partook in the intellectual achievements of the era. Its manners were adopted in a form perhaps less refined than those of the privileged classes of the *ancien régime* in France, but essentially identical with it. The nobles studied the philosophy of the Enlightenment and were fascinated by the great literature of Germany and France, and by the artistic styles in painting and music of the Baroque and Rococo. Politically, they interested themselves in court intrigues, in struggle for power, and in foreign affairs (more than in internal questions). Their dominating position in the army, their control of the guard regiments at the palace, and their hold on the court and the administration gave them the decisive influence in a state which was dependent upon the will of weak autocrats.

The Provincial Nobility. Apart from the court, the landed service-nobility in the various parts of the empire constituted the most powerful factor. This group had begun its rise under Ivan the Terrible; during the Time of Troubles it had gained pre-eminence, and under the first three Romanovs it had entrenched itself. In exchange, it was sworn to perform continued service in the armed forces or in the administration. During Peter's reign, the chief burdens of government had fallen on its shoulders, but under his successors it had tried to rid itself of as many of its obligations as possible. In 1730 some of the gentry secured the right to avoid military service on condition that they withdraw from the capital and reside on their estates. This was the first break in the system of service, and it was carried to its logical conclusion under Peter III when, in 1762, the gentry, though retaining the exclusive right to own serfs, were freed from all obligations of service and thus could become a leisure class. They were also exempted from taxation. As in France, the very existence of this class undermined the welfare of the state.

The Bourgeoisie. The bourgeoisie remained without much influence in the eighteenth century. Peter's attempts at raising the social standing of merchants and artisans had borne some fruit, but so long as the gentry retained the exclusive political power and the peasantry was held to a status of want and serfdom small progress could be made. Towns stagnated; by the end of the century less than 5 per cent of a population of about forty million lived in towns, and only part of these belonged to the bourgeoisie. Professions and commerce found little attention.

The Proletariat. In Western countries, industrial workmen began to make themselves felt in the eighteenth century, but in Russia they remained without importance. No common interest among the industrial workers could lead to the formation of a specific class for the reason that industrial labor was recruited partly from the ranks of peasant-serfs and assigned to factories; during certain seasons they regularly returned to resume their agricultural duties. A great many worked in mines owned by the state, but the more unfortunate were assigned to private enterprises.

AGRICULTURAL LIFE

The Peasants. Practically all the land of European Russia was owned by the state, the nobility, or the monasteries. As a result, approximately sixteen million peasant men and women who made up the peasantry in the middle of the eighteenth century found themselves in a sphere altogether unique. Few of them were free—with the exception of younger sons of noblemen or sons of priests who had found no other occupation, sharecroppers who had no permanent residence, and peasants in Siberia or in other outlying or recently acquired parts of the empire.

The Serfs. By far the majority of the peasants were serfs. Their status differed greatly according to region, type of bondage, and type of master.

PUBLIC LANDS. A part of the serf population lived and worked on estates owned by the state, monasteries, or by the Tsars personally, and were comparatively better off than those subject to private masters. The laws of the land, instead of the arbitrary will of a profit-seeking owner, were applied to them. But they, too, were bound to the land whose usufruct they enjoyed; they were often dependent on harsh officials; and at all times they faced the unwelcome prospect of being assigned to factories.

PRIVATE ESTATES. On the other hand, the private and hereditary serfs, who formed the majority of all peasants, found themselves in a desperate position. It was up to the landowner to regulate their lives, to arrange their marriages, to exercise jurisdiction over them, to punish and banish them, and to keep control of their personal belongings. Government regulations for the betterment of their condition remained ineffectual, for a peasant could not bring suit against his master and was exposed to merciless punishments. To be sure, there were many humane members among the landholding class; but in a general atmosphere such as existed during the eighteenth century even their humanity was but relative, and when an owner went so far as to free his serfs from servitude he often gained for them no more than the status of agricultural wage-slavery.

Obrok. As hereditary serfs, the peasants were divided into two principal groups: the obrok-paying and the barchina-rendering serfs. During the eighteenth century, the majority of those on obrok (those paying a fixed sum) lived in the less fertile northern regions where the landowners found it more profitable to ask for money than for labor. Often the results in crop raising and cattle breeding were poor, especially because peasant skill and industry were inferior to those in other parts of Europe, where crops of two or three times the value were harvested with the same size and type of land. Furthermore, the peasant's plot of land was sometimes too small to make its cultivation adequate for the maintenance of a family and the payment of steadily rising dues. To provide the necessary sums, the land was therefore frequently left to the care of women while the men tried to earn the obrok through work in a factory. Thus, labor for industry was supplied, but agriculture suffered, and the extension of the obrok system was therefore opposed by the government.

Barchina. The barchina peasants (those subject to labor services) were still worse off. They were not even free to go into factories and augment their incomes, since their labor was demanded by the masters approximately three days a week. During harvest season they were often compelled to give even more time to their lords and to neglect their own urgently needed crops.

The Mir. To avert the disastrous consequences of such a system, co-operation was emphasized and peasant holdings were treated as the common enterprise of a whole village community (mir) so that they could be looked after by all those not engaged in work for the squires. This, naturally, strengthened social consciousness among the peasants. The community had elected officials who were, however, not responsible to the members (as in the few cases where the mirs were composed of free peasants) but to the landlords, who factually, if not theoretically, owned the land. The common land was distributed by the mir and at intervals redistributed among the individual members, the state taxes and often the obrok being handled by the mir. Care was given to the aged, the sick, and the orphaned. Education was likewise under the auspices of the mir; but it was very meagre except in the Baltic provinces, which after Peter's conquest remained socially under domination of the Baltic Germans with their higher standards. Unfortunately, the mir was frequently under the influence of an indolent priest or a rich peasant (kulak) who, unmindful of his own earlier sufferings, exploited the work of his fellow men or oppressed them through loans at usurious rates. Under such circumstances, even the mir did not gain as much for the individual peasant as should have been possible; and the serf became so fearful and despondent that he denounced any innovation, even if it held definite promise for his betterment, lest it somehow be so interpreted as to heighten his distress.

HOUSEHOLDS. It is to be noted that in the eighteenth century another class came into being—the household serf—which was developed by assigning children of peasants to the household of the owner. Here they received special training and later served as domestic help, being employed for spinning and weaving and other household duties, and occasionally as musicians and teachers. From this group arose distinguished writers, artists, and scientists, some of whom received additional training in special public institutions or abroad; but the majority of them lived under pitiable conditions.

CLERICAL LIFE

The Upper Clergy. Those at the top of the hierarchy enjoyed the favor of the government and were honored with rank and distinction. They formed one of the most important pillars of the state and were to a large extent dependent upon it. Under Peter the Great, they were relieved of much of the administration of worldly church affairs, which had passed into the hands of the Synod. In 1762 church property was entirely confiscated; disposal of it by the church had been curtailed in Ivan the Terrible's time. Now it was ordered secularized; and in 1764, under Catherine, the order was executed. A state budget was introduced which provided for the maintenance of the clergy. Although this served to link the church entirely with the state and to subject the hierarchy to government direction, it was possible for the hierarchy to draw substantial incomes and lead a life of luxury as well as of influence.

The Lower Clergy. The position of the village clergy was in sharp contrast to that of the higher ranks. Though free, they formed in some respect the lowest of all classes, despised by nobility and peasantry alike. Before the eighteenth century the position of priest or "pope" had been often elective; those who bid for the lowest salaries had been not infrequently chosen. Therefore, the least qualified had monopolized many of the positions. Education among the clergy was scanty; they had to guarantee, but not to prove, that they could read and write; and they were expected to pass a perfunctory examination in religion. Not until Napoleonic times was serious theological training prescribed. Their moral standards were often equally low; many were equipped neither to teach the gospel, to preach, nor to enlighten. Their own lives set no example, and their work consisted largely in serving as useful tools of the state (sometimes in police matters) rather than in the propagation of the faith.

In Peter I's time, elections to parsonages were gradually discontinued. Instead, either popes were nominated by the diocese or, more frequently, the office of priest passed from father to son. This led to the establishment of a hereditary clerical class, which from time to time had to be purged of superfluous members; the unhappy victims were sent to factories or estates. The only advantage the village priest enjoyed, from 1738 on, consisted in being exempted from the poll tax. Otherwise he belonged to the lowest strata of the population, and until 1796 he could be subjected to corporal punishment and flogging. The wives of the popes continued to be subjected to such indignities for some additional forty years.

ECONOMIC LIFE

In the course of the eighteenth century, the population of Russia doubled, reaching more than thirty-five million by the end of the century. This caused an enormous growth in the demand for goods, but brought also severe shortages; agricultural production, especially, could not keep up with the increased needs because of lack of possibilities for an expansion of the cultivable area (particularly in central Russia). The effects of this situation were both favorable and unfavorable.

Industries. Initially, industry benefited from population growth and shortages of agricultural lands. Laborers became available. But the demand for goods rose and, despite continuing lack of capital and technical skills, factories—primarily in the textile and metallurgic fields—increased in size and number. Moreover, mines were developed in Siberia and produced large quantities of gold and coal, and the iron industry in the Urals continued to make rapid progress, so that by the end of the century it became the world leader in iron production. The immediate result of industrial expansion was that new labor shortages occurred.

OWNERSHIP. Most of the heavy industries were in governmental hands. Private industrialists were generally members of the nobility. Many acquired their factories during the times of Elizabeth, as compensation for meritorious service, just as in former times faithful servants had been awarded landed estates. They disposed of the necessary labor force because they either owned serfs and could shift these from agricultural to industrial labor, or because they could "buy" serfs ("possessional serfs") from others who could spare them, and employ them in their industries. Naturally, these industrialists possessed little training in business life and generally had to rely on managers who, especially if not recruited at a high price from abroad, likewise lacked knowledge and often honesty. State supervision and interference persisted. The owners had few outlets for their products. Most of their goods had to be produced for the government; some was for export; and only a little could be sold on the free market and even then to the gentry only. The bulk of the population had to rely essentially upon the products of their own home industries.

WORKING CONDITIONS. In the factories the workmen were illtreated and overworked. Their fundamental grievances were long hours, enforced transfer from their lands to factories, long journeys between their homes and the mines with consequent loss of pay, and irregularities in the payment of wages—low as they were. Innumerable complaints poured in at St. Petersburg; but neither investigations and regulation of wages by state officials nor the occasional confiscation and transfer of ownership of whole factories remedied the evils. Furthermore, redress was generally delayed, sometimes even beyond the lifetime of the claimant. In desperation, many workers sacrificed their small earnings and tried to buy themselves free by hiring still more wretched persons who would be willing to take their places. Others—and there were thousands of these—fled to Siberia and other possible havens of freedom.

Shirking and drunkenness among workers added another problem to industrial life. Poor helpers, like everyone else, had to be cared for in times of depression and in the event of accident and sickness. The entire system of forced labor was burdensome, and free labor and competition would have been more productive and profitable. The more industrialization advanced, the more the factory owners suffered anew from labor shortages. When, at the end of the century, the industrialists were forbidden to buy peasants and to separate them from their land for employment in mines and factories, labor shortages became critical.

Commerce. Unlike industry, commerce did not benefit as much as it should have from population growth and increased needs. The somewhat dated mercantilist policy of the government, implying a large amount of state control and monopolistic institutions, interfered with a normal development. Unlike Western Europe, the evolution did not lead to a free and unimpeded growth of Russian commerce under the leadership of a powerful bourgeoisie.

INTERNAL TRADE. Economic oppression of the vast masses of the peasants and workers accounted for the fact that the internal market continued to depend largely upon a rather small group of wealthy people. The poor still provided the main part of their needs through the production of their own food and their own tools. To be sure, state banks were established under Elizabeth and, at least temporarily, interest rates were lowered; but taxes were steadily raised and this slowed down the growth rate of internal trade. State and private monopolies were not as all-embracing as in the time of Peter the Great, but though diminishing, they continued to exist, as in the case of tobacco, rhubarb, and other lucrative commodities. An impulse for the stimulation of internal trade came from the establishment of free commerce in the Ukraine.

In Siberia, commerce developed slowly. Settlements there remained scarce, though some were established in the western parts. To protect them against nomad invasions, it was necessary to erect a fortification line extending from the Caspian Sea to Orenburg (founded in 1760) and thence to the upper Irtish region. The parts inhabited by Kirghiz tribes and consisting chiefly of barren steppe were incorporated in 1740.

EXTERNAL TRADE. Exports and imports were encouraged, and they increased when, owing to Ostermann's foresight, tariff barriers were lowered in 1728 and 1729. But his judicious policy was not persistently carried out, and by the middle of the century, extreme reverse trends prevailed. Yet, by 1800 (at least according to official figures, unreliable though they are), Russian foreign trade had increased about tenfold over 1725. Both the East and the West profited from it. Unfortunately for the Russian people, the raw materials as well as the man-hours invested in export goods were woefully undervalued, and, in a sense, exports often meant a loss for the nation rather than an advantage. They included great amounts of grain and iron in addition to traditional goods, such as furs, wax, tar, hemp, and lumber. Imports were composed likewise of traditional commodities, such as cloth, dyes, tin, colonial goods, and wines; but increasingly they consisted also of various types of luxuries fit for a gradually Westernized society. The chief Western trade partners were Holland, England, and some of the North German towns, such as Hamburg and Lübeck; in the East, China and Persia played the leading roles.

SYSTEM OF AUTOCRACY

As a whole, Russia in the eighteenth century presented the picture of a country where the concept of service to the state was paramount. Nobleman, merchant, peasant, and clergyman alike had to correlate their lives and activities with the needs of a state which was autocratically governed by the ruler. Yet, the ruler himself was not free in his decisions, for he was subject to custom and dependent upon the continued support of the most essential class, the service-nobility. In the hands of an efficient and farsighted monarch the system might have worked to common benefit; under incompetent men and women it led to grievous and often ineradicable injustices, to social rifts, to economic insecurity, and worst of all to destruction of human dignity which for centuries was to leave its scars on the nation.

PROBLEMS

1. Discuss the stratification of Russian society in the eighteenth century.
2. Discuss the service obligations for nobility and peasantry.
3. Discuss the economic significance of serfdom.

17

INTERNAL CONDITIONS IN CATHERINE'S TIMES

Significant Dates

Reign of Catherine II 1762–1796
Pugachev Revolt 1772–1774
Issuing of Charter 1785

CATHERINE II

Catherine, a German princess, was thirty-three years old when she ascended the throne in 1762. To all appearances she had accepted the Orthodox faith with much sincerity, which—to the mind of her Russian supporters—contrasted favorably with the agnosticism of her husband. Her marriage had been a failure, and after a few years she took a lover, who in due time was succeeded by eight or nine others by whom she had several children. But her love affairs and dissipations, which mirrored the concepts of the times and resembled conditions at the French court, were not to interfere with her devotion to duty as a ruler. She was an indefatigable worker, an interested student of political affairs, a diplomat, a linguist, a sculptress, painter, reader, and correspondent. Under the influence of the writings of Montesquieu, Beccaria, and Voltaire, she showed certain traits of an "enlightened, benevolent despot." But her actions hardly justify her claim to practical enlightenment. Internal improvements during her reign were limited in scope and served her personal vanity and desire for applause more than the needs of the people. Perhaps the disposal and subsequent murder of her husband and later the murder of the one other claimant to the throne, the former baby-Tsar Ivan VI, who had by now grown to manhood, left her with an uneasy conscience, made her dependent upon those who had elevated her, and prevented her from insisting on innovations lest she risk her crown.

CATHERINE'S RULE

Attempts at Reform. In 1767 Catherine set out to achieve administrative reorganization and improvement in municipal and economic institutions and to better agricultural conditions. Accordingly, she convened a commission of more than five hundred members, elected by all classes except the serfs, to deliberate the contemplated great reform. She herself wrote a rather general directive, which was applauded throughout the Continent for its liberal spirit; but it was stripped of many of its generous suggestions on being submitted to the commission. Deliberations took more than a year. No progress was made, and in 1774 the whole work was abandoned.

Failures and Achievements. Institutional changes were limited to the administrative system; the powers of the Senate were reduced and the land was redistributed into fifty-one districts, each having its own councils, courts, and administration dominated by the local nobility. Both measures served to enlarge the autocratic powers of the ruler and those of the gentry. Corruption in the administration continued to flourish as it did in the days before Catherine. As before, the inhabitants of the country were excluded by edict from participation in public affairs. Serfdom was not only preserved, but it was vastly expanded by enormous grants of public land to the gentry and by its extension to the Ukraine, where all remnants of autonomy were abolished. Capital punishment and torture were seldom resorted to, but the first had already been officially abolished by Elizabeth and the latter by Peter III; asylums and hospitals were founded, but in this case again Peter has to be credited for the initial measure. Vaccination was introduced and was propagandized. Education was extended to women, but only to those of the upper class. Schools were founded in agricultural districts and even among some of the most backward Asiatic tribes, but instruction was insufficient and the lack of understanding of local conditions sometimes led to preposterous contradictions. Only in the complete emancipation of the merchant class in 1785 and in a liberal attitude toward the Old Believers, some of whom were encouraged to return to Russia, could signs of true enlightenment be found; yet even these faded during the era of the great French Revolution (1789–95), when the privileged classes, fearing a similar upheaval in Russia, supported the passage of reactionary measures.

Court Life. The court at St. Petersburg during Catherine's reign was brilliant and extravagant. The empress surrounded herself with capable advisers, such as Panin, Sievers, her lover Potëmkin, the Princess Dashkov, and various excellent generals, as well as famous foreign scientists and philosophers. Life was fashioned along French patterns. It was a late blossoming of the culture of the court of Louis XIV. Art treasures were brought from abroad at the expense of toiling workers; French actors, dancers, and physicians were hired at great cost, and, besides Western philosophical ideas, they introduced stilted manners little in harmony with the crude pleasures enjoyed by Catherine and her court. From Germany, teachers and artisans were introduced. The foreigners eventually spread the liberal concepts of their home countries and found disciples in men like Novikov, scientist, author, and editor of a paper, *The Drone,* and Radishchev, famed for his realistic and accusatory description of social conditions in his *Journey from Petersburg to Moscow.* Both were bitterly persecuted by Catherine and exiled, but nevertheless a liberal movement took firm root in Russian society.

PUGACHEV REVOLT

Preliminary Uprisings. Since Catherine's lengthy rule of nearly thirty-five years thus marked no true progress in the social development of a country urgently in need of reform, general unrest increased. Numerous minor outbreaks occurred and a serious rising followed the pestilence which swept the country in 1770, but none brought amelioration of conditions. Eventually, a revolt broke out, which surpassed in size and violence that led by Stenka Razin one hundred years earlier, and darkly foreshadowed the collapse of the autocratic system that was to occur in the early twentieth century.

Grievances. As in the times of Razin, the revolution was directed not against the institution of Tsardom, but against the nobility. The tsarist idea was firmly maintained, because only from a supreme autocratic ruler could relief be expected from the oppressions of the landowners and a small gentry. And if such relief had not been forthcoming in the past, that was seldom blamed on the inefficiency or unconcern of the Tsars, but rather on the malevolence of the court nobility, who were accused of preventing the complaints of the poor from reaching the throne and of falsifying ukases of the Tsars. As a matter of fact, peasant delegations sent to submit petitions had frequently been waylaid en route to the capital or, if they finally did arrive, had been imprisoned and flogged.

Pugachev. The revolution broke out in 1772. In contrast to the Razin rising and despite all oppression, not the peasantry but the Cossacks (those from the Ural) acted as the driving force behind the upheaval. They had their own grievances with regard to military service imposed upon them, corruption of their officers, persecution of the numerous dissenters among them, and an edict of the government ending their right to choose their own superiors. They seized upon the occasion of a war between Russia and Turkey, and provided a legitimate basis for their rising by spreading rumors that Peter III had not died but had reappeared. Peter was vested with all manner of liberal ideas which, it is very likely, he had never cherished. He was credited with special sympathy for Old Believers, although in reality indifference in religious matters had accounted for his tolerance towards them. Once these rumors were given credence, several impersonators of the dead ruler appeared. It was a Cossack, Pugachev, who, despite differences in both appearance and age, finally emerged as the "true" Peter and was acknowledged leader of the revolution. Though less a pilot than a tool, he showed enough independence and shrewdness to engage the help and cooperation of the peasants by promising them emancipation from serfdom, religious freedom, and abolishment of military service.

Revolution. Although the interests of the peasants were no longer identical with those of the Cossacks and although many of them stood in fear of Cossack outrages, a large number thereupon joined with Pugachev, and soon the rising spread to the European part of the empire as well as into western Siberia. Had Pugachev been as able in strategic planning as in evoking the enthusiasm of the impoverished masses rebelling against their masters, the revolution might have been successful. But despite an army of more than fifteen thousand men, his siege of the fortress of Orenburg, crucial link in the defense system of the government, miscarried after exhausting attempts. In March, 1774, reaction set in accompanied by defeats. It was only by the greatest exertion that Pugachev was still able to enlist the help of new recruits, to seize the town of Kazan, and to threaten Moscow. The government answered by putting an end to the war with Turkey and, with the freeing of sufficient troops, countered the menace. Betrayed by personal enemies among the Cossacks, Pugachev was captured in August, 1774, and executed in January, 1775.

Results. As with many premature revolutions, the Pugachev revolt showed the urgent need for reforms; yet by its very lack of success it defeated any opportunity for improvement. A charter of the nobility, issued by Catherine in 1785, strengthened serfdom by placing additional burdens on the peasants, and historians have justly argued that the work of social reform was thrown back by half a century. Indeed, the revolt served to increase the autocratic tendencies in Catherine, who showed in her advancing years a reactionary attitude that made her the bitterest enemy of the French Revolution and even made her refuse, at any time, recognition of the independence of the United States.

CATHERINE "THE GREAT"

If Catherine in her internal policies showed herself hardly worthy of the surname "the Great," wisdom and steadfastness in external affairs should explain the attribute accorded her. Yet, success, rather than ability and perseverance, accounts for the title; and success was essentially achieved by a combination of favorable circumstances, able help, and weight of Russian power, while Catherine herself contributed but little. As a whole, the policies pursued under previous reigns were carried on by her. No clear pattern emerged with regard to Western European powers, and only in connection with Russia's immediate neighbors can a consistent policy, aiming at aggrandizement at the cost of these neighbors, be witnessed.

PROBLEMS

1. Discuss Catherine's claims to the title "the Great."
2. Trace the conditions leading to the Pugachev revolt.
3. Discuss the effect of the Pugachev revolt.

18

GROWTH OF RUSSIA'S INTER-NATIONAL ROLE

Significant Dates

Treaty of Belgrade	1739
First Partition of Poland	1772
Treaty of Kuchuk Kainardji	1774
Treaty of Jassy	1792
Second Partition of Poland	1793
Third Partition of Poland	1795

The era from Peter the Great to the death of Catherine the Great in 1796—the latter date marking the year when Napoleon appeared on the international scene—constituted a transition period in Russia's role in the European community. Before Peter, the country was little known and little considered in the arena of general European politics; after his death, it was a power to be reckoned with, whose might was appreciated and whose consent to international arrangements was often sought. It remained so despite, rather than because of, the work of his successors; and under Catherine II it became an integral part of Europe, a full and independent partner in the system of Continental politics.

The transition period itself was characterized by the spirit of the time, according to which foreign affairs were conducted as a private art—the art of diplomacy—practiced by rulers or ministers according to certain rules and standards of a very distinguished guild; op-

portunistic motives and personal inclinations furnish a better key to
an understanding of this period than any attempt to trace trends or
plans.

RELATIONS WITH CENTRAL AND WESTERN EUROPE

Alliances.   After Peter's death, Russia for a time continued the
policy of friendship with Prussia and France laid down by the great
Tsar. But in 1733 France tried to place on the Polish throne the
father-in-law of Louis XV, Stanislaw Leszczyński, whereas Austria
and Russia herself supported the candidature of August of Saxony.
From that time on, a strong movement was felt in Russia to abandon the Franco-Prussian side and to support Austria, which was
allied with England. This had its advantages, for Austria was a
traditional and permanent ally in the struggle with Russia's most
dangerous enemy, Turkey; also, the court at Vienna shared Russian
interests in Poland. Conversely, the change had the disadvantage of
necessitating a readjustment of relations with the English, who had
proved jealous and aggressive ever since the creation of a Russian
navy and the progress of Russia toward the Baltic Sea ports, and
whose co-operation could be counted upon only as long as a need
existed for Russian timber, tar, cordage, and other commodities, such
as grain for the British navy and home economy.

Seven Years' War.   It was the chancellor Bestuzhev-Ryumin
who most strongly advocated this Anglo-Austrian course, the course
that was pursued until 1756, when the entire policy suddenly collapsed because of a reversal of the European alliance system—which
now reflected complete disregard and neglect of possible Russian
interests. England changed sides and joined Prussia; and, in exchange, France reconciled herself with Austria. Prussia's king, Frederick the Great, had inspired this reversal of alliances, because he
hoped to recover through England the old friendship with Russia
or, at least, to secure her neutrality in the coming struggle with
Austria. However, Bestuzhev-Ryumin's anti-Prussian attitude and
Frederick's cynical remarks about the dissolute Tsarina Elizabeth
precluded such realignment, and Russia found herself on the newly
created Franco-Austrian side and involved in a war that was to last
in Europe for seven years. In the campaigns, defeats and victories
alternated. In 1760 Berlin was occupied for a few days by Russian

troops, but indifference on the Russian side and inertia of the generals rendered useless efforts to hold the city. In 1762 Elizabeth died, and her successor, Peter III, who adored the Prussian king, put a prompt end to the superfluous bloodshed; thus he renounced, and gained nothing from, a war which had little relation to the true interests of the country and which probably could not have ended with different results for Russia even with "victory."

New Diplomacy. After the war was over and Prussia and Austria had composed their differences, Russia followed a policy of amity with both the countries which it continued until the end of the century.

France. As to the Western nations, France vied alternatingly with England for Catherine's favor. Up to the outbreak of the French Revolution in 1789, Catherine, with her predilection for French *esprit* and cultural exchange, would have preferred to secure also a political bond with France; however, when the storm broke, co-operation between the revolutionary Western nation and the autocrat of the East came to nothing.

England. Relations with England after the Seven Years' War remained vacillating. As at the time of Bestuzhev-Ryumin, a faction at court—now under the leadership of Potëmkin—worked for an English alliance. During the seventies, British offers were considered, according to which, in exchange for naval support against the rebellious colonies in North America, a colony in America or on Minorca in the Mediterranean was to be ceded to Russia. The French, supported at the court by the party of Count Panin, did their best to circumvent the scheme, which eventually collapsed because of its own impracticability. The British resumed their infringements on Russian as on other nations' neutral rights on the seas; and their actions led to a dangerous rift which was aggravated by Catherine's promotion of co-operation among all northern powers against the island kingdom. However, England's final defeat in 1783 cleared the way for the resumption of normal relations. With Britain's increasing need for Russian grain and iron during the period of industrialization and urbanization, the connection soon became comparatively close. But political collaboration remained sporadic until the Napoleonic invasion of central Europe.

RELATIONS WITH NEIGHBORING COUNTRIES

Basic Aims. In contrast with her policies towards the Western powers, whose course was dominated by Western interests, Russia pursued determined self-centered aims with regard to her three neighbors Sweden, Poland, and Turkey. Seeing them weakened in their structure by the transition from absolutism to bourgeois rule or by outmoded despotism and dated feudalism, Russia consistently encouraged their internal disorders and opposed reforms in order to bring about their disintegration and absorption into the Russian commonwealth.

Sweden. With regard to Sweden, ill-feeling persisted after the conclusion of the Great Northern War in 1721, and in 1740 Sweden tried to profit from the succession disputes after the death of Tsarina Anna by making war, ostensibly for the purpose of helping Elizabeth to the throne. Elizabeth showed little gratitude. When the Swedish armies were beaten, she imposed a harsh peace which deprived Sweden of parts of Finland including the great harbor of Viborg. Later, relations improved and in several instances co-operation was achieved, such as in the northern alliance against England; but at no time were plans for the ultimate partition of Sweden lost sight of, and internal opposition to the Swedish government was regularly encouraged in order to further them. Not until 1787 was a temporary end put to Russian schemes, when Gustavus III of Sweden profited from Russia's engagements in the south and undertook a war.

Turkey. Russia consistently followed the fundamental principle of her policy regarding Turkey—namely, to gain access to the open sea in the south.

TREATY OF BELGRADE. With this objective in mind and at the same time with the aim of putting an end to the invasions of Turkish-ruled Tartars in the Crimea, the peace concluded by Peter in 1711 was broken in 1735. Persian support was bought at the cost of Baku and Derbent on the Caspian Sea, both previously conquered by Peter and now voluntarily relinquished because they seemed to offer little material advantage. The Russians were victorious; and had it not been for the desertion of Russia's other ally, Austria, the whole northern coast of the Black Sea might have been taken. As it was, the Turks secured a comparatively favorable peace (Belgrade) in 1739, dismantled the fortress of Azov, and ceded the Black Sea coast from the mouth of the Don to the Bug River—but only under the condition that Russia would neither erect military installations nor maintain a navy on the Black Sea.

TREATY OF KUCHUK KAINARDJI. The struggle was resumed in 1768 when Turkey intervened in the Polish turmoil to strengthen her northern borders, thus threatening the success of Russian domination over all Poland. Notable victories were won by the Russian army under the generals Rumiantsev, Golitsyn, Panin, and Suvorov, and this time not only the rest of the northern Black Sea coast but also the Crimea was conquered. A Russian fleet, which had left the Baltic Sea to stir risings against the Turks in Greece, sailed around Europe and succeeded in defeating the Turkish navy. Peace was finally concluded at Kuchuk Kainardji in 1774, marking the overwhelming ascendancy of Russia and carrying the tradition of Peter a step farther. The fortress of Azov passed conclusively into Russian hands and most of the Black Sea coast from the Bug River to the foothills of the Caucasus range was incorporated. The Crimea itself was constituted as an autonomous Tartar state—naturally promising little stability—and nine years later was dissolved and absorbed by Russia. The conquered territory was reorganized by Catherine's lover Potëmkin, towns and harbors were erected, schools and factories founded, and people settled; and, although many of Potëmkin's new institutions were staged, rather than real, eventually the region began to prosper. In 1796, the harbor of Odessa was founded, and it developed into the greatest market for grain exports from southern Russia.

TREATY OF JASSY. The Treaty of Kuchuk Kainardji provided also for a protectorate of Russia over Moldavia and for her right to interfere in internal Turkish affairs, should the interests of the Christians living in the Sultan's empire seem to be threatened. It was in order to throw off these stifling conditions, to free themselves from economic competition, and to forestall Russian political penetration of the Balkans, that in 1787 the Turks broke the peace. They availed themselves of the opportunity offered by Russia's illegal acts of annexing the Crimea in 1783 and of constructing a large Black Sea fleet, and once more resorted to arms. Again, fate was against them;

this time Russian forces, led by Suvorov, succeeded—though only after enormous losses—in taking the Turkish key fortress of Ismail on the Danube. In the meantime, Russia's ally Austria pushed from the northwest into the Turkish empire. But again she prematurely dropped out of the war, so that the subsequent Russo-Turkish Peace of Jassy of 1792 added little to the gains of Kuchuk Kainardji. The *de facto* annexation of the Crimea was recognized *de jure,* and some territorial gains were made by Russia, bringing the extension of her Black Sea coast to the Dniester. However, the Turks maintained their rule of the Turkish empire and the Russian advance in the direction of the heart of the Turkish empire and the Straits leading into the Mediterranean was halted. Russia's drive foreshadowed, however, future difficulties with England and Austria, which prepared to resist too far-reaching encroachments on Turkey.

Poland. Sweden and Turkey both possessed sufficient inner strength and international importance to preserve their independence; but Poland fell victim to Russian pressure and diplomacy. It is incorrect, though it has often been done, to view Poland's collapse as a result of the "greed" of her neighbors, particularly Russia. In reality, century-old oppression of the great bulk of the Polish population, oligarchic and anarchic rule, persecution of dissenting religious groups, license and arrogance on the part of a small, uneducated lower gentry, chauvinistic and aggressive policies not in line with the strength and value of existing institutions—these and resulting disintegration necessitated a radical change. The logic of events was on Russia's side.

CIVIL WARS. The beginning of the final chapter in Polish history was marked by a renewed succession struggle in 1733, when a national reform party elected Stanislaw Leszczyński as king against Russian will and Leszczyński attempted to ally himself with Sweden. Russia expelled the candidate by armed force and saw to the continuation of previous conditions through the choice of August of Saxony. After an uneventful reign, August died in 1763, and again Russia interfered in the election, using as pretexts political complications in the Polish province of Courland and the old religious differences over the position of the Orthodox within the kingdom. Eventually Catherine succeeded in having one of her former lovers, Prince Stanislaw Poniatowski, elected king. The troops which had helped him remained in Poland, and soon the Russian ambassador in Warsaw exercised greater power than the king. Thereupon, in order to recover freedom of action, new internal reforms were introduced by Poniatowski and some of the powerful noble families. These reforms were actively opposed by Catherine in order to prevent recuperation of Polish strength, and the blind Polish lower gentry joined the opposition through fear of losing their privileges. Civil war broke out, in which the peasant saw his chance and also took up arms. A triangular struggle ensued between a reform-minded upper nobility, a foreign-supported gentry, and a desperate peasantry. Under pressure from abroad the struggle ended in cancellation of the intended reforms, except for those referring to religious tolerance; Russia reserved, as in Turkey, her right to interfere in Polish internal affairs if the interests of the Orthodox Christians demanded it.

FIRST PARTITION. Catherine intended to use this privilege as a steppingstone to complete domination; but Frederick the Great, anxious to connect his outlying Prussian possessions with Brandenburg, from which they were separated by Polish western Prussia, made use of the Tsarina's simultaneous preoccupation in the Turkish war and in the Pugachev revolt, and proposed instead annexation of parts of Poland by the three neighbors Russia, Austria, and Prussia. Russia had to consent and in the Treaty of 1772 secured most of former White Russia, which in the late Middle Ages had been annexed by Poland's partner, Lithuania. A properly bribed Polish diet confirmed the cession.

SECOND PARTITION. Poland, largely confined through this first "partition" treaty to her ethnographic frontiers and relieved of most of the vexing religious problem, endeavored to rebuild on a sounder basis during the following twenty years. The elective monarchy was abolished, majority rule instead of unlimited veto power was introduced, and peasant reforms were prepared. In 1791 a new constitution was adopted which satisfied Prussian and Austrian designs, but which seemed to Russia to lay the foundation for future resurgence of the Polish threat. Again Catherine decided to interfere, and once more she was afforded the opportunity by the reactionaries within Poland. At their request, Russian soldiers were sent anew into the country and under pressure the constitution was abrogated and the old state of disorder re-established. Then a second treaty was imposed by Catherine in 1793, which provided for further cession of land, including most of ancient Lithuania in addition to the rest of White Russia. Moreover, Poland had to subordinate her external policies to those of Russia and to combine her military forces with those of Catherine.

THIRD PARTITION. The stipulations—unlike those of 1772—left no room for future free development of Polish life, and necessarily led to a revolt by freedom-loving elements within the country. Inspired by the successful defense of the newly founded French Republic against the apparently overwhelming power of monarchies encircling it, the Poles, led by Thaddeus Kosciusko, rose in armed resistance to Russian dominance. But they had to pay the penalty for past misdeeds. Unlike the French, among whom the liberal Republic could inspire devotion to a great cause, the oppressed people of Poland had no trust even in those members of their educated upper class who now promised them a different, more liberal treatment. Unwilling to help prolong, under whatever form, the domination of the old abusive ruling class, they were not inclined to shed their blood for new ideas and their proponents. The uprising of 1794 failed, and Kosciusko was taken prisoner. Warsaw surrendered to Suvorov, and the remnants of the country were divided among the three neighboring powers. Once more Russia took the largest slice, helping herself to the Baltic coast with strategic Courland.

The acquisition of two-thirds of former Poland by Russia marked the greatest territorial gain—but not an unequivocally secure or profitable one—in Catherine's time. Within two years of the last partition, Catherine "the Great" died.

PROBLEMS

1. Summarize the chief objectives of Russian foreign policies in the eighteenth century.
2. Describe the territorial changes of Russia from 1725 to 1796.
3. Discuss the role of Russia in the Seven Years' War.

19

THE TURN OF THE CENTURY

Significant Dates

Reign of Paul I 1796–1801
Suvorov's Italian Campaign 1799
Maritime League against England . . . 1800–1801

PAUL I

Catherine was succeeded by her son Paul (1796–1801), whose parentage remained unclear—perhaps even to Paul and Catherine themselves. Paul has been called "an idealist in pursuit of the Absolute"; and this description does him better justice than do many of the adverse judgments of romantic and nationalistic historians within and without Russia. Certainly he was mentally ill, as violent changes of temper and erratic orders indicate; but he was no more mad perhaps than Ivan the Terrible or possibly Peter the Great. It merely happened that the age in which he lived, unlike earlier periods, offered no scope for the display of such personalities as he represented. Generosity and sincerity were by no means absent from his make-up; and the tyranny of his actions was mitigated by a thwarted yet strong sense of duty that was manifest throughout his reign. But Paul was afraid. This is not to say that he, like many other Russian rulers, was wanting in personal courage, but that he feared the evil court intrigues about him could put a premature end to the reign which he had so eagerly awaited since the murder of his father through the thirty-four years of his mother's usurped rule. His own murder in 1801 demonstrated the justification of his fears.

THE DOMESTIC SCENE

Rise of New Concepts. Paul's rule introduced the "Modern Age" into Russia. To trace to Catherine's time the background for modern concepts of state is not difficult, but it was the end of the century which actually ushered in visible changes. "Ruling" in the old sense—in the sense of exercising absolute privilege, of pursuing private pleasure, of practicing good administration as one would in his own large household—had to make room for different standards which involved duty and responsibility. Territorial gains became identified with ideas of national will and, perhaps, of geopolitics; they were no longer exclusively linked with the personal grandeur of the ruler. Morality at the court, though not much better in Paul's time than in Catherine's, now had to live up to triumphant bourgeois standards, at least ostensibly. It was also under Paul, and not under his mother, that the first effective step was taken to solve Russia's knottiest problem: serfdom.

Bureaucracy and Autocracy. The Tsar's activities brought many arbitrary and useless measures: Censorship was strictly enforced to keep out the liberal ideas of the French revolutionists; books of scientific and literary value were indiscriminately banned; details of dress were regulated (i.e., laced shoes and round hats like those preferred by the Parisian mob were proscribed, sans-culotte costume was not tolerated) and tight, unhealthful, and impractical uniforms were introduced for the army. Through inflexible regulations, progress was stifled and imagination among officials suppressed. Arbitrary appointments and dismissals poisoned the atmosphere, and exaggerated severity hit those guilty of the slightest default in the prescribed duties; a punctilious and stifling court ceremonial undermined independent thought and action.

Military Affairs. But the short reign of less than five years brought astounding changes. With his intense interest in military affairs, Paul's first move was to remodel army and navy. Warships were reconditioned, and the army was provided with adequate and modern artillery. Training standards of sailors and soldiers were raised to meet the high standards set by Frederick the Great, if not by Napoleon. Superfluous charges were abolished and posts of command were reserved for trained officers in place of idle nobles.

Government. The administration was put on a sounder basis. The instability in the highest position, the throne—a result of the succession law established under Peter the Great and Catherine I— was abolished upon adoption of the law of primogeniture. The highest administrative units, the "colleges," made room for appointed advisers of the Tsar, who now were obliged to shoulder personal responsibility.

Education and Commerce. Catherine's hesitant proposals in the educational and commercial field were translated into practice. The University of Dorpat, great seat of learning for German scholars, was reopened. Although commercial activities suffered from Paul's veering policies in international relations, trade was encouraged. Imports of luxury goods were restricted. With government support, the Russian-American Company was founded and set to the task of exploring and colonizing arctic America. Russian rights in America were reserved north of latitude 54°40′ and guaranteed by treaties with Spain, England, and the United States. Tolerance was maintained toward adherents of the non-Orthodox faiths as well as toward dissenters.

System of Service. The principle of compulsory service to the state, abolished unilaterally for the gentry by Peter III in 1762, was revived—although the Tsar's assassination precluded its legal reintroduction. On the other hand, the burdens of the peasants were for the first time defined, if not eased; and this limitation by law of the rights of the landowners meant more than any wholesale attack on the institution of serfdom itself. It is true that under Paul as under his predecessors hundreds of thousands of peasants were still "given away" to small landowners; but at least a peasant could no longer be separated from his land like a slave, nor was the amount of his *corvée* or barchina any longer left to the arbitrariness of his master.

RUSSIA'S INTERNATIONAL ROLE

Opposition to Revolutionary France. In Paul's reign external affairs were conducted in an abrupt, moody manner; yet the historian cannot fail to recognize that the fundamentals of Russian foreign interests were at no time overlooked. At the time of Paul's accession, the basic struggle of autocracy against the Revolutionary French Republic was in the foreground. Opposition to the Republic, inherited from Catherine's reign, accounts for the outbreak of war between the two countries in 1799. French annexation of Malta, then under Tsar Paul's protectorate, and renewed disturbances in Poland, the result of French Revolutionary doctrines, were but secondary causes.

Coalition against France. The war, undertaken in alliance with England, Austria, and Holland, showed the solidly good condition of the Russian armies, which fought in various theaters of war. Foremost was the army under General Suvorov, who had been in retirement as a result of one of Paul's evil whims but who was recalled and generously accorded full and unconstrained power. Under him, a Russian army crossed half of Europe and recaptured northern Italy from the French in a campaign as brilliant as that which Napoleon had conducted three years earlier when winning the Po Valley. The very success of Russia, however, stirred up jealousy among the Austrians; and subsequently Suvorov was deserted by his allies, his plans for invading France were overthrown, and nothing was left for him but to retreat via Switzerland. Despite heroic efforts and excellent leadership, the difficulties of terrain, the resumed attacks by the French, and the lack of support by Austria brought enormous losses; and a woefully decimated army returned to Russia. Suvorov himself died shortly thereafter, and the coalition with the Hapsburgs against France ended abruptly.

Reconciliation with Napoleonic France. What followed was not so much a "reversal" of the existing system of alliances occasioned by Paul's disappointment as it was the logical outcome of changed circumstances. Napoleon's actions in 1799 and 1800, particularly his internal policies, revealed him to Paul as no longer the heir of the Revolution, but the liquidator. Such about-face tactics coincided with the autocratic principles on which the Russian state system was built, and consequently a *rapprochement* took place which opened the way to Russian politics for the pursuance of the unremitting task of opposition to England. The latter country, growingly alarmed at Russia's interference in its European system of balance, began to fear Paul's accelerated naval construction and his expansion in Asia. For during Paul's reign not only did armies participate in the Western European scene and effective fleets threaten in the Baltic and Black seas, but also troops marched in the direction of what Britain considered her "life lines," namely the

Mediterranean, Turkey, and Persia. In 1801 the territory of Georgia submitted formally to Russia and brought her within a short distance of English supply routes. The hazard to England was increased when, incited by France, Paul ordered Cossack regiments to assemble in southwestern Siberia for an invasion of India itself. The importance of the undertaking and the effect it might have had on all future times cannot be minimized—although the preparations were so incomplete and the losses so great, even before the expedition started, that success should scarcely have been expected.

THE MURDER OF PAUL

Before the rupture with England became definite, Paul fell victim to the hatred and fears of a disappointed and enraged—and possibly Anglo-supported—nobility. His political measures (designed to reduce the nobles to their previous status of servants of the state), his lack of tact in personal relations, and his arbitrary decisions had provoked their resolution to do away with him. With the connivance of Paul's oldest son, Alexander, conspirators fortified by alcohol —men whom Paul regarded as his friends and guardians—broke into his bedroom on the night of March 23, 1801, and butchered him in the cruelest manner.

Thus ended an unhappy and in many respects evil, yet important, rule that did not lack in progressive elements. Alexander, avowing his complicity in the deposal plans, denied any foreknowledge of the murder, but failed to prosecute the perpetrators of the act. Some of them mounted to high posts under him, and only after many years was the last one of them dismissed from office.

PROBLEMS

1. Discuss the change in the spirit of the age after the French Revolution.
2. Comment on the chief reforms of Paul I.
3. Describe the international position of Russia as seen by Paul I.

20

RUSSIA AND FRANCE

Significant Dates

Rule of Alexander I 1801–1825
Battle of Austerlitz 1805
Napoleon's Invasion of Russia 1812
Congress of Vienna 1815

ALEXANDER I

The first decade and a half of the nineteenth century is overshadowed by the political events stimulated by Napoleon's activities. Internal planning in Russia had to be subordinated to external needs, and little was accomplished. Alexander (1801–25), whose initiative was needed for domestic adjustments, disappointed the expectations of the progressives. Though trained in liberal ideas by his tutor, the Swiss La Harpe, and though gifted with imagination, personal charm, intellectual curiosity, and perseverance, he was superficial, lazy, unstable, and given to dissimulation. He revoked many of the abortive orders of his father but his insincerity caused the work of reform to be neglected. He surrounded himself with capable men (Speransky, Nesselrode, the Pole Czartoryski, the German vom Stein, the Corsican Pozzo di Borgo, the Greek Capodistrias) but gave little heed to their advice.

FIRST DECADE OF ALEXANDER'S REIGN

The tasks confronting Alexander upon his accession to the throne were twofold: (1) to find a solution for the numerous internal problems, the foremost being those of autocracy in a revolutionary age, of modernization of the economic structure, and of serfdom, and (2) to carry on, in the international arena, the consolidation and exploitation of Catherine's acquisitions, and to make a decision regarding a pro-French or anti-French orientation. Alexander undertook to tackle the internal issues with many plans and little action; in the external questions, he showed much vacillation, which ultimately, however, served him well on the road to further aggrandizement.

Internal Affairs. Dependent as Alexander was on the service and court nobility which had organized the murder of his father, the new emperor deemed it necessary to reinstate the Charter of the Nobility revoked by Paul I. He provided for an expansion of the educational system, but he did little to promote the professional and merchant classes. He likewise contributed little to the improvement of the national economy. As to the peasantry, he confined himself to a few, often ineffectual measures aiming at ameliorating the condition of serfdom, but he did not permit steps to be taken for its abolition. He convened committees to deliberate on administrative improvements, but while approving, like his grandmother, of humanitarian aims in general, he rejected them in practice if they interfered with the existing autocratic organization of the country. For a number of years, he was advised, though without immediate consequence, by one of Russia's most capable and interesting statesmen, Mikhail Speransky.

Speransky. Mikhail Speransky (1771–1839) was the son of a village priest. Educated first at a seminary, then at a university, he subsequently became a professor in St. Petersburg and after a short army career was appointed to the Ministry of the Interior. At the age of twenty-two, he was ennobled and, a few years later, found himself in the special graces of the Tsar. In 1809 he was appointed Secretary of State, but was dismissed in 1812 and exiled because of his arrogance, his pro-French leanings, and the intrigues of jealous courtiers. Only in 1814 was he recalled and, having lost many of his liberal ideas, he then served again under Alexander and later under Nicholas I.

Speransky's Reform Plans. Under the influence of the West, and particularly of French ideas, for which he was bitterly attacked by the famous historian Karamzin and other Slavophils, Speransky worked out projects of fundamental importance for the future development of Russia. He advocated a constitution, which would retain different class rights and, temporarily, serfdom. He proposed a modern administrative system through separation of the judicial from the administrative department, and he planned popular representative bodies in the form of legislatures which were to be elected by nobles and free peasants. Each community, district, and province was to have its own legislature and another was to be established on a national level. In cases of disagreement, each could appeal to the next higher body. At the top of the structure was to be a Council of State working directly under the autocratic ruler, whose voice was final except when infringing upon "fundamental laws." Speransky also drafted municipal reforms and church statutes; and, as governor of Siberia from 1819 to 1821, he worked on the reorganization of Siberia, which was to be divided into two governor-generalships. Under Alexander's successor Nicholas, from 1826 to 1833, Speransky made perhaps his most definite contribution by directing a new and long-overdue compilation and codification of Russian law, embracing principles of private property as well as civil rights.

International Affairs. In foreign affairs, as in internal affairs, Alexander followed the pattern set by his grandmother, Catherine. Power, glory, and expansion were his aims.

ALIGNMENT WITH ENGLAND. Alexander inherited from his father an alliance with France and an expedition against India, but he immediately reversed the course. He called back the troops en route for India, and sought a *rapprochement* with England. The greater Napoleon's ambitions, the more decidedly did Alexander pursue a pro-English policy; and when Napoleon committed the outrage of executing the Duc d'Enghien and had himself crowned emperor, an alliance with Britain was made, which first envisaged only peace and arbitration. But in fact, it soon led to war with France. In 1805, after the Austrians had joined the Allies, an army was dispatched to central Europe, where, under Alexander's command, the famous battle of Austerlitz was fought—against the counsel of General Kutuzov. The complete rout of the Russo-Austrian forces put an end to Alexander's plans. Austria was obliged to sue for peace. Only distance saved Russia.

FRENCH ALLIANCE. The state of war continued, but little action was taken until Napoleon had attacked Prussia and conquered Berlin. Then Russian troops joined with the Prussians and, after two indecisive engagements, were again beaten in the battle of Friedland in 1807. With Napoleon master of the Continent, Alexander, flattered by the victor's magnanimity toward him, concluded peace at Tilsit. Though Russian generals considered such a peace inopportune and unnecessary, Alexander expanded it into an alliance with the erstwhile enemy. He agreed to the restitution of a Poland to be formed of parts which Prussia had secured in the treaties of 1772 to 1795 and of which she was now deprived; and he joined in Napoleon's economic war against England. He closed all ports to British ships and, under the "Continental System," stopped all direct trade with Great Britain.

Disadvantages of French Alliance. For religious reasons, the treaty providing for the resurgence of Catholic Poland caused great discontent in Russia. Politically, it likewise proved disappointing, for Napoleon refused to concede in exchange the annexation of Constantinople, which Russia hoped to acquire in her war then being waged against Turkey. Equally disadvantageous were the economic consequences of the stipulations providing for England's isolation. Trade with Britain in timber, flax, iron, and grain had been a basic factor in the Russian economy, and France was unable to substitute for England. France neither needed the commodities which formed the bulk of Russian exports to England nor could guarantee a vigorous intercourse, for the British fleet dominated the sea lanes. The wealthiest and most influential class in Russia, the gentry, was severely hit; the exchange rate of the ruble sank to less than one half, and the "Continental System" undermined prosperity and respect for law. The English, experienced in piracy and smuggling, profited from the corruption among Russian custom officials and found leakages enough, so that the Franco-Russian alliance was subjected to serious strains.

Decline of French Alliance. A new meeting of Alexander and Napoleon was therefore arranged in 1808 in Erfurt; but Franco-Russian relations, governed by economic needs and political trends and not by dynastic and personal arrangements, were not improved. The French minister, Talleyrand himself, secretly advised the Tsar against concessions and called attention to the deterioration of Napoleon's position in France, to his lack of success in rebellious Spain, and to his renewed incurrence of Catholic resistance which followed his highhanded policies toward the Pope and the papal states. The French emperor thus failed to engage more vigorous Russian support in his persistent struggle with England; likewise, Alexander's aid to his French ally was only very inadequately forthcoming when war was renewed between France and Austria in 1809. Alleging the need of his forces for the continuation of a campaign against Turkey and a war against Sweden, in which he had been engaged since 1808, the Tsar ordered his troops to avoid serious action against Austria.

NAPOLEON'S INVASION OF RUSSIA

Causes.   By 1811 Europe began to speak of an impending war between France and Russia. People became increasingly aware of the incompatibility of French political ambitions with Russia's security, of the fundamentally opposed economic interests of the two countries, and of the utopianism of a Continental rule divided between Napoleon and Alexander. In view of these basic differences, minor factors resulting from the great issues constituted insurmountable obstacles to the maintenance of peace on the Continent. Thus, severe tension was caused by the failure of a plan suggested at Erfurt —according to which the alliance between Russia and France was to be strengthened through a marriage between Napoleon and one of Alexander's sisters. Lack of support against Austria in 1809 and refuge offered to French *émigrés* in Russia added to French misgivings. Increased tariffs impeded French trade in wine and other commodities. Often, new tariffs infringed on Napoleon's "Continental System," which was also circumvented, with Russia's connivance, by American and other neutral ships. Conversely, Alexander was infuriated by Napoleon's annexation of the German principality of Oldenburg (whose hereditary prince was Alexander's brother-in-law), by the re-establishment of Poland, which was contrary to Russian plans, and by French support of Turkey in defending the Straits.

Preparations.   Napoleon carefully evaluated his chances in a war against Russia and judged them favorable. He withdrew troops from Spain and secured contingents for his army from Prussia, Austria,

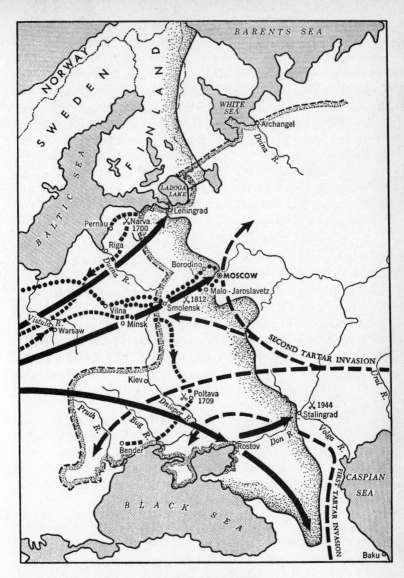

INVASIONS OF RUSSIA

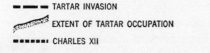

- – – – TARTAR INVASION
- EXTENT OF TARTAR OCCUPATION
- ······ CHARLES XII

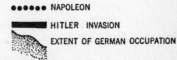

- ●●●●●● NAPOLEON
- HITLER INVASION
- EXTENT OF GERMAN OCCUPATION

and other satellites. Russia answered these preparations by composing her differences with Sweden and Turkey. The Swedish campaign of 1808 and 1809 had led to brilliant results. Russian soldiers had conquered Finland, crossed the frozen Gulf of Bothnia, and invaded Sweden proper, and in the Peace of Frederikshavn (1809) the whole of Finland had been ceded to Russia; now the Swedes—under their new crown prince, Bernadotte—were pledged to the promise of military aid against Napoleon. Likewise, Alexander succeeded in protecting Russia's southern flank; peace with Turkey was concluded at Bucharest (1812), and although Russia failed to gain her main objective, the Straits, she advanced her borders to the Pruth River (Bessarabia) and was confirmed in her protectorate over Turkey's Orthodox subjects.

Attack. With preparations completed on both the French and the Russian sides, war broke out in June, 1812. French armies of 650,000 men, half of them foreigners, crossed the Russian border at various points, the main assault being launched in the center along the Vilna-Smolensk-Moscow line. Bad weather, lack of discipline, desertions, and particularly the early breakdown of the supply system made the assault enormously difficult for the French. Nevertheless, the Russians were forced to retreat. Several generals had recommended retreat from the beginning, anticipating that Russia's wide expanse would lead to Napoleon's destruction; but their counsel went unheeded, and necessity alone accounted for Russian movements. In vain was the supreme command of the army transferred from Alexander himself to the able Barclay de Tolly, a Baltic baron of Scottish descent, and later, for nationalistic reasons, to Kutuzov. The latter endeavored to halt Napoleon's advance; but even the bloody Battle of Borodino failed to stop the French, and in September, 1812, Moscow fell to the enemy.

Moscow. Napoleon had intended to smash Russian resistance through a single mighty stroke but had been denied the opportunity by the Russian retreat. By occupying the heart of the country, he now sought to end the struggle. But again he was disappointed. Russia's scorched-earth policy had greatly weakened his position; and the masses, who might have been won by the promise of emancipation, failed to support him because he hesitated to release the revolutionary forces in Russia for fear of the reaction in Europe. His offers to Alexander for peace negotiations went unanswered.

Instead, the Russians redeployed their armies, and their church called upon all to support the national movement and to show utmost perseverance in the holy war against this pillaging, desecrating enemy.

Retreat.   In the middle of October, Napoleon was forced to withdraw from Moscow. A devastating fire, in part the result of Russian orders but in part the consequence of neglect, had destroyed stores and quarters, rendering it impossible for the French to pass the winter there. To avoid the rigors of the weather and to reach Europe through territory not yet scorched, Napoleon led his loot-laden army —now reduced by battle, disease, and desertion to 100,000 men—in a southerly direction. At Maloyaroslavets he was stopped by Kutuzov and forced onto the old Smolensk road. Overcautiousness cost Kutuzov the opportunity to destroy the enemy. He refrained from attacking in force and instead, marching parallel to Napoleon's army, harassed and whittled away at the half-starved, demoralized, weary French by costly yet successful rear-guard and guerrilla action.

BEREZINA.   After Napoleon had passed Smolensk, where, contrary to plan, he could not spend the winter for lack of supplies, the cold intensified and added to the sufferings of the struggling army. Yet the temperature was not low enough to freeze streams and swamps. Therefore, when the small Berezina River was reached, the progress of Napoleon's army was halted, and two improvised bridges had to be thrown across to allow passage. This moment was seized upon by the Russians, who attacked in force; and the frenzied crossing in icy weather, under enemy fire, over burning and breaking planks, became one of the great military catastrophes of all ages. The ensuing gruesome march from the Berezina to Vilna virtually destroyed the decimated force which thus far had saved itself from disaster. By the end of the year, the last of Russian territory was freed.

Triumph over Napoleon.   Incited by England, Alexander elected to continue the war until the destruction of Napoleon was complete. On December 30, 1812, a convention was concluded at Tauroggen with the Prussian General York, and treaties with Sweden and Austria followed in 1813. Reluctantly the country followed a policy which did not seem dictated by strictly Russian interests. Napoleon was pursued through Germany; the Allies won the decisive Battle of Leipzig; and in 1814 France was invaded. In July, Alexander and the Prussian king made their triumphant entry into Paris, and Napoleon was forced from his throne.

Congress of Vienna. Peace was concluded at Paris and supplemented by the Congress of Vienna. The question whether or not all of Poland should be ceded to Russia, and whether Prussia should be compensated for her share of Poland by parts of Saxony, very nearly led to rupture among the victors; and only the new peril arising with the reappearance of Napoleon saved the wartime alliance. While Prussian and English forces rushed to defeat Napoleon once more (Waterloo, 1815), negotiations came to a successful close. Russia received the disputed territory, and in turn granted a certain amount of autonomy and a constitution to Poland as well as to Finland. A special covenant, the "Holy Alliance," supplemented the political settlement. It was inspired by Alexander himself, who had fallen under the spell of mystical religious groups and "evangelists," such as those represented by Baroness Krüdener. The Holy Alliance stipulated that internal as well as international relations should be based on Christian ethics, and it provided for co-operation in the preservation of peace on the basis of the Viennese arrangements.

Russia thus emerged from the Napoleonic era secure in her realms, greatly enlarged, and with increased international prestige. She had acquired additional Polish territory through the Congress of Vienna; she had gained Finland in the Peace of Frederikshavn, and Bessarabia by the Treaty of Bucharest; and in 1813 she had also succeeded in forcing Persia to cede Baku. In international affairs Russia held a dominant position, and the stipulations of Vienna combined with those of the Holy Alliance seemed to give permanence to this position.

PROBLEMS

1. Discuss the difficulties of Franco-Russian co-operation in Napoleonic times.
2. Discuss Napoleon's failure in Russia.
3. Discuss the territorial aggrandizement of Russia, 1800–25.

21

THE POST-NAPOLEONIC PERIOD

Significant Dates

Period of Congresses	1818–1822
Emancipation of Peasants in Baltic	
Provinces	1816–1819
Beginning of Greek War of Independence . .	1821

FAILURE OF LIBERALISM

The effect of the Napoleonic Wars on Russian internal conditions necessarily differed from that on other European countries. In most of Europe the ideas of liberty released by the French Revolution had spread swiftly, but in Russia the broad masses had remained untouched by the new liberal trend. Its influence was correspondingly small, being limited to the narrow upper layer of society. Unlike governments of other countries, the Russian autocracy refrained from introducing reforms during the war. Increasingly a victim of obscurantism and reactionary mystical and pseudoreligious ideas, Alexander neglected internal improvements; and, his vanity flattered by his international role, he kept his attention focused on external policies. Even after peace was concluded Alexander continued to disappoint the liberals.

Polish and Finnish Constitutions. In newly acquired Poland, Alexander granted a constitution. It was more liberal than that imposed on France; but it was of a definitely aristocratic character because a middle class was wanting and the peasants were neither freed nor represented. Alexander himself became king and his brother Constantine was made commander of the army; to the disappointment of all, not even the governorship was placed in the hands of a Pole. The constitution itself was repeatedly violated in budget and other matters, and the diet was not regularly convened as stipulated. Thus, Alexander's liberalism was limited abroad as well as at home. Only conquered Finland was allowed a constitution which guaranteed a measure of self-administration.

Arakcheyev and Reaction.   In Russia, the Tsar left most of the work to "ministers" whom he had created after foreign models. With the "favorite" and virtual "vice emperor" Speransky in disgrace or assigned to lesser tasks, the general Arakcheyev came to dominate affairs. He was an honest but brutal and subservient man who lacked Speransky's vision and ability; and reaction triumphed, as it did everywhere in Europe. The police gained undue power, and strict censorship was introduced again to prevent the spreading of progressive ideas. Mysticism and religious bigotry prevailed, while liberal ideas were confined to secret societies (Freemasons, Northern Order, Sons of the Fatherland). Universities, whose number had increased, were put under strict supervision. Because of dogmatic considerations, the teaching of natural sciences was limited, and theological studies were made compulsory. To prevent popularization of "atheistic, enlightened" science, many lectures were given in non-Russian languages, and half of the professors were foreigners. Primary and particularly secondary schools fared better; although few new ones were founded, their quality was improved.

Military Colonies.   A notable innovation of the period was the "military colonies," which Alexander created in the special interest of his beloved army and which Arakcheyev, noted also for his improvements in the artillery, was charged to organize. Certain territories were set aside for military administration. In these special areas everyone was brought automatically into the armed forces, whereas the rest of the country was exempt from compulsory service. Every peasant in the military colonies was a soldier, free from taxation, looked after for life, but also subject for life to military rule. He was always in uniform; every step was supervised; his private life, including his marriage, was regulated; and his children were brought up as soldiers. At the time of Alexander's death one million men and women lived in such military colonies. By combining military service with agriculture and by freeing most of the rest of the country from the financial and personal burden, Alexander had envisaged both a financial gain for the state and economic as well as humanitarian advantages for the soldiers; but the idea as carried out proved unworkable. Soon the colonies, even those with trustworthy officers and good order, resembled prison camps; and desperate revolts, brutally suppressed, only served to aggravate conditions.

ECONOMIC CONDITIONS

Reconstruction. Economic conditions in the post-Napoleonic period were naturally poor. The public debt was staggering and continued to mount. Reconstruction, however, proceeded at a quicker pace than had been expected—even in the face of prevailing corruption. Production of cotton, flax, grain, coal, oil, and copper was raised; closer economic ties were secured with China and central Asia; expeditions were sent out to explore Russian America and other regions; and the resources of European Russia and the newly acquired territories were developed. Exports in 1814 amounted to forty-five million silver rubles (as against imports valued at about twenty-eight), and they rose steadily. However, because of undervaluation of the products of Russian soil and Russian labor, the trade balance still worked to the disadvantage of the national economy, and the government itself was close to bankruptcy.

Industries. As in other countries, factories increased speedily in size and number. Many landowners, under pressure of the government, established mills—even though the venture did not always turn out successfully. Steam power came into use in larger plants and enabled them to compete successfully with home industries. Lower cotton prices led to the establishment of scores of textile mills. This general trend was furthered by government measures; the ban on free-market selling was partly revoked, the currency was stabilized, more appropriate credit institutions were founded, and tariffs were introduced to protect infant industries. Although the system of *vochinal* workers (who were heritable property and subject to the jurisdiction of the owner) and of possessional serfs (who were granted and ascribed to industries from agricultural districts) was preserved, a change came also in labor conditions. Factory owners benefited from whatever number of serfs were set free and, instead of employing unsatisfactory forced help for which they had social responsibilities, they could draw upon an increasing reservoir of a freely shifting industrial proletariat.

Agriculture. The advance of industries, a result of economic pressure and world-wide trends and not of conscientious planning, was bought at the expense of agriculture. Little attention was given to the improvement of agricultural techniques, and production in relation to work invested remained low. As agricultural prices steadily declined, the landowners were unable to free themselves of the debts which not only the state but also they personally had incurred during the wars. The peasants, the main producers of Russia's wealth, suffered correspondingly, for the burdens were shifted to them. Again, many uprisings occurred.

Serfdom. Noticeable progress was traceable in only two areas: the discontinuation of the practice of "giving away" additional peasants into serfdom, and the emancipation of serfs in the Baltic provinces. There, in Estonia, Latvia, and Courland, the German barons anticipated future needs and unanimously freed their peasants from personal servitude (1816–19), though without allocation of land. It was an important and progressive measure, although unsatisfactory to the extent that no secure foundation was laid for the life of the peasant under the new conditions and to the extent that part of the freed serfs came to fill the ranks of an uprooted proletariat. In the rest of Russia, although the wars were over, emancipation was postponed as before. Only some 40,000 were voluntarily freed by progressive landowners during Alexander's reign, and many of them benefited but little, for they, too, slid into economic bondage created by the factory system.

DEATH OF ALEXANDER I

In 1825, when none of the high hopes which the world had placed in the genius and liberalism of Alexander I were as yet fulfilled, the Tsar died suddenly on a trip to the south. Few witnesses were present, and rumors spread that the death had been staged and that in reality, Alexander had retired to a monastery in Siberia to atone for the murder of his father and other unchristian deeds. The legend has never been conclusively disproved; but to the world, in any case, Alexander was dead.

Alexander's Legacy. In the course of the one hundred years from the death of Peter I to the death of Alexander, a peculiarly contradictory situation had developed in Russia. Peter's Westernization had aimed at the modernization of the country, at the building of her national strength, and at catching up with the Western powers. During those hundred years, Russia had acquired vast Western territories, her armies had marched across Europe to Paris, and she had gained a leading role in forming European policies. Western books, arts, sciences, and education had been introduced into the country, and many Russians visited European lands. Yet because of national pride and lack of flexibility, the distance between Russia and the West had in many ways increased. Compared to the West, her governmental system was backward, her social and educational organization retained its feudal characteristics; serfdom and illiteracy of the masses persisted, and her economic institutions lacked an enterprising middle class. Middle nineteenth-century Russia has been called "a colossus on feet of clay." Her productive forces remained underdeveloped, and the rift between the ruling groups and the progressive elements of society had widened. The governing forces bent on maintaining existing ways faced equally determined rebellious forces. An intelligentsia drawing strength from those circles which did not belong to any of the established ranks (*raznochintsi*) sought a completely new order and was ready for any sacrifice. Out of this conflict came a period immensely rich in inspiring ideas and personalities, in literary works and music, and also rife with political ferment which was to shake the foundations of Western civilization.

PROBLEMS

1. Discuss the scope and significance of Speransky's reform plans.
2. Discuss the extent of the liberalism put into practice by Alexander I.
3. Discuss the economic conditions in Russia after the Napoleonic Wars.

22

ERA OF SUSPENSE

Significant Dates

Reign of Nicholas I	1825–1855
Dekabrist Rising	1825
Russo-Turkish War	1828–1829
Crimean War	1854–1856

Alexander I has received considerable attention from historians. The promise of the young Tsar and the failure of the man, his curiously dual nature, and the fortuitous fact that he lived in an era of decision account for this preoccupation with him. But his lifework was indifferent, and his death more important than his life. To be sure, the death in itself made no incision, but it was taken as the signal for a revolution which—although of small scale, and unsuccessful at that—gained great significance in Russian history.

THE DEKABRIST RISING

Alexander's Succession. Alexander had no children, and the throne should have fallen to his eldest brother, Constantine. But because of private affairs and his dislike for reigning, Constantine had waived succession rights; yet, neither the next presumptive heir, Constantine's younger brother Nicholas, nor the government and people were properly informed. When news of Alexander's sudden death reached St. Petersburg, Nicholas therefore took an oath recognizing Constantine as Tsar, while Constantine, residing in Warsaw, did likewise in favor of Nicholas.

The Revolutionaries. The uncertainty which resulted from the confusion and, owing to distance, from the delay in proclaiming a new Tsar was seized upon by a group of revolutionaries, whose hopes for the redress of existing wrongs had been deceived by Alexander. Many of them were members of romantic secret societies which, as in other parts of Europe, were formed by students, professors, poets, idealistic officers, and members of the nobility inspired by a sense of their responsibilities toward the people. They were embittered by persistent corruption, faulty jurisdiction, police tyranny, censorship, degradation of human beings through serfdom and corporal punishment, and suppression of free thought in universities. They resented the fact that neither the new spirit which had swept Europe nor the devotion shown by all the Russian people in the defense of their country had helped to improve the lot of the common man. Using the American constitution, the French constitution of 1791, and the Spanish constitution of 1812 as their models, they accordingly worked out plans for radical changes. Abolition of monarchy and of military dictatorship, emancipation of serfs, communal possession of land, and reduction of the clergy were among the aims advocated by them. Some proposed abolition of a standing army, free access for all citizens to any trade or profession, and autonomy for subjugated nations within their ethnic borders. Others, on the contrary, demanded of these nations the sacrifice of their "national rights to political utility"; in this sense, they advocated the resettlement of Jews, who formed a state within the state, in Palestine, and they envisaged a class struggle which was to lead to state socialism and to the Russification of the empire.

The Dekabrist Revolt. Two groups were outstanding among the revolutionaries, the "Northern Society" and the "Southern Society," which counted among their leading members the guard officers Pestel and Bestuzhev-Ryumin and the poet Ryleyev. Believing the confusion after Alexander's death opportune for pressing their aims, these men, although unprepared, started a revolution in December, 1825 (Decembrist or—in Russian—Dekabrist rising). Just when accord between Alexander's two brothers was reached and Nicholas was proclaimed rightful Tsar and autocrat, they incited the soldiers of some imperial guards to keep their sworn allegiance to Constantine (an object hardly worthy of the devotion of a revolutionary) and to demand a constitution. The rising was essentially confined to St. Petersburg and two places in the south; it was vigorously suppressed, and five hundred soldiers paid the extreme penalty for their undertaking. Outrages were committed by the Tsar's troops, and finally many of the revolutionary leaders were caught. Five Dekabrists, including Pestel, Ryleyev, and Bestuzhev-Ryumin, were hanged, and thirty-one others imprisoned or exiled for life; and the revolutionaries, deprived of their leaders, were for many years unable to recover.

STRUGGLE AGAINST REVOLUTION

Autocracy. Nicholas I (1825–55) took the Dekabrist rising as a warning. As a dutiful guardian of Russian tradition he held down any liberal trend with an iron hand, and "Autocracy, Orthodoxy, and Nationalism" became the watchwords of his reign. During the thirty years of his rule none of the great problems facing the country were solved. Notwithstanding humanitarian principles typical of nineteenth-century liberalism, emancipation was again postponed. The government confined itself to convening new commissions which, after prolonged sessions during the years 1826 to 1830, 1835, 1839 to 1842, and 1844, recommended only minor changes in the existing status. Not even voluntary emancipation and the granting of small acreage to the liberated serfs was permitted the landowner, although in view of a rapidly increasing population and oversupply of laborers serfdom came to mean a grave economic burden for him. Only in cases of mutual consent by owner and serf was complete liberation allowed, provided the peasant, though freed, continued to render some state service. A special law stipulated that whole villages (but no individual peasant) might gain the right to purchase their freedom in cases where, as often happened, the landowner's estate was sold at auction.

A few additional steps were undertaken to lighten the burdens of the peasants: Their transfer to mines was forbidden; their being rented out to owners of land or factories who had no right to hold serfs of their own was stopped; and provisions were made for the care of the needy. In outlying parts of the empire, the serfs benefited by so-called Inventory Regulations, which served as a census and stipulated the amount of land and dues for each peasant.

Economy. The delay in settling the problem of emancipation reacted adversely not only on the development of agriculture, but likewise on the growth of industries, on financial policies, and on the whole Russian social structure. Essential economic improvements were retarded; yet Nicholas' capable finance minister, Kankrin, through strict economy succeeded in re-establishing Russian credit. Devalued paper money issued during the emergency was withdrawn. Some scientific improvements were introduced for agriculture, building activities were sponsored, and, through protective tariffs, industrial output was stimulated. A technological and a mining institute were founded, and monopolies were subjected to revision. Textile home industries were aided through equipment with better types of spindles and looms; and mills, particularly in the Polish parts, gained international markets.

Political Unrest. Maintenance of the existing class structure and privileges, prevalence of a powerful bureaucracy dependent upon the autocrat, and involuntary servitude combined with the socioeconomic changes which came in the wake of beginning industrialization led (in Russia, more than elsewhere) to serious difficulties. Revolts in agricultural districts occurred in alarming numbers; painstaking historians have counted as many as five hundred and fifty-six during Nicholas' reign of thirty years. Likewise, labor troubles, typical for industrialized countries, began to appear. The military colonies were reluctantly continued by Nicholas and contributed their share to the spirit of rebellion. To deal with prevailing unrest, a new department was added to the imperial chancellery; this was the famed "Third Section," which assumed police functions and soon became a byword for autocratic oppression. Through it, revolutionary movements were brutally crushed, religious sectarians were persecuted anew, censorship of books was enforced, liberal newspapers were suppressed, and universities were strictly supervised. The educational system was geared to making "good subjects" of the young; vocational training, useful for the state, was emphasized, and culture in its broader aspects was neglected.

1848. When the Revolution of 1848 broke out in Paris and swept over most of Europe, Nicholas sent troops to quell the movement in Hungary before it could reach the Russian border, and at home all possible precautions were taken. The number of students in any university was limited to three hundred, and liberal groups were checked by police spies; the Petrashevtsy circle, a radical group to which members of the highest nobility belonged, was broken up and twenty-one of their number exiled to Siberia, the novelist Dostoyevsky among them. Through these measures Nicholas himself believed he was serving the true interests of the country, the care of whose spiritual and material well-being he considered his God-ordained duty.

PROBLEMS

1. State the social theories behind the Dekabrist rising.
2. Discuss the policy of "Autocracy, Orthodoxy, and Nationalism."

23

SLAVOPHILS AND WESTERNIZERS

Significant Dates

Karamzin, *The Old and the New Russia* . . . 1811
Literary Criticisms by Belinsky 1840–1848
Herzen, *The Bell* 1857–1867
Bakunin, *God and the State* (posthumous) . . 1882

The progress of Russia's political and social conditions did not take place without sober questioning from the more thoughtful people in the country, who strove to sound the spiritual basis, the existing status, and the future direction of Russia's destiny. Two schools of thought, particularly, took part in the investigation: the Slavophils and the Westernizers. Both were separated by an unbridgeable gulf from the uninterested and inarticulate masses of the Russian people.

PHILOSOPHIES OF SLAVOPHILS AND WESTERNIZERS

Ideology. The two groups, as the names indicate, were opposed to each other because the one looked toward the "Slavic soul" for the salvation of Russia, the other toward Western methods. Despite such divergent attitudes the two groups had much in common. Adherents of one not infrequently changed over to the other or shared its views, and many held an intermediary position.

GROUNDS IN COMMON. What connected the Slavophil and the Westernizer was their mutual dependence upon Europe's great philosophers. Hume, Voltaire, Saint-Simon, and Proudhon exercised wide influence, and the great German philosophers gave direction to their thoughts. The writings of Kant, Goethe, and Schiller and particularly those of Schelling, Hegel, Feuerbach, Stirner, and later Karl Marx were scrupulously examined; and the demands of the Russian political schools were formulated either in conformity with the views of these men or in opposition to them.

Westernizers and Slavophils had in common also a love of Russia, around which all their work and efforts centered. Both feared the incompetence of the existing Russian government. Westernizers and Slavophils alike idealized the Russian peasant and defended the mir or village community—a peculiarly Russian institution in which all saw the sound foundation of the past and the basis for a desirable new Russian society. Both opposed a bourgeois society as it existed in Western countries—with "two classes, exploiters and exploited." Both hoped for a better balance between industry and agriculture, brought forth by Russian civilization. The work of both schools promoted new thoughts, led to a re-evaluation of the past, and resulted in valuable new historical and legal studies.

DIFFERENCES. They differed fundamentally, however, in their political aims. The Slavophils originally considered themselves non-political, and many became conservatives later in life. The Westernizers were avowedly radical, some of them believing in the necessity of a class struggle, others envisaging progress within the capitalistic system. Influenced by the Christian romanticism of Chateaubriand, the Slavophils worked for a spiritual reform within the Russian people. The Westernizers, on the other hand, regarded the state not as a moral but as a purely political institution properly functioning for the welfare of the individual. The Slavophils believed in Orthodoxy; religion was part of the very basis of their views and Orthodoxy expressed for them divine will and eternal truth. The Westernizers were often atheists; at least they saw no place in their system for a state religion. They believed in the rights of the individual, whereas the Slavophils opposed individualism because, in their view, it led from freedom of thought to license.

The evaluation of Peter the Great's achievements further separated the two groups. The Slavophils extolled the advantages of Russian ways before the reign of Peter. They thought that Peter's reforms had interrupted a healthy and natural development and that his work constituted a "negation of a sacred mission." They felt that it had created a barrier between classes by separating the educated from the folk. Conversely, Peter's work was held in high regard by the Westernizers, who saw Russia as but a part of Europe.

AIMS.   If the Slavophils considered the West with its industrial development, bureaucracy, and urbanization to be bad and poisonous, the Westernizers exaggerated and idealized the virtues of the West. As the Slavophils pointed out, they overlooked a lack of spiritual depth. This lack was felt particularly in the Western system of law, which the Slavophils regarded as the "law of the conqueror," with many formalities not understandable to the weak and simple, but made to benefit the strong and rich, whereas to them the Russian laws sprang deep from the roots of a "pacific people." The West, the Slavophils asserted, fostered ambition and looked for outward comfort and shallow luxury, whereas typical Russian traits were simplicity, humility, and patience—leading, they held, to true contentment.

Attitude of the Government.   The Russian government looked with equal disfavor on both philosophies, and representatives of both suffered censorship and exile. The revolutionary tendencies of the Westernizers were naturally condemned, but the ideas of the Slavophils likewise were found objectionable. It was feared that the latter would interfere with the Russification policies in the non-Orthodox parts of the empire and lead to a breakup of the national entity.

LEADING THINKERS

The representatives of both groups were numerous. Many of them were writers or at least belonged to literary circles, and some of the great Russian authors of the age, devoted as they were to social as well as literary objectives—Pushkin, Gogol, Goncharov, and later Dostoyevsky—exercised a powerful influence among them.

Slavophils.   The Slavophils represented no homogeneous group; in time, they revealed consistent changes in their philosophy, their ideals, and in the character of their aims.

NICHOLAS KARAMZIN (1765–1826) is often regarded as a precursor of the Slavophils. He believed in autocracy, which he considered characteristic of and necessary for Russia. He opposed any constitutional system as developed by Western countries, and advocated the division of Russia into fifty provinces each of which was to be ruled over by a paternalistic, benevolent governor responsible to the autocrat and directed by his Christian conscience.

IVAN KIREVSKY (1806–56) was the first acknowledged leader of the Slavophils. After studying the Greek church fathers, he arrived at the conviction that Christianity was deeper, purer, and more closely interwoven with Russian life than with that of other countries, where it had taken on a subjectivist-rationalist character. He hoped that through the Orthodox faith Russia would gain inspiration. He explained the growth of the Russian character on the basis of the historical evolution of the nation, which should not be interrupted by the influx of non-Russian ways. In the same spirit, he extolled communal ownership as exemplified by the mir. Although he acknowledged the potentialities of the United States (which, however, he considered handicapped by the one-sidedness of its English heritage), he believed that Russia would fall heir to the greatness of Italy, Germany, and France.

ALEXIS KHOMIAKOV (1804–60) extended the conclusions of other Slavophils to all Slavic people of Orthodox faith. He insisted that all Slavs were more or less similar in character, and that unlike the heritage of the conquest-minded Romans and Germans, theirs was a peaceable one. But his generalizations, unsupported by historical evidence, failed to convince the serious student.

KONSTANTIN AKSAKOV (1817–60) followed Kirevsky and Khomiakov in their explanations of Russian ways and in attesting to their peaceful character, for which he gave as example the deliberative assemblies of the past—the vieche. He affirmed that common consent, not majority rule, represented the true will of a people and that it alone could establish acceptable law. For him European ways led to the destruction of liberty; for liberty "could never survive in countries where governments and peoples were separated by divergent interests." The formation of a Russian state along European lines seemed to him destructive and practically impossible.

IVAN AKSAKOV (1823–86) survived most of the other prominent Slavophils and demonstrated by his example the dead end to which their philosophy led. Convinced, as were the others, of the decadence of the West, he personified the transition from a philosophical and religious system, founded in the soul of the people, to a practical political nationalism (Pan-Slavism) and, ultimately, to reaction.

Westernizers. The Westernizers likewise underwent a change, beginning like the Slavophils in the field of philosophy but ending with socialism and anarchism when attempting the practical application of their theories.

P. CHAADAYEV (1794–1856) may be considered as their precursor. His *Philosophical Letters,* published in 1836, exposed the cultural "isolation" of Russia, doubted the greatness of her past, and denounced Orthodoxy, which—unlike the Catholic church in Europe—had failed to provide a sound spiritual basis for the Russian mind. He extolled the achievements of Europe, its rational and logical mind, its creation of a progressive spirit, its scientific bent, and its leadership on the path to freedom.

VISSARION BELINSKY (1811–48) is considered the dominant figure among the Westernizers. He devoted his work to literary activities and, in censor-stricken Russia, literary criticism offered him the best field for the promulgation of his political ideas. He joined the Slavophils in their contention that society had precedence over the individual, but he maintained that society had to reserve room for the expression of individual activities and rights. He vigorously denied to Orthodoxy the place in Russian life assigned it by the Slavophils, believing that reason was the tool of civilization and of true justice. Knowledge, not autocracy or theocracy, he considered the main cultural power. Belinsky's chief importance lay in the influence which, after his premature death from consumption, he exercised upon the younger generation, for which he opened the road to socialism.

ALEXANDER HERZEN (1812–70), the son of a Russian nobleman and a German woman, continued and perfected Belinsky's work, though not always agreeing with him. Under the influence of the writings of Voltaire, Schiller, Saint-Simon, Proudhon, and especially Hegel and Feuerbach, he became a protagonist first for liberal and later for socialist ideas. In 1847 he left Russia, never to return. His chief influence was exercised through a paper, *The Bell* (*Kolokol*), which he published in London from 1857 to 1867 and which, though forbidden, was widely read in Russia—even by the Tsar.

Herzen believed in a combination of the aims of the French Revolution and the concepts of German idealistic philosophy. He hoped for a new law, replacing the old Roman law, which was to lead to materialistic socialism and atheism. Inasmuch as he despised a bourgeois republic as thoroughly as a monarchy, he was looking for a true folk state with the hope that in evolving it Russia would be able to skip altogether the stage of the bourgeois state. Yet, he was ready to allow for the lethargy of the people and their persistence in old ways until the practices of his new state could gradually replace them. From his exile he fought first of all for emancipation of the serfs, greeting with joy the steps taken toward such reform. After seeing emancipation come true in 1861, he increased his demands, asking for constitutional rights, common ownership of land, and self-government of the people.

MIKHAIL BAKUNIN (1814–76) went far beyond the aims of other Westernizers. Described as a "product and victim of Russian conditions under Nicholas I," he fought valiantly throughout his life in his struggle against all existing order. He was one of the great agitators of all times, a man who by extraordinary and persistent deeds tried to bring about his utopian form of society.

Born of a wealthy, cultured family, he studied in Berlin and Paris and in 1848 took an active part in the revolution in France. He never relented in his fight against organized authority. From Paris he rushed to Prague, then to Dresden, to participate in revolutions there. Twice imprisoned, twice sentenced to death and reprieved, he was finally extradited to Russia. There he spent the years 1851–54 in prison, and afterwards was exiled to Siberia, from which he subsequently escaped. He participated in the Polish uprisings in 1863, worked with the revolutionaries of Italy until 1868, and became leader of the revolution in Lyons in 1871. Denounced by Karl Marx, he was excluded from the International Workingmen's Association; in 1874 he once more participated in uprisings (at Bologna); and finally he died in Switzerland.

Ardent for action and a "dedicated" man, he denounced all compromise including that of democracy. He advocated anarchism, promulgating a "Catechism of Anarchism" which rejected all the moral concepts of his time and which demanded unrelenting, self-sacrificing struggle for the overthrow of state and church. Destruction came first with him; the new world, he thought, had to be created from the start. Freedom was his religion. Although believing in immortality, he did not believe in God. According to him, a world without God and without law could alone be free. He recognized no moral responsibility of the individual, as long as no one could escape the political and economic inequality of society as it was. This society he wanted first replaced by voluntary contracts in the sense of Proudhon. Unlike Karl Marx, who relied on the city proletariat, he believed that Russia with its millions of suffering peasants could lead the way to such a new world.

Proponents of Other Systems. Bakunin and Ivan Aksakov represent the ultimate products of Westernism and Slavophilism, both going far beyond the original principles of either school. Between them, there were many men of lesser influence, representing all shades of opinion from the theocratic and apocalyptic dreams of a Vladimir Soloviëv, from Juri Samarin's and Pisarev's and Chernyshevsky's idealistic and revolutionary systems, to the practical political programs of the materialists. They all prepared the country for a reshaping of its entire structure.

PROPAGATION OF SLAVOPHIL AND WESTERN IDEAS

Most of the Slavophils and Westernizers belonged to a small group of intellectuals, spoke only to this small group, and were known only to it. Nevertheless, their influence was enormous, for their ideas were carried into the universities and from there spread among the teachers of future generations. Professors like Granovsky and Shefirev in Moscow—representing opposing sides—contributed to the promulgation of their views. These found acceptance readily in the Russian mind because, in an age of increasing nationalism, they expressed, along with religious thought, ideas concerning the nature and future of the Russian nation. Many intellectuals came to be persuaded that such extravagant notions were not held; it was believed that Russia was "different." The most influential book insisting on the uniqueness and special individuality of Russia was Danilevsky's *Russia and Europe*. It was in the climate of opinion which engendered such views, works, and attitudes that the great reforms of Russian society were undertaken.

PROBLEMS

1. Discuss the trend of political ideas in Russia in the middle of the nineteenth century.
2. Discuss the philosophical background of the Russian thinkers.
3. Trace the transition from thought to action in the second half of the nineteenth century.

24

EMANCIPATION

Significant Dates

Reign of Alexander II 1855–1881
End of Crimean War 1856
Emancipation Proclamation 1861

ACCESSION OF ALEXANDER II

The first of the great reforms was the liberation of the serfs. The need for it had long been recognized, but emancipation was delayed not so much because of opposition to the measure itself as because of the uncertainty and fears of its implications. With tens of millions of people involved, no one doubted that emancipation would necessitate a series of additional changes, and that these were bound to interfere with the maxim of "Autocracy, Orthodoxy, and Nationalism" which Nicholas had considered the basis of the Russian state. Yet, even he realized the inefficiency of the existing system when he saw his country defeated in the Crimean War by the far inferior forces of Western nations, and shortly before his death in 1855 he advocated emancipation. His son and successor, Alexander II (1855–81), elected to support the emancipation movement. Whether he was personally moved by the liberal spirit of the age or whether he was merely convinced that revolution would break out unless the government remedied the evils "from above," he carried out the abolition of serfdom. Probably he saw in this step also a way for preserving the autocratic structure of the government. It has even been argued that emancipation was meant to serve as a new way, adapted to modern times, of exploiting the labor of the masses.

ACT OF EMANCIPATION

Despite social and political reaction under Nicholas I, the Russian peasants had also moved in the course of his reign in the direction of greater freedom and emancipation. Through the progressing conversion of part or all of their barchina into obrok services, many of them had steadily gained independence. Laws had been passed which allowed them legally to buy land. They no longer delivered most of their crops to the landlords but produced largely for a market where they could sell freely. In some regions, they found new sources of income through the raising of lucrative crops, such as sugar beets. Those who were state peasants were given a certain amount· of freedom of movement; those who were· called into military service found their term of service reduced from twenty-five years to fifteen years. Moreover, the government had established model farms and had set up agricultural training schools, which were intended to raise the initiative and productivity of the peasants. The act of emancipation constituted a logical sequence to such evolution.

Preparations. The practical solution began with the working out of certain principles and the adoption of a procedure. Abolition of serfdom was decided upon in principle, and it was further decided that personal liberty alone would not do; the peasants were to receive land as well as freedom. Likewise it was established that such land was not to be secured by confiscation, but that the landowners were to receive due compensation. The procedure was to be systematic, beginning with the gathering of all available material and the sifting and discussion of it, and ending with a finished and effective emancipation plan to be submitted to the Tsar. The cooperation of all was solicited: of the idealists who, whether as members of the intelligentsia or of the imperial household itself, advocated it for humane reasons; of the economists, who in view of population pressure and increasing scarcity of cultivable land feared the collapse of the financial structure of the empire; of the state functionaries, who found themselves unable to erect a stable, modern government upon the archaic institution of serfdom; and, most of all, of the landowners themselves.

Economic Problems of Emancipation. When work began, the problems appeared to be overwhelming. There were regions with a surplus of workers and others with too few; there were districts with rich "black" soil and others of very limited fertility; there were serfs paying obrok and earning part of their living through industrial activities and those altogether engaged in agriculture under the barchina system; there were household serfs and artisans and factory help completely separated from the soil. No uniform solution was possible; on the contrary, circumstances demanded a separate system of emancipation for each group and region. The size of future land allotments for freed peasants and the compensation to owners had to be worked out according to local conditions. The decision had to be made whether to include in the compensation a sum for the loss suffered by the owner upon being deprived of the labor of his former serf. If he was to be compensated for both land and labor, who was to pay—the state, its treasury sorely depleted after a lost war, or the peasant, who possessed nothing and could only rely on future earnings from the land to be apportioned to him? If the latter plan were accepted—and under the circumstances it appeared the only feasible one—provisions had to be made to guarantee his payments, necessarily spread over many years, by retaining some sort of control over him.

Social Problems of Emancipation. Similar unfathomable problems were raised by the social aspects of emancipation. What would be its reaction on the peasant and his productivity, which formed the backbone of the state economy? How would the shattered finances be affected? What would be the effect on the liberal bourgeoisie and on the industrialists? Certainly, the danger of revolutionary outbreaks could not be discounted if the peasants were led to expect too much; and the peasants could be prevented from too great expectations only by public instead of secret sessions of the committees charged with emancipation legislation—and this in itself constituted a danger. Furthermore, the possible effect of any measure upon the landowning nobility had to be considered, since it was this class whose services had chiefly sustained autocracy.

Method of Emancipation. In the face of these thorny problems, the task was resolutely undertaken in 1857 and was successfully carried through owing to the devoted work of the high functionaries. Committees of landowners were formed, and plans from their midst as well as from outside sources poured in. But the peasants themselves were allowed no place in the organs of the state charged with the work of emancipation. In February, 1859, an "Editing Commission" was established to sift the various programs. Under the broad-minded chairmanship of Count Rostovtsev, and later of dutiful Count Panin, and with the help of progressive statesmen such as Minister of the Interior Lanskoy and Under-Secretary N. A. Milyutin, the work was taken up by three subcommittees in its judicial, administrative, and economic aspects. It was agreed to free the serf, to grant him a land allotment, and to fix a transitory period during which he was to pay for the acquired land while still obligated to perform some of his former duties. The state was to guarantee or advance the payments to the landowner, while the peasants were to continue through the mir to repay the government for all sums advanced to him. For the fulfillment of the obligations of each peasant, the mir remained collectively responsible. Attempts by reactionary landowners to sidetrack the decisions by giving the peasants only temporary use of the land were thwarted; and heated discussions over the amount of compensation, the size of the allotments, and the judicial status of the freed peasant were brought to final conclusions. After a protracted session of more than a year and a half, the findings were submitted to a "Main Commission," which accepted the proposals of the Editing Commission with one special amendment. With joint consent of both landowner and serf, the allotment could be reduced to one quarter of the legal size, and in that case the peasant was exempted from each and every redemption payment and service. Many were to avail themselves of the opportunity and to accept a small but outright gift of land in preference to a larger piece burdened with dues.

Emancipation Proclamation. On February 19, 1861, the solemn emancipation manifesto was signed. Twenty-two and a half million peasants were thereby freed. This tremendous work, which anticipated by four years the Thirteenth Amendment abolishing slavery in the United States and which was carried out on an infinitely larger scale, was achieved without civil war and without devastation and armed coercion; and yet it provided not only for freedom but also for the economic future of the freed. In 1863 an act was promulgated which freed also the state and court peasants; and the provisions for them were still more liberal than those for the landowners' serfs.

AFTERMATH OF EMANCIPATION

Status of Freed Peasants. Enthusiasm in Russia as in all of Europe was enormous, though it was soon dimmed by a realization of the burdens still resting upon the peasants. Although an end had been made to the jurisdiction and arbitrariness of squires, full citizenship was not granted, and the peasantry was to form but a "tributary order." For a transition period of nearly fifty years, the peasant was still tied to his mir, which distributed the allotments, regulated the dues of each, and was obliged to assume joint tax responsibility for all members. Private land property was not recognized for the individual peasant, but the allocations in each village were held in common property by the mir. Unless sufficient guarantees were given to meet future obligations, no one could move from his village without relinquishing his title to a share of the common land. The burden of taxes—now payable in money or in work to the state instead of the squire—was heavy because the value of the peasants' new land was assessed very high and taxes included compensation for both land and lost bondage rights. The burden was distributed according to the number of "souls" or male workers and the amount of livestock of each peasant. The land allotments were often not sufficient, considering existing cultivation methods; from one quarter to one half of all former serfs had to lease additional land in order to make a living, and often had to lease it at extravagant rates. Misery was greatest in the fertile but densely populated blacksoil areas. Laziness and drunkenness, compatible with the status of serfdom, were not miraculously abolished nor was a feeling of responsibility or a desire for initiative engendered.

Effect on Peasants. The peasants were bitterly disappointed. Since they had not followed the proceedings, despite all publicity, the mistaken feeling grew among them that they were being deceived by greedy landowners and that the true intentions of the government were being thwarted. They resented not receiving all the land formerly tilled by them, they objected to the burdens, and they felt encumbered by a mir which was often under the undue influence of a village priest or a rich peasant (kulak).

Effect on Landowners. The landowners were not less dissatisfied. Their political and economic power and influence were greatly reduced. Only the more progressive among them succeeded in adjusting themselves to the new conditions by reasonable arrangements with their former serfs. The majority found great difficulties and lived by selling, instead of cultivating, their estates. By 1905, out of the land left to them after the emancipation in 1861, approximately one half had passed into the possession of peasants. The redemption payments from the state had been insufficient to provide the former owners with a new start, for a large part was simply used by the government to cancel existing debts and the remaining payments were made in bonds which shortly became salable only at a loss. Industries monopolized much needed help, particularly in sparsely populated northern districts, and fields remained uncultivated. In time, few among them were able to retain their princely estates and palatial homes in the capital, and quite a few even had to sell their manors and elegant houses in the provincial towns. The majority lost most of their wealth and standing, and differences within the ranks of the landowning nobility, grave as they had always been, were accentuated.

Peace Mediators. To deal with existing unrest and to quell riots, the government appointed peace mediators. Though many of them were corrupt or inefficient, their task as a whole was well performed. Many difficulties were eliminated; time helped to settle remaining problems; and despite shortcomings and dissatisfaction, the gigantic work of emancipation was carried out with an astonishing measure of quiet and success.

PROBLEMS

1. Discuss the problems of emancipation.
2. Discuss the effects of emancipation.
3. Compare the social conditions of the peasants before and after emancipation.

25

ERA OF REFORM

Significant Dates

SIGNIFICANCE OF EMANCIPATION

Emancipation introduced a new stage in Russian history—the short transition period of the "Liberal Age," which saw bureaucracy triumphant over the country as well as over the autocrat himself. The long era from Ivan the Terrible to Nicholas I, in which the service-nobility and its ideology had dominated Russian development, had come to an end with the Crimean War. The new period was more in line with the spirit of Europe than any other in modern Russian history, and it was marked by a series of progressive steps, of which emancipation was but the first.

REFORM LEGISLATION

Financial Reform. In 1862 legislation embodying some of the proposals of Speransky was set in motion to co-ordinate the financial structure of the empire with the needs of a new era. A ministry of finance and a state bank were created; and a regular budget was introduced, to be supervised by the finance minister. Tax collection was removed from the hands of private financiers, and a large government staff was organized to deal with the taxpayers, whose ranks were swelled by the multitudes of emancipated serfs.

Educational Reform. In 1863 a second great reform, that of the educational system, was undertaken. Popular education was widely extended; secondary schools were opened to women, who were also permitted—though sometimes only as auditors—to enroll at the universities. Universities were granted greater autonomy, but after the revolutionary disturbances in the seventies this autonomy was again limited through state supervision.

Judicial Reform. A third step, in 1864, consisted in the reorganization of the judiciary. In addition to an inadequate administrative setup, it had suffered from lack of competent judges, lack of impartiality, and corruption. Now, with the abolition of serfdom, the landowner's jurisdiction was eliminated, and the state assumed their functions. Secret interrogation was abolished, equality before the law was decreed, and new courts with a jury system—though limited in scope—were introduced. Special volost (district) courts for peasants and justices of the peace dealing with minor offenses were set up. The judicial agencies were freed from bureaucratic interference, trials were speeded up, and the existing tortuous process of judicial appeal was restricted. It is true that the practice did not live up to the intentions, but gradually improvements were made.

Administrative Reform. Likewise in 1864, local self-government through a zemstvo system was instituted and became a progressive factor of outstanding importance. In three separate *curiae* (estates)—landowners, the village communities, and the townspeople—delegates were elected to district and provincial assemblies. It became the task of these bodies to attend to local administration. They dealt with education, welfare, health problems, the organization of communication systems, and industrial construction; and through them state and local taxes were levied. Unfortunately, the funds at the disposal of the zemstvos were often insufficient; yet, the zemstvos, dominated though they were in practice by the landowning nobility, contributed much to the betterment of conditions and served as schools for future political leaders. In the revolutionary eighties their work, like that of the new courts, was interrupted; but later they gained increased prestige.

Revision of Censorship. In 1865 edicts were issued to reduce censorship.

Insufficiency of Reform Legislation. The great reform laws of 1861–65 altered the structure of the empire fundamentally, but years were to elapse before their practical effect was fully felt. Only gradually could sincere co-operation on the part of officials be secured and the state machinery as well as the minds of the masses be adjusted to the new situation. In the meantime the progressives, belonging to all classes of the population, became impatient. Socialist tendencies increased, and in 1863 a revolt occurred in Poland which was suppressed with unnecessary brutality. In 1866, in a growingly tense atmosphere, an attempt on the life of the "Tsar Liberator" was made.

Further Reforms. Most Russian historians take this event as a milestone marking the interruption of the reform work. Facts, however, indicate that with the accomplishment of the financial, judicial, educational, and administrative reorganization of 1861 to 1865 the legal changes necessitated by emancipation had been essentially effectuated before 1866; the execution of further adjustments in line with the trend of the times could be stopped as little by the displeasure of the Tsar at the people's ingratitude as by the appointment of reactionaries to high positions. Thus, in 1867, protective tariffs were revoked; in 1870 a reform of municipal administration along lines similar to the zemstvo government was carried out; and four years later universal military service was introduced. The number of years of service was radically reduced, a system of exemptions for breadwinners and a system of education for all soldiers were instituted, and much of the inequality and abuse resulting from the existing military organization was banned.

Beginning in 1863 and extending for three decades, various acts were passed which regulated and lightened the financial burden of the peasants under the emancipation act.

SHORTCOMINGS OF REFORM WORK

How did it happen that this enormous reform work—perhaps occasionally retarded by so-called reactionary trends yet never seriously interrupted—failed to satisfy the needs of the country? The chief causes may be found in various factors: delays in carrying out the laws in the immense country because of its often unreliable bureaucracy; antiquated agricultural methods still practiced by the peasants after their emancipation; rapid industrial development which ran parallel with and always outdistanced the administrative reform work; and dissatisfaction of the intelligentsia at the persistency of a paternalistic regime which showed no intention of giving way to constitutional or popular rule.

Agriculture. In agriculture, especially, the beneficial effect of the reform work was slow in coming. The land distribution caused widespread injustices. Many farms, owing to their small size, proved unworkable under existing cultivation methods; capital was lacking for modern improvements; and famines still occurred regularly. In the black-soil districts, the need for land to provide for a rapidly increasing population was keenly felt, but intensified cultivation profiting from mechanical inventions was neglected. Agricultural production between 1860 and 1900 was raised only slightly, and necessary government credits for extensive improvements were not available. An undue share of the crops was used for exports to secure gold needed for interest payments on foreign loans. The lazy peasant profited from the industry of his neighbors in the same mir; drunkenness and illiteracy led to low living standards. Thus, despite emancipation and judicial, financial, and administrative changes, the agricultural system of Russia was still far from up-to-date.

Industries. Conversely, industries developed far too rapidly in comparison with the over-all progress of the country; and industrial crises, in themselves a factor sufficient to cause grave difficulties and revolutionary activities, were added to the agricultural problem. To be sure, production fell shortly after the emancipation edict of 1861, because many of the erstwhile forced laborers left their working places and because lack of capital slowed down important improvements. But gradually factories adjusted themselves to the new situation, joint-stock companies were founded, and better wages and living conditions were offered. The transportation system, which had been grievously neglected, was improved. After its slow, fitful growth, which had followed the construction of the first railroad in 1838 and of the main line connecting Moscow and St. Petersburg in 1851, large-scale railroad-building activities began in 1870 under D. A. Milyutin, capable war minister and brother of the advocate of emancipation. In 1877 an additional impetus to industrialization resulted from the reintroduction of protective tariffs, although they exercised adverse influence on the price level of industrial products, since even with low trade barriers Russian industries could have found sufficient markets for their limited production.

In 1881 one of the periodic world-wide depressions hit Russia, but after 1885 industrialization again took a strong upswing.

PROBLEMS

1. Discuss the need for further reform legislation after the emancipation of 1861.
2. Discuss the attitude of the tsarist government toward reform.
3. Discuss the influence of the reforms on industrial life in Russia.

26

INTELLIGENTSIA AND PARTIES

Significant Dates

Populist Movement 1878–1884
Alexander II Assassinated 1881
Social Democratic Party 1883
Menshevist-Bolshevist Split 1903

SOCIAL CURRENTS

Intelligentsia. In an atmosphere replete with reforms that never kept pace with the needs, political agitation persisted under the direction of the so-called intelligentsia. Unlike the agitators of Western Europe, these Russian intelligentsia were not essentially bourgeois; nor were they close to the soil and the people living on it. They were recruited largely from the professional classes and from the nobility; they were city- and university-bred men distinguished by a strong social consciousness. Like the eighteenth-century philosophers of the French Enlightenment, they little valued the religious spirit of man and its expression through the church; they were socialistically inclined and were preoccupied with the material needs, the individual well-being, and the security of man.

Populists. The intelligentsia were divided into various groups and "circles." Some of the circles were not unlike the "salons" before the French Revolution, where revolutionary ideas were discussed theoretically. But many of the intelligentsia, afraid of the sterility of their endeavors unless fructified by practical knowledge and experience and aware of their lack of understanding of the masses, tried to gain a better idea of existing needs by establishing artificial contact with the people and by sharing their life. Under the guidance of Bakunin and Lavrov, they combined this purpose with an endeavor to inspire the people with revolutionary ardor. This Populist movement became known as *V narod* ("To the people"), and secret societies such as the *Zemlya i Volya* (1878-79) tried, though without success, to co-ordinate idealistic reasoning with practical demands of the day. The leading Populist was Mikhailovsky. Out of the movement arose an organization, *Narodnaya Volya* (1879-84), which embraced socialist ideas.

NIHILISTS. Others, lacking such practical experience and driven by theoretical materialism and scepticism, formed various, essentially anarchistic groups, which became known as "Nihilist" after a term used by the novelist Turgenev. The Nihilists aimed to free the individual altogether from the duties imposed upon him by family, state, and church, and to destroy the foundations of existing society through acts of terror. They recognized no other values than those of science. Whereas the *V narod* program asked for theoretical preparation, for practical experience, and for investigation of social and economic conditions, the Nihilists called for action, subordinating social to political aims. Believing in the urgency of directing general attention to the dire need of constitutional reform as an essential condition for improving the status of the masses, they proceeded to do so by means of all kinds of propaganda, using terror as their chief weapon.

Terror. Under the aegis of the Nihilists, a number of outrages were committed without regard for the lives of guilty or innocent. In 1878, when general dissatisfaction with the government prevailed because of the lack of results from the Turkish war, the first great terrorist act was committed and the chief of the secret police was killed; in 1879 the governor-general of Kharkov was murdered, as was the new chief of police; in the same year, two attempts were made on the life of the Tsar, both miscarrying but exacting the lives of innocent victims. In the following year, another attempt was made by undermining the imperial palace. In 1881 the Tsar's "dictator," Loris-Melikov—an able, progressive statesman—was the object of a plot. Co-operating with the only elected popular representation, the zemstvos, he had envisaged liberal reforms whereby the influence of the radical groups was to be reduced and a constitutional system gradually created. Finally, in March, 1881, Alexander II, while engaged in putting into practice the constitutional plans of Loris-Melikov, was assassinated by a bomb.

REACTION AND PROGRESS

Alexander III. The murder of Alexander II interrupted the progress of political reform, but did not stop the process of industrialization and social change. Under his son, Alexander III (1881–94), work on the constitution was halted, autocracy revived, and censorship returned in an intransigent form. Loris-Melikov and the imperialist N. P. Ignatiev, the Slavophil friend of the people, were dismissed. Konstantin Pobedonostzev, tutor of Alexander III and Procurator of the Holy Synod, a man of considerable ability and conservative in his attitude, but pessimistic and cynical in his views of human affairs, gained dominant influence; his assistants were Ivan Aksakov and Katkov, two former liberal Slavophils, but by now old and essentially reactionary. N. K. Bunge, finance minister until 1887, was the only prominent liberal among Alexander III's advisers.

Revival of Paternalism. The zemstvos, which had grown in importance and which had laid a basis for a certain amount of self-government, were deprived of their representative character and became a part of the civil service. The so-called Zemstvo-Liberals were persecuted when they tried to organize co-operation among the various zemstvos all over the empire and to develop the institution into a large-scale political factor, and their state-wide planning was discouraged. On the other hand, the landholding nobility regained some of its lost influence through the institution of "land captains," who were chosen by the government from their midst and charged with supervising the administration and jurisdiction in rural districts. Through the church, special influence was exercised on the curricula of the schools, and the police supervised most intellectual activities in the country. In line with Pan-Slavist programs, Russification was sponsored in the border regions, in Poland, Finland, and the Baltic countries. Under Alexander III, furthermore, persecution of Jews was intensified; they were allowed to settle in restricted areas only; certain professions were barred to them; purchase of real estate was prohibited; and schools were ordered to accept only a low percentage of Jews.

Gains of Peasantry. This return to the principle of "Autocracy, Orthodoxy, and Nationalism" of Nicholas I was not paralleled by a reactionary tendency in economic and social conditions. On the contrary, the reign of Alexander III showed the continuance of the progressive trends noticeable since emancipation. The peasantry gained considerable advantages: In 1882 the redemption payments were reduced, and in the same year an inheritance tax was introduced by the able finance minister Bunge, who thus for the first time laid the larger share of the financial burden on the shoulders of the wealthy and privileged classes. Bank credit was offered for purchases of land, and the share of the total land owned by peasants actually increased substantially. From 1883 to 1886 the poll tax was abolished, and following this the village authority over the peasant was eased by opening the way for appeals to higher courts.

Gains of Industrial Workers. The government turned its attention likewise to the needs of the working class. In 1882 child labor was regulated and working hours were reduced, and during the following eight years laws were promulgated regarding compulsory education for minors working in factories, curtailment of nightwork of women, unjust fines, and payment of wages in kind instead of money. Factory inspectors were named to enforce this legislation and to supervise the laborer's living and working conditions.

Results of Social Legislation. Unfortunately, the effect of the various steps undertaken to improve the conditions of the rural and industrial workers did not come up to expectations. One of the most important reasons for this was the rapid increase of the population, which caused continued impoverishment. Because of corruption, the application of the laws intended to ameliorate conditions often lagged behind the spirit. Moreover, on the land, the institution of land captains and the increase of indirect taxes constituted a serious check against progress. In the towns, the evolution of a modern economy brought about adversities. The laborer's low standards of living were but little improved, as the country, with its economy based on agriculture, was not ripe for industrialization. By the time of Alexander III's accession to the throne, only 8 per cent of the population lived in cities, from which new industries springing up all over the country could draw their labor supply. Living quarters, hastily and penuriously constructed, were often of a most disgraceful type. Sometimes numerous families dwelt together in large sleeping halls, and immorality, drunkenness, and filth prevailed. The health of young and old was undermined by the vices of the towns and was no longer even partly balanced by strength-giving rural activities which in earlier days had formed a vital part of the industrial serf's life. Working hours remained long; whole families were occupied in factories; and the care and education of children were sorely neglected. Thus, Russia, "backward but not stagnant," still did not catch up with the standards of Western countries.

FORMATION OF PARTIES

Liberal Parties. Alexander's vigorous rule of political conservatism and economic advance and the continuing distress of large parts of the population necessitated a change in the position of the various groups among the intelligentsia. The incoherent, utopian movements had to make room for more practical political parties. Populists, Nihilists, and Anarchists disappeared; capable organizers, both liberal and Marxist, emerged; and with their help the *V narod* movement developed into what was later called the "Social Revolutionary party" (S.R.) and the Zemstvo-Liberals gave rise to the "Konstitutional Democrats" (Kadets). In contrast to former radical groups, both these parties were progressive and fought determinedly —by the use of chiefly peaceful propaganda and with legal means —for reform, abolition of class differences, freedom of speech and press, equality before the law, a constitution, and betterment of social conditions. The S.R. interested themselves largely in agricultural life, which they wanted to transform in a socialist sense; the Kadets concerned themselves more with questions of government, with the building of a parliamentary state formed after Western models.

Revolutionary Parties. Yet, parties of a more revolutionary character were also created. One of the first Marxist groups was formed abroad by G. V. Plekhanov in 1883; and Russia's Social Democratic party was organized in 1898.

Social Democrats. The Social Democrats shared the desires of the zemstvo and popular groups with regard to equality before the law, freedom of the press, and civil liberties; but they concentrated on practical economic aims—the gaining of higher wages, better working conditions, and shorter working hours. They organized strikes and unionized workers. They had little sympathy for the Populists and their idealism and little confidence in the helpfulness of an unenlightened peasantry, but concentrated their attention on the future of the proletariat. Though active underground, they found themselves, paradoxically enough, not infrequently encouraged by secret government agents and spies who wanted to divert attention from political goals. The police, who succeeded in placing agents in key posts right within socialist ranks, actually co-operated with labor unions in the economic struggle when to do so served the political intentions of the government.

MENSHEVISTS AND BOLSHEVISTS. The growth of the Socialist party suffered at first from the smallness of the industrial proletariat and from the peasant's aversion to innovations. Violent strikes, which were organized in 1885, 1896, and, after Alexander III's death, in 1897 and 1898, were suppressed by force. Eventually, because of lack of success, the overcautious, opportunistic policies directed by Plekhanov led to a schism in the socialist movement. In 1903, at a congress in London, the break occurred over the questions of the enforcement of a strict centralized direction of the movement and of the use of violence in the revolutionary struggle. The "majority party," the Bolshevists under Vladimir Ulyanov (later known under his pseudonym "Lenin"), which was convinced of the need for revolutionary war, seceded, while the "minority," the Menshevists, continued to follow Plekhanov. By working together with other liberal parties, as in other countries, and by participating in popular agencies and representations, this more moderate wing of the socialists sought the realization of socialist objectives.

PROBLEMS

1. Discuss the position of the intelligentsia toward the social system of Russia.
2. Discuss the economic policies of the government under Alexander III.
3. Trace the emergence of political parties in Russia.

27

THE ARTS IN RUSSIA

Significant Dates

St. Sophia in Kiev Begun	1017
Icon Painting (Andrew Rublev) . . . . *ca.*	1400
Founding of Ballet School	1738
Founding of Academy of Fine Arts	1758
Founding of Philharmonic Society	1802
Dostoyevsky, *Crime and Punishment*	1866
Tolstoy, *Anna Karenina*	1875–1877

Life and conditions in every country find their expression through nonmaterial as well as material media: through the use made by people of their leisure; through the works of art produced within the atmosphere in which they live; through the thoughts expressed in their literature; through their costumes, dances, music, and play. No description of such activities can be satisfactory; for each has its own medium of expression and must be seen, heard, or felt rather than listed or described. But an indication of their scope, direction, and significance in the body politic has a place in the work of a historian.

ARCHITECTURE

The first concrete form of expression of artistic feeling in Russian culture, as with so many others, is found in architecture. As in the West, Christianity provided the moving impulse, and, except for northern Russia, Byzantine influences were predominant.

Leadership of Kiev. The early Christian churches were often shed-like buildings. The first wooden cathedral of more elaborate design was built in Novgorod in 989; it was much imitated all over the country, but wars, invasions, and fires have destroyed many of the best. The first stone church was begun in Kiev in 991. In 1017, under the influence of Byzantium and with the help of Greek artisans, the great Cathedral of St. Sophia in Kiev was begun; it was provided with many domes and beautified by mosaics and paintings. St. Sophia served as a model for future building, which combined "lusty northern strength, mystical Byzantine piety and a haunting Orientalism."

More outstanding works soon followed. They included the church of the Lavra Monastery in Kiev and, as the center of Russian power moved northeastward, numerous churches in the Suzdal-Vladimir region. Some of the most beautiful among them were of small size and located outside of the larger towns. The churches showed increased "sophistication," being built in carefully worked sandstone which added warmth and beauty to the texture of the outside walls. In the twelfth century they showed occasional Romanesque traits —added by Western masters who were invited to come to Russia. Some Western influences are noticeable also in the architecture of Novgorod, but their traces are insignificant; essentially, the Byzantine pattern prevailed in the Novgorod area as in Kiev, though with a number of local, native additions. An eightfold sloping roof covered many of the churches. In the twelfth, thirteenth, and fourteenth centuries the peculiar bulbous dome (born out of climatic considerations), which combines cupola with pyramid, was developed. It survives to this day as a mark distinctive of Russian churches.

Prominence of Moscow. In the fourteenth and fifteenth centuries the power of the Moscow grand dukes increased, and, despite their parsimoniousness, they slowly began to beautify their capital. At first they contented themselves mainly with wooden structures, none of which have survived. However, under Ivan the Great, husband of the Greek princess Sophia who had been reared in Renaissance Rome, a change occurred that was to bring Moscow to the forefront in the field of art. Now, master architects, attracted by the offers which Ivan tendered them because of their technical and engineering skills, came from many parts of Europe. The most famous were Fioraventi, Solari, and Aloisi. After having become acquainted with Russian traditions, they—and Russians under their direction—set to work to build various great stone edifices. Thus were created some of the most famous churches in the Kremlin, such as the "Assumption" and the "Annunciation." It would, however, be incorrect to say that the foreigners succeeded in introducing the art of the European Renaissance. The spirit of this mighty movement remained rather alien to the Russians, and the foreign architects had to conform to the Russian style and the rules of the Orthodox authorities. Nor were they widely imitated; to the contrary, wooden buildings in the traditional style remained predominant. In the middle of the sixteenth century, the many-colored Church of St. Basil, with its towers and domes, was erected in Moscow outside the Kremlin walls.

Among secular buildings, houses and fortifications of more elaborate constructions had already been constructed in the thirteenth century. They showed an unmistakable influence of traditions spread by the Tartar conquerors. The subservience of the Muscovite grand dukes increased these influences, which found their reflection in the palaces constructed by the numerous princes for their own safety and glorification. But a certain change came with the arrival of the Renaissance artists who built the famous stone Kremlin walls (after those of the Sforza castle in Milan), constructed some of the towers, and created new palaces, among which were the Facette (*Granovitaia*) Palace in the Moscow Kremlin.

Hegemony of St. Petersburg. Not until the late seventeenth and the eighteenth centuries did a second and all-embracing change occur. At this time, partly under the influence of Peter the Great, a radical departure from tradition led to the frank introduction of entirely Western artistic concepts. Baroque and Rococo architects were called into the country, and they built, without regard for old Russian ways, in their own manner. The most famous among them were Trezzini, Schädel, LeBlond, and, later in the eighteenth century, Bartolomeo Rastrelli and Quarenghi. The new undertakings no longer revolved around Kiev, Novgorod, or Moscow; rather, they centered on St. Petersburg. The city itself, stretching along the banks of the Neva and offering special opportunities for a lovely waterfront, was carefully planned along Dutch patterns and adorned by Western architects with buildings in the Italian, German, and, above all, French taste. Palaces, bridges, portals, and streets, if not churches, took on the stamp of a different spirit. In 1757 the Academy of Fine Arts was founded in St. Petersburg; from it were graduated native artists, many of them serfs, who at the request of their Westernized patrons and masters imitated chiefly the French and Italian schools. In the nineteenth century, the German classicist style dominated. But in Russia, as in other countries, the architecture of the nineteenth century, showed little originality; and the former spiritual and creative impulse was supplanted by an inspiration which came chiefly from commercial, military, and self-glorifying projects.

PAINTING, SCULPTURE, MUSIC, BALLET

Painting.   The history of painting follows a different path. Introduced during the eleventh century through frescoes of Greek masters, the art of painting was soon adopted by Russians. In the course of the centuries, various schools emerged, among which those of Kiev, Suzdal, Novgorod, Moscow, and "Stroganov" stand out. In painting, as in architecture, what was later created in St. Petersburg represented not Russian but Western taste.

School of Kiev.   Inasmuch as the first great Russian painters came, like her architects, from Greece, Russian disciples in Kievan times adhered strictly to the style set by Byzantium. They painted icons * and adorned the inside walls of the churches with frescoes. Mosaics were also made, but these were done almost exclusively by Greeks who came to Russia. In all three media—panel painting, fresco, mosaic—individuality was subordinated to prescribed patterns, and rather than inventing new forms, the artist prided himself in continuing the style set by his predecessors. Since naturalism might appeal to the eye and thus "deprive the soul of clear recognition," the artist placed the accent not on realistic but on abstract representation. He imitated the elongated figures of the Greeks, and he used symbols which were customary—and therefore understood even by the unlearned worshipper. He tried to express sacredness

* Icon: Defined in terms of use in the Eastern Orthodox church, an icon is a panel painting containing the image of Christ, the Virgin Mary, or one of the saints. The figures are characteristically highly stylized and symbolic, and are generally placed against a gold background. Gestures and the manner in which the drapery, hands, and face are rendered follow closely traditional formulas. There are also icons made of silver or other metals.

and saintliness and to draw the spectator into another, unworldly sphere—onto the path of salvation. With their pure colors, their gold and blue, the icons particularly show unusual beauty, depth, simplicity, and grace.

SCHOOLS OF SUZDAL AND NOVGOROD. As Kiev declined, the art of painting icons flourished—particularly in Suzdal and Novgorod, where, far from Byzantium, it was enriched by indigenous local tradition. Now, red, yellow, and green came to supplement blue and gold. This art reached its peak in the fourteenth century with Theophanes the Greek, who had come to Novgorod at an early age.

In the fifteenth century, new Byzantine influences on Novgorod's art contributed to the production of additional masterpieces—primarily icons; and the importance of fresco painting was reduced.

SCHOOLS OF MOSCOW AND "STROGANOV." Moscow art flourished at the same time as that of Novgorod. Notwithstanding its rather recent origin, foreign domination, and economic adversities, Moscow had become early a cultural center of Russia. The greatest figure there, and the most famous painter of all Russia, was Andrew Rublev, whose tender, timeless work is comparable to that of Giotto and other inspired masters of the early Renaissance. Rublev was not a solitary figure. Several disciples shared with him the beautiful achievements of Russian icon painting, and the art flourished despite Tartar occupation and Western influence. It failed, however, to progress in the fifteenth and sixteenth centuries; despite the emergence of a great painter, Dionysius, it was cheapened and finally degraded by conventionality and a mercenary spirit. Unlike the situation in the West, the church succeeded in stifling the further evolution of painters through its opposition to pictures of secular topics; and despite the examples of the great Dutch, German, and Italian artists, Russian painting became untrue to the spirit of its time.

An attempt to revive the greatness of earlier ages came with a school named after a member of the rich Stroganov family. This school tried to recapture the spirituality and simplicity of the works of the past great masters, and it excelled through the elegance of its color schemes, the use of gold coloring, and the minute care in every detail. But the decline could not be arrested. Book illuminations, which had reached a certain perfection earlier, likewise lost in inspiration, and the illustrations and woodcuts of the period cannot compare with the great contemporary achievements in Germany and other Western countries.

WESTERNIZED ART. In the seventeenth century, secular topics were increasingly treated; foreign teachers began to arrive and introduced many of the naturalistic concepts prevailing abroad. In particular, the art of portraiture spread. The technique was improved by the introduction of perspective and attention to background. Yet, it was not before the eighteenth century, after the foundation of the Academy of Fine Arts, that painters of eminence appeared. Although old church art persisted, in particular among the Old Believers, the interest of the painters was directed largely to secular themes, and their horizon was widened through travel and studies abroad. But even so, lack of originality and imitation of the French and Italians prevailed.

MODERN SCHOOLS. The first masters of independent merit appeared in the second half of the eighteenth century. More came after 1800, in the Romantic period, with Levitsky, Bryulov, and Ivanov; and in the nineteenth century the genre picture (Venetsianov) began to arrive on the Russian national scene. By then, the Academy, whose influence on the development of arts had been beneficially felt during the earlier period, had assumed a dogmatic character, and in 1863 a number of members revolted against it. A patron of art, Paul Tretyakov, supported their ideas, and a new school arose which, instead of imitating foreign tastes, took its inspiration from Russian history and daily life and marked the rising spirit of "social consciousness." Its followers in the second half of the nineteenth century, N. Gay ("Crucifixion"), I. Repin ("Barge Haulers on the Volga," "Ivan the Terrible and His Son"), V. Surikov ("Execution of the Streltsi"), and others, belong to the best masters of their times. They introduced a period when Russia, influenced by the Impressionists and Expressionists, shared in the international development of painting. The constant social preaching of the artists, however, was eventually resented, and the period before the First World War witnessed a return to earlier purely aesthetic concepts.

Sculpture. Traditional rejection of the making of plastic images of man almost completely checked the development of sculpture in Russia. Some bas-reliefs constituted almost all we know of Russian sculpture during the first seven hundred years. Only with the introduction of Western tastes in other fields did Russian work in sculpture also begin. Even then, only foreign masters excelled, the best known monuments being those created by the elder Rastrelli and the statue of Peter the Great by Falconet.

Music. In music, Russia produced, until the nineteenth century, little that gained recognition beyond the national borders. Russian folk songs, with their "elemental power" and expression of tenderness and melancholy, were deep and inspiring musical treasures. Collections of these folk songs exist, and many of their themes and rhythms have found a reflection in the masterpieces of later periods. A musical notation, such as Europe adopted around A.D. 1000, was not known in Russia. Sacred music was based on Byzantine traditions and underwent little change. Individual works, such as the majestic medieval Latin hymns or the compositions of the Renaissance and Reformation, were not created. In the eighteenth century opera was introduced from Italy. The first Philharmonic Society was founded as late as 1802, when the works of the Germans— Bach, Haydn, Mozart, and Beethoven—inspired the Russian world. But in music, the Russians emancipated themselves, more speedily and effectively than in other fields, from foreign influence. They imbued their compositions with such spirit as to give them significance beyond national borders. Glinka (d. 1857), with his *Life for The Tsar,* introduced the great period of Russian music. In the agitated times of emancipation and reform when national aspirations and social questions involved every artist of feeling, Musorgsky (1839–1881; *Boris Godunov*), Tchaikovsky (1840–1893; symphonies, *1812 Overture*), and Rimsky-Korsakov (1844–1908; symphonies, *Scheherazade,* collection of folk songs) created their immortal works. In the twentieth century, Rachmaninoff and the "modernists" Scriabin, Stravinsky, and Prokofiev maintained the tradition of Russian accomplishment, versatility, and social consciousness.

Ballet. Of special interest is the development of a Russian specialty—the ballet. As part of theatrical productions, it owes its formal origin to the West, but it soon developed independently and fused artistic conceptions of the West with those derived from Russian folk dances and national traditions.

BEGINNINGS OF BALLET. The first performance of a play took place in 1672 before Tsar Alexis. It dealt with a biblical topic,

Esther, and it was succeeded by a dance performance, *Orpheus and Eurydice,* and by another biblical play, *Holofernes and Judith.* After Alexis' death, reactionary tendencies prevailed, and the stage was closed except for private performances. The theater was revived by Peter; and in 1735 the first regular ballet was staged before Tsarina Anna by Landé, dancing master of the Military Academy. In 1738 he founded "Her Majesty's Dancing School," accepting pupils from the age of seven on, many of them children of serfs; and ballet presentations soon became fashionable. The topics were mainly of foreign and mythological origin, but gradually folk dances and Russian themes gained in importance. By the beginning of the nineteenth century the ballet was well-established: the government supervised and paid for the school; children of serfs were enrolled in it; no one could leave before the lapse of ten years; the star, rather than the ensemble, was emphasized; and musical composition, mimicry, and pantomime were greatly improved. The Mazurka from Glinka's *Life for The Tsar* was staged and a great director, Didelot, and excellent performers increased the reputation of the Russian ballet.

ZENITH OF BALLET. After Didelot—through bad administration and conventionality, poor education, and low moral standards—the work of the school was menaced until, in the 1850's, reforms were introduced. Under the direction of two Frenchmen and with the help of fine dancers, the ballet re-established its reputation and became foremost in creative and inspiring methods. Through grace, as opposed to "acrobatics," the St. Petersburg ballet gained fame and world-wide appreciation. It maintained this reputation because of its faculty for consistent evolution, reform, and resistance to outmoded traditions. In the 1890's it witnessed a great revival; and men like Sergei Diaghilev and Michel Fokine, supported by musicians and painters of merit and training in ballet composition and by the great dancers Anna Pavlova, Adolph Bolm, and Vaslav Nijinsky, led the art of Russian ballet to new heights.

LITERATURE

In literature, as in the other arts, Russia, until the eighteenth century, did not offer the scope, variety, unique artistry, and philosophical depth which characterized the contemporary achievements of Italy and Germany, France and the Low Countries, and Spain and other regions. Perhaps a number of important works were lost during the long troublous periods of Russian history—during the Tartar period, the *Smuta,* or the various revolutions. Only in the last two centuries have scholars unearthed some literary works which may constitute a permanent treasure of world literature.

Early Literature.   For lack of a Slavic alphabet, literature did not antedate the ninth century. The earliest works after the creation of the alphabet by the two "apostles of the Slavs" were, of course, of a religious nature. Many of them were translations. The *Nestor Chronicle,* the first Russian historical work, dates from the eleventh century and was followed by other chronicles—for example, those of Novgorod and Pskov. About the same time some *Lives* of the saints and other church writings were composed. In the twelfth century, church literature was created in the Suzdal region; and during that same period the most prominent work of medieval Russian literature, an epic, *The Lay of Prince Igor,* originated. Fables, folk songs, and epic songs (the *byliny*), constituted likewise an important part of the Russian art of expression, but most of them were passed on orally from generation to generation and were not collected and written down until the eighteenth and nineteenth centuries. In the late fifteenth and the sixteenth centuries, religious controversies and increased contacts with the West led to intensification of literary activity. The printing press was, however, not introduced until the middle of the sixteenth century and played but a small role for another two hundred years.

Linguistic Reforms.   In the times of the Patriarch Nikon, Tsar Alexis, and especially Tsar Peter, interest in foreign works increased, and many imitations and translations were published; but not even under Elizabeth, vaunted for her Russian leanings, was native literature fostered. Likewise, the three outstanding writers of the time of Catherine the Great—Novikov and Radishchev (both pamphleteers as well as literary men) and G. Derzhavin—failed to reach the level of contemporary European poets. Perhaps Russian authors were restricted by state supervision and censorship, and by differences between the written and the spoken word, and particularly by the complexities of alphabet and grammar. Linguistic studies in any case had to precede other accomplishments and to pave the way for poetic literary expression. Three names were chiefly connected with this task: Lomonosov (1711–65), professor at the

Academy of Sciences and a polyhistor, philosopher, poet, historian, physicist, and chemist; Karamzin (1766–1826), historian and poet, whose romantic novel, *Poor Lisa,* was a milestone in the field of the Russian art of writing; and Zhukovsky (1783–1852), famous for his grammar and translations.

Nineteenth Century. Once the new basis for literary expression was laid, writers of ability and profundity were not lacking. In line with the spirit of the nineteenth century, interest in religious, philosophical, psychological, and social aspects, rather than in literary problems and fantasy, dominated. Although Russian writers greatly admired and were influenced by German idealism, by Schiller and Goethe, as well as by the romantics Schlegel and Fichte, art for art's sake and classical serenity and detachment never gained widespread favor in Russia. "Art [is] an expression of the spirit and tendency of society in a given epoch," said the great literary critic Belinsky, and, added Herzen, "Man is not born for logic alone,— but also for the social-historical world of moral freedom and positive action." It is in this spirit and in a definitely national yet "all human" atmosphere that the greatest works in Russian literature and their creators must be viewed: Pushkin (1799–1837), famed for his poetry, for *Boris Godunov,* and for *Eugene Onegin;* Lermontov (1814–41), known for *A Hero of Our Times;* Gogol (1809–52), who wrote *Dead Souls* and *The Revizor;* Turgenev (1818–83), author of *Fathers and Sons;* Dostoyevsky (1821–81), writer of *Crime and Punishment, The Idiot, The Brothers Karamazov;* and Tolstoy (1828–1910), who wrote *Anna Karenina, War and Peace,* and *The Death of Ivan Ilyich.* In an interplay of nationalism and practical religiosity, the prominent Russian poets demonstrated their deep trust in the Russian people and in Russia's destiny.

The literary tradition of the great Russian authors and their many distinguished contemporaries was continued in the following generation by Anton Chekov (1860–1904), D. Merezhkovsky (1865–1941), V. L. Andreyev (1871–1919), and the fighter for the new revolutionary world to come, Maxim Gorky (1868–1936).

PROBLEMS

1. Discuss the foreign influences on Russian art.
2. Discuss the importance of "social consciousness" among Russian artists.
3. Discuss the scope of artistic achievement in nineteenth-century Russia.

28

RUSSIA AND EUROPE

Significant Dates

Greek War of Independence 1821–1829
Russo-Turkish War 1828–1829
Peace of Adrianople 1829
Revolt in Poland 1830–1832
Treaty of Unkiar Skelessi 1833
Straits Convention 1841
Crimean War 1854–1856
Peace of Paris 1856
Revolt in Poland 1863

The rhythm of domestic change in Russia is traceable also in external affairs. A distinct connection between international and internal policies can be observed, for instance, in the defeat in the Crimean War and its reaction upon the emancipation of serfs, in the Congress of Berlin and nihilistic activities, and in Far Eastern involvements and the Revolution of 1905.

RUSSIA AND WESTERN EUROPE

The century from the Congress of Vienna to the outbreak of the First World War was a period of relative peace (or at least no great conflict), embracing all major nations. Only once, in the Crimean War (1854–56), did Russia become involved in a war with any of the great Western powers. Otherwise her political role in relation to them was confined to diplomacy. Immediately after the Napoleonic period, Russia's position was of great weight; in the course of the century, however, it diminished and did not resume primary importance until the last two decades of the century.

Relations with the Great Powers. The victories which Russia's armies had gained during the Napoleonic Wars and the role which she had played at the Congress of Vienna caused many European statesmen to fear for the balance of power in Europe and to work for a redress of that balance. Many of their policies were aimed therefore at reducing Russian influence on the international stage as well as in internal European affairs. Austria's minister Metternich, the leading diplomatic figure of the time, endeavored to check by his diplomacy the impact of Russia—at least in Central Europe. More determined still was England's policy. Refusing cooperation in international affairs as provided for by the Holy Alliance, she gradually assumed a position that was to become one of the chief obstacles for Russian ambitions throughout the nineteenth century. On the other hand, Prussia saw her advantage in maintaining friendly contact with her eastern neighbor, and France too built up a satisfactory relationship with the erstwhile enemy.

Principle of Legitimacy and International Congresses. Basic for Russia's diplomacy after 1815 was the "principle of legitimacy" agreed upon at Vienna. Its purpose was as far as possible to guarantee all "legitimate" rulers their pre-revolutionary territories and powers. With this aim in view, Alexander I, capably supported by his foreign minister Nesselrode, opposed revolutionary movements and interfered in favor of the existing order wherever it was threatened. He participated in a number of congresses—at Aachen (1818), Carlsbad (1819), Troppau-Laibach (1820–21), and Verona (1822). Besides attending to immediate questions such as withdrawal of the occupation army from France, reduction of French reparations, and regulation of the American slave trade, he saw to it that the agitation of liberals in Germany, Italy, and Spain was suppressed, and he interfered in the struggle for independence in South America. Even in Greece, when a war of independence broke out, he supported the "legitimate" rule of the Sultan, notwithstanding the fact that Russia had long coveted domination of Constantinople and the Straits. Soon, however, the struggle of the Greeks and with it the whole "Eastern Question" (i.e., the rule of the Turks in Eastern Europe and Asia Minor and the traffic in peace and war through the Bosporus and Dardanelles) took on a form which also forced Russia to break with her policy of adhering to the principles of Vienna.

NEAR EASTERN PROBLEM

During the eighteenth century and Napoleonic times, Russia's chief preoccupation in external affairs had been with her northern and western neighbors, Sweden and Poland. During the nineteenth century, Russia centered her attention upon the south, upon Turkey and the Straits. Until 1914, the strategic Near Eastern problem runs like a red thread through the history of Russian international activity in Europe, giving direction to her plans and her wars and alliances. Yet, despite many a victorious enterprise against Turkey and notwithstanding the dissolution of the Ottoman empire, the gains were insignificant; the goal, Constantinople, was not reached, and by 1914 Russia had hardly improved her position over that in 1815.

Greek War of Independence. The Greek War of Independence, a revolt against Turkish rule, began in 1821. As long as Alexander lived, Russia observed the principle of legitimacy; but his policy was reversed under his successor. Constantinople seemed too important. Again and again, Russia had been stalled in her drive. At Tilsit and Erfurt, when she had demanded from Napoleon a free hand with regard to Turkey, Napoleon, who called Constantinople the "capital of the world," had refused concessions and insisted he would never permit the city to fall into Russian hands. Later, Russian troops had marched triumphantly into far-away Paris, but Constantinople not so far away had proved beyond Russia's reach. Now, the Greek War of Independence opened new possibilities. In 1826, by the Treaty of Akkerman (1826), the Turks were forced to respect previously undertaken obligations regarding Christian minorities in the Balkans; and when they again procrastinated, intervention in favor of Greece was decided upon. In conjunction with France and England, Russia dispatched a fleet to force the Sultan to accept Allied mediation between him and the insurgents. Against the original intention of refraining from active participation in the armed conflict, this Allied armada struck a military blow at Turkey and destroyed, at Navarino, the fleet which had come from Egypt to support the Sultan.

Turkish War. The attack was represented in the English Parliament as an "untoward" accident, and was certainly unwelcome to the British to the extent that it increased Russian influence in the Mediterranean. They therefore withdrew from further action, with the French following in their wake. But the dismayed Turks declared a holy war, and Russia decided to profit by this opportunity and continued her campaign. While General Paskevich seized the fortress of Kars in the Caucasus sector, the main body of the Tsar's troops, led by General Diebitsch, crossed the Balkan mountains with great difficulties and took Adrianople, key to the road to the Straits.

Adrianople. Defeated Turkey was obliged to sue for peace in 1829 (Adrianople). She ceded all her territories in the Caucasus and accorded Russia a protectorate over the Danubian provinces of Moldavia and Walachia. The treaty marked an important moment in history, for Russia established herself thereby as protagonist of the Christian states in the Balkans in their struggle for independence from Turkey and as a power on the Balkan peninsula. With her sponsorship, Greek independence was declared and guaranteed by the European powers, and Serbia as well as the Danubian principalities gained autonomy.

Unkiar Skelessi. A new success was scored in 1833, when a rising of the Egyptians forced Turkey to appeal for help to the European powers. In exchange for assistance, the Sultan concluded the Agreement of Unkiar Skelessi with Russia. This treaty accorded the Tsar the right to use the Bosporus and the Dardanelles for his warships and closed them to other nations, thus establishing a virtual Russian protectorate over Constantinople. The treaty was supplemented in the same year by an arrangement with Austria which provided for co-ordinated policies of the Tsars and the Hapsburgs toward Turkey.

Straits Convention. The position thus gained, however, could not be maintained against the misgivings of England and France, which in 1838 seized upon the opportunity afforded by new troubles between Turkey and Egypt to weaken Russia's protectorate. This time, in alliance with Austria and Prussia, they did not allow Russia to act independently, but insisted upon their right to have a voice in affairs pertaining to Turkey and the Near Eastern problem. After long negotiations, which were complicated by France's desire for prestige and her alignment with Egypt, a new convention was concluded in 1841. It replaced the Russian protectorate over the Straits by an international guarantee.

CRIMEAN WAR

Outbreak. The Straits Convention did not settle the Near Eastern problem, nor did it satisfy Russian ambitions or compose Anglo-Russian rivalry. It also failed to arrange the question of protection for Christians in the Balkans, among whom the Catholic minority looked for French, and the Orthodox majority for Russian, support; neither did it protect the vast French economic interests in the Near East. In 1850 the struggle was resumed when Louis Napoleon, then President of France and thirsting for recognition and glory, demanded from Turkey the right of French control over holy places in Palestine for the protection of Catholic monks. This reopening of the Eastern question induced Tsar Nicholas not only to demand like privileges for the Orthodox clergy and a protectorate over all Orthodox Christians, but also to suggest to England in 1853 a final settlement of the whole Near Eastern problem—the outright partitioning of Turkey. The offer, which ran counter to the British policy of keeping "life lines" through the Mediterranean unimperiled and of maintaining economic privileges in Turkey, was categorically declined. Suspicions and fears in London rose to a high pitch, and the Turks were incited by England to reject a Russian ultimatum demanding a protectorate over their country. Tsarist troops thereupon invaded the Danubian provinces, and the Sultan, relying on British backing, declared war. Prussia took no part in the hostilities, and Austria confined herself to keeping a menacing but noncombatant attitude so long as Russia did not transgress on the Danubian region. But Britain, France, and later Piedmont actively intervened in favor of the Turks; their fleets sailed through the Straits into the Black Sea; and the Crimean peninsula was invaded.

Defeat. The Allied forces reaped little glory. Poor leadership and bad organization led to unnecessary loss of human life and waste of material, and ultimate success was due only to the technical inferiority and still greater incompetence of the Russians. Corruption of the bureaucracy, failure of the supply system, and lack of equipment and particularly of medical help rendered useless the bravery of the Russian soldiers and the valiant efforts of such capable leaders as General Totleben, defender of the key fortress of Sevastopol. In view of their losses and the exhaustion of their finances, the Russians were obliged, after Tsar Nicholas I's death in 1855, to put an end to the struggle—which seemed to prove the superiority, at least militarily, of a "degenerate" yet industrially developed Western world.

Peace of Paris. Peace was concluded at Paris in 1856. In pushing Russia's frontiers back and stripping her of naval power, it served mainly English interests. The mouth of the Danube and parts of Bessarabia and of earlier conquests in the Caucasus region, as well as the fortress of Kars, were forfeited by Russia; she had to renounce any existing or future unilateral protectorate in Turkey, to remove her warships from the Black Sea, and to scrap her shore fortifications.

Political Reorientation. The stipulation dealt a severe blow to Russia and led to a reversal of her policies. The old foreign minister Nesselrode was replaced by A. M. Gorchakov; a *rapprochement* with France was promoted and the alliance with Austria, which had proved so unsatisfactory, was discontinued. A firmer alliance was sought with Prussia, where Gorchakov's friend and "pupil" Bismarck came to power in 1861; and steps were taken to recover lost prestige through enterprises in the Far East.

POLAND

The realignment in foreign affairs, combined with the internal reforms of 1861, made it possible for Russia to meet a crisis which arose in 1863. This time not Turkey but Poland was involved.

Revolution of 1830. The Poles had been granted autonomy within the Russian empire by the Congress of Vienna: Their country, "Congress Poland," which corresponded approximately to existing ethnographic facts, had been made a kingdom with Russia's Tsar as king of Poland, and they had been accorded a separate administration and constitutional rights. But this arrangement had deprived them of coveted eastern territory and had failed to satisfy their national ambitions. The resultant unrest led to infringements on Russian suzerainty, and in 1830, following uprisings in Paris, a revolution broke out. Faced by the brutal might of the Russian army under Diebitsch and Paskevich, and hindered by their own disunity and the greed and reactionary spirit of their leaders, the Poles emerged defeated and deprived of many of their previous rights.

Revolution of 1863. When the Revolution of 1848 swept Europe, Poland dared not join in the movement; but in the following decade, after the Crimean War and during the early reign of Alexander II, Tsar-Liberator, hopes in Poland were reawakened. Alexander's conciliatory attitude encouraged the Poles to demand concessions and territorial aggrandizement. Unrest grew and culminated in 1863, after the introduction of a revised conscription law, in a new revolt. With the assistance of Bismarck and because of continued disunity among the Poles, this revolt also was suppressed and resulted in the abolition of Polish autonomy. Emancipation of the serfs was decreed; and in order to break the hold of the Polish nobility and gain the sympathies of the people, it was carried out under particularly generous conditions for the peasants. Measures for the Russification of the country were proclaimed and harshly, though unsuccessfully, applied.

Internal consolidation and recovered prestige opened the way for Russia to concentrate again on her most important foreign problem and to resume her Balkan policies.

PROBLEMS

1. Discuss Russia's drive to gain domination of the Straits.
2. Discuss the influence of Russo-Turkish relations on Anglo-Russian relations.
3. Describe the status of Poland under Russian rule.

29

INTERNATIONAL REORIEN-
TATION

Significant Dates
Three Emperors' League . . 1872–1878, 1881–1887
Russo-Turkish War 1877–1878
Congress of Berlin 1878
Franco-Russian Entente   1891
First Hague Peace Conference 1899
Second Hague Peace Conference 1907

RUSSIA AND THE BALKANS

Abrogation of Black Sea Clause. The first move in Russia's renewed drive for the penetration of the Balkans consisted in the abrogation of the most burdensome stipulation of the Peace of Paris. In 1870, while the attention of the world was focused on the Franco-Prussian War and the collapse of Napoleon III's empire and while England and Austria were preoccupied with the issues arising from these, Russia swiftly repudiated the clause which banned the maintenance of warships on the Black Sea.

Background to War with Turkey. Emboldened by the inability of their treaty partners to challenge the act, the Russians undertook the next step and began to reclaim from the Turks the parts of Bessarabia ceded at the Peace of Paris. Their drive gathered momentum under the leadership of the Pan-Slavs, who, as political heirs of the Slavophils, preached the collaboration of all Slavic na-

191

tions, the common interests of all Orthodox peoples, and the "great civilizatory mission" of the tsarist empire.

EXPANSIONIST PAN-SLAVISM. The chauvinistic ideology of the Pan-Slavs went back to the seventeenth century when a Croatian, Krizhanic, had advocated the unity of all Slav peoples. The German Herder, with his interest in, and respect for, Slavic folk traditions, and the Czechs Kollar and Palacky in the nineteenth century had contributed further to the idea; but not until the revolutionary year 1848 had it taken on a practical political meaning. A first Pan-Slav Congress was held in Prague, and although it found little support from the Russian authorities, the movement grew. A second Congress followed in 1867 in Moscow under the direction of the Russian Slavophil Pogodin, who, in extravagant lyrical pronouncements, had extolled the role and superiority of the Russian world. Dostoyevsky, Danilevsky, and Ignatiev indirectly or directly contributed to the Pan-Slav program. The government, out of caution, remained averse to the exaggerated expansionist demands of the Pan-Slavs, their anti-British and anti-German propaganda, their denunciations of the "competitive and oppressive" system of the West, and their bellicose insistence on the "salvation of all Slavic brethren from oppression."

CONCLUSION OF THREE EMPERORS' LEAGUE. Behind the profession of lofty Pan-Slav aims stood the practical desire for the possession of Constantinople. The Russians realized, however, that no possibility existed for taking the city against the concerted opposition of the European powers. They therefore made a number of compromises, the most important of which consisted in the renewal of good relations with the Austrian empire. So long as Russia and Austria had been confronted by a strong Turkish power threatening the existence of both, they had found collaboration expedient; but when the Turkish danger subsided and Austrian and Russian spheres in the Balkans moved closer together, tension arose, increasing in proportion to the growing ethnic and religious aspirations of Slavophilism. These aspirations ran counter to Austria's plans for aggrandizement and her resolve not to permit the emergence of a strong Slavic power which, like the old Ottoman empire, could threaten her from the rear. Now, however, a reconcilation of Russian and Austrian aims was sought; and a willing hand was lent by Bismarck, chancellor of Germany, who was anxious to strengthen his newly created empire through friendship with his eastern neighbor. Under his auspices, a "Three Emperors' League" was formed in 1872, based on the analogous monarchic structure of Russia, Austria, and Germany.

RESURGENCE OF THE BALKAN PROBLEM. The alliance was never wholehearted: Austrian and Russian policies in the Balkans remained opposed despite formal co-ordination, and Germany's feelings were alienated when in 1875 Gorchakov, fancying himself in the role of a European arbiter, interfered in Franco-German relations. Nevertheless, the alliance survived and enabled Russia to pursue further her Balkan plans. She had not long to wait for a propitious moment. In 1875 and 1876 continued Turkish oppression led to revolts in Bosnia, Herzegovina, and Bulgaria. Promptly Russia and Austria dispatched an ultimatum to the Sultan, known as the "Andrassy Note," and—Germany, France, and England concurring—demanded from him long overdue reforms in favor of the Christian states in the Balkans. The Turks made promises but took no action, and the revolts spread. In 1876 Serbia and Montenegro declared war against Turkey.

The Turkish War. This situation gave Russia the sought-for opportunity to resume her Near Eastern drive. After assuring herself of Austria's acquiescence by a convention (at Reichstadt) and by subsequent agreements, which set aside Bosnia as Austria's and Bessarabia as Russia's sphere of influence, she actively intervened with the Sultan on behalf of the revolting Balkan nations. The Pan-Slav Ignatiev was sent to Constantinople where he took up the cause of Serbia and Montenegro, demanded the cessation of Turkish oppression, insisted on the introduction of reforms which tended to break up the Turkish empire, and thus tried to re-establish Russian hegemony in the Balkans. In vain did England sponsor an international conference in order to prevent the Russians from solving the Near Eastern problem in their own way. The negotiations brought no result, and Russia declared war on Turkey in April, 1877. Despite a valiant defense of the fortress of Plevna by the Turks and the persistent incompetence of Russia's military and administrative leaders, the tsarist army, greatly outnumbering the enemy, eventually reached the gates of Constantinople.

PEACE OF SAN STEPHANO. At this point the advance was halted by the decision of the Russian general staff not to risk a long, costly, and possibly unsuccessful assault on the Turkish capital and by the action of the British, whose fleet entered the Marmara Sea and threatened to fulfill Turkish hopes for intervention. The Russians decided to conclude peace (San Stephano, 1878). They forced Turkey to recognize the independence of the Slavic nations in the Balkans, created—under their own protectorate—a large autonomous state of Bulgaria with a port on the Aegean Sea, and recovered Batum and Kars. By also demanding recognition of additional rights for Christians within the Turkish empire, they intended to secure permanent domination of Turkish affairs.

CONGRESS OF BERLIN. This Russian solution of the Balkan problem might have brought a beneficial and durable settlement; but in going beyond the Reichstadt Agreement it antagonized the Austrians, who found their own Balkan plans menaced; and, more important, it revived the familiar fears in London. Disregarding the inefficiency and barbarity of Turkish rule, England demanded, under threat of war, a revision of the Treaty of San Stephano; and the Russians found themselves in no position to oppose her. After separate negotiations in Vienna and London, an international congress for the settlement of the Eastern problem was convened in 1878 in Berlin. Bismarck presided as mediator and "honest broker"; Disraeli represented England and Gorchakov, Russia—the latter being a rather unfortunate choice, for he was old, deaf, and vain, and his claim of "having saved European peace" in 1875 had cost him the friendship of the Iron Chancellor. At the Congress, the British did not yield; determined to make war rather than allow the execution of the Treaty of San Stephano, they found support from Bismarck who, faced by the alternative of a European conflict, resolved to support their demands. The Russians were forced to rescind the Treaty of San Stephano, to consent to a radical reduction of the territory assigned by them to Bulgaria, and to forego access to the Aegean Sea by means of a Bulgarian port. The border lines of the Christian states, whose independence was recognized, were redrawn—unsatisfactorily for them and for Russia. The Straits were once more closed to all non-Turkish warships; and the cession of the port of Batum to Russia was made dependent upon its complete demilitarization.

RAPPROCHEMENT WITH FRANCE

The Congress of Berlin marked a turning point in Russian external relations. It exposed the unreliability of any power combination in which the Russian and the Austrian empires were partners; it proved England's resolve to impede Russian access to the Mediterranean even at the cost of war; it divulged Germany's primary concern with friendly relations with Austria and England; and it demonstrated France's inability to help Russia within the existing system. Russia therefore devoted the ensuing thirty years to attempts to build up a different, more reliable alliance system and to temporize in questions referring to Turkey and the Straits.

Reinsurance Treaty. The threatening reorientation of Russia's foreign policy caused grave misgivings in Germany. Bismarck considered friendship with the Slavic neighbor "the pivot" of German security and exerted himself to the utmost to have the Three Emperors' League renewed, for it had lapsed at the time of the Congress of Berlin. Afraid of any combination of hostile powers such as had threatened Frederick the Great when Russia was allied with Austria and France during the Seven Years' War, he sought to tie together again the interests of the three empires. In 1881, he finally succeeded in overcoming Russian resentments remaining from the days of the Congress of Berlin and in preventing a Russian-French *rapprochement,* and the League was renewed. Moreover, in order to avoid new friction, Bismarck endeavored to direct Russian attention to tasks and opportunities in Asia. But the Balkan problem could not be subdued. In 1885 troubles flared up in Bulgaria and again proved the incompatibility of Russian and Austrian plans with regard to the Balkans. Not even Bismarck's skill, prestige, and acknowledged peaceableness could restore harmony among the three empires. The League expired, and in 1887 Bismarck found himself forced to renounce the idea of renewing it. He had to confine himself to preserving friendship with Russia through a separate secret alliance. This so-called "Reinsurance Treaty," defensive in intent, served the cause of understanding only briefly; for in 1890 Bismarck was forced to resign, and without his support the Reinsurance Treaty was allowed to lapse. Once more isolated, Russia this time turned to France.

Entente with France. Friendly relations between Russia and France had existed for some time and had been fortified by French loans to Russia after Germany, because of political disappointments, had closed her money markets to Russia. Upon the lapse of the Reinsurance Treaty in August, 1890, therefore, an official political agreement was made, and an exchange of diplomatic and military courtesies followed. In August, 1891, despite the Tsar's reluctance and against the protests of liberal and socialistic-minded quarters in France which recognized the threat to peace, an entente was established. It provided for consultation in international questions and mutual support in case of war. In the following year France, envisaging difficulties with both Germany and England, supplemented it by a military convention of aggressive character, and in 1895 and 1896 the treaties were disclosed to the world. Russia gained economically, for she received further loans of almost one billion dollars which were fundamental to her progress on the road to Westernization and industrialization. Politically, the balance was less favorable. On the one hand, Russia could use France as a counterweight and emancipate herself from dependence upon the central powers. On the other, she became subservient to chauvinistic French interests and found herself launched on an anti-German policy which, contrary to her growing trade interests, would lead to a long-drawn-out tariff war with Germany. She also saw the security of her western border imperiled and continued to be thwarted in her Near Eastern plans.

Relations with Other Powers. Several vain attempts were made to escape this political bondage without losing access to the French money market. In 1899 a conference was held at The Hague at Tsar Nicholas' suggestion in an endeavor to halt the armament race and ease the financial burden on Russia. In 1905 an agreement was signed at Björkö by which the Tsar and Emperor William II tried to revive the former friendship between their two countries; in 1907 a second peace conference was held at The Hague; and in 1908 a new convention was entered into with Austria at Buchlau, dividing the spheres of interest in the Balkans and laying a basis for a new advance on Constantinople. But the Hague peace conferences failed to promote the cause of disarmament and understanding; the Björkö negotiations were disavowed and blocked by both Russia's and Germany's foreign ministers—the one out of consideration for

France, the other for Austria. The Buchlau bargain, in fact, turned out to the unilateral advantage of the Austrian empire. Whereas Russia encountered an insurmountable obstacle in England when trying to secure her share of the deal, the Austrians, to the utmost indignation of Russia, quickly grabbed the parts allotted them.

Thus, after one hundred years of diplomacy, the Russians found themselves still hopelessly stalled in the pursuance of their primary aim—the seizure of Constantinople. England still blocked the free exit from the Black Sea; Austria frustrated Russian Balkan schemes; Germany, whose friendship had been forsaken and who consistently supported Austria, threatened the western border; and France dragged Russia into Western European problems alien to the needs of the tsarist empire. Combined with internal difficulties, the whole situation boded ill for Russia.

PROBLEMS

1. Discuss the relations between Germany and Russia, 1870–1905.
2. Trace the causes for the Franco-Russian alliance of the 1890's.
3. Discuss the antagonism between Russia and Austria, 1870–1905.

30

RUSSIA AND THE UNITED
STATES

Significant Dates

RELATIONS UP TO THE AMERICAN
CIVIL WAR

Russia and the Birth of the United States. It is of special interest to survey separately the relations between the United States and Russia. That the revolutionary foundation of a new commonwealth in opposition to its legitimate suzerain would find the approval of autocratic Tsarina Catherine, who ruled Russia during the American War of Independence, could hardly be expected. Yet, disagreements with England over the question of neutral rights on the seas forced Catherine to assume a friendly attitude towards the United States.

Opening of Official Relations. The first hopes of the new United States concerned recognition of American independence, initiation of official relations, and regulation of commercial inter-

198

course. As early as 1780, Francis Dana was sent by the Continental Congress on a mission to Russia, and in the last few years of the eighteenth century, Rufus King was commissioned to carry on negotiations. But in neither case, despite the unremitting efforts of the United States, was recognition extended by Russia. More than a quarter of a century elapsed before official relations were opened in 1809, in the midst of the Napoleonic era. At that time a minister to St. Petersburg was appointed in the person of John Quincy Adams, and Russia named Count Pahlen for the post in Washington; A. Dashkov was made chargé d'affaires; and consulates were established in both countries.

Napoleonic Period. The results of Adams' mission were disappointing; a commercial treaty could not be concluded, for Russia insisted on political concessions as well as economic arrangements. Anxious though she was, because of Napoleon's Continental system, to replace the English with American carrying trade, she insisted on a formal acknowledgement of her claims in North America (which extended, territorially, from Alaska to the Columbia River and to trading posts even farther south). Economically, recognition of Russian trade monopolies there was demanded. The prolonged negotiations were broken off in 1812 when Napoleon attacked Russia and forced the Tsar into an alliance with England, against whom the United States in that very year went to war. To bring the contradictory situation to an end, Russia offered her mediation between the United States and England. This proposal was anxiously accepted by the Americans; envoys were immediately dispatched, but the British refused to negotiate and the Americans were obliged to return empty-handed. Nevertheless, friendly contact was maintained with Russia, which in 1814 again was asked to sponsor peace with England. Yet, even after the signing of the Treaty of Ghent, the urgently desired commercial treaty with Russia was not concluded because political demands still stood in the way. Claims were brought forward by Russia not only on territory in America south to 51° north latitude, but also on the entire northern Pacific Ocean, which Russia wished to declare a mare clausum; and these claims were emphasized by the renewal of the Russian-American Company, which had been founded by Paul I with the Tsar himself as a stockholder. Furthermore, no recognition was to be extended by the United States to the revolting Spanish colonies in South America.

Political Accord. The South American issue was eventually eliminated, first by United States recognition of Colombia in 1822 and then definitely by President Monroe's message to Congress on December 2, 1823. But Russian demands on the northwest coast remained, and not until the next year was a political settlement reached. Since the returns from the commercial investments in their American colonies were small and did not warrant a great military outlay for protection, the Russians finally declared themselves ready to conclude a treaty. Latitude 54°40′N. was recognized as the southern border of Russian America, and the United States undertook to refrain from trade with Russian settlements there.

Commercial Treaty. Once political accord was reached, efforts for a trade agreement were resumed. After several attempts, yet not before the abrogation of the "Tariff of Abominations" in 1832, the long-delayed commercial treaty was concluded. Its immediate importance was small, for at the time Russo-American trade did not exceed one million dollars, of which Russian exports, mainly in hemp and iron, comprised about three-quarters; but the expectations of southern planters for increased cotton exports to Russia warranted the effort.

Dissatisfaction with Political Accord. Soon the commercial treaty began to overshadow the political agreement of 1824, and when in 1834 the ten-year period stipulated for the latter had passed, it was not renewed. During its course, Americans had continued to smuggle goods into Russian settlements on the West Coast; they had violated the stipulation banning shipments of munitions, arms, and liquor to the Indians; they had insisted on a different interpretation of Russian rights in the zone down to latitude 54°40′N., Russia maintaining her right of jurisdiction, the United States allowing only that of settlement. Little chance for improvement existed; and, dissatisfied, Russia gradually lost interest in her American possessions. Some of these were eventually leased to the British Hudson's Bay Company; others were sold; and after the gold rush of 1848 had thoroughly altered the balance of power on the Pacific coast, Russia's colonial activities were increasingly directed to the vast spaces in Siberia.

Russian Weakness in America. The advent of the Crimean War further modified Russia's attitude. Alaska, lying open to seizure by England, would certainly have fallen to the enemy had not the British preferred an agreement with Russia to refrain from extending the theater of war to North America. For they realized that public opinion in the United States favored Russia and would never permit expansion of British rule contrary to the Monroe Doctrine. But Russia could not indefinitely rely on such a favorable constellation; indeed, hardly was the Crimean War over when new threats to Alaska arose. In 1863 a Polish uprising occurred, and the Tsar feared that it would be used as a pretext for a new attack by England and France. This time the Russian-American possessions would be unprotected, for the United States was engaged in a civil war and the Russian fleet lacked appropriate support, coaling stations, and harbor facilities in the Pacific. Considerations of this kind led to the dispatch of the Russian Pacific fleet to the United States. This measure was popularly interpreted as an act of good will towards the abolitionist North (Russia had abolished serfdom two years earlier), but it was to serve also as a safety measure for the Russian ships which, anchored in a neutral port, could hope for protection against possible British raiders.

RELATIONS SINCE THE AMERICAN CIVIL WAR

Sale of Alaska. The recurring threats to Alaska caused the Russian government to consider seriously liquidation of Russian-American ventures and the sale of all possessions there. But objections to such a program were raised. Some feared a disturbance of the balance of power in the Pacific area and the possible emergence of the United States as a strong rival; others anticipated an imperialistic policy in the United States, which, once in possession of Alaska, might be desirous of extending its influence to the Asiatic continent. Again others considered the commercial disadvantages of selling Alaska, realizing its potential wealth, its use within the world-communication system, and its importance for shipping and telegraph lines. However, advocates pointed out that the sale of the colony would bring a substantial profit and that Russia should secure this rather than incur new expenses for defense which might yet prove inadequate. They felt that in view of vast migration of Americans to their West Coast and the resulting pressure, the continued possession of Alaska would disturb relations with the United States, as it had before; and they demonstrated that in the past the economic benefits had been disappointing. Furs were exhausted; little gold had been discovered; and, because profits could not be realized, the Russian-American Company itself had allowed its charter to expire in 1861. It was also feared that money invested in Alaska would divert attention from more profitable schemes nearer home. After full consideration, the government decided in 1867 to sell Alaska for $7,200,000—a small sum as measured by present standards, but at that time considered adequate by Russians and exorbitant by Americans.

Conflict of Interests. After the sale, friendly relations prevailed until the death of Alexander II. But with the accession of Alexander III, and more so when Nicholas II came to the throne, public opinion in America altered. Persecution of Jews and failure to introduce a constitutional system in Russia formed the ideological background for growing tension, and by 1903 ideas of official protests were entertained by the United States. Practical differences, however, played an equal, though never avowed, role. Imperialism on both sides of the ocean had brought American and Russian spheres close together in the Pacific area. Russia had established herself in Vladivostok, Manchuria, Sakhalin, and the Kurils, and the United States had penetrated beyond Alaska to Hawaii and the Philippines. Disturbances in China had opened the way for American commercial expansion, and an "open-door policy" was proclaimed which conflicted with monopolistic Russian penetration of the Chinese empire. The Boxer Rebellion and American insistence on the maintenance of China's *status quo* increased the tension. When the Russo-Japanese War broke out, the sympathies of the United States as well as her financial support went to the Japanese; and this aroused the bitter resentment of Russia. But fears of Japanese hegemony—after Japan's surprising victories—put an end to anti-Russian agitation and prompted Theodore Roosevelt to offer his mediation to the belligerents. The Peace of Portsmouth and subsequent steps towards constitutional government in Russia did much to bring about a gradual reversal of popular feelings. Russia's delegate, Count Witte, helped to spread a favorable opinion, convincing American press representatives as well as influential American Jews of future improvements within the tsarist empire.

Thus, revived hopes for improved domestic conditions in Russia coupled with comparative unconcern regarding her external policies prevailed in America. But new difficulties arose once more from the Jewish question when Russia subjected naturalized American Jews of Russian origin, who were visiting Russia on business, to restrictions imposed on them before their naturalization. Under pressure primarily from the New York community, and despite steadily improving trade figures, the trade treaty of 1832 was unilaterally abrogated by the United States in December, 1911. Thereafter relations remained cool, and not until after the overthrow of the tsarist government and upon America's entrance into the First World War were correct relations reestablished.

PROBLEMS

1. Discuss the difficulties experienced by the United States with Russia during the first fifty years after gaining independence.
2. Discuss the factors prompting Russia to sell Alaska.
3. Describe the causes of discord between the two countries at the turn of the century.

31

EXPANSION IN ASIA

Significant Dates

Annexation of Georgia 1813
Annexation of Amur Region 1854
Founding of Vladivostok 1860
Treaty of Peking 1860
Conquest of Central Asia 1865–1881
Occupation of Merv 1884

THE "FRONTIER"

Like the westward movement in America, the eastward expansion of Russia bears witness to the historical hunger of all agricultural peoples for more land. There, as in the United States, the movement was spasmodic. All fields of human endeavor were touched, so that several separate "frontiers"—political, agricultural, economic, and cultural—can be discerned, each progressing eastward and southward, one following the other.

Advance of Frontier. The changes of the political frontier may be surveyed in four stages: (1) from 1580 to 1650, expansion from the Urals to the Pacific, in a general northeastwardly direction, followed by a hundred years of intensive exploration; (2) from 1785 to 1830, conquest of the lands between the Black and Caspian seas; (3) from 1850 to 1860, annexation of the Amur River region and penetration through Manchuria, followed by economic exploitation; (4) from 1865 to 1885, incorporation of Transcaspia and Turkestan, and penetration of central Asia.

CAUCASUS

Annexation. The first stage, which had brought the great expeditions and explorations of the famous foreign academicians Bering, Gmelin, and Pallas, ended with the mapping of the confines of Siberia in the second half of the eighteenth century. The second stage, which meant a shift of direction, consisted of an unrelenting struggle for possession of the area between the Black and Caspian seas. This region was of high value because it included the strategic passes and roads through and around the Caucasus range and possessed the economic advantage of considerable mineral wealth, particularly oil. Although inhabited by different nationalities—Armenians and Georgians—the territory belonged geographically and politically to Persia and Turkey. Peter the Great in his time secured some of the Persian sectors in the eastern Caucasus region, but under his successors these had to be relinquished. During the reign of Catherine II, encroachments were made on the Turkish parts and culminated in the submission of local princes in Georgia; but no definite Russian suzerainty was established. Under Paul I, further expeditions and negotiations were undertaken; yet only during Alexander I's rule, in 1813, was the full incorporation of Georgia, including Baku, accomplished. The struggle for the surrounding land went on for another decade or more. It was not until the Treaty of Adrianople (1829) that Russia could consider all of the Caucasus as hers, together with the lands extending south to the strategic town of Erivan.

FAR EAST

Period of Neglect. The third stage of Russian movement eastward comprised expansion beyond Siberia. Until the nineteenth century, Russian progress there had been slow. After the exploration of the country, attention had been centered less on its exploitation and expansion than on discoveries in other regions. A number of expeditions were undertaken, such as that around the world in 1803, another to explore the coast of America in 1815, and an antarctic expedition in 1819 to 1821, while in Siberia proper the government confined itself to administrative reforms. According to plans drawn by Speransky the region was divided into two governor-generalships, and some attention was paid to the settling of the land.

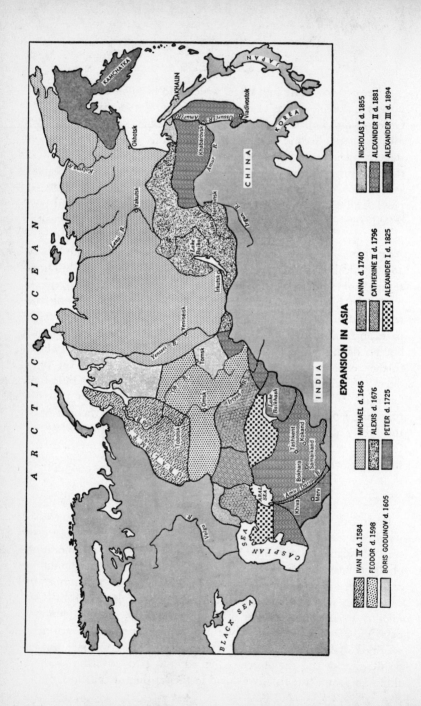

EXPANSION IN ASIA

IVAN IV d. 1584

FEODOR d. 1598

BORIS GODUNOV d. 1605

MICHAEL d. 1645

ALEXIS d. 1676

PETER d. 1725

ANNA d. 1740

CATHERINE II d. 1796

ALEXANDER I d. 1825

NICHOLAS I d. 1855

ALEXANDER II d. 1881

ALEXANDER III d. 1894

Revived Interest. In the middle of the nineteenth century, when England's Opium War against China had divulged the weakness of the Chinese empire, Russian expansionist policies in Asia —slowed down ever since the Treaty of Nerchinsk in 1689—were resumed. A commission was set up to investigate economic opportunities in the Chinese border areas and particularly in the region of the Amur River. In former times, the chief trading objects had consisted of gold, rhubarb, silk, damask, and tea, which were exchanged for Russian furs; and the tsarist government had, for over a century, reserved for itself a monopoly in these commodities and had thereby stifled connections with China. Now, however, new entrepreneurial forces came to the fore, and these, grown in a laissez faire atmosphere, represented new economic interests, such as mining, fishing, and private trade. The committee reported about the changed conditions and, prompted by it and by new nationalistic trends, the government undertook the second step. In 1847 it appointed N. Muraviëv governor-general of eastern Siberia. His initiative and energy were called upon to change the existing policy of passivity. Under his leadership, Russians infiltrated into the Amur region and, contrary to the stipulations of Nerchinsk, founded a city, Nicholaevsk, on the Amur estuary. Soon thereafter the island of Sakhalin and territory in Korea were occupied, and in 1853 Alexandrovsk was built on the De Castries Bay. Peasants were settled in the Amur region and, for the sake of defense, organized as Cossacks; and an "Amur Company" for promotion of Russian interests was founded.

Annexation of Amur Region. The Crimean War, which broke out in 1854, further stimulated these activities, for in view of the imminence of a Franco-English attack in the Far East, Muraviëv was forced to strengthen and expand Russia's hold. Chinese protests notwithstanding, he took possession of the whole course of the Amur. Specially built steamships were sent down the river to its mouth to protect and provision the new settlements and, despite the unhealthy climate, thousands of colonists were assigned to the region of the Amur's estuary. Chinese immigrants were attracted, and solid fortifications to protect against possible landings of the enemy were erected.

Crimean War. In the same year, 1854, a combined Franco-English fleet opened hostilities by attacking the fortress of Petro-

pavlovsk in Kamchatka. Despite the seizure no advantage was
gained, and in 1855 the British and French shifted the scene of
action southward in an attempt to destroy Russia's Far Eastern fleet.
They succeeded in blockading the Russians in what they took for a
bay west of Sakhalin; but in reality, this bay was an open waterway
through which the Russian fleet sailed unharmed while its enemies
lay in wait at the southern entrance. In the following year, the
Treaty of Paris put an end to the futile campaign.

Treaty of Peking. After the Crimean War, in 1858, the annexation of the Amur region was legalized by a treaty with China.
Pressed by British infringements in the south and threatened by
Russia in the north, the Chinese agreed, through the Convention of
Aigun, to the cession of the left bank of the Amur and, through the
Treaty of Tientsin, to commercial privileges for Russia not unlike
those granted earlier to England. Two years later, when the British
and French occupied Peking in order to put down a Chinese independence movement, the Russians extended their hold and founded
Vladivostok on Chinese territory. In the same year, 1860, they also
made a new treaty at Peking—whereby they acquired both sides of
the Amur estuary in addition to all the country south to Vladivostok. China was forced to agree to a new border along the Ussuri
River and to economic and diplomatic concessions. In addition, the
Russo-Chinese border in central Asia, in Turkestan, was subjected
to a revision; and it was to this latter region that Russia, from 1860
on, began to shift her attention.

CENTRAL ASIA

Early Failures. Ever since the early eighteenth century, the
country lying east of the Caspian Sea had attracted Russian interest.
During the rule of Peter's niece, Anna, local princes in the regions
of the storied cities of Khiva and Bokhara had pledged their submission to the great neighbor. But not until the following century
did political and economic reasons call for steps beyond formal submission. Only then did imperialism, missionary spirit, industrialization, and the attendant race for raw materials and markets
revive the desire for the neglected region. For, despite its deserts and
mountains, Turkestan was rich in hemp, tobacco, silkworms, and
cattle, and it possessed unexploited subsoil wealth. Moreover, Khiva

was famed for its gold mines, its horticultural opportunities, and its horse-breeding areas. In 1834 Russian domination was therefore extended east of the Caspian Sea, and five years later an expedition against Khiva was undertaken. Unprepared for the extremely rigorous climate, it came to a disastrous end, but not without alarming the English, who saw an additional sphere of conflict added to the many already existent in areas situated between their possessions and lifelines and those of Russia.

Conquests. For two decades after the failure of the Khiva expedition, no further attempts were made by Russia; the humiliation of the Crimean War, however, released a new urge to resume activities in central Asia. This prestige motive was coupled with a realization of the strategic need for securing the southern borders of Siberia against possible British inroads and for eliminating the pillaging attacks of roving tribes. Furthermore, the demand for cotton by the textile mills of Moscow and Narva grew steadily, and it seemed possible to partially satisfy it with the products of central Asia. A few enterprising and energetic governors, such as General Kaufmann, were aware of these trends, and a period of rapid and highly successful expansionist activity was initiated by them. In 1865 Tashkent was seized; in 1866 Bokhara was invaded and in 1868 ancient imperial Samarkand fell; in 1873, after great losses, Khiva was taken; and in 1876 Kokand was occupied. The inhabitants, many of them Mohammedans, were brutally subjected, and thousands fled across the Chinese border. Turkestan itself was constituted a governor-generalship. In 1881 Geok-Tepe was stormed, and under the leadership of the harsh governor-general of Transcaspia, General Skobelev, Turkomania was added to previous conquests.

Conflict with England. Imperialism triumphed. With increased misgivings the English watched the steady approach of Russia toward India. Determined not to yield, they emphasized their own aspirations and determination; they had their queen crowned "Empress of India"; they occupied Baluchistan; and they made wars and treaties with Afghanistan. Yet, the Russian drive advanced inexorably: in 1884 Merv submitted to Russia, opening the road to Herat, gateway to India. Remembering the days when Persia, acting for Russia, had taken possession of Herat in 1856, the British now decided to put a definite stop to the Russian advance; they negotiated a treaty delineating the northern frontier of Afghanistan, beyond which the Russians were not to go.

Economic Penetration.   This enforced pause in the advance of the Russians turned out to their own advantage, for instead of wasting their strength by further expansion, which would have served none but some private banking and trading interests, they began to consolidate their rule in the conquered areas. They strengthened military installations, promoted cultural interests, and opened the country by constructing railways. The economy of the occupied territory was remodeled, new markets were created, and new products, especially cotton, were grown. Despite great difficulties, the trans-Caspian railway line in 1888 was continued to Samarkand and later to Orenburg and Tashkent; and strategic stations and ports were built at the crossroads of the tradeways. The whole area was made part of the economic, political, and strategic structure of the empire. Ultimately—though only in postrevolutionary times—the civilization of the West and of European Russia reached the native populations of central Asia.

Persia.   After Russia's position had been consolidated in Turkestan, her influence was spread further. Particular attention was paid to Persia. The trans-Caspian and Transcaucasian lines were extended to the borders of that country and a number of concessions were gained. Russia was granted the right to install telegraph service in Persia, to organize steamship companies, to veto foreign railroad construction, to build up fisheries, and to found a bank for financing imports from Russia. A special hold over Persia's internal affairs was gained by receiving, as a guarantee for Russian loans, the privilege of supervising the country's income from customs duties. Economic relations became very lively: Russia exported sugar, oil, and textile goods, and imported cotton, fruits, opium, rice, and fish, so that by 1914 the total value of trade exceeded sixty million dollars.

PROBLEMS

1. Trace the regions of chief expansionist interest of Russia in Asia.
2. Discuss the political and strategic significance of Russian expansion in Asia.
3. Discuss the economic advantages derived for Russia from Asiatic expansion.

32

RUSSO-JAPANESE RIVALRY

Significant Dates

Trans-Siberian Railroad	1891–1903
Leasing of Port Arthur	1898
Russo-Japanese War	1904–1905
Capitulation of Port Arthur	1905
Naval Battle of Tsushima	1905
Peace of Portsmouth	1905

TRANS-SIBERIAN RAILROAD

Railroad Planning. Important though the results of railroad building and economic penetration of central Asia turned out to be, the most ambitious commercial scheme of Russia in the second half of the nineteenth century concerned Siberia and the Far East. From approximately 1850, plans for railroad connections there had been proposed for strategic, economic, and cultural reasons. Regardless of its original efficiency, the existing mail and river transport system, which extended over thousands of miles, was no longer adequate; not even the steamship lines, operating since about 1840, sufficed to provide for the growing population and the demands of the Far Eastern military forces. It was, therefore, first proposed to supplement the steamboat service by railroads which were to connect the main river network; and later, a through line extending from the Urals to the Pacific was suggested. As in the United States, the advantages of a northern, a central, or a southern route were for a long time vainly debated, while an attempt was made to gauge also the implications of the construction as such. Some feared undesirable economic, social, and international repercussions; conversely, others considered these unimportant in comparison with the railroad's strategic and commercial value.

Construction of Trans-Siberian Railroad. No practical step was undertaken until 1884, when a line was constructed across the Ural range connecting the Volga and the Ob basin and servicing the mining districts in between. Although this railroad eventually formed no part of the trans-Siberian system, which was to run to Irkutsk between 53° and 55° north latitude, it served to stimulate final planning. In 1891 actual work on the main line was begun and simultaneously carried on in different sections, reaching Irkutsk in 1898. Because of climate and expense, the last section—from Irkutsk to Vladivostok—presented the greatest difficulties. Eventually, Chinese permission was given to lay track through Manchuria; and in 1903 the trans-Siberian railroad, extending five and a half thousand miles to the shores of the Pacific Ocean, was completed. Constituting at first a drain on the resources of the government, it began to show profits from the year 1913 on; and only the First World War interrupted further progress.

Demographic Consequences. As in the United States, the railroad thoroughly transformed the country. Economic growth was stimulated, and a vast influx of settlers began. In 1861, after almost three hundred years of occupation, Siberia had contained no more than five million inhabitants; and during the thirty-year period following emancipation of the serfs, despite offers of free land and exemption from military service, immigration had accounted for little more than half a million colonists. In contrast to this record, the twenty years following the start of the railway project saw an influx of approximately four million additional settlers. Before the outbreak of World War I, more than eleven million people inhabited the country, and great opportunties existed for many millions more.

Political Consequences. Politically, the railroad changed the picture by upsetting the balance of power in the Far East, affecting English as well as United States interests, Japanese aspirations, and Chinese conditions. In view of China's impotence and America's continentalism, counteraction was left to the initiative of the British and the Japanese. Both were determined to halt Russia's further advance and to prevent any scheme for establishing a hegemony on the Pacific coast. England had witnessed Russia's approach in the Near East to the Straits of Constantinople, in the Caucasus region to Persia, in central Asia to Afghanistan; she had seen the tsarist empire extend its feelers into Tibet and toward distant colonial prizes: Siam and Abyssinia. She now feared the emergence of additional spheres of conflict and so seized the opportunity to check Russia through collaboration with Japan.

RUSSO-JAPANESE WAR

Russo-Japanese Relations before 1900. Japan had entered into relations with Russia in 1855, but Muraviëv's occupation of Sakhalin had quickly brought dissensions. Europeans had reached Sakhalin in 1649, but since it held little attraction for them, it had formed an unchallenged field of activity for the Chinese and also, from about 1785, for the Japanese. Russia did not put forward claims until 1807, and Muraviëv's occupation of the island was the first practical evidence of her interest. The resulting conflict with Japan was not settled until 1867, when a convention stipulated common rights for Russia and Japan. This agreement, naturally of no permanence, was terminated in 1875, when Japan ceded her rights in Sakhalin to Russia in exchange for the Kuril Islands. Twenty years later difficulties again arose when Japan, jealous of Russian railroad construction and penetration into Chinese territory, attacked China, defeated her, and wrested from her vast territorial and commercial concessions. Russia, in conjunction with other European powers which were interested in the independence of a weak and exploitable China, forced Japan to relinquish a part of her spoils. Following the example of various Western powers which had imposed trade concessions and annexed harbors from impotent China, Russia secured in 1898—to the great dismay of Japan—a twenty-five-year lease of the very harbor, strategic Port Arthur, from which Japan had just been forced to withdraw. The Russo-Japanese tension came to a climax during the Boxer Rebellion in 1900, when Russia extended her sphere by occupying Mukden and, instead of evacuating it after the suppression of the Boxers, made it an important railroad center and a flourishing commercial town.

Outbreak of War. Japan was thus deprived of access to a region she considered important for her strategic security, vital for her surplus population, and necessary as a market for her coal and cotton exports and as a source for needed wheat, rice, and beans. Moreover, Japan found herself thwarted in Korea where her aims had led to strife with Russia. She also saw Russia gain steadily increasing dominance over China through the establishment of banks, the granting of loans, and, for the sake of guaranteeing interest payments on these loans, the installation of Russian supervisors of the Chinese customs office. In order to retrieve the lost ground, Japan therefore looked for allies and found unexpected support in England. In 1902 the two nations entered into a formal alliance. Thus backed, Japan started negotiations for Russian withdrawal from Manchuria; and as these did not bring results, she swiftly struck at Russia in 1904. The attack not only served Japanese interests, but put Japan in the role of an agent for various European powers: for France, which desired to see Russia more dependent upon her alliance; for Austria, which wanted the Tsar's attention diverted from the Balkans; and for England, which was determined to halt Russian progress in the Far East.

Peace of Portsmouth. The war itself turned out disastrously for the Russians. Although they won many an important battle and although within a year the Japanese were in serious financial straits, the victory was Japan's. Port Arthur was lost; and in the great naval battle of Tsushima the Russian Baltic fleet, after a long cruise around Africa, was virtually annihilated. Because it underestimated Japanese strength, possessed weak communication lines, conducted a war from a distance of thousands of miles, and was hindered by hostile public opinion at home and abroad, the Russian government found itself forced in mid-1905 to accept the mediation of Theodore Roosevelt and to enter into peace negotiations. Owing to the ability of Russia's plenipotentiary, Count Witte, and his shrewd estimate of Japan's financial weakness and material exhaustion, and as a result of American and English fears lest Japan emerge a more potent power on the Pacific than they desired her to be, the peace turned out to be less harsh for Russia than anticipated. It was concluded at Portsmouth, New Hampshire. It stipulated that the long-promised military evacuation of Manchuria was to be carried out forthright; that Port Arthur and half of Sakhalin were to be surrendered; that fishing rights in Russian waters were to be granted to the Japanese and their special interests in Korea recognized. But no indemnity was exacted from Russia, nor was she compelled to relinquish her railway line through Manchuria.

Thus ended, for the time being, the Russian advance in the Far East.

PROBLEMS

1. Discuss the political significance of the trans-Siberian railroad.
2. Trace the relationship of Russia and Japan until 1904.
3. Discuss the interests of the great powers in the outcome of the Russo-Japanese War.

33

REVOLUTION OF 1905

Significant Dates
Reign of Alexander III 1881–1894
Reign of Nicholas II   1894–1917
October Revolution 1905
First Duma 1906

The war with Japan released a long-threatened revolution in Russia. Because of the government's failure to adjust itself to the changing conditions produced by rapid industrialization, social legislation and political growth had been constantly endangered. In 1894 Alexander III's son, Nicholas II (1894–1917), last of the Romanov rulers, had come to the throne. He may have been personally engaging, well-intentioned, and devoted to his duty, but he was also narrow-minded, autocratic, and politically weak and inconsistent. His inability contributed to the misery of the people, to revolution, to war, and to the end of his dynasty.

REIGN OF NICHOLAS II

During the first decade of Nicholas' reign, an attempt was made to continue the paternalistic course set by Alexander III. The dominant figures in this period were Pobedonostzev, who exercised his enormous influence over the Tsar to prevent concessions to liberalism, and Count Sergei Witte, appointed in 1892 by Nicholas' father to the post of Minister of Finance.

216

Introduction of Modern Economy. Witte, a Westernized statesman of considerable ability, who was politically a conservative but economically a progressive, never found himself in the good graces of the Tsar or in the favor of the people. Ruthlessly efficient, he made, nevertheless, outstanding contributions. He concluded trade treaties, granted subsidies for industries, and introduced protective tariffs; he had railroads built, secured loans from abroad, introduced the gold standard, and developed new industrial centers, such as the rich Donets basin.

INDUSTRIAL PROGRESS. Although per capita production lagged considerably behind Western European countries in the thirty years before World War I, Russian coal output climbed more than tenfold and iron production was twice tripled, so that Russia became the third largest producer of these materials in the world. Some of the largest factories of Europe were founded near Moscow and Narva, and the number of spindles in the textile mills was increased to nine million. Russia rapidly climbed to fourth place among the world's textile producers. Large crops of cotton were grown in newly acquired regions of central Asia, and Russia was able to free herself by more than 50 per cent from her dependence on foreign, mainly American, cotton imports. Oil production in the Baku region was doubled; platinum production provided nine-tenths of the world supply; the paper industry was extended; and copper, silver, gold, zinc, and manganese were mined in increasing quantities.

FOREIGN LOANS. But this enormous progress was bought at considerable sacrifice. Loans from abroad, proffered chiefly by France, could be secured only at the expense of political concessions, which later were to contribute to Russia's involvement in the First World War. Outside influences increased; commercial activities were channeled in an unfavorable direction; and the fruitful supplementation of mutual needs of Russia and Germany suffered. Forced and unprofitable exports became necessary to establish further credit and guarantee punctual interest payments. Customs tariffs for needed goods had to be raised. The cycles of prosperity and depression haunting the industrialized nations struck Russia also; and the country, already confronted by its many political and social problems, was exposed to all the consequences which the full impact of industrialization and radical economic shifts had brought about.

Agriculture. While so many endeavors centered around industrialization, the problems of Russian agriculture did not receive
sufficient attention. Capital was channeled into industry, and needed
improvement and modernization of the cultivation of the land were
neglected. Yet, intensive instead of extensive farming would alone
have offered a solution of the agricultural problem. Rapid population increase sharpened the difficulties. The individual peasant relying on the collective, the mir, often did not show a sufficient sense
of responsibility. Laziness and drunkenness continued to prevail,
and the periodic redistribution of much of the peasants' lands by
the mir deprived them of an interest in improving what they had.
Unrest among them increased once more, even though joint tax
liability of the mir had been canceled in 1903 and flogging had been
abolished in 1904.

The Church. The church likewise did nothing to further a
healthy evolution. Under the control of laymen and dominated by
a large bureaucracy interested in maintaining its property, it served
the state and the existing system rather than its members. The standards of the village priest were often only too low; his poverty interfered with his duties and often forced him to supplement his income
by secular activities, such as working or renting land. The intelligentsia and the workers took steadily less interest in religion, and
many students of theology quit the service. No one was allowed to
withdraw from the Orthodox church once he was a member, or
change his religious adherence; those belonging to other faiths, including the Old Believers, were discriminated against. Only after
1905, when Pobedonostzev had been removed from the office of
Procurator, did the Old Believers gain at least a greater measure
of freedom. But a thoroughgoing reform for the sake of reducing
state control, improving clerical standards, and broadening liberty
of conscience was also then avoided.

Administration. Up to 1905, no progress at all was made in the
political sphere. Nothing was done to introduce an order adapted
to modern conditions, except insofar as Alexander III had shown
the way. The men in leading positions, and in particular Nicholas
II himself, could not even maintain the existing order. Among
the rapidly growing, immensely diversified population, and in view
of much social mobility and the penetration of both the aristocracy

and the bureaucracy with modern constitutional ideas, faith in autocracy was lost.

Law and Civil Rights. The situation was worsened by half-hearted compromises which the autocracy made in legal affairs. It sought to bring them more in line with advanced Western concepts, yet it simultaneously rejected constitutionalism and opposed the liberal policies of the zemstvos. Jews, whom the emperor personally disliked, were persecuted more ruthlessly than ever; Orthodox sectarians were subjected to similar sufferings; and an intransigent policy of Russification of border lands was carried out. What had remained of autonomy in Poland, in the Baltic states, the Ukraine, and in Armenia was destroyed. Finland suffered most: The guarantees given her under previous reigns were disregarded, and in 1899, under the pretext of unconstitutional demands by the Finns, the autonomy of the country and its legislature were abolished.

Revival of Terroristic Acts. As a result, popular discontent and tension increased, and shortly after 1900 new terroristic outbreaks occurred. In 1902 the minister of the interior was assassinated; in 1904 the hated reactionary finance minister Plehwe, who the year before had replaced the able Witte, was murdered; in the same year the governor-general of Finland was killed.

REVOLUTION

Road to Revolution. Within ten years of incongruous administration, the country thus headed toward radical change, and the struggle prepared by the liberal and Marxist intelligentsia came to pass. A second stage of Nicholas' rule began in 1904 and lasted until 1907. However, only Western, and mainly Anglo-Saxon, thinkers considered as a true accomplishment the progress made during these years in the direction of Western democratic concepts. In Russia, the trend toward democratic liberalism was regarded by most as being of not more than temporary use; if it were to serve the good of Russia, it would have to lead promptly to the next stage. For, in the minds of Slavophils, Westernizers, and adherents of autocracy and socialization alike, liberal bourgeois ways were typical for Western countries; in Russia, they were to make room quickly for a society based less on individualism than upon a communal spirit, and Russia's future was to be anchored in Russian and not in Western ideas.

BLOODY SUNDAY. The forces for reform found an opportunity for pressing their demands when, in 1904, the government, engaged in war against Japan, needed their support. In November representatives of the zemstvos (whose activities had been allowed to increase after Plehwe's assassination) met in St. Petersburg and asked for popular representation and civil liberties. As their demands were not heeded, notwithstanding the fact that defeats in the war revealed the weakness of autocracy, more radical groups took over and began to organize strikes and foster disorders. These culminated on a January Sunday in a great procession of workers—men and women who, under the leadership of a priest, Father Gapon, marched to the Tsar's palace to present a petition asking for political freedom, equality before the law, lower taxes, and better working conditions. In the absence of Nicholas II, the marchers were received with rifle fire, and "Bloody Sunday" ended with the murder of hundreds of the defenseless, singing petitioners.

October Revolution. Agitation for violence and strikes was thereupon renewed. New unions were formed, and mutinies in the army and navy occurred. In February the ruthless Grand Duke Sergius was assassinated, and late in February the Tsar found himself compelled to make a first concession by promising the convocation of a consultative representative assembly, a Duma. Such representation—to be elected by three separate *curiae,* the landowners, townsmen, and peasants—failed, however, to satisfy the demands; and agitation was renewed. The zemstvos organized new nationwide congresses of their various delegates; the intelligentsia increased their propaganda; the factory workers formed revolutionary unions; and even the peasants, who had so far remained inactive, began to stir, joining with their co-operative associations in political demands for more land and full civil rights. In August the Tsar found himself compelled to make a second promise—the granting of popular representation with wider consultative tasks and the right to propose drafts of laws. But even this new concession failed to stem the tide. The Socialists steadily gained in strength; and in October a general strike was staged by quickly formed revolutionary councils (soviets), paralyzing all activities. Revolution was now in full swing. Leadership was assumed by the Socialists under Khrustalev and Trotsky and by the Kadets under Milyukov; and many members of the various professions hastily formed unions of their own and joined in the movement.

COMPROMISE. Fearful disorders followed, which the government found impossible to curb even with the most ruthless measures. Mutinies flared up in the navy and, with somewhat less vigor, in the army. The nationalists rose in Finland, the Baltic states, Poland, and the Ukraine; the Jews vigorously supported the revolt against their oppressors; the peasants attacked landlords and pillaged estates; and strikes spread throughout the country affecting the whole economy of the nation. In the midst of the turmoil, Count Witte was reappointed by a frightened Tsar and given special powers. He determined upon a decisive concession promising fundamental civil liberties and regular popular representation with a certain amount of legislative power. This, in connection with extensive promises given several weeks later regarding franchise, appeased the liberals and, combined with energetic support to all conservative groups, isolated the Bolshevist-dominated soviets. Pobedonostzev, for three decades evil genius of the Tsars, resigned and with his elimination the issue became clearly a struggle for power between government and soviets. The former received support from France as well as Germany and succeeded toward the end of the year in arresting the revolution. When in December the soviets called for renewal of the general strike and for further violence, the government acted energetically. With the help of the army, risings were suppressed, the members of the soviets were arrested, additional promises regarding the franchise were made, and then elections for the Duma were held.

CONSTITUTIONAL REGIME

First Duma. Although the revolution failed entirely to fulfill the demands of the Socialists, it did satisfy to a certain extent those of the liberals who saw at least a beginning made in the establishment of a constitutional government. The Tsar and the Russian authorities benefited from this situation, for the opposition was now clearly split. In May, 1906, the Duma convened. According to Witte's plan, it was elected by *curiae* of large and small landowners, the former enjoying plural vote, and of an urban population likewise divided according to property and profession. Suffrage was indirect and unequal; clergy, students, soldiers, and nomads possessed no vote at all. Nevertheless, the peasant representatives and the Kadets held the majority; and Count Witte, who had assured the Tsar of a "pliant Duma," was dismissed.

DISSOLUTION OF DUMA. The life of the first Duma was short. Through so-called "fundamental laws," control of the finances and of the military forces as well as special legislative powers, and thus supreme authority, still remained reserved for the Tsar, and the government was responsible to him personally. The representatives tried to do away with such prerogatives and to push through a truly liberal program. Demanding a general amnesty, control of the budget, expropriation of landowners, factory reforms, and parliamentary ministerial responsibility, they still found their aims irreconcilable with those of the government, which after a short time summarily dissolved the assembly.

Agrarian Reform. Revolutionary activity was promptly renewed. Some of the ex-representatives convened at Viborg, Finland, to protest and to continue their work until the convening of a new popular representation. The government—now under P. Stolypin, a man of energy and progressive leanings, yet a political conservative and supporter of tsarism—countered with efficient and sometimes brutal measures. On the one hand, it resumed repressive steps, and on the other, many social and peasant reforms were decreed "from above." The peasant, whose remaining balances on the redemption tax had been canceled in the previous year, was now allowed to claim his land, possibly in one piece as inviolate private property, enclose it, and to leave his village community at will, yet retain his share of property. By this measure (which, of course, could only gradually be carried out) Stolypin succeeded in avoiding the partitioning of the landowners' estates and in dividing the peasantry, the more wealthy members of which were satisfied and began to lend their support to the government.

Second Duma. Meanwhile, elections for another Duma had been held, and they turned out as unfavorable as those for the first Duma; for, although the Kadets lost rather heavily, the Socialists, who had not participated in the first Duma, won many seats. In a more radical assembly, inciting speeches were made, and again demands for extensive changes were formulated. This led to the dissolution of the second Duma.

Third Duma. The Tsar now chose to alter arbitrarily the electoral law. Through a different *curial* system and redistribution of electoral districts, the peasants and workers were deprived of some part of their votes, and the representation of the always obstructive national minorities, foremost the Poles, was drastically cut, whereas the landowners and wealthy classes gained additional franchise. The third Duma, elected according to the new method and convened in November, 1907, was consequently chiefly composed of conservatives and moderates. Though not representative of the Russian people as a whole, it introduced for the first time some sort of representative government in Russia and, as it happened, exercised considerable influence on national and international relations. Although its legislative powers were intended to be small and censorship of newspapers and books was enforced anew, it succeeded in gradually extending its influence. A number of progressive measures were worked out, not the least among them being measures for the betterment of agricultural conditions and a plan for universal education to be completed in practice by 1922.

The third Duma served its full term from 1907 until 1912 and was in turn followed by the fourth Duma. The parliamentary system as embodied in these two Dumas introduced the third stage in Nicholas' rule, which belongs to the history of the First World War.

PROBLEMS

1. Discuss the significance of the work of Witte for the economic growth of Russia.
2. Discuss the chief causes of the Revolution of 1905.
3. Discuss the aims of the agrarian reform work under Stolypin.

34

ROAD TO WORLD WAR I

Significant Dates

Formation of Triple Alliance 1883
Formation of Triple Entente 1907
Austrian Annexation of Bosnia 1908
Balkan Wars 1912–1913
Outbreak of First World War 1914

The Revolution of 1905 and the Japanese War ended an era of autocracy and imperialism without introducing a period of healthy national growth. The short "liberal era" which followed from 1907 to 1917 was one of reluctant and essentially fruitless governmental compromise with enemies at home and abroad. In domestic affairs these compromises, stimulated by the rapid economic expansion of the country, tended in the natural direction of greater freedom and social improvement, but failed to satisfy the progressives, whether liberal or Marxist. The gulf between government and populace remained unbridged.

INTERNAL CONDITIONS

The Court. At the head of the government was Nicholas II, inspired by his concept of duty yet unaware of the trends and needs of the time. His strong-willed wife, Alexandra (a German princess educated at the court of Queen Victoria of England, where she had gained an ill-balanced notion of her position) began to dominate the political scene, and insisted in a semireligious way upon an auto-

224

cratic form of rule which her weaker husband was scarcely able to maintain. Behind her stood a number of strange religious and medical figures (the famed Rasputin prominent among them) who, though not always wrong or evil-intentioned, often used their influence for personal gain. A large and despised police force, employing spies and counterspies, was necessary to support the tsarist system.

The Government. The chief ministers of the period were conservatives and bureaucrats. Many of them possessed considerable ability and were earnestly devoted to their tasks. With the aid of a class of educated and privileged officers, landowners, and administrators, and under the supreme authority of an absolute Tsar, they endeavored to guide the country along careful, beneficial, and paternalistic lines. The most important among them was P. Stolypin, a controversial figure who in 1906 had introduced the peasant reform and who was assassinated in 1911.

The People. On the other side stood the intelligentsia and the masses, including the various national groups which formed part of the empire. All opposed the government, but for varied reasons and with different objectives. Intelligentsia and commercial groups demanded representative government patterned after the Western bourgeois states; they hoped to secure thereby greater freedom, extensive civil rights, and better social conditions. The proletariat envisaged a classless society, either of an anarchic character or under proletarian dictatorship; they were imbued with Marxist principles by radical organizers and, although as yet weak, were most ably led. The peasants, faced with land shortage, desired the abolition of the large estates and additional land allotments for themselves. The Jews demanded equality and quite naturally joined the ranks of the dissatisfied, for they were still persecuted despite the warnings of far-sighted ministers such as Witte and Stolypin. The Finns, Poles, Armenians, and the Ukrainians, who were becoming more nationality-conscious, sought independence or autonomy.

Economy. The population of the Russian empire early in the twentieth century numbered about 150,000,000. The industrial workers, though rapidly growing in numbers, constituted a rather small minority. This distribution necessarily influenced the advance of the Russian economy.

INDUSTRIES. Despite the political rift between government and governed, considerable economic progress was made; favorable economic legislation was passed by the third and, from 1912 on, the fourth imperial Duma. Industries advanced at a rapid pace and economic expansion took place in various directions. Internal and external trade increased, and foreign money markets became readily accessible to Russian enterprises. Living standards for the towns and for the industrial population as a whole were bettered, and educational facilities were spread by the zemstvos.

AGRICULTURE. In the villages, various forms of local government (with elected assemblies) and of co-operatives contributed to the advancement of peasant interests. Stolypin's peasant reform of 1906, which had broken the mir and communal ownership, did not succeed, however, in improving the lot of all peasants. Many who lived in the overcrowded black-soil districts or who possessed neither the industry nor the knowledge to improve their lands found themselves in as wretched circumstances as before and were forced to sell out and join the ranks of the landless proletariat. But there were other millions who, possessing a spirit of enterprise, benefited from the change. Certainly, the rise of a large class of small independent peasant proprietors was stimulated. The productivity of the land was increased; and, through reclamation projects in the old parts of Russia as well as in Siberia, the area under cultivation was considerably extended.

EXTERNAL CONDITIONS

Foreign Entanglements. But as in the times of the Crimean War and the Russo-Japanese War, economic progress could not outweigh political dissatisfaction; and if there were external complications, lack of success was likely to topple the precarious balance. It was therefore of grave consequence when the government found itself inextricably involved in the complicated and war-breeding system of alliances which marked the late nineteenth and the early twentieth centuries. Indeed, the lost war against Japan entangled Russia still further in this system, for now she was compelled to seek a *modus vivendi* with her two most persistent antagonists, England and Japan. Treaties with both were concluded in 1907.

Treaty with Japan. Through a convention with Japan it was arranged that southern Manchuria would be reserved as a sphere of Japanese interest; and Korea was completely renounced by the Tsar and annexed by Japan in 1910. In exchange, Russia secured northern Manchuria, where the town of Harbin became a center of Russian activities and a railroad terminal. Settlers were attracted, a flourishing trade was built up, the mineral wealth of the country was exploited, and industries of large scope were founded. Russia also received a free hand in Outer Mongolia, although nominal Chinese suzerainty was retained there. Although the hold of the rich Chinese merchants persisted and counteracted Russian efforts to foster a separatist movement, new treaties made in 1912 and 1913 with Japan as well as China guaranteed the Tsar additional rights and extended them even to Inner Mongolia.

Treaty with England. The treaty with Japan found its counterpart in that with England. While the one limited Russian advances in the Far East, the other stopped Russia in central Asia and on the approaches to India. The agreement reached between the respective foreign ministers, Grey and Iswolsky, was to a certain extent the result not only of the lost Japanese war but also of friendlier public opinion in England, which followed the introduction of a parliamentary regime in Russia. It also sprang from jealousy of the German advance in the Near East, where a railroad line was planned to connect Berlin and Bagdad by way of the Balkans and the Turkish empire, thus cutting through the hypothetical communication lines of both Russia and England. The Anglo-Russian treaty was intended to consign to the past all differences between the two nations. It dealt particularly with the rivalry of the two countries in Persia and stipulated that England should keep out of northern Persia while Russia should recognize southern Persia as a British sphere of influence. Subsequently, Russia promised also to refrain from penetration into Tibet and Afghanistan. In exchange, England extended loans and, upon occasion, equivocal political backing to the tsarist government.

Triple Entente. Though the treaties served to eliminate causes of discord, they unfortunately did not further the cause of peace; rather, they form chapters in the melancholy story of how the nations "backed into" World War I. For while differences between Russian and British imperialism were composed, a general system of alliances was furthered which in itself bore the seeds of war. The rearrangements increasingly tied Russia financially to France and England, who shortly owned three-quarters of all foreign investments in Russia, and made possible the finishing touches to the Anglo-Franco-Russian "Triple Entente," which implied grave political obligations for Russia.

Relations with Germany. From that time on, every European incident assumed proportions far beyond its inherent importance and led to tests of strength between the "Triple Entente" and the "Triple Alliance," the latter consisting of Germany, Austria-Hungary, and vacillating Italy. In many instances, Russia was but a pawn of the Western powers. She found herself opposing Germany when her own interests would have dictated a sympathetic attitude toward that country—inasmuch as the political preponderance which Germany had possessed in Bismarck's time no longer existed, the customs wars of earlier periods were composed, and almost one third of all Russian foreign trade was carried on with Germany. The fears regarding the construction of the Bagdad railway were overcome in 1910 by an agreement at Potsdam, and the line itself was extended to provide for Russian needs. In the winter of 1913 to 1914, another source of friction was eliminated when the German General Liman von Sanders, who had been sent to reorganize the Turkish army, was appointed to another post at Constantinople.

Relations with Austria. Yet there remained the alignment of Germany and Austria, and Austrian interests continued to be incompatible with those of Russia in the Balkans. Russia and Austria watched each other jealously, in some cases preventing by mutual arrangements the progress of one at the expense of the other—as during the Turko-Greek War in 1898 or the Macedonian revolt of 1901—and in other cases taking advantage of a momentary opportunity. In 1908, when the so-called Young Turk revolt threatened to rejuvenate and reform the decaying Ottoman empire, common fears of a resurgence of Turkish power drove them once more to concerted action. At Buchlau they concluded an agreement which permitted Austrian annexation of Bosnia and Herzegovina and gave Russia free passage through the Straits. But in actuality this agreement brought new hostility, for Austria, acting quickly, annexed the region set aside for her, whereas Russia, facing the opposition of the Western European powers, found herself unable to take her share. In the resulting bitter diplomatic struggle, Germany supported Austria's questionable action.

Relations with Turkey. The Buchlau bargain and its failure demonstrated the impossibility for Russia to come to a beneficial understanding with Germany as long as the latter country insisted on backing Austrian expansion southeastward. It also strengthened Russian determination to gain domination over the Straits, as previously arranged. Every opportunity was taken to achieve this aim by weakening Turkey, forestalling Austria, and gaining the consent of other powers. On this basis, Italy was allowed in 1911 to wrest Tripoli from the Turks, and in 1912 a war which Serbia, Bulgaria, Greece, and Montenegro declared on Turkey was greeted as a step towards the desired goal.

Sarajevo. The results of the Balkan War of 1912, which could not be checked by the halfhearted intervention of the great powers and which was followed in 1913 by a second war among the victors, were in line with Russian hopes. Except for the territory contiguous to Constantinople and the Straits, Turkey was expelled from Europe; Austria's neighbor, Serbia, was enlarged and strengthened; and the whole situation remained sufficiently unsettled to foreshadow further favorable changes. Indeed, less than one year later an incident occurred which led to the next—and this time general —struggle. For on June 28, 1914, the Austrian Archduke Francis Ferdinand was murdered by a Serb national in the Bosnian town of Sarajevo. The outrage led to an Austrian ultimatum to Serbia with demands beyond those warranted by the murder; and, despite the guilt of some Serbian government agencies, Russia decided to take up the cause of her Slavic sister nation. In an atmosphere of chauvinism and imperialism, Russia's allies of the Triple Entente and Austria's partners in the Triple Alliance failed to counsel moderation. Hostilities began, and though wise statesmanship might have localized actual warfare, they were allowed to spread to Germany, France, and England. Thus began the First World War.

INVOLVEMENT IN WORLD WAR I

For the Russian government, the war was certain to turn out disastrously. The weakness of the existing social system, the pressure of new ideas, and the lack of progressiveness, combined with dependence upon uncongenial allies, portended defeat no matter what the military results. Nevertheless, Russia entered the war. Aside

RUSSIA IN 1914

from the spirit of the time, the immediate practical political causes why she did so on the side of England and France may be approximated as follows:

1. *The existing system of alliances,* the Triple Entente and the Triple Alliance, which bound the countries to military support of their allied partners even when their interests were not directly involved. Thus, French thirst for revenge and Anglo-German naval and trade rivalry pushed Russia into action.

2. *Russian resentment against Germany,* surviving from the defeat at the Congress of Berlin, 1878, and the fear that Germany herself was to assume the leading role in the Near East. This resentment was increased by rumors that Germany had pushed Russia along the road to war with Japan and toward defeat and that, notwithstanding Germany's conciliatory attitude in the question of the Bagdad railway and the Liman von Sanders mission, she was endeavoring to draw Turkey into her own sphere.

3. *The leanings of some Russian circles,* particularly of the intelligentsia, toward a parliamentary system and civil liberties as found in France or England, which seemed to them preferable to the parliamentary but paternalistic part played by the German imperial government.

4. *Irreconcilability of Russian and Austrian intentions* in the Balkans, fear of loss of prestige there if support were not given to Slavic Serbia, and hope that war would bring an opportunity for realizing domination over the Straits.

5. *The annexation of Bosnia* and the attitude of Vienna towards the Slavic nations in the Balkans and even toward those within the Austrian-Hungarian monarchy, which the revived Pan-Slavist movement regarded as the greatest threat to the fulfillment of its own mission.

6. *A bellicose spirit of nationalism,* prevailing in Russia as in France, Germany, Austria, and other countries. It expressed itself in the role and influence of the military, in the attitude of political leaders and of many intellectuals, in speeches and publications, and especially in the reports of the daily press.

7. *Personal intrigues* of diplomats, which were fostered by selfish, vainglorious men such as the Austrian Berchtold and the Russian Iswolsky. The position of the "autocrat" Nicholas and of the German emperor formed no political reality, despite all claims to divine rights, family ties, and personal friendship; the rulers' influence was

in effect subordinated to the independent play of diplomatic forces and popular trends.

On August 1, 1914, war broke out between Russia, Austria, and Germany. France joined Russia according to treaty obligations, and England entered the struggle three days later. The war came at a moment when, despite the great advance of the previous fifty years, the urgent problems besieging Russia—those of landownership, of industrialization, of democracy and class society, of education, and of strategic security—still remained unsolved.

PROBLEMS

1. Discuss the internal conditions foreboding ill for autocracy in the event of war.
2. Trace the steps towards the opposing political alignments of the Triple Entente and the Triple Alliance.
3. Discuss the factors which drew Russia into World War I.

35

WORLD WAR I

Significant Dates

WAR

The Early Campaigns, 1914–15. The Russian plan for the conduct of the war collapsed during its initial stages. While the Central Powers had calculated on a quick northward push from Austria into Russia, the Russians had intended to throw their forces southward, to invade Austria in Galicia and gain the support of the Slavs living in the region. But owing to the weakness of the French, the occupation of Galicia had to be interrupted; and instead, in order to divert German pressure from France, an attack on East Prussia was made. This saved France, by forcing the Central Powers to shift troops from their western to their eastern front, and thus perhaps constituted a decisive factor in preventing German victory in the First World War; yet it did not benefit Russia, for it resulted in terrible defeats in Prussia at Tannenberg and the Masurian Lakes. By the end of 1914 German armies under Hindenburg stood deep in Polish Russia, and the city of Łódź was lost. A Russian winter offensive failed to dislodge all of them, and only in Galicia were advances made; but lack of supplies endangered the newly won positions there. In the summer of 1915 a German-Austrian counter-offensive occurred which forced Russia to give up her conquests, and at the end of 1915 the Russians had evacuated all occupied foreign territory, while the enemy pushed beyond Kaunas, Warsaw, and Brest Litovsk. Likewise, Russia's allies in the Balkans were beaten, and Bulgaria joined the Central Powers.

The Brusilov Offensive, 1916. Despite these reverses, the Russians were called upon by their Western allies in 1916 to again relieve the critical situation in France. A new attack, called the "Brusilov" offensive after the commanding general of that name, was therefore launched. The Russians succeeded in re-entering Galicia and won over many Slavs fighting in the Austrian army. But the advance constituted a Pyrrhic victory; for the terrific cost in men and matériel undermined the physical strength as well as the morale of the army, and more was lost than gained. Furthermore, Rumania, whose entry into the war was hailed as a welcome aid, proved a drain on Russia. Unprepared, she was soon defeated by the Central Powers; the country was occupied, and the Russian lines were exposed at their southeastern flank.

Rasputin. By the end of 1916, the Russian position had become precarious. Although fifteen million men had been mobilized, success in the field was lacking, and the economy of the country was disrupted. The original patriotic wave of enthusiasm roused by the "great venture of war" had subsided; people and soldiers understood neither the causes nor the objectives of the war, nor did they cherish the immediate prospects. The number of prisoners and deserters multiplied, enormous losses influenced the temper at home, and the whole country became weary of war. Moreover, confidence in military and political leadership was fast waning. Prompted by his concept of duty, the Tsar, despite all warnings, had assumed personal command of the armies in the fall of 1915 after the great military disasters of that year. But owing to his military inexperience and his essential ignorance of the status of Russia—resulting from his autocratic seclusion—he proved unequal to the task. Increasingly he came under the influence of his wife, who through foreign education, autocratic pretensions, and mysticism was far removed from an understanding of popular trends and who followed blindly the advice of her friend Rasputin. This man had gained complete ascendancy over her when, apparently miraculously, he had saved the life of her son, a hemophiliac. She believed implicitly in his prophecies, some of which, perhaps because of his common sense, had come to pass. Because of his outward humility, mystic religiosity, and brusque manners—his coarseness, corruption, and debauchery notwithstanding—she regarded him as the incarnation of the spirit of the Russian peasant masses. Soon Rasputin dominated court intrigues, interfered (not always incapably) in state business, gave directions even to military authorities, chose and dismissed ministers, and directed the decisions of the Tsar. Twice he was removed from the court, but his influence over the Tsar and Tsarina was such that he was recalled both times. His role reflected the level to which conduct of public affairs had sunk in Russia. His financial malpractices, shameful private life, and unfortunate influence did not come to an end until December, 1916, when members of the nobility and of the court, who feared for the survival of tsarism, decided to do away with him. He was invited by them to a banquet and there murdered.

Domestic Difficulties. The action came too late to save the reputation and the throne of the imperial family. As in the times of the Crimean and the Japanese wars, dissatisfaction was rife among the people. The inefficiency and waste of the bureaucracy were overwhelming; the military forces were left short of ammunition; and intended army reforms were not carried out. Heavy industries lacked the materials which they could no longer get from Germany, their former chief supplier; and skilled labor was unavailable in many fields. Despite improvements during the course of 1915 when the first military reverses demonstrated the critical situation, co-operation between government and people was wanting, and in view of prevailing low educational standards a realization of the issues at stake could not be evoked among the masses. Revenues dropped not only because of Russian isolation from abroad, but also because of prohibition of alcoholic beverages, which had provided a large share of excise taxes.

Growth of Opposition. Politically, the war accentuated the existing internal tension. Under the influence of the Tsarina and Rasputin, appointments to high offices were often injudicious; the war prime ministers, Goremykin, Stürmer, and Trepov, and most of their colleagues were essentially chosen from the conservatives and showed little ability and often still less uprightness. Their weakness strengthened those forces which the government had always tried to suppress; and the laboring class and the peasants, profiting from the wartime boom, increased their power. The intelligentsia, partly represented in a "Progressive Bloc" of the Duma, profited also from war conditions, and they soon seized some of the governmental functions and pressed for a parliamentary system embodying rights similar to those of the peoples in Western Europe.

REVOLUTION

February Revolution. In November, 1916, the final attack on the government was opened with a speech by Milyukov, leader of the Kadets in the Duma, who denounced the inefficiency or traitorous intent of the existing tsarist regime. The murder of Rasputin in the following month increased the tension, and in February, 1917, bread riots broke out in Petrograd (St. Petersburg). Strikes increased day by day. In vain did the president of the Duma, M. Rodzianko, and others beseech the Tsar to appoint a government which possessed the confidence of the people. Further disorders occurred and were accompanied by clashes with the police. On February 25 these culminated in a mutiny of the Guards, who when ordered to fire upon strikers and bread rioters turned upon their own officers and sided with the masses. On the same day, the Duma was dissolved, and the government ceased to function. To the cries for bread were now added demands for sweeping political changes. The Tsar tried to hurry back to Petrograd, but was stopped on the way and persuaded to abdicate. Subsequently he and his family were arrested. His brother, who was named successor instead of the sickly son, refused to reign without popular consent; and a Provisional Government, representing the "Progressive Bloc," was formed by a committee of the Duma. Prince Lvov, liberal head of the zemstvos' Union, became prime minister; Milyukov, foreign minister; and A. Kerensky, leader of the Social Revolutionary party, minister of justice.

THE PROVISIONAL GOVERNMENT

The Provisional Government. The new regime was rooted in the middle class, which comprised but a small fragment of the Russian masses; as Leon Trotsky later pointed out, it was not truly revolutionary, since the change meant essentially that those who through economic position and education had, *de facto,* influenced affairs before, now officially assumed power. Being unprepared, they depended largely upon spontaneously formed councils (soviets) of soldiers and workmen. Thus, the new government was forced on a middle road and, lacking a broad basis, into a dead end. Its desire not to disorganize the country in the midst of war was greater than that for immediate execution of social and political reforms.

THE SOVIETS. From the beginning the radical forces, though inferior in numbers, proved exceedingly powerful and determined, and they were responsive to many of the smoldering trends set in motion by the Russian masses. For the time being, however, the soviets, which represented these radical forces, were quite willing to allow the Provisional Government to bear both the official burden and the responsibility. They confined themselves to the organization of their own agencies and through these exercised an effectual but illegal influence; government authority was actually split. The soviets instituted an "Executive Committee" of their own and took precautions against the return of autocracy. They undermined discipline among their opponents, abolished officers' ranks, and demanded peace, while disseminating antibourgeois propaganda. Realizing the hesitancy of the government, the soviets incited the peasants to seize the long-coveted land and aroused the workers to take possession of their factories. When Nikolai Lenin (hurried from Switzerland through Germany with the consent of the German High Command) arrived in Petrograd in April and Leon Trotsky arrived from America in May, the real struggle began; for Lenin, denouncing the Provisional Government as subservient to bourgeois England and France, demanded immediate concentration of all forces upon truly revolutionary tasks.

INCREASE OF RADICALISM. The first swing to the left—typical of all revolutions—soon came with the question of ending the war "without annexations and without indemnities," as demanded by the soviets. In May, two right-wing ministers, including Milyukov, who adhered to imperialistic war policies on the side of England and France, resigned. But the soviet representatives who replaced the outgoing ministers belonged essentially to the moderate Menshevist wing and failed to sufficiently strengthen the government. Reforms were postponed, in particular those concerning distribution of land, and the general desire for peace remained unfulfilled. Instead, a new and mighty offensive was undertaken in July, intended to serve as much the strengthening of the government at home as the cause of the Allies abroad. This "second Brusilov"—or "Kerensky"—offensive achieved surprising success in its initial stages, but it could not be sustained. Its failure coincided with growing difficulties at home; economic deterioration, rising inflation, and struggle over the nationality rights of Poles, Finns, and Ukrainians brought a severe crisis and led to the withdrawal of all Kadet ministers from the government.

RESIGNATION OF GOVERNMENT. This moment seemed opportune to many Bolshevists, who within the radical soviets made up but a small left wing, to launch a bid for power, or at least an attempt to increase radical influences and to push the country farther along the road to revolution. Relying on the revolutionary mood of the masses which had been evidenced in June in a convention of delegates from the soviets all over the country (First All-Russian Congress of Soviets), they organized riots and sponsored strikes, and finally incited uprisings. These, however, were quickly checked by government forces. Lenin had to go into hiding and Trotsky was arrested. Nevertheless, Prince Lvov, following the example of the Kadet ministers, now resigned, and Kerensky became prime minister. General Brusilov was replaced by General Kornilov.

KERENSKY. Kerensky, though vain and ambitious, was patriotic and possessed of ability; but he proved unequal to the task of guiding the imperiled nation and of directing the course of the revolution. He lacked the support of the army, which felt that resistance to Germany was useless; and he failed to make preparations for peace. He could not rely on the garrison of Petrograd, which was important because of the continued German advance on the capital. Likewise, he found himself unable to establish a working coalition with the soviets, to gather all military resources of the country, and to reorganize resistance. In September his authority and good faith were further shaken by a coup which General Kornilov undertook in order to seize power. Kornilov marched on Petrograd, but his troops deserted his cause and the scheme collapsed, thus adding to the revolutionary agitation of the day.

Achievements of the Provisional Government. Under such conditions, constructive work, which normally the Provisional Government might have achieved with considerable benefit to the Russian people, became impossible. Even so, what was done was by no means negligible. An end was put to autocracy and the entire tsarist system and, in September, Russia was declared a republic; the nationality problem was courageously, though not always judiciously, attacked; the Poles and Finns were started on the road to independence; co-operatives were supported instead of private enterprise; legislation was enacted concerning civil rights, prison reform, equal rights of women, universal suffrage, and religious freedom. Yet, the most pressing problems—the question of further prosecution of the war, the scope of internal reforms, and the partition of land—were postponed by the Kerensky government. The military position of the country deteriorated rapidly, and the whole empire, disorganized and irretrievably split, was faced with dissolution. It was in this situation that the chance for gaining control presented itself to the Bolshevists.

Evaluation of February Revolution. Often the question has been asked if the process of change going on since 1861 did not guarantee further progress which could satisfy needs and demands of the Russian population. Marxists deny that such a development was possible under the inexorable logic of historical evolution. Others hold that Russia's involvement in World War I prevented the further successful pursuit of the goal. Still others argue that the direction of change toward a liberal capitalistic system, based on individualism, was undesirable—at least for Russia. And there are those who insist that it was only the conspiracy of a few eminently able revolutionaries which drove Russia onto the path toward reconstruction under the socialist banner. Whatever the opinion, the fact remains that by 1917, Russia was well on the road to overcoming her "backwardness." War and revolution gave a new turn to Russia's history. This did not mean, though, that all former trends were reversed; indeed, in many respects the element of continuity was accentuated.

PROBLEMS

1. Discuss the domestic influences checking the successful progress of the war.
2. Describe the February Revolution and its relationship to the soviets.
3. Discuss the achievements of the Kerensky government.

36

INTRODUCTION OF BOLSHEVISM

Significant Dates
October Revolution; Soviets Seize Power . . . 1917
Peace of Brest Litovsk 1918
First Soviet Constitution 1918

OCTOBER REVOLUTION

Bolshevik Realism. Neither determination, nor political organization, nor the use of physical force suffices to explain the rise of the Bolsheviks to power in 1917. The essential causes for their success must be sought in their realization of the ultimate trends of the revolution and in their readiness to face and satisfy the two chief demands of the Russian masses—peace and land. In order to gain these objectives, they undermined the authority of the Kerensky government not only with the industrial proletariat, but also with soldiers and peasantry—those segments of the population which theoretically did not contain likely Marxist recruits. Kerensky was unable to offer more attractive aims, and his assumption of dictatorial powers lacked a sound basis; it was not backed by the armed forces and thus remained without political reality.

Bolsheviks in Majority. Late in September, shortly before elections for important town and provincial soviets were held, new strikes and food riots occurred. The Bolsheviks profited from these anarchic conditions; promising nationalization of land as well as of banks and industries, elimination of the bourgeoisie, election of a Constituent Assembly, and—most of all—peace, they secured for the first time a majority in the soviets. Trotsky was elected president of the Petrograd Soviet. The government—which could rely on the Social Revolutionary and the Menshevik parties only, neither one of which was ready to identify itself with the masses and fulfill their wishes—was thus forced into trying to gain Bolshevik support. The Bolshevik leaders increased their propaganda for "direct action," formed their own "Red Guards," and furthered the disorganization of the regular armed forces. As a result, soldiers quit the ranks in steadily increasing numbers, while peasants continued to seize lands of proprietors and began to plunder and murder.

"Victory of Socialism." In October Lenin returned to Petrograd where, ostensibly for the defense of the capital, he organized a "Military Revolutionary Committee" which assumed the right to countersign orders issued by the regular general staff. Through Bolshevik dominated "soldiers' soviets" Lenin also secured control of the Petrograd garrison, of the Peter and Paul fortress, and, indirectly, even of the army in the field. Relying upon such formidable backing, he proceeded to prepare an armed uprising. Too late did Kerensky order countermeasures. The authority of his government was insufficient, and he could not even rely on the functioning of the bureaucracy, whose services had actually broken down in the meantime. A "Pre-Parliament," convoked by him early in October, 1917, to bridge the time until the convening of a constituent assembly, failed to support his measures. The Bolsheviks grew stronger daily; and on the night before the convening of an "All-Russian Congress of Soviets" on October 25 * they executed a long planned coup. They seized railways, bridges, telephones, and banks in the capital and thus gained control of the central communication system; when Kerensky left to secure help from the army, the members of his government, who had meanwhile sought refuge in the old imperial Winter Palace, were captured. This put an end to the Provisional Government. The Pre-Parliament was abolished, and Lenin proclaimed the "victory of socialism." Without much difficulty, Bolshevik rule was extended to Moscow.

* Up to February, 1918, Russia used the "Old Style" Julian calendar which at that time differed from the Gregorian calendar, used in the West, by 13 days. The Revolution took place on October 25, 1917, according to the Russian calendar (hence "October Revolution") or on November 7, 1917, according to the Western calendar.

Bolshevik Legislation.   Once in power, the Bolsheviks, in contrast to the hesitant Provisional Government, acted with speed and energy. They disregarded personal and political consequences and concentrated on two fundamental objectives—nationalization and peace. A "Soviet of the People's Commissars" assumed executive power—with Lenin as chairman; Rykov, commissar for the interior; Trotsky, commissar for foreign affairs; and twelve other members. One of these, Stalin, became commissar for nationalities. Within less than three months, from October, 1917, to January, 1918, the most radical changes were enacted. All large estates of state, church, and private owners were confiscated and turned over to volost land committees. Workers' control over the means of production and over the sales and finances of industrial and commercial enterprise was established. While this step, which later led to complete nationalization, affected at first only about 20 per cent of all Russian factories, it did embrace the key production centers. Eight-hour day work laws and legislation for the protection of women, children, and mine workers were passed. Civil ranks and classes were abolished, and social insurance and price regulations were introduced. Banks were nationalized, and banking was declared a state monopoly. All tsarist prewar loans were declared null and void. By decree, only civil marriages were legally recognized; registry of all births was required; equality was decreed for legitimate and illegitimate children; and divorce by petition of one or both parties was made possible. Measures for expansion of educational and library facilities were adopted, and separation of church and state was instituted.

Bolshevik Administration.   In December a "Supreme Council of National Economy" was created and the food supply for the capital, although remaining insufficient, was augmented. The foundations for a special "Red Army" were laid. The country was reorganized on a federal basis; provincial soviets were charged with regional administration; and a People's Court with elected members was instituted. The poor were encouraged to seize the property of the wealthy—especially their lands. Revolutionary tribunals were constituted to deal with cases of sabotage, treason, or even opposition. Special agencies were formed to supervise the press (censorship), and a new police force (Extraordinary Commission—"Cheka") was formed.

The nationality problem of the empire was resolutely attacked on the promised basis of the rights of the people to self-determination.

To be sure, the Soviets, through intrigue or force, did their utmost to establish everywhere their own brand of government; however, where they did not succeed, the various national groups were authorized to constitute themselves as independent states. Following the Finnish and Polish example, Bessarabia and the Caucasus regions availed themselves of this right. Later, the Baltic states—Estonia, Latvia, Lithuania—gained independence. The Ukraine, on the other hand, which as early as June, 1917, had proclaimed itself an autonomous republic, did not achieve the formation of a solid independent government. Bolshevik, monarchist, German-sponsored nationalist, and White Guardist governments, and, more effectively, one established in December, 1918, under the Social-Democrat Petlyura succeeded each other without bringing about the constitution of a Ukrainian state. Separatist tendencies contended with pro-Russian and Pan-Slav nationalism in the Ukraine.

Dissolution of Constituent Assembly. A last blow was dealt the dying liberal system when in January, 1918, the recently convened Constituent Assembly was summarily dissolved. Elected in November, it was chiefly composed of Kerensky's Social Revolutionaries and of Mensheviks. The Bolsheviks were determined to make interference with their program impossible, and upon losing the fight for the presidency and the first test vote, they immediately withdrew. Within twenty-four hours, supported by the galleries and the Petrograd garrison, they dispersed the convention.

PEACE

Armistice. With equal assurance, speed, and radicalism, the Bolshevik government turned to external affairs. Immediately announcing its intention to conclude an armistice, it confronted the world with a demand for peace on a nonimperialistic basis, without annexations or indemnities, and with self-determination for all peoples. Since England and France (and later the United States) refused to negotiate on such a basis, whereas the Central Powers declared themselves willing to accept the terms, separate peace was decided upon and armistice negotiations commenced in November.

Soviet Dynamics. Despite their military and domestic predicaments, the Bolsheviks were in no wise in a weak position. Taking

up the cause of workingmen the world over, they had reason to hope
that by using propagandist speechmaking and by prolonging the
negotiations, they would be able to rouse the working masses in Germany and, perhaps, in the Western countries. They knew the
strength of their appeal to self-determination of the people, which
threatened to sway the minorities in the Austrian-Hungarian empire; and they were also aware of the military difficulties besetting
the Central Powers, who were anxious to shift troops from the east
to an endangered front in the west.

Peace. The Russian delegation handled the situation astutely,
but was unable to come to an agreement because Germany, after
seeing the Russian border states released from Russian suzerainty,
wished to control them. Furthermore, the Central Powers were
resolved not to permit self-determination or political dissolution in
their own realms and were as intent upon averting revolution in
their own countries as the Russians were anxious to promote it. As
no progress was made and as the Germans were threatening resumption of hostilities, the leader of the Russian delegation, Leon Trotsky, finally declared that he would sign no formal peace, but that his
country would withdraw from war and forthwith cease combat.
Such action, however, was unacceptable to the Central Powers, who
countered by first concluding a separate peace with the Ukraine and
then, in February, 1918, reopening the campaign against Russia. By
a vigorous push deep into the country they forced the resumption
of negotiations and now, under stricter conditions, secured the conclusion of a formal peace (March, 1918, Brest Litovsk). The Russians
bitterly denounced the dictate as imperialistic and as a blow to the
working class; but in order to fulfill the domestic promise for peace
and to maintain Bolshevik rule, they nevertheless signed it.

CONSTRUCTION OF SOCIALIST STATE

Nationalization. The cessation of hostilities was utilized by the
Soviets to concentrate on the work of building a socialist society in
Russia and of spreading the Marxist doctrine from this center to the
other countries of the world. With this in mind, the Bolshevik government concentrated its attention, notwithstanding increasing internal disorders and foreign intervention, on the task of reshaping
the entire national system. Between February and December, 1918,
many new laws were promulgated.

AGRICULTURE. Private ownership of all land, including that of the peasants themselves, was abolished. The previously "socialized" land was declared nationalized, and all property rights in land were assumed not by the peasants who worked it but by the state. Anyone who wanted land to cultivate without hired labor could get it from the state. A central food control was introduced, prices were fixed, a corn monopoly was established, and, with the help of the armed forces, grain control was taken over by the state and a share of the harvest was collected from farms. Special "Committees of Poor Peasants" were set up to prevent the clandestine resurgence of wealthy landowners. In February, 1919, the first state (Soviet) farms were created; collective farming was sponsored with the aid of state loans; and the establishment of farm associations (artels) was furthered.

INDUSTRIES. Some industries, such as the metallurgic and paper industries, were completely nationalized; others, such as the textile industry, had individual factories, rather than having the entire industry appropriated by the state. All coal mines, oil fields, and railroads were declared public property. In May, 1918, the first "All-Russian Congress of the Soviets of People's Economy" met and set in motion the process of planning typical of later Soviet policy. Projects were devised for the financing of state industries and trade establishments. Co-operatives were incorporated into state institutions; a "People's Commissariat for Food Supply" took over sugar, meat, textile, and other retail establishments; and the tobacco, oil, and sugar trades became state monopolies. All foreign trade was nationalized and turned into a state monopoly. The right of inheritance was abolished. A new "Labor School Statute" with emphasis on manual training was promulgated.

Soviet Constitution. These changes were embodied in the fundamental law or constitution of July 10, 1918, which at first covered only a part of the former empire, Russia proper. Under the dictatorship of the proletariat, it provided for a "Federation of Soviet National Republics" in which all class divisions were abolished. All peoples of the Federation were declared equal and sovereign by a decree issued later in October, and, at least on paper, their right to self-determination and secession from the Federation was reasserted. The abolition of private ownership of land, banks, and all means of production and transportation was confirmed and their right of inheritance annulled. War, imperialism, and colonization were denounced. Anyone could profess any or no religion. The church was no longer recognized as a juridical person; it could own no property and was fully separated from the state. Education was henceforward given free of charge. Universal military training was ordered and the duty to work established. Supreme authority was vested in the "All-Russian Congress of Soviets," which was to elect an "Executive Committee," which in turn chose the highest state functionaries in the "Council of People's Commissars." Local and district soviets were created and their jurisdiction circumscribed. Suffrage was confined to soldiers, laborers, and peasants; but the representation accorded to the industrial workers was a multiple of that of the peasants in proportion to their numbers. Parties, aside from the Communist, were abolished. Merchants, *rentiers,* and former members of the police, of the ruling house, and of the clergy were disenfranchised.

Results of Bolshevik Revolution.   In less than twelve months, the Bolsheviks thus not only extirpated the roots of autocracy as they had existed in Russia for hundreds of years, but they also demolished by law the foundations on which a "liberal democracy" could be built. As envisaged by nineteenth-century radicals, the stage of the bourgeois state was skipped. Instead, true to Marxist concepts, the legal foundations for a new type of society were erected in which classes were leveled and in which, after a transitional stage of the dictatorship of the proletariat, equality was to reign; in which the church as a political factor was eliminated, and private property, ownership in land, and wealth of every kind were abolished; in which the means of production and most of those of distribution passed into the hands of the state, which was ruled by soviets of formerly "exploited" classes. But it remained to be seen to what extent, if at all, this transformation could in practice be accomplished.

PROBLEMS

1. Describe the methods applied by the Bolsheviks in gaining power.
2. Discuss the immediate measures carried out upon assumption of power by the Bolsheviks.
3. Discuss the importance of external peace for the survival of Bolshevik rule.

37

CIVIL WAR

Significant Dates

Outbreak of Civil War 1918
Allied Intervention in Russia 1918–1920
Death of Nicholas II 1918
Polish-Russian War 1920–1921

While the work of socialization was in progress, Russia found herself exposed to internal disorders and external dangers which had been equaled only during the Time of Troubles. As then, national unity was broken and a triangular or multilateral struggle raged in which external and domestic, political and social issues were hopelessly confounded. There were the Bolsheviks or "Reds," rulers of Russia and fully on the defensive, and the counterrevolutionaries or "Whites," divided into many incoherent groups of former officials, nobles, military men, Westernized liberals, moderate socialists, Cossacks, and separatists. There were external enemies. On the one hand stood the Germans, favoring the Reds in Russia proper because they were responsible for the withdrawal from the war, but attacking them in the newly created border states of the Baltic region and in Poland and the Ukraine—all of which the Central Powers wished to dominate and use as buffers against the rising social danger. On the other hand stood the Allies—France and England, joined by the United States—equally apprehensive of the "Red peril," but at first particularly anxious to reopen an eastern front against Germany. They continued their interference on the side of the counterrevolutionary Whites long after the war with Germany was terminated.

There were also the Japanese, interested in the more practical aim of wresting Far Eastern territory from an apparently disintegrating Russian empire.

REDS AND WHITES

Foreign Intervention. Civil war began immediately upon assumption of power by the Soviets; Allied intervention followed five months later. The first efforts of the Whites, commanded by two former chiefs of staff, General Alekseyev and General Kornilov, came to naught in the spring of 1918; and new operations under a more efficient leader, General Denikin, were begun from the Ukraine and the Caucasus. Simultaneously with Denikin's campaign, Allied intervention was undertaken. In April, 1918, the British and Japanese landed in Vladivostok, and they were followed in August by contingents from the United States, which was interested as much in checking Bolshevism as in keeping an eye on its allies, the Japanese. In the summer British troops descended on Murmansk; they were followed by French and, in September, by American detachments. English forces landed also in Estonia, Russia's western gate, and at Baku in the south, while French help, military and financial, was extended to Denikin's army. Thus Soviet Russia found herself menaced from north, south, east, and west, cut off from the seas, and isolated from contact with other nations.

Comparison of Reds and Whites. The Bolshevik government struggled against the overwhelming force of its enemies until October, 1920, when French, English, and American troops were finally withdrawn and civil war was ended. The Bolshevik government managed to survive only because of the lack of co-ordination of its enemies—the natural consequence of their utterly divergent aims. On the side of the Soviets were patriotism, enthusiasm, and fear—patriotism to defend the country against foreign invaders, enthusiasm to promote a "classless society," fear (on the part of the masses, and particularly of the peasants) of losing the economic advantages gained through the Revolution. On the side of the Whites were expert military men, zeal for constitutional freedom, and the vast resources of the foreign interventionists. But the Whites lacked a common objective. Some were desirous of the return of monarchy, others of some kind of democratic republic; yet all were in the unhappy position of fighting their own country and were unwilling to make the necessary social concessions. They fought in separate groups over interrupted lines of communication, and there were many unreliable subordinates lacking in discipline. The Bolsheviks, on the other hand, had the strategic advantage of easily defensible interior lines, unified command, and a devoted Red Army, capably organized and led by men like Trotsky. The Whites were also dependent upon help from foreign powers which, like the Poles in the Time of Troubles and Napoleon in 1812, did not understand the social aspects of the struggle.

Civil War Fronts. The only objective common to all Whites was the overthrowal of the Bolsheviks; and until November, 1918, the chief aim of the foreign powers consisted in the reopening of a second front against Germany. In November, 1918, after the end of the First World War, the allied aim, because of the growing appeal of Bolshevism, became identified with that of the Whites. But very little was effectively done to make their cause triumphant, and at no time was concerted action carried on. When in May, 1919, Denikin launched his main offensive in the south, the other fronts wavered; and, although he almost reached Moscow, he had to give up his drive near Moscow for lack of support. In the following year, he was replaced by a leader with more statesmanlike abilities, General Wrangel, who operated until November, 1920, in the Crimea but achieved no better results. In the fall of 1919, the western group under General Yudenich pushed from Estonia eastward to Petrograd; but neither Denikin nor the Allied forces co-ordinated their actions with his. Indeed, the Allies were forced just at that time to quit the northern sector and to flee from Archangel; thus, Yudenich's attempt also miscarried. When the White forces in Siberia under General Khorvat, Admiral Kolchak, and Captain Semënov started their operations, they met with the same fate. Favored not only by their remoteness from Soviet strongholds and easier access to foreign supplies, but also by the social and economic structure of Siberia, they actually came closest to success. They sponsored an autonomy movement which resulted in a provisional Siberian government with headquarters at Omsk, and in November, 1918, Admiral Kolchak was proclaimed "supreme ruler" of all of Russia. But the Bolshevik power of resistance, combined with dissensions in Kolchak's own camp, overwhelmed him. After holding out until February, 1920, he was betrayed, captured, and executed. The Siberian autonomy movement, sponsored and artificially upheld by the Japanese, collapsed.

EFFECTS OF CIVIL WAR

Chaos. Intervention and civil war led to an almost indescribable amount of destruction of material and moral values, and normal standards of life were undermined. In the towns almost all public services ceased to function, medical help for the sick became unavailable, schools were closed, and families were dispersed. In addition to the organized resistance groups, roaming bands of all kinds were formed which contributed to the agony of the country: war veterans who could not reach their homes; young people who were orphaned or who had left their homes because of the general disintegration; German war prisoners, released but unable to gain their homeland; and others.

Among these was a large band of Czechs, numbering forty to fifty thousand men, who had joined the Russian armies after deserting the Austrians. After the Treaty of Brest Litovsk, they were to have been shipped to the western front in Flanders. They reached Vladivostok, their port of embarkation, but at the instigation of the Allies they were turned back into Siberia to fight the Bolsheviks. Joined by Kadets, Social Revolutionaries, and Cossacks, they seized large sections of the Siberian railroad and marched upon Moscow. Only after entering European Russia were they repelled. They returned to Siberia, where they terrorized the population, sometimes fighting against the Soviets, sometimes joining the Red forces. An indirect result of their actions was the death of Nicholas II, the last Romanov ruler. When in January, 1919, a Czech detachment reached the region of Ekaterinburg (Sverdlovsk) where the monarch had been brought, he and his family were executed by their Red guards, lest they be liberated by the Czechs.

Polish War. Following the civil war, although in many respects a part of it, there occurred an external war against the Poles which resulted from Poland's support of the counterrevolutionaries in the Ukraine. The Poles had established an independent nation in November, 1918. With chauvinism immediately seizing the country again, they had used the occasion offered by Russia's civil strife to annex Lithuanian and White Russian regions which had once belonged to their medieval empire. The war, beginning in May, 1920, with their occupation of Kiev, might have been disastrous for them —the Reds ousted them in June and actually reached the suburbs of Warsaw—had they not rallied on their own territory and received the help of the French, who were particularly insistent in their opposition to Bolshevik rule. Thus, the tide turned in August, 1920, and the Reds were forced to retreat from Warsaw and to yield their conquests. In May, 1921, Russia was obliged to consent to the Treaty of Riga, which deprived her of all territory coveted by the Poles, notwithstanding the decision of a commission under Lord Curzon, which, in accordance with ethnographic realities, had fixed a different, more equitable, eastern border for Poland.

Famine. While the Poles were penetrating into Russia, at the end of 1920, a new disaster befell the country and added to the horrors of civil and external war and the accompanying Red and White terror which had cost hundreds of thousands of lives. A terrible famine occurred—as much the result of war, revolution, and peasant dissatisfaction as of the experimentation with new social systems and methods. It hit different parts of the country in different degrees, and it was especially severe in the cities. But military intervention being over, the outside world was now willing to intervene with helping hands. Foreign churches, nations, and humanitarian groups, such as the Quakers and the Red Cross, took part in relief, and the efforts of men like Fridtjof Nansen and Herbert Hoover served to ameliorate the worst suffering.

Survival. Despite famine, economic collapse, internal and foreign wars, physical demolition, and the destruction of existing law and the disintegration of society, the Bolshevik government survived; but it was only a gigantic effort of the people and a large scale reversal of the accepted program that saved the Bolshevik system.

PROBLEMS

1. Compare the respective aims of the Reds and the Whites during the civil war.
2. Discuss the reasons for the Bolshevik success.
3. Discuss the implications and effects of the Polish-Russian War of 1920.

38

RECONSTRUCTION

Significant Dates

Lenin 1870–1924
Comintern Established 1919
New Economic Policy (N.E.P.) 1921
U.S.S.R. Created 1922–1923

The year 1921 brought the adaptation of Communist Russia to demands and needs within a non-Communist world. The dominant figure in achieving this adjustment was Nikolai Lenin. It was he who reinterpreted Marxism in order to fit it to the needs of the time and of the new Russian society.

MARXISM AND LENIN

Marxist View of History. The founder of the doctrine which Lenin sought to put into practice was Karl Marx (1818–1883). Marx had interpreted the political and social evolution of mankind as a process subject to natural laws and not dependent upon human will. According to him, human will and all human activities are determined by, and a reflection of, laws of nature which govern the process of social evolution and which demand continuing change. Progress is brought about by an incessant struggle of opposite forces, leading eventually to a communistic society that embodies the highest ethics of man. The struggle has been in the past a conflict between classes, between those who own property (which according to Marx meant those who have appropriated other people's labor) and those who are dependent upon them and exploited by them. It has now entered the last stage, with the proletariat emancipating itself and striving to set up a classless society. A new generation of man will be created and the state, law, and all means of coercion will become superfluous. The creation of these new conditions will be hastened by the unrelenting efforts of revolutionaries.

Forty-five years after the death of Marx, his dreams appeared to have come close to realization—owing to the work of Nicolai Lenin.

Lenin. Born in 1870, Lenin (Vladimir Ilich Ulyanov), the son of a school superintendent belonging to the lower nobility, became involved at an early age in the revolutionary struggle. The execution of his older brother, who had participated in an assassination attempt on Alexander III, left a deep impression upon him. After finishing his law studies he traveled abroad and came in contact with leading *émigré* socialists. Thereafter he actively engaged in revolutionary work. He was arrested in 1895 and exiled to Siberia in 1897. Released in 1900, he again went abroad, living alternatingly in Munich, Zurich, Geneva, and Paris, editing one revolutionary paper after another (*Iskra, Vperiod, Zvezhda*), and writing pamphlets, letters, and instructions. He participated in the Socialist Party Congress of 1903 in London and there assumed the leadership of the forces, opposing any compromise solutions with bourgeois trends. He thus caused a break in the ranks of the socialists, which brought the establishment of the Bolshevist wing. He held firm to his views through the time of the Revolution of 1905 (which for a short time brought him back to Russia) and through the difficult years 1907 to 1912, when Stolypin's reform work in Russia greatly reduced the appeal of the socialist program. His chances revived when war broke out in 1914 and led to a new crisis within Russia. Unwaveringly, he opposed the war, demanding that the proletariat use its arms to fight the ruling propertied classes rather than their brothers abroad; and when tsarist rule was overthrown by the Duma and an amnesty extended to socialist leaders, he found his chance to put his ideas into practice.

Like many of the great figures in Russian history, Lenin possessed a dual personality. Utterly ruthless in his methods, sacrificing without compunction the lives of hundreds of thousands, both guilty and innocent, he yet had a heart of feeling and his actions were dictated by humanitarian considerations. He was a practical follower of a materialistic school, but simultaneously a fervent adherent of a faith which included many idealistic elements. In the same way as Bismarck, he considered politics as "the art of the possible," and was ready to compromise without losing sight of his ultimate aims. He assumed dictatorial powers in a society intended to be the most democratic; and although he misjudged the chances for the Russian experiment in other countries, he proved a farsighted, soberly evaluating statesman for his own country. His ability as an orator was not outstanding, yet he knew how to inspire people and to command their loyalty.

CONDITIONS AT END OF CIVIL WAR

International Position.   Until he suffered a stroke in 1922 and then, diminishingly, until his death in January, 1924, Lenin guided the transformation of Russia into a smoothly operating "Soviet Union" and re-established her international position. He achieved this despite much division and opposition within the ranks of his own adherents. By the end of 1920, the Soviets had succeeded in gaining official recognition from their four Baltic neighbors, Estonia being the first of these nations to sign a treaty with them. Commercial intercourse was also secured with Germany and Sweden. In 1921 Poland, Turkey, and Afghanistan extended their recognition; and in 1922 the first great power, Germany, followed. Russia's former allies, however, who enjoyed greater freedom of action than Russia's neighbors, remained aloof. Since the Soviets had withdrawn from the war in 1917, they were refused a voice in the peace conferences and in planning a future which they had not helped to prepare. A meeting to ascertain their wishes, held on the Turkish island of Prinkipo, came to naught, since the Allies insisted on consulting also the counterrevolutionaries (who, however, refused to appear). As a consequence, the new Europe was drafted by the Western powers not only without the co-operation of defeated Germany, but likewise without that of Russia; and it showed all the shortcomings of a one-sided arrangement. The Soviet Union bitterly denounced the Versailles Treaty (although it rescinded the stipulations of its own peace treaty of Brest Litovsk) as a continuation of the old imperialistic policies of Western powers, and predicted the collapse of the Versailles system before the proletarian advance.

Comintern. In opposition to the traditional "war-breeding" policies of the Western powers, a new "international ideal" was set up in Russia by the institution of the Third International (Comintern). Under Lenin's leadership the first Congress of the Comintern was held in 1919, and a second followed in 1920. These congresses were directed "against chauvinism as well as pacifist hypocrisy" and aimed at world peace through world revolution, at abolition of capitalism in all countries, and at federation of Communist parties everywhere. Nationalization of the press and confiscation of factories, lands, buildings, and banks in all countries were demanded. In advanced countries, the aim was to be achieved by revolts of the proletariat, in colonial areas by risings of the oppressed. Support was given to Communist revolts abroad, such as those occurring in Hungary and Bavaria.

Economic Weakness. The real test of the Soviets' strength and future position, however, depended less upon their relations with other European powers than upon their ability to consolidate their rule and to build a society at home which could secure for the Russian people benefits unparalleled in tsarist times. A proof of their strength was the success of the new government in surviving the civil war; but the growth of their system depended upon the success or failure of economic reconstruction.

INDUSTRIES. By 1920 industrial productivity had fallen by 50 per cent or more; and in the oil, coal, and metal industries it amounted to no more than 10 per cent of the prewar level. Food and fuel were lacking, money was worthless, and black markets and speculation flourished. Nationalization of industries, extended to embrace all enterprises and completed in 1920, had been carried out in a haphazard way by inexperienced officials sometimes for purely ideological reasons, sometimes for the sake of revenge. Managerial experience was also lacking. Labor had to be conscripted; workers were sent against their will wherever needed; and the advantages of nationalization which should have resulted from correlation of industries, standardization, and planning were more than outweighed by discontent and disillusionment. Contrary to their hopes at the beginning of the Revolution, the workers had not become employers; instead government agencies and officials now controlled their labor, using former owners and foremen as industrial managers and mercilessly punishing slackness or non-co-operation.

AGRICULTURE. In the field of agriculture, conditions by the end of 1920 were equally desperate. Productivity had sunk to a new low; no peasant was interested in producing more than his own needs demanded; and anti-Communist feeling ran high among the peasantry. The state, and not they, had legally, at least, taken over all the land and had partitioned and redistributed it. Farms were both unlucrative and overcrowded; for bad conditions in the cities forced millions to migrate to the land. Moscow had declined to one million inhabitants. Compulsory grain deliveries, brutally enforced, lessened interest in tilling the soil and thus caused widespread famine.

TRADE. Unfortunately, even where production was still adequate, it often failed to serve its purpose because the distribution system was disrupted. For the most part normal trade had come to a standstill, black markets operated everywhere, and exchange by barter prevailed. In 1920 all private trading had been prohibited; small factories, shops, and stores were closed; the owners were arrested and their goods confiscated. House owners were dispossessed, the homeless being quartered in any available room. Gold, silver, and jewelry in excess of certain small amounts were confiscated, and all cash had to be deposited with the state bank. Consumers' co-operatives were brought under state control, and food was rationed through a system so arranged as to discriminate against those who belonged to the former privileged classes—this in itself serving as a political tool and lever.

NEW ECONOMIC POLICY

In the face of these conditions and the discontent of the masses, the Soviets in 1921 relinquished, at least for a transitory period, the original program and, against much opposition by radicals, accepted a compromise with Marxist ideology. This compromise covered all phases of public life and became known as the N.E.P. (New Economic Policy). In order to revive production, to increase the output of the individual workingman, to re-establish the transportation system, to reanimate a feeling of responsibility among all citizens, and to check spreading discontent, a series of fundamental changes was undertaken.

Reorganization of Economy. The introduction of the new system was prompted by a mutiny of sailors which occurred in March,

1921, at Kronstadt. After three years of experimenting with communistic organization, a department for economic planning was now created (Gosplan) which began the task of scientifically outlining measures for Russia's political, economic, and social development. A considerable amount of private trade was reintroduced and, to stimulate it, the hoarding of cash and the functioning of private mutual banks were no longer prohibited. Not only was the individual's rights to property partly recognized, but permission was given to leave to heirs sums up to five thousand dollars—a considerable amount for then existing conditions. Large factories were removed from the control of the workers and brought directly under that of the state; small factories were allowed to be operated by private owners, although at times, for lack of capital, they remained dependent upon the state. Considerable differentiation was now made in the remuneration of the worker on the basis of the quality and quantity of his work. Money recovered its value. Co-operative societies gained new concessions. Treaties with capitalistic countries were concluded, and concessions were granted to foreign private entrepreneurs.

In agricultural districts, where discontent with the political structure was greatest, requisitions of grain according to fixed quotas, regardless of the size of the harvest, were stopped. Instead, the peasant was allowed to sell on the free market that part of his crops which exceeded a certain percentage of his harvest. A program of rural electrification was worked out to increase agricultural production and to raise the tiller's living standard.

Evaluation of N.E.P. The N.E.P. marked a retreat from the uncompromising theoretical position of communism. It abolished the delivery quotas formerly imposed on the peasants and some of the restrictions on trade. It allowed a certain new accumulation of wealth (through savings accounts), rights of inheritance, and differentiation of wages. Politically it brought a firmer union of the Soviet peoples and greater restraint in the promotion of world revolution. It was, therefore, bitterly denounced by some groups within the Communist party who insisted that it prevented the progress and success of the cause of the proletariat. It does not seem, however, to have constituted a permanent renunciation of the communistic goal, since it did preserve the nationalization of the banks, land, and large industries and accentuated Communist educational aims. At the same time, it did continue to discriminate against the members of the former wealthy and ruling groups and of the church. In all, the N.E.P. probably did not sacrifice more ground than special conditions temporarily demanded. Its results in any case justified the expectations. Although communistic principles and the classless society were endangered, and although poverty, low wages, and lack of such essentials as fuel persisted, the Soviet regime was saved. The first winter following the inception of the plan was hard. Famine and epidemics ravaged the country, all food rations for workers had to be reduced, and church goods were confiscated to help purchase food for the starving. But under the new policy, and with the help of relief organizations, many Russian peasants resumed work on the land, and agricultural production increased rapidly. Trade and industrial production followed, and illegitimate dealings were curbed. Technical experts were secured, railroads regained their pre-Revolutionary standards, and attention was devoted to education and recreation. A normal, though very low, state budget was drafted, and further planning was put on a sound basis.

Labor and Land Codes. The plan was supplemented in 1922 by a Labor Code and a Land Code. The Labor Code provided for collective agreements through trade-unions of the workingmen. The regulations regarding working hours and labor of women and children were revised, and new laws were passed for health and accident insurance. Old-age insurance, however, was postponed until 1928. The Land Code abolished "once for all" private property in land, forests, and rivers, and forbade purchasing, selling, and mortgaging, while providing for gratuitous leasing if the land were kept under cultivation. Many of the changes were embodied in the fundamental law (constitution) which was re-edited in 1923 on the basis of the political events that had taken place simultaneously with the economic recovery under the N.E.P.

Revision of Constitution. In December, 1922, the first Congress of the United Soviet Socialist Republics had been held and Joseph Stalin had delivered the main report. A Union of Soviet Socialist Republics (U.S.S.R.) was declared, comprising the Russian, Ukrainian, White Russian, and Transcaucasian republics, the last consisting of Georgia, Azerbaidzhan, and Armenia. This union ended all separatist tendencies, which had been particularly strong in the Ukraine. Foreign policies, foreign trade, over-all economic planning, the army, civil and criminal legislation, and education and health services were unified for the whole country. Supreme authority was vested in a central executive committee, which in turn elected a presidium of nineteen members; and executive powers were retained by a Council of People's Commissars.

PROBLEMS

1. Discuss conditions in Russia at the end of the civil war.
2. Discuss the advantages and dangers of the New Economic Policy.
3. Describe the organization of the U.S.S.R. under the constitution of 1923.

39

THE STRUGGLE FOR POWER

Significant Dates

Death of Lenin 1924
Tenth Jubilee of Revolution 1927
Banishment of Trotsky 1928

THEORY AND REALITY

Party Friction. The N.E.P. solved, but also created, economic problems. At the same time, through departure from original socialistic theory, it exercised far-reaching influence on the ideological development of Soviet Russia as a Communist state, and harmony within the ranks of the revolutionaries was endangered. In May, 1921, before Lenin had even formulated the new policy, dissatisfaction came to the fore, evidenced by the resignation of G. Zinoviev, one of the prominent Bolshevik leaders. In the following year, the government found it necessary to reinstate the Cheka (secret police), known since as the Ogpu, and to outlaw tendencies conflicting with the official party program. In time, disunity and difficulties increased, revealing a tripartite rift between government forces, antirevolutionaries, and ultrarevolutionaries. Failing health prevented Lenin from settling the struggle which soon engulfed two of his most influential collaborators, Trotsky and Stalin. Shortly before his death, an open clash occurred at the Congress of the Communist Party which had been convened to discuss problems of economic reorganization, social insurance, and international relations with Western capitalist powers. Sharp controversies arose among the contending factions, and in an atmosphere of distrust and acrimony, demands were promptly voiced for the forceful suppression of all dissenters and of all factions within the party.

Break in the Party. After Lenin's death the need for demonstrating unity and determination, lest the Western world seize a chance for overthrowing the Communist regime, held the party together. A. I. Rykov was chosen chairman of a new government, S. S. Kamenev became vice-chairman, G. V. Chicherin continued as commissar of foreign affairs, and Trotsky took over the commissariat of war. The party itself was reorganized, and despite their disagreements, Zinoviev, Trotsky, and Stalin remained members of the Central Committee and of its executive committee, the Politburo. Stalin was also renamed Secretary General, an office which he had held since 1922. N.E.P. policies were reaffirmed and plans were drawn for balancing the budget, increasing exports, and further reducing "profit-seeking private capital." But peace within the party did not last. The existing breach was widened by acrimonious denunciations among the various factions, and before the year 1925 was over Trotsky was stripped of his powers.

Stalin and Trotsky. The struggle in the party was, as always, evidenced by ambitious personalities. The most outstanding were those of Trotsky and Stalin.

TROTSKY. Leon Trotsky (Bronstein) was born in 1879, offspring of a well-to-do Jewish family. At the early age of 19, he was arrested for revolutionary activities and in 1900 was banished to Siberia. He escaped in 1902 and made his way to England. There he participated in the London Congress of 1903 but vacillated for some time between the positions of Plekhanov, Martov, and Lenin, sympathizing with the more liberal trends of the Menshevists as well as the fervent revolutionary zeal of Lenin and his Bolshevists. For a time, he collaborated with Lenin on the socialist newspaper *Iskra*. In 1905 he returned to Russia and became the outstanding leader of the revolution. After its failure, he was imprisoned and exiled once again to Siberia. He escaped again and eventually reached Vienna where he lived and worked—later in Switzerland, Germany, and France, as well—on leading socialist *émigré* newspapers. During the First World War, he was as unrelenting in his opposition to the war as was Lenin. When the Revolution of 1917 broke out, Trotsky was in

New York; he immediately hurried back to Petrograd and placed himself at Lenin's service. A professional revolutionary and an intellectual, Trotsky was a founder and originator of ideas rather than their executor.

STALIN. Josef Stalin (Dzhugashvili), born in the same year as Trotsky, was the son of poor Georgian serfs. His mother sent him to study for the priesthood, but owing to his Marxist attachments he was expelled from the seminary and became a clerk and a revolutionary agitator. He, too, worked on socialist newspapers, participated in international socialist congresses (Stockholm, London, Vienna), and was several times arrested, sent to prison, and exiled. After 1912, he stood in the front ranks of the Bolshevist group, and he became one of the editors of *Pravda*. News of the February Revolution reached him in exile in Siberia, and he was the first of the Bolshevist leaders to arrive in Petrograd. A practical politician, Stalin was essentially an accomplisher and executor of ideas.

Issues and Struggle. Overshadowing issues stood behind the two men. These issues concerned essentially the relationship of the individual to society and his right to self-assertion and initiative within the communistic world. This basic problem led to clashes on questions of party discipline, party policies, planned economy, and the immediate practical issues of tactics regarding the furthering of world revolution, the training of the young generation, the relationship of town and country, the communization of the peasantry, and the right to independent trade-unions and other agencies outside the party. Trotsky, who was essentially a theoretician and who never held a position of final responsibility, generally advocated the liberal and anarchic side of the program and a materialistic, classless, and communistic world; Stalin, a practical statesman, emphasized the need for adjustment to existing conditions and for discipline, which he considered necessary to guarantee the success of the revolution and the preservation of a proletarian dictatorship in Russia. Both insisted upon their exclusive understanding of true materialistic socialism and upon their adherence to and furtherance of it, and each accused the other of betraying the work of Karl Marx and Lenin.

Stalin's Triumph. After a bitter struggle, success came ultimately to the party of Stalin, not only because he controlled the better organization, the Communist party itself, but also because of the realism of his policies and the inherent disruptive tendencies among his opponents. Trotsky, who several times recovered his position in party and government, was unable to hold the opposition together. Ideological issues divided it into so-called "right" and "left" oppositions. Prominent members among the rightists were Rykov, Bukharin, and the trade-union leader Tomsky; the dominant figures among the leftists, aside from Trotsky, were—at least at certain times—Kamenev and Zinoviev. In 1926 the latter three were successively deprived of their positions. In 1927 Trotsky was expelled first from the Central Committee, then from the party, and in the following year he was banished to Siberia. Kamenev and Zinoviev (who recanted) escaped with a light sentence of exile to European Russia. Even in Siberia, Trotsky continued his opposition and intrigues, and in 1929 he was expelled from the Soviet Union for organizing secret anti-government societies. He went first to Turkey, then to France, to Norway, and finally to Mexico; wherever he was he hurled denunciations and accusations at the Stalin regime. In 1940 he was murdered in Mexico City, a victim it has been said (but never proved) of Stalin's vengeance. In Russia, his followers, the so-called Trotskyites, were persecuted with unrelenting bitterness; many fled or were banished to remote regions, and many perished.

PARTY POLICIES

Party Congresses. The party struggle against the Trotskyites could never have been won had it not been supplemented by constructive political and economic programs worked out by the party. In the early years of the revolution, party congresses were regularly held and were of great significance because they acted as a barometer of popular trends and frequently challenged the policies of the leaders. Later, they were no longer regularly convened and lost some of their democratic importance. In line with centralizing trends, power shifted by the end of the 1920's almost entirely to the party leadership, which formed the "Central Committee," and to its executive agency, the "Politbureau"—the latter consisting of from five to ten members. Party congresses then served mainly to ratify and propagate the programs of the leaders. Of special importance was the fourteenth congress, held in December, 1925, during the course of which a vast industrialization plan was announced; all forces of the Soviet Union were called upon to co-operate lest the capitalistic West, recently strengthened by the Locarno Pact with Germany, put an end to the Communist experiment. Also, a change in the policies regarding the peasantry was proposed. One year later, at the fifteenth congress of the party, which was remarkable for its intransigent attitude towards the opposition, the reshaping of Soviet agriculture was again emphasized, and a change became noticeable in international policy, inasmuch as the drive for world revolution was slowed down. Stabilization in Germany and most other countries rendered the outbreak of world revolution problematic, and only England, hit by a crippling strike of the miners, and China, disturbed by civil warfare, seemed to offer any prospects. Hence, co-operation with capitalist countries to secure credits for industrialization was envisaged.

Tenth Anniversary of Revolution. The following year, 1927, brought the tenth jubilee of the Red Revolution. At the celebration in November, Stalin reviewed the achievements of the past and announced plans for the future. Chief points of the program were the creation of a mighty industry, the radical abolition of private property among peasants and the collectivization of villages, the spread of education to eliminate illiteracy and drunkenness, and the extension of diversified cultural activities. Provisions were made to reduce or cancel the debts of all poor peasants, to decrease taxes, and to raise old-age and veterans' pensions. The death penalty was to be abolished, except for treason, desertion, and corruption; equality for women, wherever still lacking, was to be provided for; and a general amnesty for former political opponents was granted. In foreign affairs, peace, self-determination of the peoples, and intercourse with all nations replaced earlier formulas.

PROBLEMS

1. Discuss the issues involved in the struggle between Trotsky and Stalin.
2. Discuss the role of the party in the building of Soviet Russia.

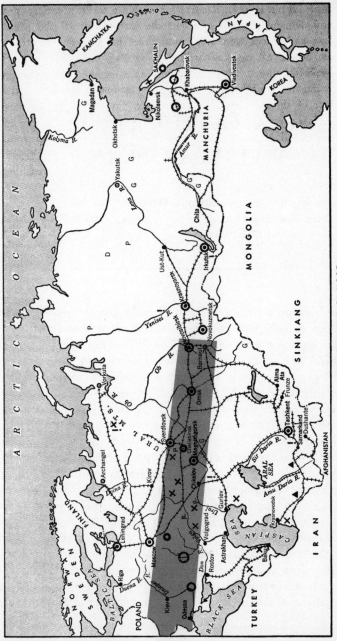

ECONOMIC MAP OF U.S.S.R.

○ MINING AND MANUFACTURING CENTERS   ✕ OIL   ▲ COTTON   G GOLD   P PLATINUM   D DIAMONDS   ++++++ MAJOR RAILWAYS IN ASIA

░ Shaded area = main agricultural belt. North of shaded area = main timber belt. South of shaded area = desert and mountain zone. Along Arctic coast = tundra.
Important Crops: Wheat, Sugar Beets (esp. in Ukraine), Rye, Oats, Maize, Potatoes, Cotton (esp. in Central Asia).   Important Mines: Gold, Silver, Copper, Zinc, Nickel, Bauxite.
Important Industrial Centers: Moscow, Leningrad, Donbass, Urals, Kuzbass, Caucasus, Tadzhikstan, Eastern Siberia for Steel, Machinery, Chemicals,
Textiles, Oil Refineries, and Hydroelectric and Atomic Energy Stations.

40

ERA OF THE FIRST
FIVE-YEAR PLAN

Significant Dates

First Five-Year Plan 1928–1932
Liquidation of Kulaks 1930

It has been argued that political consolidation, crowned by the constitution of 1936, was gained at the cost of economic and social reaction, beginning with the N.E.P. in 1921. However, the Soviet government never lost sight of the socialist program, the execution of which alone could give permanence to the new society; and in many essentials, the N.E.P. was abandoned before 1925. Its replacement by a new order seemed, aside from the political issues, the more urgent because in the course of years speculation in essential commodities increased and began to hamper a steady flow of goods. The quality of industrial work did not improve, and an oversized bureaucracy lacking experience failed, despite its numerous controls, to co-ordinate the national economy. The private entrepreneur had recovered almost one-tenth of the wholesale trade and approximately one half of the retail trade, but fearing renewed expropriations he lacked a feeling of security and therefore sought quick and often extravagant returns for his services. Although industries had steadily gained over agricultural activities, they were still insufficient to provide, in a hostile world, much needed equipment for the country's defense. Medieval and modern production methods still existed side by side.

THE NEW PLAN

In order to overcome the difficulties and to end the mixed private and socialist economy, it was decided to reorganize the planning commission of the N.E.P. and to appoint eleven members who were to work out a co-ordinating plan for all activities—economic, political, cultural, military—in all parts of the empire. During the years 1925 to 1928 this state planning commission (Gosplan) drew the first "Five-Year Plan" (*Piatiletka*), which constituted not so much a final ukase as a program subject to revision while in progress.

Political, Cultural, and Strategic Aspects. Politically, the Five-Year Plan envisaged the strengthening of a socialist society through elimination of resurgent private enterprise. Independent entrepreneurs were to be eliminated through taxation and government competition. Credit facilities were to be withheld from them, freight service for their goods restricted, high rents exacted, and personal discrimination imposed—extending even to their children, who were excluded from universities. Likewise, private enterprise in agriculture was to be curbed, and the liquidation of the so-called kulaks, who formed the wealthier part of the peasantry, was started. Culturally, the plan provided for improved working and living conditions, for extended educational facilities, and for reduction of illiteracy. It laid a new basis for the scientific investigation of Russia's resources and potentialities. Strategically, it outlined better distribution of defense installations throughout the empire and aimed at emancipation from foreign countries and from foreign basic materials.

Industrial Aspects. But the most important section of the plan dealt with economic issues. It stipulated the method and provided the means for the industrial transformation of the country. The over-all productivity of labor was to be increased and definite quotas were set which were to be reached within a specified period. Coal mining in the Donets basin was to be speeded by mechanization, as was steel and iron production. New metallurgic plants were to be erected in Krivoi Rog, in Zaporozhe, on the Kerch peninsula, and in Siberian Kusnetsk, along with a pig-iron and rolled-metal combine at Magnitogorsk, more oil wells in the Caucasus, and truck and tractor works in Stalingrad. Automobiles were to be manufactured in Nizhnii Novgorod on the basis of a contract with Henry Ford, who was to supply parts and technical advice. Prospecting for oil was to be carried out in Asia. The plan provided further for electrification, the importance of which had been emphasized by Lenin. The largest European power plant was to be built in connection with a new dam across the Dnieper at Dnieprostroy. Thousands of kilometers of roads with stone surface were to be laid, and a railroad (*Turksib*) connecting Turkestan and Siberia was to be completed.

Agricultural Aspects. The industrial transformation under the First Five-Year Plan was paralleled by agricultural changes which equaled the industrial innovations in economic importance and surpassed them in social significance. The tension between industrial and agricultural workers—the one representing the proletariat with Marxist tendencies, the other constituting the backbone of individualism and private property—was such as to endanger the whole Soviet structure. A process of leveling was necessary to reconcile the diverging classes and to distribute equitably the economic burden. The Trotskyites had recognized the problem early; and the party under Stalin, though disavowing its precursors, followed their lead when outlining the first Piatiletka.

DISSATISFACTION OF PEASANT. Essentially, the Revolution disappointed the peasant. By 1905 he had possessed in full private ownership about 40 per cent, and by 1914 more than 50 per cent, of the cultivable land. He had since seized the estates of crown, church, and nobility, but had then been deprived of his new acquisitions and of all he had previously owned by the fundamental laws of 1918 which permitted no personal ownership whatever. Not even the usufruct was unequivocally accorded him, for by fixing prices and requisitioning grain and by taxation and socialization of farms, the state deprived him of freedom of action. During the time of "War Communism" (i.e., between 1918 and 1921), committees of Poor Peasants—sometimes directed by those who had remained poor through laziness, drunkenness, or inability—had interfered with successful agriculturists. As a result, many peasants had begun to produce for their own needs only, and though their own consumption increased and their social level was raised, the country as a whole suffered direly. The government found itself forced to intervene; and quotas were fixed by which the peasant had to contribute to the national food supply. Wherever these quotas were not met, grain was collected from him by force. This regulation—ruthlessly enforced—led to grave disturbances and ultimately to counterrevolutionary movements. It was therefore changed in 1921, when the N.E.P. allowed again, within limits, private trade in agricultural products and reintroduced taxation instead of compulsory grain delivery.

NEED FOR RURAL REFORM. The N.E.P., however, failed to offer a solution to the agricultural problem as such, for the gulf between the interests of worker and peasant remained unbridged. The wealthier peasant, the kulak—better off than his neighbor whether by virtue of greater ability and industry or by virtue of shrewdness and skill at exploiting others—began to prosper again; and, leasing more land, he threatened the concept of a classless society. Backward methods of production persisted and coercive measures with regard to collective farming hindered expansion of the sowing area. The First Five-Year Plan, therefore, undertook the task of industrializing agriculture, transforming the peasant into a laborer, and stamping out the main protagonist of individual farming, the kulak.

COLLECTIVE FARMING. For this purpose large mechanically equipped farms were to be created on which the land was cultivated collectively or co-operatively. Peasants who accepted the new system were jointly to own and use all facilities except expensive machinery, which was rented from so-called "tractor stations." A collective farm (*kolkhoz*) was required to raise and deliver to the state a certain amount of produce—the type of produce being to a large extent fixed by over-all planning commissions. Wheat, rye, oats, potatoes, sugar beets, and industrial crops were predominant. What was harvested above the quota had to be used to meet the financial obligations of the kolkhoz and also to pay the tractor station. The remaining surplus could be sold on the free market and the income used for distribution among the members or spent on cultural and other improvements. Speculation in grain was forbidden.

THE KOLKHOZ. A kolkhoz represented an economic and social unit which drew up budgets, paid taxes and expenses, set aside reserves, and divided the common income according to the amount and quality of work performed. It consisted, on an average, of seventy-five families, each of which could maintain personal ownership in house, garden, fowl, and a few animals. A specific measure of productivity on the common land was fixed for the individual farmer, who was obliged to invest between 100 and 150 days' work to meet his quota. Production above the required quota increased the peasant's share in the kolkhoz' profit or reduced his required working time, so that industrious peasants had extra time for attending to their own gardens and for extending their hours of leisure. Strict discipline, enforced by fines and premiums, was observed; "labor brigades" under the command of "brigadiers" attended to the daily requirements. Outside help, except by experts, could not be hired, and negligent members could be expelled. But voluntary withdrawal was also possible, although it involved loss of the share in the common land. A general meeting of the members decided most common problems.

THE SOVKHOZ. The kolkhoz was to constitute the chief form of agricultural organization, but it was to be a transitional step only toward a "higher" form resting on completely nationalized, state-owned, and state-run farms, called *sovkhoz*. Sovkhozes already existed, but they comprised only a very small percentage of the cultivable area of the country. They contributed little to the food supply, serving mainly as experimental farms and as models for kolkhozes.

Trade Aspects. In the period between 1918 and 1928, the official attitude toward trade and traders had alternated between radical rejection of all private trading activities and an attitude of compromise and concession. The Five-Year Plan intended to give stability to new forms of trade which were in line with socialist concepts.

DOMESTIC TRADE. During the period of civil war and intervention, trade—together with all other economic functions—had stagnated and did not revive until the era of the N.E.P. in 1921, when co-operatives, and later private companies, were allowed to function again. But as in industry and agriculture, reaction set in after 1925. State-owned "syndicates" and co-operatives found increased government support and favors, and subsequently the Five-Year Plan stipulated that most wholesale and retail trading activities were to be monopolized by the state.

FOREIGN TRADE. Unlike internal trade, external trade had from the beginning been forbidden to private enterprise, and throughout the period of the N.E.P. it remained an exclusive state monopoly.

The urgent task of achieving the greatest possible self-sufficiency (autarky), the need for careful planning of imports so that they would satisfy the demands for industrialization, and the possibility of using the country's growing buying power for political ends and revolutionary objectives actuated the government to keep its hold on foreign trade. A People's Commissariat for Foreign Trade took charge of exports and imports, trade treaties were concluded, and Soviet buying agencies (e.g., the "Amtorg") were established abroad. If necessary, concessions would be granted to foreign capitalists.

EXECUTION OF PLAN

With great enthusiasm, the execution of the gigantic Five-Year Plan—duly propagandized—was undertaken. Owing to the great exertions of all and in spite of the depression in capitalist countries, its fulfillment could be announced in 1932, one year ahead of schedule.

Industry. During the four years of the plan's execution, the industrialization of the Soviet Union made rapid progress. Coal, steel, oil, and especially electrical power production increased at an enormous rate. Russia regained a place among the industrial nations of the world. The Turksib railroad was opened on May 1, 1930, the Dnieprostroy dam in 1932, and great accomplishments could be registered in all other undertakings. Yet, there was much criticism, and the official figures given to substantiate the advance made were assailed as to their correctness. Failure of the transportation program was only too evident; and the low productivity of the laborer, his wastefulness, and the poor quality of his work were criticized. His lack of interest, a result of low wages, and the excessive costs of production owing to his laxity were pointed out. Too much centralization hampered local initiative; the bureaucracy caused unnecessary delays and through its distrust antagonized skilled technicians, who because of existing shortages generally had to be recruited from former bourgeois circles or from abroad. Actually, some of these technicians were accused of sabotage, others of treason; they were tried, and this action led to severe international repercussions. Furthermore, the existing tension between peasant and industrial worker was not sufficiently alleviated, for the former felt that he still carried the chief burden of the national economy without

benefiting in equal measure from the fruits of the country's industrialization. Food, fuel, and many amenities of life were still lacking
everywhere, particularly because a large percentage of the national
income was reinvested in capital assets; thus living standards were
not raised. Ideologically, there were many doubts (supported by the
Trotskyite opposition) regarding the possibility of permanent socialist success unless the Communist system were to be supported
by all nations of the globe.

Agriculture. Changes and advancement in industry were in
many respects more easily achieved than in agriculture. Not only
were they less dependent upon the vagaries of nature, including the
weather, and the slowness inherent in the natural process of growth,
but they also met fewer obstacles in human relations. The urban
proletariat was differently trained and had different standards and
mores than the peasantry. Much more effort was needed to convince
the agricultural producer of the benefits of the newly planned
system.

COLLECTIVIZATION. Enthusiastic young men were sent to extol
the value of collectivization and preach the advantages of large,
scientifically administered farms. Apart from the propaganda, special privileges consisting of lower taxes and postponement of debt
payments were extended to those who joined. Where these induce-
ments were not sufficient, force was employed. In 1930 a law was
passed which made it possible legally to confiscate land, houses, and
other possessions of all who could be considered kulaks; these were
brutally expelled from collectivized regions. So great was the official
ardor that Stalin himself had to warn against excesses and to insist
on the individual's right to join or not to join collective farming.
By the end of the First Five-Year Plan, about three-quarters of the
arable land was under cultivation by collective or co-operative farms.
In some regions the percentage was higher, as in the Ukraine, the
Caucasus, and the lower Volga region. In the less-fertile northern
parts, collectivization was undertaken on a smaller scale, perhaps
because the government planners needed agriculturists with personal initiative and individualistic spirit to help increase the agricultural production of these not sufficiently exploited regions.

EFFECTS OF COLLECTIVIZATION. The results of collectivization,
bought at the price of incredible suffering by millions of former

well-to-do peasants, were in many respects gratifying. Modern cultivation and cattle-raising methods could be introduced and the burden of the individual was lightened through the use of machinery. In contrast to the mir, the members of the kolkhoz enjoyed more equal rights, better medical care, and wider educational facilities. Agricultural output reached prewar standards in 1930 and surpassed them thereafter. Industrial crops were grown and found ready markets in the numerous processing factories. Politically, collectivism had the advantage for the government in that it enabled the state to exercise stricter supervision of the individualistic agriculturist, for it could exercise control through tractor stations upon which each kolkhoz depended for its needed machinery. The desired leveling process could thus be carried on, and the food supply for the urban worker, who formed the backbone of the Communist system, could be guaranteed.

Trade. Within three years of the initiation of the First Five-Year Plan, private trade declined from 40 per cent to about 15 per cent of the total, and this trend continued thereafter. Price ceilings were imposed on private companies, advertising was banned, and competition was limited; yet prescribed standards were required to be maintained. Nevertheless, a certain amount of private retail trade survived, for, despite much higher prices and manifold handicaps, buyers were attracted by better service, by the greater variety of goods offered, and by their availability without rationing.

PROBLEMS

1. Discuss the aims of the First Five-Year Plan and the main difficulties facing its completion.
2. Discuss the introduction and significance of collective farming.
3. Describe the importance of the foreign trade monopoly for the Soviet system.

41

LIFE IN THE 1920's

It had always been an axiom of socialist thinkers that the transformation of a capitalist into a socialist society would create a new type of man. The Soviet government set itself promptly to the task, in order to accelerate the process, not only of changing the economy of the country but also of modernizing Russian family life, educating all classes and all nationalities of the empire, opening professions to married and unmarried women, and adopting new standards of working conditions on a basis of equal rights and opportunities for all. These great aims, the leaders believed, warranted even very harsh measures. They explained them, and excused themselves at the same time, by pointing out the exigencies resulting from a period of transition linking a capitalist and a socialist era. As a result of the stern measures they took, the suffering of the individual was often very great.

THE FAMILY

The effect of the upheaval of 1917 on the daily life of the average Russian was overwhelming. All existing standards of morality were affected. Concepts of honesty were undermined. People, who in other times would never have injured others, would now betray, steal, and even commit murder. Family life and institutions—long regarded as the foundation of a bourgeois society—suffered particularly; destructive forces released by the Revolution as well as the creative intentions, transformed into law, of the new regime contributed to their collapse. Yet, the dissolution of all accustomed ties proved to be only temporary. Once the period of violence was over old mores of the Russian people began to reassert themselves, and the laws proposed in the early stages with so great a fervor were in large part rescinded. In December, 1917, a decree was published (and in 1918 this was succeeded by a law) which stipulated that only civil marriage carried legality. Marriage formalities were reduced to registration; and divorce was facilitated—all that was demanded being a simple notification from one marriage partner to the other, and, if necessary, an agreement regarding the care of the children. Illegitimate children gained equal rights with legitimate ones. Abortion was legalized in 1920.

Gradual Reversal of Policy.   Immediate practical results were felt in the relationship of parents and children. Homes of rich and poor were broken up, and political disagreements between the older and younger generations, combined with economic changes, added to the disintegration of society. Roaming bands of orphans and fugitive youths became a public nuisance and menace. Famines, poor housing conditions, and redistribution and relocation of millions of people contributed their share to the disorder. These changes, losses, and sufferings could be justified only if the Soviet government had been faced with the necessity of creating a new and stable basis for social relationships by re-establishing and then by bettering prewar living conditions. But poverty and internal ideological struggles prevented efficient measures. Since no law could change the fundamental concept of monogamy and since promiscuity was checked by forces inherent in nature and in pre-established social conventions, normal family life slowly returned. A new Family Code which was published in 1927 and which, in line with reaction against the N.E.P., once more sought to introduce the original aims of the Revolution, proved to be short-lived.

Position of Women.   In line with the professed ideals of the Soviet government, attempts were made with the changes in family relations to improve the social position of women and to guarantee them equality with men. Local laws among "backward" ethnic groups allowing polygamy and child marriage were abolished, and prostitution was fought everywhere. Positions in all professions were opened to women, and their pay was raised to equal that of men. For the sake of employed mothers, nurseries (*crèches*) and kindergartens were founded, and mothers were guaranteed their normal wages for a period of six to eight weeks before and after childbirth (this time span was considerably reduced in the period from 1930 to 1944). Yet the percentage of women engaged in working for a living did not increase until industrialization was accelerated in the interest of national defense, when the labor shortage was painfully felt. The Communist party then began to exercise pressure upon all who were not otherwise engaged, and women undertook to seek employment, preferably in light industries. During the Second World War more than half of all persons employed were female; in the medical field, their numbers reached almost 75 per cent of the total.

EDUCATION AND SCIENCE

While the concepts of family life were undergoing constant changes, the Soviet government found it necessary to pay much more attention to the education of the young generation. Plans for abolishing widespread illiteracy had been laid by the tsarist government; the Soviet rulers carried out revised plans, but in addition to such an aim they envisaged also the broader one of building an educational system which would open opportunities to all for technical and university training, according to ability and without regard to birth and family background. They furthermore experimented with methods already tried in progressive schools of leading Western countries—such as Germany and Switzerland—and based on greatest possible freedom for the pupils. Their foremost educational aim was "scientific enlightenment" of the young Soviet citizen.

Education.   In 1918 the first Soviet Uniform School Statute was promulgated. It reduced the customary discipline of tsarist schools, deprived the church of all influence, and emphasized manual instead of intellectual training. But relaxation of discipline in the period of civil war led to an exodus of pupils from the schools and also to a great decline in the number of educational institutions —two factors which combined to lower the already deficient scholastic standards. Only after political stabilization was achieved in

1923 could a new statute of the "Uniform School" be worked out to check the growth of ignorance. Unfortunately, there was, in the face of large increases in the number of attending pupils, a serious lack of teachers.

THE POST-REVOLUTIONARY SCHOOL. The new statute emphasized the teaching of social relationships and reduced emphasis on mastery of facts and methods. A program of "complex themes and projects" was outlined, paralleling so-called progressive trends in other countries; but it did not work because broad concepts, such as nature or society, were made topics for discussion among pupils who had not acquired even the most elementary knowledge. The same year, 1923, brought a reorganization of universities. Like the school program, it led to a lowering of former scholastic standards, for discrimination was exercised against the intelligentsia and their children, regardless of ability, and preference was given to Communist workers. Moreover, strict ideological supervision hampered the free development of professor and student.

END OF EXPERIMENTATION. The years 1925 to 1930, consequently, led to a revision of the entire educational system. Political indoctrination was reduced and, despite lack of competent teachers, emphasis was placed instead on reading, writing, arithmetic, language, geography, and literature. Compulsory primary education, planned in tsarist times but unfulfilled because of the outbreak of war, became a fact for almost all of Russia, regardless of race or religion. The introduction of a simplified alphabet helped to carry out this program. Discipline also was reintroduced; and physical culture received special attention, with stress on co-operative sports which simultaneously served military demands.

Science. When the Communists took over Russia, the study of the natural sciences flourished and the Academy of Sciences enjoyed high rank in the world. Founded in 1725, its fame had rested during its initial stages mainly on foreign, particularly German, scholars; the physicist Euler, the botanist Steller, and the natural scientists Gmelin and Pallas were among its most celebrated members. The first Russian of great repute was Lomonosov, and after him the Academy became a truly national institution. During the nineteenth century, its members held distinguished places in their fields—Petrov and Lenz in physics, Ber (Baer) and especially Pavlov (nervous reflexes) in biology, Mechnikov in physiology, Chernyshev and Vernadsky in geology, Belopolsky in astronomy, and Soloviëv and Kluchevsky in history. In addition, many outsiders, such as Mendeleyev, who developed the atomic table, enjoyed equal or greater fame.

Soviet Academy of Sciences. Lenin recognized the importance of maintaining existing standards. Science was furthered in every way, and the geologist Karpinsky was elected president of a reformed Academy. But only after the consolidation of the country following the period of civil war was it possible to continue the great tradition. Branches of the Academy were set up throughout the country to train scientific personnel, stimulate interest, and broaden the basis of technological studies. Various divisions were created for natural sciences, history, literature, economics, and other fields. By 1939 there were some one hundred and fifty institutions, museums, and observatories in existence. Eminent men emerged or continued their studies begun in tsarist times; the historians Pokrovsky, Volgin, and Tarle, the physicians Bogomolets, Burdenko, Filatov, and Stern (first woman member of the Academy), the physicist Kapitsa and the chemist Semënov, the agriculturist Michurin, and many others in all fields of science contributed to the advancement of mankind's understanding of natural and social forces.

Academic Freedom. The state took an interest in their work and —through the establishment of laboratories and research institutes and through "authors' certificates," prizes, honors, orders, and cash premiums for inventors—endeavored to stimulate the greatest possible productivity. On the other hand, the state supervised the attitudes of its scientists and the political significance of their work. If their views or teachings were contrary to the accepted ideology, they were removed or their work was disavowed. In 1929 almost one third of the members of the Academy, including some of its most distinguished men, were purged, and again a few years later the work of others was interrupted and their books were revised or disappeared from the market. Thus, science both profited and lost through state interference; but as a whole the achievements in Soviet Russia, though not reaching in originality and scope the level of the United States or Germany, kept up with the standards of Western countries.

ARCTIC INSTITUTE. One of the special fields of Soviet scientific endeavor was the arctic regions, their possibilities, problems, and resources. In 1930 a separate institute was created to continue work which had been carried on from the time of Peter the Great. This comprised investigating the wealth in iron, zinc, gold, and furs of Russia's arctic regions and the cultures of the inhabitants; it comprised also establishing communication lines and transportation centers for the dawning air-borne age. Under the direction of Professor Schmidt, and often with the help of involuntary labor, considerable advance was made. Ports were founded, and the northeastern passage became a regular trade route. Attempts were even undertaken to develop the arctic regions for agricultural production, but—partly because of inadequate and inefficient personnel—progress was slow.

LIVING CONDITIONS

Naturally, the Soviet government was aware of the close relationship of family life, education, and general living conditions. All efforts to improve these met, however, with great difficulties. The Revolution of 1917 had ruined the high standards of the upper class without improving immediately the economic situation of the workingman; only his social position had been changed. The task of bringing about an amelioration also of his economic conditions was therefore re-emphasized during the period of the N.E.P. as well as during that of the First Five-Year Plan. The achievement of the aim, however, depended first of all upon a vast increase of industrialization and production, and this in itself was to bring grave hardships.

Wages and Prices. During the period of the N.E.P., wages had risen considerably. By 1928, there was much less inequality of income than Russian subjects had known in tsarist times; yet, unlike the years immediately following the Revolution, differences did exist. Sixty per cent of the population drew medium wages about two to four times as high as the lowest and two to four times less than the highest. These inequalities were modified, though, by the fact that rationing regulated the supply of goods, that many prices were fixed, that rent controls were imposed, and that, for lack of production, even those who possessed large incomes could not buy many things. Wage differences resulted from various factors: salaries were often paid on the basis of piece work, hard workers receiving more than others; bonuses and prizes were awarded; and certain types of work, such as that of the higher bureaucracy, were more generously rewarded than the work of the manual worker, and the work of the industrial laborer more generously than that of the peasant.

Unfortunately for the population, prices as well as wages rose. Goods fixed at low prices could be purchased only within the allotted scanty rations and often necessitated waiting in long queues. Up to 40 per cent of the total wages was withheld at the source for taxes, trade-union dues, social insurance (old age, funeral), and educational projects. The withheld wages served also to build sanitariums and to provide free medical and dental care, although if specialists were called in, they were allowed to charge an extra fee.

Working Hours. An eight-hour working day was introduced after the Revolution, and during the times of reconstruction this was lowered to seven. Unemployment disappeared by 1930; thereafter a shortage of labor arose which caused the government to exercise economic and other pressure on people so that they would accept jobs wherever needed under the Five-Year Plan and stay on the job. Experiments were also made with the abolition of Sundays and the introduction of uninterrupted workday weeks; factories were operated without pause, and workers labored in shifts of five or six days, followed by a holiday which differed according to the shift. But this plan caused confusion and dissatisfaction, ruined industrial machinery by overworking it, and made impossible common enjoyment of holidays. The number of working days per year was scarcely less than in prewar times, and two weeks of yearly vacation just balanced the loss of the religious holidays celebrated in tsarist times.

Living Standards. As a result of general conditions, living standards remained very low. The shortage of housing was terrible, and whole families had to be pressed into one or two rooms, without private cooking or washing facilities. Food remained extremely scarce. In many families, there had to be several wage-earners in order to achieve a minimum of comfort. Slack work was severely punished, job changing was made difficult, and absenteeism was bitterly denounced. Since political reliability could not be expected from every worker, strict supervision was exercised; and this often poisoned the atmosphere. Office workers and intellectuals from tsarist times, even though most of them served loyally, worked under particularly adverse conditions; only with difficulties could they find security in the new society. Those who were considered unreliable were shifted without compunction to distant regions; families were broken up, productive work was interrupted, and intense misery resulted.

PROBLEMS

1. Discuss the influence of the Bolshevist Revolution on family life.
2. Discuss the influence of the Revolution on educational standards.
3. Discuss the position of women in the U.S.S.R.

42

RELIGION AND THE ARTS

Significant Dates

Disestablishment of Orthodox Church . . .	1918
Arrest of the Patriarch	1922
League of Militant Atheists Founded	1925

It was only during the 1930's, after the full stabilization of Stalin's power and the elimination of all opposition, that the functionaries of the Communist party secured a complete hold over all aspects of public life. During the fifteen years following the Revolution, however, there existed much room for experimentation, discussion, and individual activity. Intellectual life was vigorous, and conditions were in flux. Thus, in the field of religion, we find not one single pattern, but various divergent trends. Some groups defended the existing church, others tried to imbue it with a new spirit, and again others sought to abolish it altogether. In the various fields of art, there were men who adhered to tradition as well as those who were receptive to new tendencies; unhampered they created significant works out of the richness of their own gifts. An irreparable loss for Russia was caused, however, by the emigration of many excellent scholars, writers, and artists. Some left their country immediately after the outbreak of the Revolution; others tried for a number of years to adjust to the new conditions but eventually gave up and left.

RELIGION

In twentieth-century Russia, which found its inspiration in Karl Marx's materialistic conception of history, a conflict between scientific and metaphysical thinking was inevitable. This was not altogether a continuation of the nineteenth-century European conflict between science and religion, which had resulted from widespread implicit faith in the progress of mankind through a deeper understanding of the laws of nature and their application to human affairs. The conflict in Soviet Russia was more of a practical than a philosophical nature; science was promoted as a means rather than as an idealistic end, and religion was fought as a material obstacle rather than as an outmoded attitude.

Attack on Orthodoxy. After the overthrow of tsarism, the Synod of the Orthodox church, which Peter the Great had introduced and which under Pobedonostzev had exercised such unwholesome political influence, was abolished by the Provisional Government. It was replaced by a patriarchate in Moscow such as had existed before Peter's time, and the metropolitan Tikhon became the first holder of the office. True to the liberal concepts of the February Revolution, full equality was guaranteed to all faiths. Upon seizure of power by the Communists, further steps were undertaken. To be sure, Karl Marx, who had seen in religion the "opium of the people" and believed that together with the bourgeois society religion would die a natural death, had not been in favor of violence against believers—nor was Lenin. The latter considered religion a private affair of each citizen, even though he held that a good Communist or party member could not remain neutral in the struggle against it. Yet, both had always feared the church as a political opponent, as a servant of the forces opposed to a socialist society. They had centered particularly bitter attacks on the Russian Orthodox church, which had always been closely linked with tsarism and which, owing to its anti-rationalistic attitude, had done so little for the material advancement of the people. Once in power, the Bolshevik government abolished therefore all privileges of the established church, confiscated its lands together with those of all other proprietors, ordered the separation of church and state, and did little to protect churchmen who found themselves attacked by local Communist agencies.

Reaction of the Church. In the face of the new forces, the church authorities acted blindly and severely and preached opposition and revenge. Even in Kerensky's time, they had failed to consider the numerous aspects in the life of their church which stood in dire need of reform, and in a *sobor,* held in the summer of 1917, they had shown an intransigent, reactionary spirit. After the Soviets had taken over the government, they continued to mix in political affairs. They denounced the Soviets' foreign policy and refused to part with their treasures (even those whose surrender would not have affected Christian duties). They supported the White armies, propagated anti-Semitism, did nothing to relieve famine and suffering, and answered the relatively moderate measures of the Soviets with denunciations and refusals of reform and compromise. As a result, many former adherents left the church, and persecutions of churchmen by zealous Communists increased. During the famine years, official confiscations of jewels, gold, and silverware were carried out, and a number of outrages occurred, including the desecration of churches and the murder or execution of priests, monks, and higher churchmen. Catholic and other denominations were similarly affected. Yet, church services were not prohibited, and many people frequented, as before, the places of worship.

The "Living Church."   While the assault on the church brought, as many faithful felt, a purification of the church, others even within the church believed that elimination of the unconcerned church members was not enough, that a thorough reform, also in dogmatic aspects, had to be carried out, and that the church owed the government a more positive attitude. Thus came into being a movement called the "Living Church." It demanded that the gospels, not the church canons, be taken as the basis of religious teachings, that celibacy be abolished for the higher clergy, that monasteries become "working communities," that communion be celebrated "in remembrance," and that humanitarian tasks be given more attention. At a great church *sobor* in 1923, the representatives of the Living Church, though by far in the minority, pushed through some of their demands. They managed also to "depose" Patriarch Tikhon.

Compromise.   The efforts of the Living Church, which found but slight support from a government essentially disinterested in religious life, miscarried when Tikhon, who had been under arrest for some time, reversed the course of the official church. Fearing that an inner split would perfect its ruin, he issued a statement abjuring his former opposition to the Soviet government and exhorting his flock to obey the state as God-ordained authority. Later, he even severed connections with the bitterly antagonistic churches of the *émigrés*. His acts led to a *modus vivendi* between church and government. Theological publications were again allowed, obstacles to the use of the churches were removed, and some theological seminaries were reopened. But the clergy did not regain citizenship rights until much later, and the government remained adamant in refusing any public religious instruction of children under eighteen years of age. Eventually, most of the adherents of the Living Church returned into the fold of the official church.

League of Atheists. In 1929 the position of the state toward the church was clarified by a law, which reasserted the church's right to exist and, even though discriminating in many practical matters (including food rations) against its officials, gave it also greater financial freedom. In exchange, the church endeavored to prove its loyalty to the state. But a new danger arose from another source —the foundation of a League of Militant Atheists.

ACTIVITIES. In the period of the First Five-Year Plan, the membership of the League climbed, reaching eventually more than five million. As an antidote against religion, it spread scientific information which conflicted with biblical stories and interpretations; it advocated a new morality, a new "humanitarian" culture, as opposed to that of the Christian churches; it instituted new rites to take the place of those of the church; and it tried to influence the education of old and young through books, pamphlets, and exhibits. It also spread information about frauds of the church in tsarist times and exposed the political servitude which the church had shown to the "oppressive" tsarist government. Under its auspices and under Communist pressure, polls were held and, "by request of many communities," churches were closed wherever possible. Universities, newspapers, cinemas, and trade-unions held religious institutions up to ridicule, and the spreading of science was used as a counterweight against "religious superstition."

DECLINE. Despite these attacks on the religious life in the Soviet Union, the church still managed to hold its own. It saved a large part of its wealth, it kept on functioning, and it retained the right to train new personnel in its seminaries and to operate monasteries. About half of the church buildings remained in its hands. The population, though mainly the older generation and those on the land, still crowded into the churches, and even urban workers, who were most affected by the anti-religious propaganda, came to visit them —at least for baptisms and funerals. Actually, by the end of the First Five-Year Plan, the Militant Atheists had already spent their main forces. Their appeal was declining, and the government evidenced lack of interest in religious affairs rather than active interference in the League, lest by creating "martyrs" an opposite effect be reached. Apparently, the government was also concerned with unfavorable repercussions abroad.

ARTS

During the years of its struggle against the church, the Soviet government never lost sight of the people's desire for pageantry as well as for spiritual nourishment, and, partly as a measure against religion, it fostered interest in music, theater, art, and literature. Even during the years of civil war, it sponsored artistic and literary activities in line with the tradition of tsarist times. A special organization, the "Proletcult," and the "Trade-Union of Art Workers" were founded to stimulate artistic creation and align it with political trends. But the accent on social consciousness, in accord with the basic concepts of the new state and the introduction of state sponsorship, public ownership of the publishing houses, and censorship, contributed to limiting the artist's initiative. On the other hand, commercialism in art, including film and radio, was eliminated; press sensationalism was suppressed, and new ways for influencing the masses were adopted, exploiting the educational and technical possibilities of the new age.

Literature. The development of all arts in Soviet Russia followed, as a whole, political trends. In the period up to 1921, destructive, negative, and revolutionary productions prevailed; from 1921 to 1933, experiments in new forms of expression were carried on; the period from 1934 until 1941 witnessed a revival of the national tradition; and the years since 1941 reflected war and victory.

NOVEL AND POETRY. In the first five years after the Revolution, some of the best writers of Russia left their country, and only a few of them, such as Alexei Tolstoy, returned. Nevertheless, the literary production was then, as well as during the years following the initiation of the N.E.P., very rich. Among the outstanding figures were distinguished masters of tsarist times, such as Maxim Gorky, Alexander Blok ("The Twelve"), and Vladimir Mayakovsky (poems). In the beginning they worked in full freedom and could indulge in experiments with modern artistic forms and abstract topics as well as with a new realism and purposeful revolutionary themes. Gradually, however, opposition to "decadent, bourgeois tastes" was demanded of all. Neutrality was rejected and, in line with Lenin's view that literature also had the task of serving the Revolution, preference was given to those who showed a positive attitude toward the Communist world and Communist aims. For this reason, although "great variety of form" was still permitted in the middle twenties, individualistic poets like Pasternak, or satirists like Zoshchenko, were looked at askance. On the other hand, young authors like Fadeev ("The Nineteen"), Ehrenburg ("Julio Jurenito"), Sholokhov ("And Quiet Flows the Don"), and Ilf ("Twelve Chairs") made their way to the front. They gained not only official approval but applause from the Russian public, and some of their works were accepted abroad as outstanding contributions to world literature. They drew their inspiration largely from the stirring period of the Revolution; later, in a more shallow way, they occupied themselves with the "heroic" times of the Five-Year Plan and the impact of industrialization.

THEATER AND FILM. The theater and the film were considered by the Communist government as particularly useful mediums for spreading the party creed, and both received much attention from the authorities. In quality of performance, the theater after 1918 had difficulty in challenging the standards of earlier periods; yet it flourished. Great new dramas or comedies were, however, not written, and as for other branches of the arts, considerable difficulties arose toward the end of the twenties, when supervision, exercised at first by an association of the writers themselves and later by the party bureaucracy, was increased.

Radio and film, expressing as they do the modern age, showed considerable accomplishments. The film in particular benefited from inspired authorship and eminent directors, such as Sergei Eisenstein.

Music. The path of musical development paralleled that of literature. The government and party showed their interest in it as a means of educating the masses and as an expression of "Soviet culture." On the basis of Communist principles, social aspects were emphasized over aesthetic problems. In 1924 an Association of Proletarian Musicians was founded which lasted until 1932 and then was replaced by a Union of Soviet Composers. The trend was against sentimental, romantic, and abstract forms and favored folk traditions and other forms thought to be intelligible to the average citizen. Two composers of pre-Revolutionary days, the popular Miaskovsky and Prokofiev, retained their high rank; but here a member of the younger generation, Dimitri Shostakovich, succeeded in sharing and later surpassing their fame.

Painting and Architecture. In painting, little of durable value was created. Upon assumption of power, the Bolsheviks dissolved the Academy of Fine Arts and nationalized all great art collections; but, productively, they added little to existing treasures. Far more was achieved in the realm of architecture, where they sponsored gigantic undertakings in industrial expansion, in city planning, and in public buildings. Commensurate with the spirit of the age, the accent was put on functional ends. Here it was also possible to evoke interest and cultivate talent among the many nationalities of the Union, whose advancement remained one of the chief concerns of socialist rule.

PROBLEMS

1. Discuss the causes of the collapse of the Communist fight against the church.
2. Describe the contributions of Soviet art.

43

EVOLUTION OF STALINISM

Significant Dates

Great Party Purges 1934–1938
Trade-Union Reform 1935
Stalin Constitution 1936

The great upheavals and changes, which the era of revolution, civil war, N.E.P., and the First Five-Year Plan had brought, were followed not by years of quiet evolution but by new struggles, terrors, and finally war. These years are intimately connected with two personalities: Stalin and Hitler. It was the latter whose policies increasingly forced the Soviets to concentrate on building a socialist society in one country rather than on a world-wide scale, and even to seek "collective security" with capitalist nations. And it was Stalin who, realizing the situation, resolutely set to this task by increasing centralization of all administrative and economic power in his own hands, and by speeding up collectivization, industrialization, and militarization at the expense of the living standards of the nation. He ordered tightest supervision of all activities—political, economic, cultural—and eliminated with brutality all possible opposition. The number of those who perished, guilty or innocent, will probably never be known, nor the number and suffering of those who, persecuted and banished, had to contribute in labor camps to the building of Stalin's empire. On the other hand, Stalin approved also a new constitution which on paper reiterated the humanitarian aims of socialism and which was to give the legal basis for the Soviet system in the age of the dictatorship of the proletariat.

PURGES

During the 1930's, the fight against all who dissented from the official party policies broadened considerably. As in earlier years, the Soviet leadership was divided, with some in favor of vigorous revolutionary action, and others, though not less determined with regard to the aim of a Communist society, advocating a more cautious attitude. As a shrewd politician, Stalin, through his key position as Party Secretary, committed himself to neither side. He used sometimes the one, at other times the other to serve his own ambitions and further the growth of the Soviet system and empire.

Rightist Opposition. The expulsion of Trotsky from the Soviet Union in 1929 had by no means decided the question of supreme power among the Soviet leaders. Stalin saw to it that as soon as Trotsky had left the party leadership the fight was extended to the "right opposition." The right's insistence before the Party Congress of 1927 that everyone should enjoy the privilege of criticism, although he might be compelled to obey the final party decisions, was rejected. In May, 1929, Rykov was removed as chairman of the Council of the People's Commissars, an office taken in 1930 by Molotov; in June, Tomsky lost his position as head of the trade-unions; and in July, Bukharin was deposed as head of the Comintern. In the following year, a great trial was started against another rightist group, the "Industrial party," which was accused of Menshevik heresy. Denounced for conspiring with foreign enemies, principally England and France, and for sabotaging the industrial program by false propaganda and incorrect planning, all participants were condemned.

Trials and Executions. In the following decade, Stalin accelerated the process of disposing of all forces which he considered a threat to the Communist government and to his personal rule. From 1934 on (when the murder of one of Stalin's friends, Kirov, in Leningrad was interpreted as an attack on Bolshevik rule), each year witnessed trials, courts-martial, purges, and executions. Rightists and leftists alike found themselves accused and repeatedly tried, and ultimately all lost their positions and many their lives. Tomsky committed suicide. Zinoviev and Kamenev after "confessing" their guilt were executed in 1936, as were Bukharin and Rykov in 1938; each time many followers died with them, while less conspicuous figures were imprisoned or exiled. In 1937 the purges were extended to the Red Army, and Marshal Tukhachevsky and seven other generals were executed after a secret court-martial. Those who escaped trial but who were not considered fully reliable were removed from their offices, so that in 1939, when the Second World War began, few of the prominent leaders of the Bolshevist Revolution held leading positions in Russia.

STALIN CONSTITUTION

Expulsions, trials, purges, and executions constituted the negative side of Stalin's program. Times demanded, however, positive steps, and as a statesman, Stalin was well aware of it. In particular, it seemed necessary to him to construct a firm legal foundation for his government. As a challenge from the outside increased and the chance for world-wide expansion of the Communist system and for the "withering away of the state" in Marx's sense receded, he undertook the task of sponsoring a new constitution attuned to the specific needs of the Russian Soviet empire. It was promulgated in 1936.

Socialist Basis.   Like the pre-existing law, the Stalin constitution provided for a Union of Soviet Socialist Republics based on socialist ownership of the means and instruments of production. Socialist ownership would consist (1) in the form of state property (land, subsoil wealth, banks, factories, the bulk of the dwelling houses, state farms, and transportation already belonged to the state), and (2) in the form of co-operative enterprises (including collective farms, kolkhoz markets, and farm machinery). But in addition, the law would now allow for a small private economy as long as this was based on the personal labor of peasants and artisans and excluded the use of the labor of others. Personal property within defined limits would be permitted; and savings, houses, and furniture could be inherited. The guiding principle was not the slogan "To each according to his needs," but "From each according to his ability; to each according to his work."

Political Structure.   The Union was now composed of eleven republics: the Russian, Ukrainian, White Russian, Azerbaidzhan, Georgian, Armenian, Turkmen, Uzbek, Tadzhik, Kazakh, and Kirgiz; to these were added, during and after World War II, the Karelo-Finnish, Moldavian, Lithuanian, Latvian, and Estonian republics. (The Karelo-Finnish Republic was eliminated again in 1956). Among all republics, the Russian Republic was not only the largest, but also the dominant. Each republic possessed sovereignty except for the powers exercised by the Union, which included questions of war and peace, defense, foreign trade, economic planning, taxes, banking, transport, and communications. Each retained on paper the right to secede. International relations formed part of the tasks of the Union until an amendment of 1944 allowed Union republics to enter into direct relations with foreign states. In addition to the Union republics, there existed Autonomous republics and Autonomous regions and National districts which were organized along parallel lines but which enjoyed a lesser degree of independence. Special guarantees were given the numerous ethnic minorities in the Union; they were allowed to develop their cultural heritage and to retain their own languages and their customs and individual institutions as long as these remained "socialist in content."

Executive, Legislative, and Judicial Structure. The highest authority of the Union was vested in the Supreme Soviet, which consisted of a Soviet of the Union and a Soviet of Nationalities, both elected by the people for a term of four years. The Soviet of the Union was composed of one delegate for each 300,000 of the population; that of the Nationalities, of a fixed number of delegates representing each Union republic, each Autonomous republic, and each Autonomous region. The Supreme Soviet possessed exclusive legislative powers and was charged to elect the presidium of the Supreme Soviet and to appoint the government (the Council of People's Commissars), which exercised the highest executive and administrative functions. It likewise chose, for a five-year term, the highest judicial organ, the Supreme Court of the Union. In practice, its role was limited; its sessions turned out to be rather short since decisions were mainly made in advance and little discussion took place. Moreover, its presidium had the power to act for it whenever it was not in session. On the other hand, there existed thousands of local and district soviets which met frequently and within the restricted areas of their competence possessed considerable influence.

In the legal hierarchy, there existed, besides the Supreme Court of the Union, Supreme Courts of the various republics and Special Courts as well as People's Courts. These were to be elected for each district by its citizens for a three-year term; area, regional, and territorial courts by corresponding soviets for five years; and supreme courts of Autonomous and Union republics for a similar term. Unlike the practice in the United States, no separation of powers was introduced; the final authority was vested in the legislature, which, after fully debating issues, generally took decisions unanimously.

Rights of Citizens. The constitution guaranteed all individual citizens full equality regardless of race and nationality, even though in practice discrimination against some groups, such as the Jews, occurred; punishment was provided for those who preached race prejudice or inequality. Each citizen received the right to employment and to payment for his work—a right ensured by the "elimination of the possibility of economic crises and the abolition of unemployment" because of the "socialist organization of the national economy." He had the right to rest, to leisure, to maintenance (in old age, sickness, and disability), and to education. Women were assured of equal rights with men in all fields. Freedom of conscience—i.e., of religious worship as well as of disseminating antireligious propaganda—was likewise ensured to all. Freedom of speech, press, assembly, and demonstrations were proclaimed, as was inviolability "of the person" and "of the home of the citizen," including privacy of correspondence. Universal military service was made compulsory, and offenses against public property were punishable.

Franchise. The most important change, compared with previous constitutions, consisted in the elimination of the disabilities formerly imposed on priests, merchants, and ex-members of tsarist authorities. Now that the bourgeoisie was virtually eliminated, all citizens were to be equal, with equal ballot rights. Candidates for office were to be nominated by public organizations, such as the Communist party, trade-unions, co-operatives, youth organizations, and cultural societies. The election of deputies was secret, and deputies were subject to recall at any time by a majority of the electors. However, only the name of one candidate, chosen though he may have been after considerable debate, appeared on the election lists, and pressure was exercised on everyone to vote.

Amendments. The constitution itself could be amended by a two-thirds majority in the Supreme Soviet of the Union. During the following decades, numerous amendments were actually voted.

COMMUNIST PARTY

Membership. The Communist party was mentioned only twice in the constitution and was defined as the "vanguard of the working people in their struggle to strengthen and develop the socialist system," and as the society of the "most active and politically most conscious citizens in the ranks of the working class." It was the only party in the Union, and admission was difficult. In 1918 it counted about 115,000 members; in 1923, 75,000; by 1928, however, it had increased to about one million out of a population of one hundred sixty million, but repeated purges kept it down to a nucleus of devoted adherents. New members were often recruited from suborganizations such as the Communist youth group, the Comsomol. After 1928 membership continued to fluctuate; yet by 1941 the party counted two and one half million members. The decision to end the system of periodical purges and to admit millions of soldiers to the privileges of membership brought a large influx of new members during the Second World War.

Position of Party. The party was given no official status as a government agency, but it held vast powers. Through its members, its youth organization, and its right to nominate candidates for offices, it secured a dominant position in internal affairs; and through its connection with the Third International it exercised extensive influence in foreign policies. The decisions of its executive committee, the Politburo, were of no less importance than those of the Soviet government, whose directing members—particularly Stalin himself—generally held positions in both. The party exercised influence on law courts, whose task it was to further the interests of the proletariat.

Trade-Unions. Factory soviets and trade-unions, which at the beginning of the Revolution assumed great responsibilities, soon lost their importance. The nationalization of industrial plants made their control by the workers illusory, and in line with this development trade-unions began to function as government agencies. Although trade-unions strove to protect the interest of the workers, the nature of the Soviet state, which accorded many privileges to the manual worker, turned the trade-unions into executors of the government's over-all policies; and these were not necessarily in line with the specific interests of each individual group of workers. The head of trade-unions, Tomsky, fell out of favor with the party leadership over just this question, and his resignation and later suicide were the result of his disagreements over the position of trade-unions as instruments of the state. However, Stalin ordered a change in 1935, and "democratization" of trade-unions was provided in order to enable them to represent the workers' cause to the government rather than vice versa.

FINANCES

State Control of Finances. Unchecked by trade-unions and controlled by a party which did not allow for deviations, the government as conceived in the Soviet constitution found itself in a unique position. In contrast with capitalistic countries, where the authorities find checks on their power through the strength of private capital, the Russian government enlarged its constitutional supremacy by securing direct control over practically all the financial resources of the country. During the first few years after the Revolution, these were necessarily small, and most of the state's income was derived from confiscation and disposal of the wealth accumulated in tsarist times. Printing of paper money likewise served to bridge the initial need. But, in line with the N.E.P., a state bank was founded in 1921, and the entire banking system was changed. Whereas during the time of civil war the existing private banking facilities had simply been taken over by the state, an intricate branch system of the central bank was now introduced; special credit institutions for the various branches of trade and industry were created, and in 1923 Soviet savings banks were founded. All financial operations were made dependent upon the state and its planning commissions, which issued loans to buyers who in turn used these to advance payments to their suppliers. Money markets, as known in capitalistic countries, ceased to function in Soviet Russia.

Currency. The year 1922 brought also a currency reform and a stable money unit, the chervonets, guaranteed by a 25 per cent bullion reserve. Two years later, the chervonets was replaced by the ruble which was fixed at one-tenth of a chervonets. Lacking intrinsic value and serving only as a means of facilitating the exchange of goods and services within the country, the ruble was artificially kept stable and in 1936 was pegged at 19 American cents. This exchange rate remained until after World War II, when it was changed to

25 cents. The commodities produced in Russia and at the direct disposal of the government served to guarantee its value. Foreign debts contracted by the Soviet state were conscientiously honored, and many internal loans for financing industrialization were successfully floated. The interest rate of 8 to 9 per cent in 1929 sank by 1940 to 3 to 5 per cent, but many issues carried no interest at all and instead were raised as lottery loans.

Budget. The budget increased enormously. In 1922, when stabilization began, it amounted to one and a half billion rubles; by 1929, it was eight times as high; and during the following twelve years it increased again eightfold.

REVENUES. The main income was derived from the surplus ("gains") of state-owned industries and from the sales tax of the co-operatives. These surpluses corresponded to the profits of industries in capitalistic countries, which in the true sense of the word did not exist in Russia. Within its socialist society, not supply and demand but the needs of the state governed the profit or surplus, and prices were fixed sometimes below cost, sometimes far above, but in all cases according to over-all plans and general political considerations. The rest of the state income was made up chiefly of income and inheritance taxes, many heavy indirect taxes, and customs revenues. In the early years of the Soviet Union's existence, the income taxes were based on class principles, private traders paying up to 55 per cent of their often small earnings, journalists and actors paying from 18 to 30 per cent, workmen and employees still less, and peasants from 3 to 30 per cent. The inheritance tax was graduated, reaching a maximum of 90 per cent.

EXPENDITURES. On the passive side of the budget, the main expense factors were those for defense and for industrialization, the latter actually constituting less an outlay than a capital investment. Smaller amounts were disbursed as health and educational obligations and as interest on government loans.

PROBLEMS

1. Compare the centralization of power in the U S.S.R. and in the United States.
2. Discuss the relationship of Soviet government and Communist party.
3. Describe the financial basis of the Soviet government.

44

LIFE IN THE 1930's

Significant Dates

Second Five-Year Plan 1933–1938
Re-establishment of Family 1935
Restitution of Disciplinary School 1936
Third Five-Year Plan (initiated) 1938

The Stalin constitution promised the Russian peoples many rights
and liberties and entitled them to great expectations, but the reality
differed sharply from the ideals set forth on paper. In every respect,
the years 1932 to 1940 constituted a period of great strain. The government realized that huge investments in plants, agriculture, and
capital goods were needed before the population could hope for
living standards that would approximate those of Western nations.
Accordingly a second and third Five-Year Plan were worked out
which made the highest demands on the industry of the people.
Under the slogan "He who does not work shall not eat," the population was driven to ever greater exertions. The example of the coal
miner Stakhanov was taken as proof that far greater productivity
was possible than had been demanded so far by the authorities, and
the quotas for everyone were substantially raised. In addition to the
pressures resulting from the acceleration of industrialization, there
was a general insecurity—a result of the denunciations and purges
of political leaders, artists, scholars, and large numbers of peasants
and undistinguished persons.

ECONOMIC CONDITIONS

The First Five-Year Plan was declared fulfilled and overfulfilled in 1932. Although proud of the achievement, the government was, however, by no means blind to criticism. The Second and Third Five-Year Plans were consequently drafted after careful consideration of the preceding Piatiletka's shortcomings. They were much more detailed and specific than the First.

Second Five-Year Plan. Besides the political goal of furthering a classless, socialist society, the main goals of the Second Plan consisted in the improvement of living standards through an increase in production of consumer goods, more rational distribution of work, and improvement in the quality of goods. The pace of introducing innovations was slackened; but better equipment, standardization, mechanization, further electrification, and greater mastery of production techniques were to make possible the doubling of the output of goods.

Objectives in Industry. The Second Five-Year Plan provided for a geographic redistribution of industrial centers through the construction of plants close to raw-material sources in the Caucasus, Siberia, and central Asia; special funds were set aside for the erection of steel mills, coal mines, and power stations east of the Urals. Money was also allocated in proportionately greater amounts for improving the transportation system through the electrification of railroads, for opening new waterways (such as the White Sea-Baltic, the Moscow-Volga, and the Volga-Don canals), and for increasing the number of motor vehicles, airplanes, and steamboats.

In addition, the Second Five-Year Plan provided for the doubling of real wages and a reduction in prices, so as to improve standards of living. Food rations were actually abolished in 1935; but, as a result, prices rose and soon equaled those formerly paid on the free market. The educational system was extended, vocational schooling was improved, and polytechnical training was made compulsory. Model schools were built in each district, and research institutes were endowed with sufficient funds. The circulation of newspapers was raised. A better health service was instituted through erection of nurseries, health resorts, and sanitariums, and plans were worked out to replace private housekeeping by large "socialized" housekeeping through the introduction of a catering system and through the sale of semiprepared food or part-ready meals.

OBJECTIVES IN AGRICULTURE. The Second Five-Year Plan also prescribed the doubling of agricultural production, which was to be achieved through completion of collectivization, additional tractor stations, and better scientific methods. Production quotas were substantially raised. New crops were to be introduced, deserts exploited, marshes drained, and virgin regions tested for agricultural possibilities. Those kulaks who had managed to survive the liquidation of their class were now permitted to return if they were deemed politically reliable, and they could become members of the collective farms.

RESULTS. After five years, the government published figures indicating the successful accomplishment of the plan; it stated that in industry the desired quotas had been reached and that productivity of the average laborer had been doubled. In agriculture the plan had resulted in increased food production, in the extension of the area under cultivation, and in an adequate supply of industrial crops. Socialism made further progress. Collectivization had reached a high of 90 per cent of all existing farms. With the introduction of some modern bakeries, meat-packing houses, and refrigeration methods, a start was also made toward better distribution and higher average consumption. Private producers and traders accounted for no more than 6 per cent of the total Russian production and turnover. However, one specific development caused alarm. In response to Stalin's speech on May 4, 1935, calling for greater individual productivity, a worker by the name of Stakhanov had cut several times as many tons of coal as required of each miner; and soon thereafter a peasant woman, Maria Demchenko, had raised far more per hectare than her expected quota. This seemed to indicate that the goals had been set too low and that there existed a possibility of increasing the industrial and agricultural output through greater exertion by each citizen. Consequently, the year 1936 was proclaimed a "Stakhanov year." Stakhanovite clubs were founded by those who greatly exceeded their quotas; and the state supported them through bonuses, privileges, and special rewards. "Shock brigades" formed from these clubs were to set the working pace, "socialist competition" was extolled, and over-all quotas for the average worker were substantially raised. As in capitalist countries, wages for the workers were more and more differentiated, according to the amount of work performed; distribution of ration cards was used by factory managers as a spur for production and discipline; and efficiency standards were revised.

Third Five-Year Plan. As a result, a vigorous countermovement set in. "Star performances" were bitterly condemned since they often did not affect the average output but instead led to the production of faulty goods and the misuse of tools. Discontent among workers increased, and justified fears were voiced regarding the re-emergence of a privileged group within the proletariat. The Third Five-Year Plan, approved by the party in 1939, but beginning to function in 1938, reflected these sentiments.

UNSOLVED PROBLEMS. This Third Plan—which, because of the war, could not be fulfilled—is of importance only inasmuch as it throws light on earlier shortcomings and subsequent trends. It differed essentially from former plans in that the industrialization program, though again emphasized, was "decelerated" and "gigantomania" was denounced. The need remained for greater individual productivity and rational working methods. The plan accentuated again an increase in consumer goods, stimulated textile production, and tried to remedy the unsatisfactory housing situation. Two problems found special attention: labor discipline and defense needs. In order to further the former, non-steady workers were deprived of their preferment for living quarters, social insurance was reduced for them, and absences from work were punished by loss of vacation. Leaves for women during pregnancy were shortened. And managers who did not enforce government decrees were subjected to heavy fines. As to the other problem, defense, up to one-quarter of the national income was set aside for military purposes, new oil resources were developed, factories were relocated in remote regions, and regional self-sufficiency was increased. Vigilance was strengthened not only against "wreckers" in factories, but also against possible saboteurs within the ranks of the planning commissions.

ACHIEVEMENTS. As a whole, the three five-year plans transformed Russia from an essentially agricultural country into a country with a balance between agriculture and industry. Hitherto unknown skills and advanced tools were introduced, and backward regions developed. Industries were expanded, and Russia became once more a leading producer in the world. A vastly improved transportation system, though overcrowded, brought material and cultural assets to and from all parts of the country. The five-year plans thus strengthened the socialist, classless state and constituted the world's chief experiment in a state-planned economy.

But in a world which moved everywhere toward industrialization, reform, and better social conditions, the five-year plans fell short of the goals of securing the Russian workingman living standards commensurate with his effort. Furthermore, despite guarantees in the constitution, they failed to provide for the acceptance and spread of individualistic freedom which the theory of the communistic state demanded. In many respects, the development followed the pattern set by tsarist Russia, for geography, geology, and climate, and the attitudes and traditions of the Russian man composed a background which, materialistic and purely economic thinking notwithstanding, could not be changed beyond a degree compatible with normal processes of growth.

Foreign Trade. During the five-year plans, a change was gradually effected with regard to the type of exports and imports. Raw materials such as furs, timber, oil, and such agricultural products as wheat had always constituted the bulk of the country's foreign trade; and in the first years after the Revolution these commodities continued to lead among Russia's exports. Often they were sold at very low prices in order to pay for imports urgently needed for economic as well as political reasons, and this led to bitter accusations of dumping and to grave international tension. In time, successful attempts were made to shift to manufactured goods, which could still be sold at low prices because of the living standards within the country, but which benefited the country's economy. However, the level of foreign trade before the Revolution was reached at no time after it. The total volume remained low, and toward the beginning of the Third Five-Year Plan it was further reduced when political considerations brought a shift from Germany and England, formerly Russia's best customers, to the United States, which offered less promising markets.

SOCIAL AND CULTURAL CONDITIONS

While revolutionary changes were taking place on the political and economic scene, an almost reactionary trend marked the path of events in the social and cultural spheres. The experimentation of the twenties was followed by a re-emphasis of old values. The family was accorded again an important place in Soviet life; differences in wages and living standards became more pronounced; education retrieved pre-revolutionary concepts of discipline and systematic training; and "petty bourgeois" tastes infiltrated artistic production.

Family Life. In 1935 the whole socialist theory of the family was revised. Under pressure of economic and demographic factors and despite the denunciations of those who feared an interruption in the development towards a socialist society, the family was again recognized as the foundation of the state. Abortion, which at one time had reached a level 50 per cent higher than births, was forbidden unless medical reasons made it necessary. Laws were promulgated in 1936 providing bonuses and tax exemptions for large families. The divorce rate was checked by law in the same year; and in 1944 further stringent conditions for divorce were imposed, including high fees and an investigation into the reasons. Common-law marriages no longer received the protection extended to legal marriages. To counteract the possible revival of pre-revolutionary family influences, the government confined itself to measures promoting social intercourse and a community spirit through the organization of numerous political and other meetings in clubs, rest houses, and educational institutions.

Living Standards. The routine of daily life during these times was strenuous. Housing shortages remained a big problem, and production of consumer goods lagged far behind the needs of the growing population. Competition—so-called "socialist competition" —having become extremely keen, put undue strain on each individual citizen. The span between incomes continued to widen; wage differences were accentuated by extra rewards given in the form of better housing, use of cars, longer vacations, and professional prizes. In the kolkhoz, gains derived from cultivation of one's private plot—possibly at the expense of common tasks—also caused differentiation. The working day became longer; by 1940 a six-day week and an eight-hour day officially existed. Sunday was, as a rule, allotted as a day of rest. Strict punishments were imposed on those guilty of shirking work, careless handling of machinery, or stealing "socialist property."

"Slave labor" camps in Siberia and in arctic regions were filled with many who would have willingly co-operated at the places for which they were trained, and these workers led a particularly sad life. Under the pretext of tasks necessary for society as a whole, involuntary work with all its attendant distress was enormously increased. In time supervision was not relaxed, but augmented, and both the Second and the Third Five-Year Plans provided for special vigilance and strictest control.

Education. In the field of education there was a trend to recapture the spirit of earlier Russia and to renew pride in the life and development of the country. No longer was everything rejected that had happened under "feudal and tsarist oppressors," but Russia's evolution was explained rather in terms of a necessary historical path, leading to a socialist commonwealth. Together with this view was adopted much of older educational methods. Naturally, history came again into its own and constituted a focus of national interest.

SCHOOLS. The number of schools increased rapidly; likewise, more years of schooling were demanded of the pupils. For the higher schools children of skilled personnel were granted equal attendance rights with Communists; in universities, although technical training was still favored, the traditional faculties were re-established and served to promote an understanding of scientific and technical methods as well as of the relationship of science to human life and society. By 1936, the former authority of the teacher returned, grading and examinations were revived, and strictest discipline was insisted upon. Even school uniforms again appeared.

ADULT EDUCATION. Inasmuch as the family had been deprived of much of its significance and many of its tasks, and inasmuch as the church had lost its dominant position, various new institutions had to be created to supplement the educational work of schools and universities. The Comsomol attended to ideological indoctrination as well as to physical training of the young; beginning in 1936 it also took a growing interest in raising the cultural level of its members, in teaching them discipline, and in strengthening their moral fiber. Adult and evening schools, which were opened in all parts of the country and conducted in languages of the various nationalities, brought the elements of education to all Soviet citizens, young and old. Press, radio, motion pictures, and lectures of all kinds were devoted to the spread of learning, information, and social theory. Museums were sponsored everywhere. Thousands of libraries were founded, thus making available over one hundred and fifty million popular books and almost as many volumes for research.

Religion. Whether the overwhelming economic tasks of the 1930's prevented the government from occupying itself with church affairs or whether it deemed such occupation unnecessary since the revolutionary path would anyhow lead to its withering away, the religious life in the Soviet Union became increasingly free from interference. The Atheist movement had not succeeded in winning over the masses or in erecting an efficient bulwark against a religious revival. Persecution of the church had served rather to purify the organization, and those who despite all threats had held fast to their beliefs constituted a firmer and stronger basis than the church had previously possessed. The government could not fail to recognize the inefficacy of the antireligious drive; and spurred by the threat arising from an emerging Nazi power in Germany which made national unity imperative, a completely new course was charted. In 1936 the "historical mission of Christianity" was officially recognized, and the Stalin constitution eliminated the existing disabilities of the clergy. Support was withdrawn from the Militant Atheists (whose official organ, the *Bezbozhnik,* had ceased to appear in 1934), tolerance was propagated, and although public religious instruction of children remained prohibited and some new persecutions (chiefly against those suspected of political opposition) occurred again in 1937–38, religious feast days were reintroduced and church bells sounded again.

Arts. Artistic life during the 1930's, just as religious life, was made to fit into the program of the Soviet government and the Communist party. Individualism was condemned, and those "idealistic" and "formalistic" trends which had occupied artists during the twenties were denounced. Instead of allowing experimentation with mere artistic forms and expressions, party and state demanded from every author, painter, and builder a positive and optimistic attitude toward the socialist society—which had to be expressed through a "realistic" presentation of it. A heroic pose and a sentimentality was often thereby introduced which rendered futile the efforts of many an individual artist to give form to his thought. Political denunciations and purges contributed to silencing those who might pursue a lonely path removed from the scene of Soviet reality. As a result, little was produced that could gain acclaim beyond the Soviet borders. Authors like Alexei Tolstoy, Pasternak, and Ehrenburg, or composers like Shostakovich and Khachaturian, who earlier had produced remarkable works, found themselves hindered in their creative activity.

Costs of Reconstruction. The 1930's saw a radical change in the material conditions of the country, a tremendous growth in its productive capacity, its educational facilities, its governmental establishment, its national power. But at what price? Mercilessly, like the governments of Ivan the Terrible or of Peter the Great, the government headed by Stalin drove the population on, regardless of human lives, human rights, and human suffering, of justice and truth, and of freedom of movement and of expression. The crimes committed by the party, the government and by zealots were numberless. The present was sacrificed to a potential better future—a future which, the historian ventures, might have been achieved more safely and possibly more speedily by more humane methods. The legacy of this period, in Russia and abroad, poisoned the minds of an entire generation.

PROBLEMS

1. Discuss the main difficulties in completing the work outlined by the various five-year plans.
2. Describe the relationship between the state and art.

45

FOREIGN RELATIONS I: EUROPE

The vast expanse of Russia and her enormous resources in natural wealth and manpower made it possible for the Soviets to carry out at home the experiment of socialism which the revolutionary leaders originally considered feasible only if undertaken on a world-wide scale. But in her foreign policies, Russia had to adapt herself to the pattern imposed by the international community of nations and the traditions of capitalistic powers. While so doing, she nevertheless did not lose sight of her primary objectives. These consisted, up to 1934, in the preservation of the Soviet system in Russia and the spread of Communist ideology abroad. Territorial aggrandizement, Pan-Slav ambitions, and imperialistic aims were denounced and rejected; the ways of traditional diplomatic intercourse were likewise temporarily given up, and economic agencies, trade headquarters, and information bureaus attended to many diplomatic functions. After 1934 a more traditional path was followed. Throughout, however, opportunities for the furtherance of communism were seized as they offered themselves, giving Soviet foreign policies a constantly changing and unfathomable appearance. This impression was heightened by the fact that the Soviet government was able to

ANGLO-RUSSIAN RELATIONS, 1856–1950

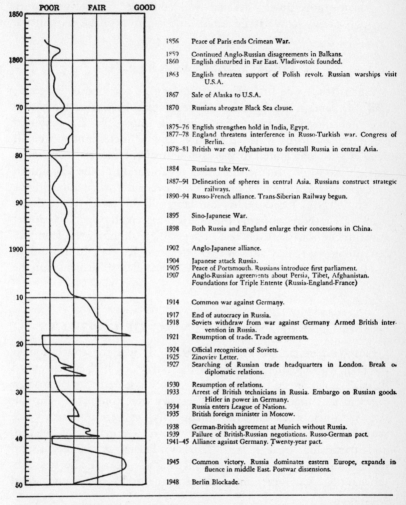

1856	Peace of Paris ends Crimean War.
1859	Continued Anglo-Russian disagreements in Balkans.
1860	English disturbed in Far East. Vladivostok founded.
1863	English threaten support of Polish revolt. Russian warships visit U.S.A.
1867	Sale of Alaska to U.S.A.
1870	Russians abrogate Black Sea clause.
1875–76	English strengthen hold in India, Egypt.
1877–78	England threatens interference in Russo-Turkish war. Congress of Berlin.
1878–81	British war on Afghanistan to forestall Russia in central Asia.
1884	Russians take Merv.
1887–91	Delineation of spheres in central Asia. Russians construct strategic railways.
1890–94	Russo-French alliance. Trans-Siberian Railway begun.
1895	Sino-Japanese War.
1898	Both Russia and England enlarge their concessions in China.
1902	Anglo-Japanese alliance.
1904	Japanese attack Russia.
1905	Peace of Portsmouth. Russians introduce first parliament.
1907	Anglo-Russian agreements about Persia, Tibet, Afghanistan. Foundations for Triple Entente (Russia-England-France)
1914	Common war against Germany.
1917	End of autocracy in Russia.
1918	Soviets withdraw from war against Germany Armed British intervention in Russia.
1921	Resumption of trade. Trade agreements.
1924	Official recognition of Soviets.
1925	Zinoviev Letter.
1927	Searching of Russian trade headquarters in London. Break of diplomatic relations.
1930	Resumption of relations.
1933	Arrest of British technicians in Russia. Embargo on Russian goods. Hitler in power in Germany.
1934	Russia enters League of Nations.
1935	British foreign minister in Moscow.
1938	German-British agreement at Munich without Russia.
1939	Failure of British-Russian negotiations. Russo-German pact.
1941–45	Alliance against Germany. Twenty-year pact.
1945	Common victory. Russia dominates eastern Europe, expands influence in middle East. Postwar dissensions.
1948	Berlin Blockade.

ANGLO–RUSSIAN relations have been tense except for brief periods of co-operation against a common enemy. Rivalry began in the time of Peter the Great when Russia started to build a navy on the Baltic and to change the balance of power in Europe. In the nineteenth century it was sharpened by Russia's growing influence in the Balkans and her advance to the Mediterranean, as well as by rivalry in the Far East and central Asia. In the first half of the twentieth century, reorganization of the British empire and questions of economic and strategic control in the Middle East did not relieve tension.

pursue simultaneously two different lines of policy—the one represented by its official foreign service, and the other by the Comintern which, the government insisted, was connected with Russia only through party channels and acted independently in all its policies.

FIRST PHASE: ISOLATION

Versailles. The first phase of Soviet rule was one of isolation; civil war, foreign intervention, and geographical seclusion made normal intercourse with other nations virtually impossible. The professed Communist aim of world revolution and self-determination of all peoples also contributed to the exclusion of the Soviets from international decisions; furthermore, the organization of the Comintern as a means for achieving their ends prevented participation in the undertakings of the capitalist and imperialistic world whose diplomats were busy rearranging the political map of Europe. The Soviet government was denied a seat at Versailles, although the Communist problem as such and Western fears of Russia's future aspirations influenced the decisions of the Versailles statesmen and the treaty which they contrived.

SECOND PHASE: REOPENING OF CONTACTS

First International Treaties, 1921. It was the conclusion of the civil war and the adoption of the N.E.P. in 1921 which ended Russia's isolation and introduced a new phase into Soviet foreign relations. A number of important treaties were completed—particularly with neighbors—and diplomatic activities were resumed. Peace with Poland, commercial arrangements with Germany and Sweden, and friendship treaties with Turkey, Persia, Afghanistan, and Outer Mongolia were concluded. Russia's voice was also heard in other international questions, such as the neutralization of the Aland Islands.

Relations with Western Europe. But in its relationship with Western European nations and America, the Soviet government made little progress. Although it offered substantial economic advantages and succeeded in opening commercial intercourse with England and Italy, its repudiation of prewar debts and its communistic orientation and propaganda prevented the re-establishment of normal diplomatic relations. In 1921, the Russians were again excluded from an international congress, the Washington Disarmament Conference; and, when in the following year they were invited to a conference held at Genoa, they found few common interests with their former allies.

RAPALLO, 1922. In their political isolation the Russians turned to the other great isolated nation of Europe, their former enemy, Germany. Exposed to the demands of foreign oil concessionaries, hindered in their international policies by Western diplomacy after Versailles, and defeated in their proposals for general disarmament by Allied opposition under French leadership, they made advances to Germany. Their proposals were well received, for Germany's foreign office under Minister Rathenau envisaged the resumption of Bismarck's policy, which had held friendship with Russia the pivot of German security. In exchange for *de jure* recognition by Germany, a treaty was concluded at Rapallo, near Genoa, which provided for close economic and political collaboration. Together, the two countries soon exercised influence of great importance in international affairs. When the French in 1923 marched into the German Ruhr and when the Allies decided to hand over the territory of Memel to Lithuania, the Soviet government showed its political orientation by denouncing both acts and by further strengthening its economic ties with Germany.

RECOGNITION BY WESTERN EUROPE, 1924. In order to prevent exclusive co-operation of Russia and Germany, the Western powers thereupon began more serious negotiations with Russia; and in 1924, while the United States still held aloof, England, Italy, and France extended official recognition to the Soviet government and supplemented their move by trade treaties. A number of smaller countries, including Norway, Austria, Greece, Hungary, and Mexico, followed their example.

LOCARNO, 1925. This second phase of Soviet foreign policy ended in 1925. Many advantages were gained by the Soviets during this period; they now enjoyed both official recognition and economic relations with most European powers as well as close co-operation with Germany. But by 1925—the year of the Locarno Pact—it became evident that the Rapallo system was not to last and that Soviet isolation persisted. Before the Locarno Pact was concluded, recurring incidents had already alarmed the Russians. A diplomatic agent, Vorovsky, had been murdered in Switzerland, and no satisfactory action was taken by the Swiss government; in Germany, the Russian trade headquarters had been raided in search of political propaganda material; and in England, a storm was raised over the so-called "Zinoviev letter" which purported to contain instructions by the Russian minister Zinoviev to the British Communist party and was interpreted as official Russian interference in British internal affairs. Furthermore, the French and English persisted in their opposition to disarmament. After the Locarno Pact, Germany concluded a nonaggression agreement and continued her commercial connection with Russia (even extending credit of three hundred million gold marks) but politically she began to veer away and to reorient herself toward the Western world. This was followed by her entry into the League of Nations and her participation in conferences at Geneva, from which the Soviets felt excluded as long as the Vorovsky affair was not satisfactorily settled.

Threat of Renewed Isolation. Facing an increasingly united Western world, the Russians thereupon began to turn their attention to eastern Europe and central Asia, and to advocate as a countermeasure an Eastern Bloc or "Eastern Locarno." At first they were not successful; for in 1926 a totalitarian government under Pilsudsky was established in Poland, which instead of accepting Russian advances allied itself with Rumania and tried—though without success—to form an anti-Soviet alliance with the Baltic states. The Russians thus found themselves stalled in their external policies, and the report of the government submitted to the All-Soviet Congress in 1927 reflected the fears of the Soviet leaders. It depicted the situation as critical, with England a persistent opponent and France an ally of hostile and reactionary Poland and Rumania. Ignoring the intrigues of the Comintern, the Congress called attention to the raids upon the Soviet embassy in China and upon the Soviet trade headquarters in London (which led to a temporary rupture of diplomatic relations with Britain), to the murder of the Communist leader Voikov in Poland, and to incidents in Persia, Switzerland, Italy, and Greece—all of which were inspired, it was asserted, by "imperialistic" headquarters in Paris and London. It denounced the League of Nations as an organ of French and English imperialism neglecting its task of promoting peace; it deplored the

GERMAN-RUSSIAN RELATIONS, 1870–1950

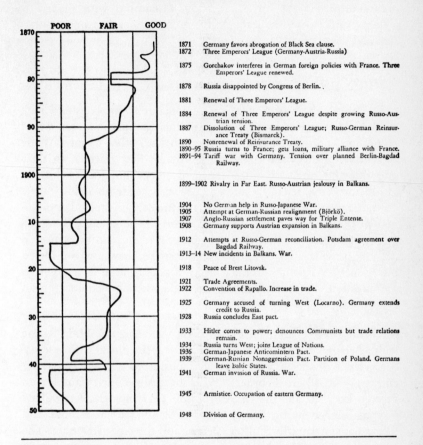

1871	Germany favors abrogation of Black Sea clause.		
1872	Three Emperors' League (Germany-Austria-Russia)		

1875   Gorchakov interferes in German foreign policies with France. **Three** Emperors' League renewed.

1878   Russia disappointed by Congress of Berlin. .

1881   Renewal of Three Emperors' League.

1884   Renewal of Three Emperors' League despite growing Russo-Austrian tension.

1887   Dissolution of Three Emperors' League; Russo-German Reinsurance Treaty (Bismarck).

1890   Nonrenewal of Reinsurance Treaty.

1890–95 Russia turns to France; gets loans, military alliance with France.

1891–94 Tariff war with Germany. Tension over planned Berlin-Bagdad Railway.

1899–1902 Rivalry in Far East. Russo-Austrian jealousy in Balkans.

1904   No German help in Russo-Japanese War.

1905   Attempt at German-Russian realignment (Björkö).

1907   Anglo-Russian settlement paves way for Triple Entente.

1908   Germany supports Austrian expansion in Balkans.

1912   Attempts at Russo-German reconciliation. Potsdam agreement **over** Bagdad Railway.

1913–14 New incidents in Balkans. War.

1918   Peace of Brest Litovsk.

1921   Trade Agreements.

1922   Convention of Rapallo. Increase in trade.

1925   Germany accused of turning West (Locarno). Germany extends credit to Russia.

1928   Russia concludes East pact.

1933   Hitler comes to power; denounces Communists but trade relations remain.

1934   Russia turns West; joins League of Nations.

1936   German-Japanese Anticomintern Pact.

1939   German-Russian Nonaggression Pact. Partition of Poland. Germans leave Baltic States.

1941   German invasion of Russia. War.

1945   Armistice. Occupation of eastern Germany.

1948   Division of Germany.

THIS chart should be read in conjunction with that on page 307 showing trends in Anglo-Russian relations. It indicates that good German-Russian relations meant general peace for Europe, as a rule, and that bad ones were to be interpreted as an alarm. Two critical moments came, first, in 1890 as a result of the dismissal of Bismarck and nonrenewal of the Reinsurance Treaty, and, second, in 1934, as a result of the consolidation of Nazi power over Germany. In view of Russia's persistent need for industrial goods and Germany's continuous demand for grain and raw materials and of the normal absence of territorial competition, the lack of harmony can be explained not by diplomatic disputes or tariff wars but by extraneous issues—the Balkan situation and a European balance-of-power system. After World War II the extension of Soviet domination deep into the heart of Germany created a new situation which adversely affected the relations of the two countries.

failure of disarmament and the resultant needs for military preparedness which reacted unfavorably on the internal progress of communism. Except for a precarious friendship with Germany, Turkey, and Persia, the leaders thus found no comfort in the international situation.

THIRD PHASE: INTERNATIONAL COLLABORATION

The third phase of Soviet international relations consisted in a reversal of policies: in abatement of their propaganda for world revolution and in increased collaboration with other nations. While continuing their policies towards Germany, they relented in their opposition to England and, in need of crucial imports, established satisfactory commercial relations; they also began to modify their attitude toward France, despite her alignment with Poland and Rumania. Both England and France welcomed the change. Resigned to Soviet refusal to honor prewar debts and to Russian insistence on making proselytes for Soviet political doctrine, they now considered the re-entry of Russia into the concert of nations as at least a step in the direction of stabilization and the reconstruction of the European Continent.

Kellogg Pact and East Protocol. In August, 1928, Russia added her signature to the Kellogg Pact. But she did so with reservations, for without disarmament she considered the agreement ineffectual. Finally, in February, 1929, she realized her plans for an Eastern Locarno, and the "East Protocol" (Litvinov Pact) to outlaw war was signed by the Soviet Union, Poland, Latvia, Estonia, and Rumania, and later by Turkey, Persia, and the city of Danzig. The pact was a demonstration rather than an effective weapon, and it needed practical supplementation such as was achieved only later through nonaggression pacts with some of the participants. Yet, it reassured the Soviets and constituted a victory in their drive for security, making possible a less intransigent attitude in their over-all policies.

Normalization of Foreign Relations. This phase of Soviet postwar diplomacy lasted until 1934. In addition to the East Protocol and the normalization of foreign relations, it brought resumption of

Anglo-Russian relations in 1929 and a nonagression pact with France in 1932. Litvinov replaced Chicherin, who had headed the Soviet foreign office through the years of the N.E.P. and the East Protocol, and emphasized the continuity of Soviet foreign policies in the direction of watchful co-operation. As minor incidents occurred in Poland or Finland, they were more easily disposed of and a *modus vivendi* was found even with regard to Japan and other countries hostile up to that time. Indeed, foreign affairs were gradually subordinated to the great tasks set by the First Five-Year Plan, and in a time when the economies in the capitalist countries were suffering a most severe setback, nothing seemed so beneficial for the advancement of Soviet aims abroad as successful and constructive activity at home.

Realignment. In 1933 Adolf Hitler came to power in Germany. At first his advent did not mark a departure from the path already followed by Germany. Although vigorous verbal attacks were launched against the Communist system, economic relations with Russia remained in effect untouched. Yet, as a precautionary measure, Russia's attitude toward France became increasingly conciliatory, and special efforts were made to preserve satisfactory relations with neighboring countries and with England. More important events occurred, however, in non-European countries. In America, a change of administration in the United States brought, finally, official recognition of the Soviet government there—a move not imitated by most Central and South American republics, which withheld recognition until the time of the Second World War. In the Far East, on the other hand, war clouds gathered, and renewed Japanese restlessness constituted a peril to the Soviet system.

SUMMARY

The development of Russian foreign relations with Europe from 1918 to 1934 thus shows successive phases of isolation, struggle for recognition, end of isolation through the Rapallo Treaty, and a renewed feeling of isolation following the Locarno Pact. This situation was relieved by continued economic co-operation with capitalist countries and ultimately, in 1929, by the "East Protocol." Not until Hitler began actively and aggressively to influence international relations in 1934 was another change called for.

PROBLEMS

1. Discuss the significance of the German-Russian alignment after Rapallo.
2. Discuss the factors impeding a *rapprochement* of Russia and the Western European nations.
3. Describe the relationship between Russia and her neighbors.

46

FOREIGN RELATIONS II: ASIA AND AMERICA

Significant Dates

CENTRAL ASIA

Russia's international relations in Europe were essentially governed by forces beyond Soviet control; in relations with Eastern countries, however, it was the Soviet government which held the initiative.

Abrogation of Imperialism. Promptly upon their assumption of power in 1917 the Communists denounced the imperialistic policies of their predecessors and subsequently abrogated the advantages which Russia had secured at the expense of weaker nations in Asia, including those advantages gained by the Anglo-Russian Agreement of 1907. They gave up the former protective attitude toward Oriental peoples and renounced banking rights, collection of debts, monopolies, and all other one-sided privileges. Then as soon as civil war ended in 1921, the government, true to its promise, concluded treaties of amity on a basis of equality with Persia, Afghanistan, Mongolia, and Turkey. The last-named power obtained the fortress of Kars (captured by Russia in 1878), and in exchange

315

Turkey released Batum which was then incorporated into Georgia. In 1922 when Georgia, together with parts of Armenia and Azerbaidzhan, formed the Transcaucasian Republic and entered the U.S.S.R., Batum returned to Russian possession.

Rise of Russian Prestige.   The Soviets were greatly strengthened by their policy of equality and co-operation, and thus succeeded indirectly in reducing English influence. The propagandistic value was particularly felt in Persia and Afghanistan, the two countries most resenting British interference. Russian prestige was also enhanced in Turkey, where Russia refrained from participating in the demilitarization of the Straits undertaken by the Western powers in 1923.

Trade Agreements.   Once political understanding was reached, trade agreements followed. Treaties were concluded by the Soviet Union with her Near Eastern neighbors in the years from 1924 to 1927, and in every instance they proved highly successful. By 1927 Russia held second place in a vastly expanded Persian trade; a strong upswing in commerce with Turkey could be noted; and Afghanistan and Mongolian trade showed a corresponding rising curve, as did Sinkiang (Chinese Turkestan), with which an agreement was made in 1925.

Political Effects.   The Soviet policy of moderation was fruitful while it lasted. Reversals set in only when reviving nationalism in Russia as well as among Russia's partners, accompanied by economic difficulties, disturbed the balance.

ADVANTAGES.   Russia's economic relations in central Asia were especially favored by geographic conditions. Russia was more closely connected than any other power with these areas, and raw materials produced by them were welcome for Siberia's industrialization. The foreign-trade state monopoly could therefore be relaxed in central Asia, and free private trading on a primitive bartering basis was permitted, benefiting the native populations; special tariffs were applied to goods reaching Russia across her eastern borders. Moreover, political resistance to Soviet ideological infiltration was slight in the "backward" East, where indeed one of the neighbors, Mongolia, herself abolished private property, expelled formerly dominating Chinese merchants, and began large-scale nationalization. In Sinkiang, likewise, Chinese influence and financial domination were reduced.

LIMITATIONS. The balance sheet was less favorable in the Near and Middle East. After 1931, the pace of the initial successes could not be sustained; rising nationalism and religious revival checked the progress made by the Soviets. Reversals were also noticeable in economic relations with Turkey; Persia introduced high protectionist tariff walls; and world depression exercised an adverse influence even in remote central Asiatic countries. Yet, as a whole, the decade from 1921 to 1931 had fundamentally changed the economic status and the political balance and opened satisfactory prospects for the Soviet future.

FAR EAST

While the Communists were making steady progress in central Asia, they were unsuccessful in penetrating the Far East, where their social theories clashed with more firmly established societies. The creation of a separate state in Siberia during the civil war and its continuation as a "Far Eastern Republic" after Admiral Kolchak's death in 1920 had reduced Russian prestige and continued to influence Soviet policies adversely even after the collapse and liquidation of the "Far Eastern Republic" in 1922.

China. The greatest difficulties were encountered in China. There Russia had to deal with several factions. The Kuomintang party, Sun Yat-sen, the Christian General Feng, Marshal Chang Tsolin of Manchuria, and after Chang Tsolin's death, his son, each took a different attitude toward the Soviet regime in Russia and strove to use the Communist ideal or Communist peril as a tool for exercising pressure and gaining hegemony in internal Chinese affairs. Under these circumstances, Russia's offers of friendship, her avowal of a renunciation of imperialistic aims, and her willingness to conclude trade agreements remained unavailing, and her sincerity was challenged by the various factions. Furthermore, Russian ideological and economic penetration into Sinkiang and into Mongolia, both of which were used as centers to spread Communist propaganda, constituted a potential threat to China's territorial status and security.

CHINESE EASTERN RAILWAY. Among the many issues, one problem was of special importance: It concerned the ownership and management of Russia's Chinese Eastern Railway. For with regard to the railway, the Soviets insisted (in contrast with their policy with regard to tsarist imperialistic ventures elsewhere) on the maintenance of their full prewar rights. They did so even in the face of the fact that, since the construction of the line, an enormous influx of Chinese settlers into railroad territory occurred, strengthening thereby the ties of the territory with China. Negotiations were therefore protracted; and although a treaty in 1924 established diplomatic relations with the Chinese government, provided for equal rights, and arranged joint management of the railroad, no lasting settlement was reached. The railway continued to constitute a problem influencing national status as well as the most diverse international interests. France, Britain, the United States, and Japan all considered the railway a paramount asset strategically and economically; and fearful for their own positions, they sought to forestall the expansion of Russian power and of Communist ideas. Under their influence, and as a result of antirevolutionary intrigues, the 1924 treaty was cancelled; in 1926 Russian directors of the railway were taken into custody by Chinese agents and Soviet property was confiscated; in 1927 the Russian embassy was searched by Chinese soldiers; and in 1929 the Soviet consulate in Harbin was raided and delegates assembling for a meeting of the Third International were arrested. Diplomatic relations were broken, and only after a Russian invasion of Manchuria and prolonged negotiations at Nikolsk Ussuriisk was the *status quo* with regard to the Chinese Eastern Railway restored in December, 1929. But this arrangement postponed rather than solved the problem. Eventually the solution came in an unexpected direction as a result of the Sino-Japanese conflict in 1931.

Japan. The intervention of Japan on the Asiatic continent meant a threat to Russia. Russia and Japan had been hostile from the very beginning of the Bolshevik regime, and Japan had been a leading interventionist in the early period of Soviet rule. She had invaded Siberia, trying to secure a permanent foothold there, first with the help of Admiral Kolchak and later through the autonomous Far Eastern Republic. But in 1922, after the Washington Disarmament Conference, she was forced to withdraw; and in 1925 official relations were established with the Soviet government. Japan consented not only to refrain from interference in Siberia, but also to abandon her occupation of Russian northern Sakhalin, though she retained fishing rights and oil concessions there.

SALE OF CHINESE EASTERN RAILWAY. The existing status was disturbed anew in the early thirties when Japan began to intervene actively in China. Her successes brought an aggressive and militarily strong power instead of a disunited China to Russia's back door and made it necessary for the Soviets to take vigorous countermeasures. A second track was laid for the trans-Siberian railway, industrial centers were shifted eastward, immigration was furthered through reduction of taxes and corn deliveries, and the Far Eastern army under Marshal Blücher was greatly strengthened. Simultaneously, negotiations with Japan were undertaken which, in 1935, led to a fundamental change. In order to keep peace, Russia liquidated the most persistent object of contention in the Far East by selling her share of the Chinese Eastern Railway. Ownership was transferred to the Japanese-sponsored country of Manchukuo, and the Soviets received a payment of one hundred and seventy million yen. This transaction altered the balance of power in the Far East and affected the interests of various great powers, but again failed to constitute a permanent solution.

UNITED STATES

While the Soviet government struggled to maintain its position in Asia, changes occurred in its relations with America. The key to the American situation was held by the United States, which had recognized the Kerensky government on March 22, 1917, but failed to open diplomatic relations with the Bolsheviks. For almost five years the United States continued—despite the extinction of the Provisional Government—to regard Kerensky's ambassador, Boris Bakhmetev, as official Russian representative, refused to receive the Soviet envoy, C. A. K. Martens, and threatened his deportation. In the meantime, in order "to guard military stores," she participated in the Allied expedition for intervention; in August, 1918, she sent expeditionary forces to Vladivostok and in September, 1918, to Archangel. These forces stayed on after the armistice with Germany was concluded and, under the pretext of enabling the

Russian people "to choose their government freely," aided antirevolutionary armies. Only in June, 1919, and April, 1920, were they withdrawn from Archangel and Siberia, respectively.

First Relations. While the expeditionary forces were still in Russia, William C. Bullitt was sent to the Soviet government to report on the situation. His visit did not lead to the resumption of official relations; and only limited private trade was allowed in July, 1920. In the following year American relief was extended to the suffering people under Herbert Hoover's direction, and in 1922 the Soviets were permitted to establish an Information Bureau in Washington.

Commercial Intercourse. Thereafter, considerable trade developed. Exports to Russia climbed between 1922 and 1930 from thirty to more than one hundred million dollars (after that declining) while imports jumped from one to fifteen million. The needs of the Soviet government for agricultural and industrial machinery accounted for the amount of exports, whereas Russian imports, although including some ore shipments, remained essentially confined to luxury items such as furs and caviar and therefore never reached considerable figures. Yet, notwithstanding trade developments, official recognition was persistently denied by the successive United States Secretaries of State—Hughes, Kellogg, and Stimson—partly because of Soviet repudiation of prewar debts and confiscation of American private property, partly because of Communist propaganda, sponsored by the Soviet government, in the United States. Public opinion essentially supported official United States policy, but it was governed less by financial considerations than by religious issues, political ideology, and aversion to state planning and interference.

Diplomatic Recognition. Not until November, 1933, after the Democratic party had taken over the administration of the United States, was a diplomatic settlement reached. In exchange for official recognition, the Communist government promised to refrain from propaganda in the United States and to safeguard the lives and peaceful work of Americans in Russia. Bullitt was now sent as official representative to Moscow, and Alexander Troyanovsky came to Washington. Yet, relations remained half-hearted; religious persecution and party purges irritated American sentiments; no satisfac-

U.S.-RUSSIAN RELATIONS, 1860–1950

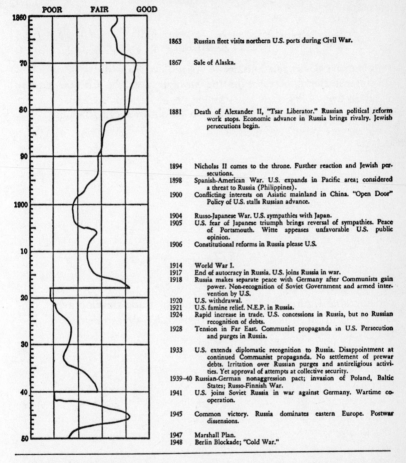

1863	Russian fleet visits northern U.S. ports during Civil War.
1867	Sale of Alaska.
1881	Death of Alexander II, "Tsar Liberator." Russian political reform work stops. Economic advance in Russia brings rivalry. Jewish persecutions begin.
1894	Nicholas II comes to the throne. Further reaction and Jewish persecutions.
1898	Spanish-American War. U.S. expands in Pacific area; considered a threat to Russia (Philippines).
1900	Conflicting interests on Asiatic mainland in China. "Open Door" Policy of U.S. stalls Russian advance.
1904	Russo-Japanese War. U.S. sympathies with Japan.
1905	U.S. fear of Japanese triumph brings reversal of sympathies. Peace of Portsmouth. Witte appeases unfavorable U.S. public opinion.
1906	Constitutional reforms in Russia please U.S.
1914	World War I.
1917	End of autocracy in Russia. U.S. joins Russia in war.
1918	Russia makes separate peace with Germany after Communists gain power. Non-recognition of Soviet Government and armed intervention by U.S.
1920	U.S. withdrawal.
1921	U.S. famine relief. N.E.P. in Russia.
1924	Rapid increase in trade. U.S. concessions in Russia, but no Russian recognition of debts.
1928	Tension in Far East. Communist propaganda in U.S. Persecution and purges in Russia.
1933	U.S. extends diplomatic recognition to Russia. Disappointment at continued Communist propaganda. No settlement of prewar debts. Irritation over Russian purges and antireligious activities. Yet approval of attempts at collective security.
1939-40	Russian-German nonaggression pact; invasion of Poland, Baltic States; Russo-Finnish War.
1941	U.S. joins Soviet Russia in war against Germany. Wartime co-operation.
1945	Common victory. Russia dominates eastern Europe. Postwar dissensions.
1947	Marshall Plan.
1948	Berlin Blockade; "Cold War."

AMERICAN–RUSSIAN relations of the past were determined essentially by absence of common interests—permitting the growth of either country without affecting the other. The Alaskan problem was liquidated before becoming an obstacle to friendly relations. Far Eastern regions possessed sufficient inherent strength to withstand an imperialistic clash of the two countries, and American isolation prevented the rise of dangerous international issues. In the twentieth century, Russia (which had previously touched United States interests primarily in the Pacific area) began to assume greater importance in the Atlantic and European sector. Ideological as well as practical political issues began to concern the United States after the weakening of France, England, and Germany as outposts of the civilization to which America belongs.

tory arrangement regarding prewar debts was reached; and, contrary to Soviet guarantees, propaganda for world revolution did not subside.

PROBLEMS

1. Compare Soviet relationships to Asiatic nations with tsarist ones.
2. Discuss the importance of the struggle over the Chinese Eastern Railway.
3. Discuss the difficulties prevailing in Russo-American relations.

47

ROAD TO WORLD WAR II

Significant Dates

COLLECTIVE SECURITY

The year 1934, which brought the consolidation of Hitler's power in Germany, marked a turn in Russian foreign policy. Nothing could be expected of a Germany which outlawed its Communist citizens, appealed to all anti-Soviet forces abroad, and indifferently watched the deterioration of existing political bonds. Moreover, Germany rejected a Soviet proposal for the guarantee of the independence of the Baltic states, which Russia considered indispensable for her own security. Faced by the specter of renewed isolation, the Soviet government turned with determination to European neighbors and to the West and found response from an apprehensive world. Small nations like Czechoslovakia, Rumania, and Bulgaria, which so far had challenged the Soviet system, hastened to recognize it now; nonaggression pacts with Poland, Latvia, Estonia, and Finland were prolonged by ten years; political and economic bonds with France were strengthened to forestall the surrender of France to German influence; and ultimately Russia joined the League of Nations.

League of Nations. At its inception the League had been intended by its founders, among its manifold purposes, as an "alternative to Bolshevism"; and Russia, which had not been invited to the drafting of the Covenant, described it in the words of Lenin as "an alliance of world bandits against the proletariat." She essentially feared not the League but the forces behind it, and from the outset was antagonized by Persian, Finnish, Georgian, and other complaints which together with Soviet Far Eastern policies were made topics of denunciatory discussion before the League Assembly.

RAPPROCHEMENT. After the adoption of the N.E.P., Russia, although refusing to become a member, co-operated with the League to a limited extent. She permitted the League's relief work under Fridtjof Nansen and later participated in the League's conferences on public health and the prevention of epidemics. Although after the murder of Vorovsky her attendance at Geneva meetings was deemed impossible, Russian co-operation, wherever economically or propagandistically advisable, was forthcoming and could be witnessed in connection with questions of labor standards and in international economic and financial policies.

SOVIET ENTRY INTO LEAGUE. Politically, however, Russia oriented herself with nonmembers, such as Germany and Turkey; and not until Germany's entry into the League and the growing need for credits from the West changed the situation was closer co-operation with the League itself considered. In 1927 Litvinov was for the first time dispatched to Geneva to attend a disarmament conference. Chiefly for propagandistic reasons, he made sweeping proposals; and though after rejection of his plan he suggested less drastic measures, his excessive zeal antagonized rather than persuaded the other members. In 1932 another disarmament conference was held, which was again attended by the Soviets but with no better results. After Hitler had come to power, a change in the attitude of the Russian delegation occurred: Its members were increasingly willing to compromise on international issues, and in 1934, in view of the circumstances, the Soviet Union formally joined the League. It thus officially attested its desire to shift from isolation and independent action to collective security together with capitalist countries.

Participation in Collective Security. The results of this new trend in Russian foreign policies were evidenced in the year 1935.

The deterioration of relations with Germany was officially avowed, and Germany was accused of violating the Treaty of Versailles, notwithstanding the fact that this treaty previously had been bitterly denounced by the Russians themselves.

NEGOTIATIONS. In March, 1935, the British foreign minister Anthony Eden made a personal call at Moscow to discuss collective security; two months later the French minister Laval journeyed to Russia and concluded a Franco-Russian "East Pact"; and after him, Czechoslovakia's foreign minister Beneš arrived for the signing of an assistance treaty. Thus, Russia began to dominate the international scene. But since common fears rather than mutual interests constituted the link, the Soviet government took care to strengthen its position through independent measures as well. As the capitalistic world, beset by depression and fascism, seemed to be approaching its gravest crisis, special stress was laid upon ideological propaganda. The Comintern received increased unofficial encouragement, and utmost support was given to other organizations such as the Profintern, the Antifascists, and the League of the Godless.

CHECKS TO COLLECTIVE SECURITY. Such action, in turn, adversely influenced collaboration with the Western powers, whence protests soon were voiced against the proselytizing activities of the Communists. Instability of relations with the West thus continued to prevail, and consequently Russia took steps to renew her former neighborly relations with Germany. This was achieved not only by a new trade treaty, but also by an invitation to Germany to join the Franco-Russian "East Pact." Yet, collective security remained the watchword, and the bonds with Western Europe were not severed. Common action for security was advocated in the case of Italy's aggression in Abyssinia, and adherence was pledged to the Montreux Convention regarding the Turkish Straits and to the United States-Franco-English Three-Power Naval Treaty.

Growth of International Tension. Two new areas of friction emerged in 1936. The one, Spain, where Fascists undertook to overthrow the republican government, soon became the most serious international issue testing the respective alignments of the great powers. Most European countries intervened on one side or the other, splitting the Continent. The Soviet government lent its forces —first financially, later militarily—to the republicans. The other area, the Far East, developed similar threatening aspects when, despite the recent sale of the Chinese Eastern Railway, clashes with infiltrating Japanese occurred on the Manchukuo frontier. The Soviets found themselves compelled to strengthen further their army there, and a new treaty for mutual aid and consultation was concluded with the Mongolian republic. Before the year ended, the interconnection of the two events and their significance—at least for Russia—became evident when in November, Germany, which in its anti-Communist drive had encouraged and supported the revolt in Spain, concluded an "Anti-Comintern Pact" with Japan. Soviet Russia thus found herself threatened from two sides and was forced to seek collective security with redoubled energy, through co-operation at Geneva as well as outside the League of Nations. She also concluded a nonaggression pact with China and held conferences in Moscow with the foreign ministers of Sweden, Latvia, and Turkey. Still, the dangers to the socialist commonwealth from the side of capitalism abroad continued to increase. Italy officially joined the German-Japanese Anti-Comintern Pact in 1937; the propaganda of the Comintern alienated the Western powers and America; the republican cause in Spain—unsupported except by Russia and a few thousand volunteers from other countries—became hopeless despite Litvinov's urgent appeals in Geneva; and the Japanese steadily advanced in China and Manchukuo.

COLLAPSE OF COLLECTIVE SECURITY

Munich, 1938. In the fall of 1938, the Russian policies, painfully pursued on the road to collective security through co-operation with Western powers, collapsed. When Hitler threatened war because of alleged aggressive acts on the part of Czechoslovakia, England and France deserted the cause and without consulting Russia submitted to the Nazi leader's demands. Not only did they participate (at Munich) in a decision over Czechoslovakia from which the Soviets were excluded, but by permitting the partition of the country—treaties notwithstanding—they caused a breach in the existing defense system of Russia. The latter found herself once more isolated; her obligations toward Czechoslovakia were automatically canceled by France's refusal to come to the aid of the Czechs, and although refusing recognition of Germany's acts, the Russians were in no position to avert their execution.

German Nonaggression Pact, 1939. Six months later, the incorporation of the rest of Czechoslovakia into Germany revived hopes in Russia for collective security as the Western nations now realized the impossibility of ever satisfying Nazi greed. In April, 1939, negotiations between Russia, France, and England were undertaken for a military alliance. But Western inability to gauge the respective threats of nazism and communism, combined with lack of military preparedness, resulted in the breakdown of the parleys. Litvinov, who saw the fundamental principles of his foreign policies collapsing, thereupon resigned; his successor, Molotov, renewed negotiations, but they led again to failure. Meanwhile, negotiations secretly undertaken with Nazi Germany promised results; and in August, instead of a Western alliance, a trade and nonaggression pact with Germany was concluded. The U.S.S.R. intended thereby to preserve her own neutrality in case the capitalist countries fought one another, or to postpone direct involvement in war while her own preparations could be completed. But the Western world was shocked by the sudden change of Russian policies and, paralyzed, watched the outbreak of war on September 1, 1939.

Invasion of Poland. The first act consisted in a German invasion of Poland and the prompt defeat of that country. Sixteen days later, in view of the end of the Polish state and the concomitant dissolution of treaty obligations, Russian troops invaded Poland from the east. They occupied almost half of the country and divided it with Germany; through an amity treaty with Hitler, a new common Russo-German borderline was established. This act ended the period of collective security and introduced a last phase in Russian international relations where the accent was placed on the individual nation's military power and its unrestricted use for survival.

Invasion of Finland. The division of Poland was supposed to serve Russian security and to stop any further German advance eastward, particularly in the direction of Russia's Baltic harbors—which would have constituted a most serious menace, for since the times of Ivan the Terrible and Peter the Great, access to the Baltic Sea was justly considered a basic principle of Russian independence. Well aware, however, of the possibility of just such a German push, the Soviets tried to forestall it by pacts with Lithuania, Latvia, Estonia, and Finland. With regard to the three Baltic states, negotiations supported by threats led to "mutual assistance agreements" in October, 1939; but those with Finland broke down and, after a number of frontier incidents, an attack was launched on that country on November 30, in order to secure by force advantageous military outposts in the event of an attack from the west. Because of this act of aggression, which was interpreted as a chauvinistic desire for aggrandizement and dissemination of communistic principles, the Soviet Union was expelled from the League of Nations. But she carried on the war, and after a protracted campaign, which divulged many military shortcomings, she conquered Finland and forced her to cede her eastern provinces together with the fortress of Viipuri (Viborg) as well as rights to ports and fortifications along her south shore.

Absorption of Baltic States. The gains in the Baltic area still did not seem sufficient to guarantee the Soviet position, and therefore, under ever-increasing pressure and with the help of indigenous Communist groups, "friendly" governments were imposed on Lithuania, Latvia, and Estonia. In July and August, 1940, the three nations were transformed into Soviet republics and entered the Soviet Union. These changes were recognized by Germany in the following January, and an agreement was made for population exchanges and frontier revisions.

Outbreak of War with Germany. The Nazis, however, had been disturbed especially by Soviet demands on neighboring Lithuania and by the Soviet invasion of Finland and had contrived to break the agreements. Consequently, aside from fundamental political and ideological differences, they failed in decisive negotiations with Molotov in November, 1940, to settle many practical issues in other regions—such as questions referring to the Balkans and the Danube area. The Soviet government was aware of the danger of a complete break with Germany and worked feverishly to strengthen its military position. It changed the tone of its propaganda; it concluded a neutrality pact with Japan and granted her fishery rights; and it engaged in negotiations with the United States. At home, Stalin was named chairman of the Council of People's Commissars in order to assemble all forces, and the army was reorganized on the basis of the experience of the Finnish war. On June 22, 1941, the expected and inevitable happened. In accordance with the logic of Nazi doctrine German armies invaded Soviet territory. Rumania, Finland, and later Slovakia and Hungary followed the German lead;

and eventually also Italian and Spanish contingents joined the Nazi forces. Thus began the struggle for the survival of the Soviet system.

PROBLEMS

1. Discuss the attitude of Soviet Russia toward the League of Nations.
2. Trace the changes in Russia's international position, 1934–1939.
3. Discuss the actions of Russia toward her Western neighbors, 1939–1941.

48

WORLD WAR II

RUSSIAN ARMY

Birth of the Russian Army. War found Russia militarily well prepared. From their accession to power, the Bolsheviks, in the midst of a hostile world, had given due attention to the defensive strength of the country and the preservation of its military tradition. This tradition can be traced back to the time of Ivan the Great, who had put an end to the disorganized nomadic and feudalistic fighting methods of the Middle Ages. Conscious of Russia's special geographical conditions, Ivan preserved some of the fundamentals of warfare which had proved valuable through the centuries. As he was provided with sufficient manpower in his vast realms, he employed large armies so that by sheer weight he could overpower the enemy; he fostered the art of guerrilla warfare; and he knew how to take advantage of climatic conditions—of long and arduous winter seasons when rivers and swamps were frozen and allowed swift movements of appropriately equipped Russian forces, whereas heavily armored enemies were frustrated. And he likewise adopted methods which Tartar and other invaders in their long and successful campaigns had shown to be of special value in the wide, sparsely populated stretches of the Eurasian plains. Mobile Cossack units and lightly armed cavalry from Ivan's time supplemented the heavy cadres previously in use. Under Ivan III's grandson, Ivan the Terrible, artillery was modernized and strengthened, constituting from then on a weapon of pride to the Russians. Also, a special well-disciplined force, the Streltsi, was created as a bodyguard directly responsible to the Tsar.

Army under Peter I.   In the following century, when the Ukraine was incorporated, Zaporogian Cossacks increased the military power of Russia. Their absorption into the army made changes necessary, and these were carried out by Prince Golitsyn (Regent Sophia's lover) and especially by Peter the Great. The most important reform consisted in the abolition of the "tables of rank," by which positions of command had been accorded nobles on the basis of hereditary rank and seniority, but which were now replaced by a system of promotion based on ability. Furthermore, the Streltsi, who like the ancient Roman Praetorian Guards had gained undue political influence, were wisely suppressed. Peter replaced them by "imperial guards," the Preobrazhensky and Semenovsky regiments, which were composed of strictly professional and disciplined troops created after European models. Peter also established a navy—the result of his experience at the siege of Azov, his acquisition of ports on the Baltic Sea, and his personal interest in maritime affairs and in shipbuilding.

Army in Later Eighteenth Century.   Although the Russian navy was allowed to decay under Peter's successors, the army gained in strength and importance during the eighteenth century. Under Anna as well as under Elizabeth, Catherine, and Paul, it was regularly reorganized and came to match contemporary standards of Europe; military dress, discipline, tactical training, mechanical equipment, and particularly artillery were consistently improved. Toward the end of the century, a gifted leader emerged in the person of Suvorov, who, in his Turkish and later Italian and Swiss campaigns (and notwithstanding many mistakes and the ultimate failure of the latter), showed strategic as well as tactical ability hardly inferior to that of Napoleon.

Napoleonic Era.   Peculiarly enough, the long warfare during the Napoleonic era, which had brought terrible defeats at Austerlitz and Friedland and victories in the campaigns of 1812 and 1813, produced little progress in the military field. In 1812 the overall Russian strategy was based on resistance and reliance upon geographical conditions, and it did not reflect scientific studies commensurate with those of the period. Thus, the campaigns turned out to be costly, and the war was unduly prolonged; the severe criticism of the Russian generals and their tactics by later generations seem justified.

Modernization of Army. Innovations, however, were introduced by Alexander I after the fall of Napoleon. With the help of the able artillery general Arakcheyev, "military colonies" were established which marked a radical departure from prior ways of recruiting troops; but corruption and antiquated social conditions checked their success and retarded the evolution of military science. The weaknesses of both army and navy and of their commanders were demonstrated in the Crimean War, and the need for radical reform became evident. It was carried out in 1874 when, after the completion of fundamental social reforms, compulsory military service was introduced. It showed tangible results in the war of 1878 and in World War I. But the auxiliary services remained inefficient and leadership incompetent, and the valor of the individual soldier could not compensate for the shortcomings of organization and strategy.

Creation of "Red Army." When the Bolshevists seized power, a thorough change was made in the organization and direction of the military forces. Many of those in command were eliminated—in some instances for no other reason than their position in former tsarist society. "Revolutionary Order Number One" abolished all distinctions of rank. Although a number of tsarist commanders were retained, new politically reliable leaders were also appointed; and all were subjected to the supervision of political commissars and soldiers' councils. Furthermore, a new military force was improvised in 1917 as *"avant-garde* of the proletariat," and war-weary soldiers and reluctant peasants were demobilized. The Red Army proper came into being on February 23, 1918, and under the able direction of men like Trotsky gained in strength and efficiency. During the civil war it saved the Bolshevik government.

Mechanization of Army. After the end of the civil war and the intervention by the Allies in 1921, the Red Army was reduced from five and a half to one and a half million men, and by 1925 it amounted to no more than six hundred thousand. Trotsky was replaced as chief of staff by M. Frunze, and the term of military service was lengthened. In the meantime a new officers' corps, indoctrinated with revolutionary ideas, was trained; its authority was gradually increased; and ultimately regular officers' ranks, including that of marshal, were reintroduced. Military orders were likewise renewed; and in 1931 the gradual numerical strengthening of the forces was begun, resulting in 1936 in a military establishment of no less than two million men. During this period, industries were keyed to the needs of defense; the equipment was bettered; a modern artillery and aviation corps was built up; and, after many disappointing years, even the tank corps and the air force began to live up to modern requirements. The constitution of 1936 provided again for compulsory military service, and great efforts were made to evoke a new feeling of national pride. In 1937 Revolutionary Order Number One was officially revoked, and in the same year purges were carried out to rid the military forces of all possible traitors; suspicious leaders were tried and executed. Among them was as distinguished a general as Marshal Tukhachevsky, who had helped to organize the Red Army, had fought in the civil war against Denikin and against the Poles, and had served as Chief of Staff of the Red Army and as Deputy Commissar of War.

THE CAMPAIGNS

Preparations against Nazis. The organization of the Soviet military forces was thus completed when the Second World War broke out. But experience in the field was still lacking. Incidents on the Manchukuo border had not taught them the art of large-scale operations, and the occupation of eastern Poland in 1939 presented no problem to Soviet military leadership. It was the Finnish War undertaken in November, 1939, which constituted a true test, and it divulged grave shortcomings: Initiative was lacking; bureaucracy hampered action; equipment was sometimes faulty; and the Finnish defenses on the Mannerheim Line were broken at last only by overwhelming numbers. The following year was, therefore, used for a correction of exposed deficiencies and for the adaptation of new methods which Soviet military analysts observed abroad in the triumphant campaigns of the Germans. The commanders were, however, circumspect enough to prepare for defense as well as for attack. They modified their tactics according to experience derived from foreign invasions incurred in previous centuries on the part of Tartars, Poles, and French, and they prepared for a possible assault from the west as well as the east.

Nazi Strategic Plan. The blow fell in June, 1941. At a time chosen because no other front except a minor one in Libya existed for them, the Germans invaded Russia with some two hundred divisions. Their objectives, to be achieved in a lightning thrust, were threefold: to seize Leningrad after a quick advance through the Baltic countries and to isolate Russia from the Baltic Sea; to gain Moscow over a central route, as formerly used by Napoleon, and to disrupt the converging Russian transportation system; and to grab the coal- and food-producing regions of the south and to deprive the Russians of fuel and provisions. They hoped to find support from a discontented population.

Nazi Failure. In every direction, the Germans came within sight of their objectives, but in none did they gain them. Leningrad was reached on August 21, 1941, and besieged in vain until January, 1944. The main blow against Moscow was slowed down near Smolensk, and an unsuccessful three-month battle for the capital began on October 13, 1941. On the same day, in the south, a siege of Sevastopol was started; but the fortress was not taken until June, 1942, and it was recovered in May, 1944. The *blitzkrieg* thus bogged down; contrary to Nazi calculations, winter overtook the German armies, which, like all invaders, suffered intensely, and in the next year their strength was insufficient to continue the threefold thrust. The onslaught, therefore, was largely confined to the south, where the whole Black Sea coast, the Ukraine with the Donets coal basin, and parts of the Caucasus region were occupied. But the key to the southern defense system, the city of Stalingrad, which dominated the vital lower Volga basin with all its communication lines and which was besieged in September, 1942, could not be taken. A Russian army under Marshal Zhukov defended the city heroically in a bitter five-month struggle which turned out to be decisive for the outcome of the war. The entire German VI Army was captured, and the remaining Nazis began their retreat. In the following summer, 1943, they staged a temporarily successful counteroffensive near Kursk; but despite the fact that Russia's allies failed to establish a second

front and confined themselves to aerial blows, Russian progress
—efficiently furthered by American lend-lease aid—could not be
halted.

Russian Victory. Deliverance came in the year 1944: In June,
the Allied invasion of Normandy opened the long-expected second
front, and in September, Finland, Rumania, and Bulgaria capitu-
lated. The Germans were forced farther and farther back, although
they continued to defend themselves with great fortitude; their retreat from the Baltic countries, central Russia, the Donets basin, and
the Ukraine was slow, and terrible devastation was wrought in the
abandoned regions. The advance of the Russian armies to Warsaw,
which was taken in January, 1945, to Königsberg, which was captured in April, and to the Oder River, which was crossed in the same
month, was extremely difficult and demanded utmost valor, skill,
and perseverance. The final battle of Berlin was most savage, and
not until May 8, 1945, did the Germans capitulate.

War against Japan. As it later became evident, no systematic
co-ordination of German and Japanese strategy existed throughout
the war. No Japanese attack in the Far East endangered the military
operations on Russia's western front, nor did it become necessary to
divert forces in men or material for action in the East. Notwithstanding the German-Japanese alliance and the Anti-Comintern
Pact, treaties for fishery rights (and others) were successfully negotiated between Russia and Japan, and thus a comparatively small
force sufficed to guard Russia's eastern border. Not until August 8,
three months after the defeat of Germany, did hostilities break out
in the Far East, and that was instigated by Russian, not by Japanese,
action. But determined fighting was confined to a very brief period.
Japan had already suffered decisive defeats, and the weapon of the
atomic bomb had been loosed upon the country. For Japan there was
only one solution, and she quickly surrendered on August 14, 1945.

WARTIME DIPLOMACY

At the beginning of the war, under the impact of the first Nazi
assault, Russia made many concessions to gain the full support of
a suspicious world. She accepted the Atlantic Charter and signed the
"Declaration by the United Nations" (January 1, 1942); she concluded a twenty-year assistance pact with England (May, 1942) and

lend-lease agreements with the United States (June, 1942); ultimately she declared the formal dissolution of the Comintern by its executive committee (May, 1943—but revived in new form in October, 1947). Soon after the German advance was stopped, a different course, however, was taken, and this found its expression in cleverly timed denunciations of the Allies for failing to open a long-promised second front, in territorial claims on Baltic regions and Bessarabia, in a neutral policy toward Japan, and, most important, in a steadily hardening stand with regard to all arrangements sought by Russia's allies in the course of wartime negotiations.

Relations with Western Nations. While the Western nations fought for "victory," for the defeat of nazism and all it stood for, and lacked a realistic concept of postwar political relationships, the Soviets at all times kept in mind precise goals beyond victory. Exploiting both military reverses and military successes, they put before the American and English demands which meant a vast expansion of their power after the defeat of Germany.

NEGOTIATIONS. In the pursuit of their aims, the Soviets participated, in May, 1943, in a postwar Food Conference at Hot Springs, Virginia; in July, 1943, in a Monetary Conference at Bretton Woods; in August and September, 1944, in a Security Conference at Dumbarton Oaks; and in April, 1945, in the first United Nations Conference at San Francisco. On the other hand, they refused to take part in an International Civil Aviation Conference, emphasizing thereby their resolve to maintain freedom of action and especially to guarantee the security of the Union not only through international agreements but also through independent military preparation. The negotiations soon gave proof of a new distribution of power.

On the diplomatic stage, the point of gravity had shifted eastward (as never before in the history of the Western world) into spheres of Russian predominance: In December, 1941, Eden visited Moscow; in August, 1942, Churchill met Stalin there; in October, 1943, both Eden and Hull, Secretary of State of the United States, traveled to Moscow; in November, President Roosevelt and Prime Minister Churchill went to see Stalin in Teheran, the most easterly meeting place yet of any great international conference. In October, 1944, Churchill was again in Moscow; in December, the Frenchman de Gaulle visited there; and in February, 1945, Churchill and Roosevelt once more traveled east to meet Stalin at Yalta in the Crimea.

TEHERAN AND YALTA. The most important meetings were those of Teheran and Yalta. It was there that Stalin secured concessions for Russia which were to lay the basis for her postwar domination of all of Eastern and half of Central Europe. At Teheran, the Soviets gained assurances not only of full military support through a second front, but also promises of territorial gains in Europe as well as in the Far East. At the same time, they succeeded in postponing decisions regarding the postwar organization of Germany, Poland, and China until the moment when a more favorable military situation would have improved their bargaining position. At Yalta, the Teheran policy was pursued further. In exchange for a promise to declare war on Japan within three months of Germany's surrender, Russia was guaranteed parts of the former Japanese empire and influence in the affairs of Korea and China. She was also allowed to retain all the Polish territory up to the Curzon Line, which she had seized in accordance with her amity pact with Hitler. (Poland was to receive German lands as "compensation" for what she was to surrender to Russia.) In addition she was given German territory along the Baltic coast, including the port of Königsberg. Furthermore, Russia was promised the occupation of eastern Germany, billions in reparations, and the use of forced labor of millions of Germans. Dismemberment of Germany was envisaged, but final agreement about it was postponed as well as decisions about the future government of Germany, about Berlin, and also about the future governments of the various eastern European states. Finally, Stalin secured the introduction of a veto right in the Security Council of the planned United Nations.

Relations with Neighbors. Through his negotiations with his allies, Stalin, having denounced early the principles of the Atlantic Charter, prepared the way for Russian domination of his country's immediate neighbors. He proffered demands for general recognition of the absorption of the Baltic states into the Soviet Union; and in April, 1943, the U.S.S.R. broke relations with the then existing Polish government. In time, the struggle between Russia and her allies over the form of a new Polish government friendly to Russia increased and came to a climax when, in January, 1945, a Communist-dominated counter-government, formed at Lublin, was officially recognized by the Soviets. As to Czechoslovakia and Yugoslavia, both instituted regimes primarily acceptable to Russia, and treaties of amity were concluded with them. Japan, too, bowed to her mighty neighbor, even before Russia joined in the hostilities, by consenting to a withdrawal from long-held coal and oil concessions in northern Sakhalin.

Relations with Enemies. The only part of Soviet policy which remained unclear and vacillating throughout the war was that toward her enemies. The desire for impressing particularly Germany and Finland with the advantages of the Soviet system, and the realization that at all times co-operation between Germany and Russia had brought great benefit to both sides, conflicted with the general desire to avenge the Nazi invasion and atrocities, with the fear of Western influences in the new Germany, and with the hope for annexations and reparations. A "Free German Committee," founded in Moscow in 1944 and composed of German refugees and war prissoners including high ranking generals, was only half-heartedly supported; and eventually a stern, oppressive policy was promoted. As for Finland, Rumania, Bulgaria, and Hungary, it was subsequently decided to bring them entirely into the Russian orbit, whereas Italy, occupied by the Allies, was left to the Western powers.

THE HOME FRONT

Wartime Economy. The military strength of the Soviet Union had to be strained to the utmost, and the most gigantic demands had to be made on its economy. The German occupation of White Russia, the Donets basin, parts of the Caucasus, and other industrial regions and the destruction of plants in centers like Leningrad, Moscow, and Stalingrad necessitated shifts of industries eastward on an unprecedented scale. Labor had to be drafted from the ranks of women and children as well as men unfit for military service. Whole population groups were transferred east of the Urals. Production of consumer goods, except those serving barest necessities, was discontinued. Concessions were made to farmers by relaxing the strict regime of the kolkhoz, and, lest survival should be endangered by lack of food production, the government shut its eyes to expanding private cultivation of land. New industries were built in Siberia, and through lend-lease from the United States shortages in vital weapons had to be overcome. Black markets were tolerated, for despite resulting inequalities in distribution, they too contributed to fulfilling needs. Through new taxes and loans, all available money was channeled into the treasury.

The price in human effort and material goods was extremely high, but under the pressure of war the Russian people provided the necessary manpower and carried the financial burden. Without the help of foreign contingents, they fought the war on Germany's eastern front; they built the new industries through their own efforts; and notwithstanding the substantial aid from abroad—aid that may well have meant the decisive balance at the critical stages in 1942 and 1943—the bulk of the military requirements was provided by the Russian peoples.

Wartime Social Policy. The impact of the struggle on social conditions within the U.S.S.R. was not uniformly in line with the desires and ideology of the Soviet state, nor were its consequences forseeable. For the sake of efficiency, political commissariats in the army were abolished, officer-ranks were accentuated, and "patriotism" was extolled—all of which conflicted with the international tendencies of Marxist teachings. Socialist experiments in education or family organization had to be relinquished, and freedom had to be further curtailed. The policy of racial toleration could not be maintained; ruthless population shifts occurred such as that of the so-called Volga-Germans who in two centuries had contributed so much to the development of the Volga region. Supervision of the political activities of the whole population had to be increased rather than relaxed since hundreds of thousands, disappointed with the Soviet system and objecting particularly to collectivization, co-operated with the enemy. Hitler failed, though, to avail himself of these opportunities and did not even make use of a whole volunteer army made up of many Ukrainians under the Russian general Vlasov, which had gone over to the German side.

Social policies were affected also by sudden and close contact with foreign countries, with intelligent and prosperous capitalist enemies as well as with allies, and this influenced the political outlook of many soldiers and administrators. Elements of doubtful loyalty came to the fore. These changes heralded a major shift in the sociological structure of the Soviet Union.

Wartime Church Policy. Special concessions were made to the Orthodox church which, immediately upon the outbreak of war, held services and prayer for Soviet victory, celebrated Stalin, and collected money to support tank battalions. The government reciprocated by re-establishing full freedom of the churches, and in September the chief atheist newspaper was discontinued. Two years later the metropolitan of Moscow, Sergius, was for the first time received by Stalin, and thereupon elected Patriarch, thus filling a position vacant since the death of Tikhon almost a score of years earlier. A "Department for Orthodox Church Affairs" was established under the Council of the People's Commissars and began to constitute, as of old, a link between state and church. Religious seminaries were reopened, and a reconciliation was effected with the Orthodox religious groups of *émigrés*. When in January, 1945, after Sergius' death, the metropolitan Alexis was enthroned as Patriarch, the Orthodox church had gained a recognized place within the new Russian society.

PROBLEMS

1. Trace the historical development of the Russian army.
2. Discuss the effect of World War II on Russia's internal conditions.
3. Discuss the relations between Russia and Japan during World War II.

49

THE POSTWAR ERA

Significant Dates

The years from the end of the war in 1945 to Stalin's death in 1953 constitute the postwar period, properly speaking. They were years not only of physical reconstruction but, in many respects, also of a return psychologically and culturally, to prewar conditions. In order to increase heavy industries, the government demanded new exertions on the side of the population and again postponed improvements in living standards; it insisted on strengthening the military establishment; and it subjected every Soviet citizen to renewed, strict supervision of all his activities. In external affairs, the years were a time of expansion. Contrary to the promises made to the world in the Atlantic Charter, yet with the consent of Russia's partners who themselves had drafted the Charter, the policy of vigorous aggrandizement prepared in war-time negotiation was now successfully pursued. Besides annexing large territories, the Soviets imposed regimes subservient to their interests wherever Soviet troops were stationed. The postwar years were thus used for a vigorous assertion of Russian power.

EXTERNAL POLICIES

War and victory furthered enormously a spirit of national pride. As early as the 1930's, the government had begun to cater to it: by emphasizing the glories of Russian (i.e., pre-revolutionary) history, by extolling military heroes like Suvorov, Kutusov, Alexander Nevsky, by re-introducing orders and titles, and by laying claim for Russia to numerous scientific inventions, such as the telephone, Bessemer process, incandescent lamp, submarine, and radio—which the world had long been wont to assign the United States, Germany, England, or Italy. Evidence of this new nationalism was provided by the change of the oath the Soviet soldier had to take: In the original Red Army, the soldier had sworn to serve the interests of the working class of the whole world and to liberate all workers in order to create a socialist order and establish the brotherhood of all peoples; now he was obliged in the first place to serve his home country, to obey, and to safeguard Russian secrets. In a like spirit, paragraph 58 of the Criminal code was revised. This paragraph, which had initially provided punishment for those who had betrayed the Soviet order, was revised in 1934 to include as a punishable offense a great variety of acts which normally would never have been deemed detrimental to the nation. After the war, its meaning was again broadened and from then on could be interpreted to comprise any kind of information which even conversationally might be given to Russians about happenings abroad or to foreigners about the Soviet Union. Nobody could thereafter be sure whether or not he had committed a punishable act. In such a spirit of nationalism, postwar foreign policies were carried on.

Postwar Diplomacy. As soon as the hostilities ended in 1945, the fruits of the wartime effort were conscientiously harvested. The territorial acquisitions which were made included, besides the Baltic states which had been incorporated in 1940, Finland's Karelia and her arctic shore line, eastern Poland, parts of Germany's East Prussia, Czechoslovakia's Ruthenian lands, Rumania's Bessarabia, and Japan's Southern Sakhalin and the Kuril Islands. In addition, a strong Soviet hold was established on Finland, Central Germany, Czechoslovakia, Hungary, Yugoslavia, Albania, Rumania, Bulgaria, and in Asia on Manchuria and northern Korea. Soviet power was also felt—often through the activities of Communist parties—in outlying regions, such as western Germany and Sweden, France and Italy, India and China, and particularly Greece, Turkey, and Iran. The conflict resulting from this development found its reaction in the councils of all nations and was sharpened by the development of a process for the release of atomic energy which gave the United States a temporary advantage in the military field.

Potsdam Conference. In July and August, 1945, a conference was held at Potsdam. Stalin, Truman (who had replaced Roosevelt after the latter's death), and Attlee (who had succeeded Churchill in the midst of the conference after a landslide vote for the Labor party) represented the victorious nations. The atmosphere was strained, for the United States and England had come to realize the dangers implied in the expansion of Russian power and the difficulties of working with the Soviets, whose interpretation of agreements often differed sharply from theirs. They yielded, however, to most of Stalin's demands with regard to the organization of the occupation of Germany, the territorial ambitions of Poland, the question of reparations, and the influence of the Soviet Union on the formation of governments in the areas occupied by the Soviet army.

Preparation of Peace Treaties. After Potsdam, the heads of the three strongest powers did not soon meet again. But the foreign ministers came together, and their conferences—complicated by the admission of a powerless but vociferous France—failed to settle existing differences. No fewer than eight meetings took place: at London and Moscow, in 1945; at Paris and New York in 1946; at London, Moscow, Paris, and again London in 1947. Except for peace treaties with the minor allies of Germany, which were the result of many unsatisfactory and perhaps dangerous compromises, no major issue was settled. Even where agreements were reached, they were so vaguely formulated that they soon led to divergent interpretations.

The Communist Appeal in the West. Endless international talks did not prevent the Soviet Union from pursuing the aim of further extending her power through action and propaganda. However, the emphasis on the Russian national tradition and the many ideological compromises made for the sake of securing practical advantages for Russia proved to be obstacles to the spreading of the Communist doctrine. The strong amity movement toward Russia

after the end of the war was interrupted. Most free elections of subsequent years in Italy, France, the Scandinavian countries, and other
West-European nations revealed that Communist parties in these
countries were unable to maintain their earlier appeal for the masses.
In Germany and Austria—and beyond their borders—the behavior
of the Russian troops, the exploitation of prisoners and workers
through forced labor, the spoliation of the countries, the transfer of
vital peacetime industries and the redistribution of land ownership,
and the shifting of populations after annexations disheartened even
those who had been sympathetic to Russia. Only a few, and eventually unsatisfactory, economic agreements could be made with western European countries, such as Switzerland, Sweden, France, and
England.

The Communist Appeal in the East. A different development,
however, took place in the East. Although demands reminiscent of
Pan-Slav imperialism spread fears in Turkey, Iran, and many Mohammedan countries, communism became of major significance in
India, Burma, China, Indonesia, and the Malay Peninsula. Likewise,
in eastern Europe communism made considerable gains. With the
help of Soviet military power Communist governments friendly to
the Soviet Union were established between 1945 and 1947 in Poland,
Hungary, Rumania, and Bulgaria, and in February, 1948, through
a coup very disheartening to the Western powers, also in Czechoslovakia. These various countries were bound together by the organization of a mutual "Information Bureau" (the Cominform, which
in 1947 took the place of the former Comintern) and by a Council
of Economic Mutual Assistance founded in January, 1949. Only
Yugoslavia under Marshal Tito, though ideologically communistic,
gained an increasing amount of independence from Moscow, constituting thereby a dangerous gap in the structure of socialist unity
and paving the way for heretical nationalistic developments within
the communistic world.

Opposition to Communism. The expansion of Russian power
in the East and the growing resistance of the West gave the United
States an opportunity, as the chief representative of the forces opposing the Soviet ideology, to take action at least in those parts which
were not occupied by Russian forces and which because of their
maritime position were deemed of special strategic importance

Soviet infiltration in Korea, in Iran (which, in addition to its wealth in oil, was important because it dominated the approach to the Indian Ocean), and in Greece and Turkey (which controlled the approaches to the Mediterranean) was vigorously and successfully opposed through economic and military aid. Notwithstanding Soviet protests, a policy of aid for the preservation of strategically important smaller countries ("Truman Doctrine") was energetically pushed. In June, 1947, the program of resistance was expanded by a proposal (Marshall Plan) that all nations of Europe should combine to work out a plan for the re-establishment of economic prosperity, and the United States supported the execution of the plan by economic aid. The Soviet government—fearing that this proposal would lead to a decline of Communist strength through economic recovery and, possibly, to virtual domination of Europe by the United States—refused its participation after brief consultation with England and France; and the smaller nations in the Soviet sphere followed Russia's lead. Finally, between February and July, 1949, a military alliance was formed by the United States, Canada, and a number of Western European countries called the North Atlantic Treaty Organization (NATO), which guaranteed mutual protection and envisaged the supply of arms by the United States.

Discord in the United Nations. The struggle between those adhering to Western democratic principles and those in sympathy with Soviet aspirations necessarily soon engulfed the newly formed United Nations organization, where eventually the two blocs faced each other and where decisions on most critical issues were made impossible by the fundamental opposition of the postwar aims of the United States and the U.S.S.R. The latter, generally backed by a minority only, made extensive use of her veto right; through her actions, the fate of many extraneous issues spanning the whole globe—from Argentina to Palestine, from Indonesia to Iran—was deeply affected. Particularly critical disputes occurred in connection with plans for the control of atomic energy, so that the commission dealing with the problem had to give up its work in May, 1948; the Russian government continued thereafter to insist on a complete ban of atomic weapons, although it demanded a veto right over any possible control agency. In 1949 the U.S.S.R. succeeded in exploding an atomic bomb of her own.

"Cold War." By 1950, the lines were clearly drawn between East and West. Each tried to consolidate its holdings and to add to its sphere the two major areas separating East and West—Germany and China. As to Germany, Russia endeavored early in 1948 to compel Western concessions through a blockade of Berlin, but in May, 1949, in the face of determined Western resistance whereby the city was supplied through an air lift, the attempt was given up. In the same year, however, the Soviets did tighten their hold on their zone of occupation in Germany by installing a Communist-oriented German government—an act which meant a virtual division of the country, and thereby a success for Russia and a loss to the Western world.

Still greater advantages were gained in the Far East. Between 1946 and 1948, under allied pressure, Russia gradually withdrew from the areas in Manchuria which had once been under Japanese control and which were, after the war, occupied by Soviet forces. When her troops left, however, control was not given to the central Chinese government; rather it was played into the hands of the Chinese Communist party. Thus strengthened, the Chinese Communists succeeded in 1949 in securing their hold over practically all of China, with the exception of Formosa and a few small off-shore islands. In the following year, they concluded a thirty-year friendship and assistance pact with Russia.

Korean War. Once China was gained, a new Communist advance was planned—this time in Korea. This country, which had been under the rule of Japan, was divided, like Germany, into occupation zones, with the Soviets receiving the northern and the Americans the southern area. Provisions for a joint administration did not work; free elections for the Korean people to decide their future were not allowed; and soon the government of the North was secured by indigenous Communists. The Russian occupation forces were thereupon withdrawn, and in 1950, the Communists ruling North Korea invaded South Korea. The United States decided to prevent any further Communist expansion and sent an auxiliary army to South Korea. Communist China supported the northern forces, and Russia sent them material and supplies. Fighting raged over most of the land, but neither side could gain a complete victory. Finally in 1953, peace negotiations led to a truce at the 38th parallel, and a buffer zone was set up.

ECONOMIC AND CULTURAL AFFAIRS

The wartime economy of the Soviet Union had forced upon the country rearrangements and relocations of production centers which after the war were made the basis of new planning. With confidence and foresight, what was undertaken under the pressure of the moment and what often seemed an undesirable measure was turned into a productive move and into a positive good. Thus, the Russians actually profited by the great eastward transfer of industrial plants when the German invasion threatened the Donets basin and other industrial regions. New permanent centers were established in the Urals, Siberia, and central Asia; the old centers served after their recovery as additional facilities. The loss of raw-material sources, including agricultural produce, became the starting point for increased surveying activity and led to the discovery and development of new and strategically safer regions. The destruction of homes and plants was made the beginning for reconstruction along more modern lines; and even the wrath of the people over the devastations wrought by the invader, as well as their dismay at the scorched-earth policy of their own government, was turned into productive channels. Women, Stakhanovites, and all other patriots exerted themselves with renewed effort to build new industries and collective farms. Writers, scholars, scientists, and artists contributed their share.

The Fourth Five-Year Plan. In 1945 the Fourth Five-Year Plan was drafted. It provided, like earlier ones, first of all for an increase in heavy industry and then for the strengthening of Russia's defenses, and for a rise in her agricultural production. This part of the program made quick progress. The plan further provided for the rehabilitation of war-damaged regions and for the incorporation of the economies of the acquired territories into that of the Union. The contributions of each region to the country's economy were carefully apportioned, and everywhere scientific research was pushed. With the knowledge that the aftermath of war tends to reduce the productivity of victor and vanquished alike, the government took care to provide incentives for hard work. An eight-hour working day was reintroduced and the customary provisions for better housing and living conditions were made.

CURRENCY REFORM. In connection with the objectives of the Plan, a currency reform was carried out in 1947. It served to put the ruble on a sound basis, made it possible for the government to reduce prices and raise the buying power of the average citizen, and provided stability so that industrial output could be increased. It also envisaged social aims. Hoarded money was forced out of hiding, and those who clandestinely had become wealthy during the war had to uncover their ill-gotten gains and lost most of them—in addition to incurring punishments. Socialist trends were thus strengthened through a leveling process.

RESULTS. The execution of the Fourth Five-Year Plan was keyed to fulfillment within four years. Enormous loans were successfully launched and increasing numbers of wage earners were put on a competitive piecework basis for individuals and groups. War prisoners, draftees from occupied areas, and political dissenters from within Russia herself were forced into involuntary labor in mines, lumber camps, and industries. Despite all efforts, timber and oil production lagged, but in most areas great advances over prewar standards were made. Coal and steel production climbed sharply; the cultivated area was increased; reclamation projects were undertaken; and agricultural productivity reached the prewar level by 1949 and surpassed it thereafter. Experiments first with small work units and later with large combines of kolkhozes were, however, not very successful. A sharp drive in the direction of agricultural cities (*agrogorod*) to replace normal collective farms had to be given up, and only a gradual reduction of the number of kolkhozes, through fusion of small units, could be carried on.

Political and Social Conditions. In a sense, the new Five-Year Plan reflected tensions within the Soviet Union. There were soldiers who, having seen the comparatively prosperous conditions of the average peasant and industrial worker in central Europe, came back —just as those after the Polish wars or after the Napoleonic invasion —not only with booty but also with unwelcome ideas. There were members of national groups, "displaced persons," whose refusal to return to their annexed countries meant a threat to future loyalties. There were officers who had too long enjoyed the privilege of commanding positions and the distinction of rank, and their readjustment to civilian life was a challenge to the "classless society." And there were peasants who had unlawfully appropriated collective land for private use. Unrest reigned, as for instance in the Ukraine, where Nazi ideas had not infrequently reflected the wishes of some of the population, and punishment and purges followed in the wake of victory.

ADMINISTRATIVE ADJUSTMENTS. In February, 1946, the first elections to the Supreme Soviet since 1937 were held; some 99 per cent of the voters went to the polls and almost all endorsed the candidates on the ballot. Stalin retained the unmatched power he had enjoyed in wartime, and Nicholas Shvernik succeeded Kalinin (who died shortly thereafter) as chairman of the Presidium of the Supreme Soviet. Molotov, the foreign minister, was succeeded by Vishinsky; and the minister of foreign trade, the chief of staff of the army, the chairman of the state planning commission, and many minor army officers were replaced. The Communist party, which had swelled during the war years, was carefully screened and repeatedly purged; the administration was streamlined; the "people's commissariats" were replaced by "ministries," as in Western countries; and a thoroughgoing financial reform was carried out. Renewed emphasis was placed on the spreading of the Communist doctrine, which was, however, modified by national aspirations; and armies and foreign representation of their own were allowed to constituent Union republics, two of which (White Russia, Ukraine) held seats in the United Nations.

SOCIAL POLICY. Administrative changes went hand in hand with determined social action. Measures were taken against graft, corruption, speculation, and crime, and a campaign was waged against hooliganism and anti-social behavior. There were also measures taken against idleness of young people—the children of privileged groups such as officials, scientists, party bureaucrats, and managers, who constituted a layer of society not unlike the "gilded youth" of 1795 after the French Revolution and who through their indulgence in fashionable, Western-inspired literary and artistic tastes as well as in undesirable social and asocial activities aroused the anger and fears of government circles. Efforts were made, aside from devaluation of the ruble, to reduce differences in living standards. Rations were abolished and prices in state stores were revised and equalized. Plans for a mighty housing program were laid.

CULTURAL POLICY. Special attention was given to writers and scholars. Largely under the personal supervision of Stalin's protégé Zhdanov, extensive "thought control" was exercised. Poets and artists were hindered in their creative efforts if they did not gain the approval of the party bureaucracy. Men working in fields as remote from immediate practical objectives as linguistics were made to conform in their conclusions to a prescribed socialist ideology, and grave damage ensued in some fields—as was demonstrated in the area of biology, where Lysenko's theories caused a thorough deterioration of standards. Contrary to the long-proved concepts of Mendel and Morgan about genetics, Lysenko insisted on the heredity of acquired traits through the determining influence of environment.

Neither was the field of religion spared. The government prescribed the dissolution of the Uniate church and engaged in a violent anti-Catholic campaign—which the papacy countered in July, 1949, by excommunicating all active Communists. It shut its eyes to anti-Semitic activities of its agents, fearing perhaps, with the revival of the Jewish state Israel, a dual allegiance of Jews.

The Iron Curtain. The combined political, economic, and sociological issues besieging the Russians in the early postwar period led the Soviet government to maintain its aloofness toward the outside world while reorganizing within. It prohibited marriages between Russian citizens and foreigners, prevented radio communications and other news from abroad from reaching the population, and made travel to and from foreign countries practically impossible. Since the Western powers on their side also imposed some restrictions, chiefly of an economic and military nature, there developed a line which sharply separated eastern and western Europe. Known as the "iron curtain," this line ran approximately through the center of Germany down to the Adriatic Sea. It reduced to a minimum the contacts between the peoples of the Western democracies and the Soviet peoples.

Democracy. Peace and security—the longings of the peoples after the destruction of war—were thus sadly undermined by the division of the world into two camps. Not even the word "democracy," which had been a prime mover in the struggle against nazism and fascism, retained a common meaning; ideologies separating the totalitarian and socialist from the liberal and capitalistic world clashed anew.

50

"COLD WAR" AND "COEXISTENCE"

Significant Dates

Death of Stalin	1953
Launching of *Sputnik*	1957
Khrushchev as Premier	1958–1964

In March, 1953, Stalin died. With him, an entire phase in the development of the Soviet world—which he had directed for thirty years—came to an end. No one was there to take his place, nor was it the intention of his heirs to permit anyone to assume a role similar to the one he had played. Changes in Russian policies were to take place. Internally, greater accent was put on the amelioration of living conditions, and externally, improved relations with the Western world were—at least temporarily—sought.

POLITICAL SCENE

Stalin's Successors. Georgi Malenkov, born in 1902 into a "bourgeois" family, succeeded Stalin as Premier. Intelligent and hard working, he was reputed to be conciliatory. Production of consumer goods was increased, amnesties were granted, labor camp conditions were improved, and Stalin's secret police chief Beria was tried and executed. But soon new inner-circle rivalries broke out, and in 1955, Malenkov was removed from the premiership. The predominant role thereupon fell to Party Secretary Nikita Khrushchev who, like his predecessor, had excelled as a party administrator. It was he who, early in 1956, made a historic speech in which in the name of the Communist party he rejected the cult of Stalin, the "cult of the individual," and in its place extolled the Leninist principle of "collective leadership." Khrushchev's administration lasted until 1964. He soon disposed of the collective leadership (old Communists like Malenkov, Molotov, and Bulganin were banished), and in 1958 he became Premier as well as Party Secretary, combining once more the two most important offices in the Soviet Union. Changes were made in the office of head of state, which was assumed first by Brezhnev, then, in 1964, by Mikoyan, and in 1965 by Podgorny; and in 1961, the Presidium of the Party's Central Committee was reduced in number. When Khrushchev himself fell from power, partly because of his own growing "personality cult," partly because of the failure of his agricultural program and the rise of tension within the Communist orbit, a new collective took over, with Brezhnev as Party Secretary and Kosygin as Premier. Significantly, this change-over brought no grave disturbance, thus demonstrating the measure of governmental stability which had been achieved.

Coexistence. With the anti-Stalin agitation came a softening of Russia's foreign policy. In July, 1953, the Soviet government had cooperated in halting the Korean War; subsequently it initiated a policy of "coexistence" which was to replace the "Cold War." It reduced its land forces and resumed negotiations with the Western powers. A large-scale personal diplomacy was initiated, and Khrushchev and other high Bolshevik officials visited one country after another in Asia, Europe, and America.

RELATIONS WITH WESTERN POWERS.   In the course of the first few years after Stalin's death, promising signs for the possibility of East-West "coexistence" appeared. The Soviets entered into new negotiations with their wartime allies and, especially at a meeting in Geneva, carried them on in a friendly spirit. But as years went by, the dilemma about how to reconcile coexistence with the professed world revolutionary aims increased.

The 1950's. In 1955, the Soviets concluded a long-delayed peace treaty with Austria, and they initiated diplomatic relations with Western Germany, despite the fact that this resurging country aligned itself with the West through the North Atlantic Pact as well as through European economic organizations. They also made efforts to heal the rift with Tito's Communist Yugoslavia and for this purpose dissolved the Cominform. But even while seeking during these years arrangements with the Western nations the Soviets refused to permit free elections for all of Germany, and in subsequent foreign minister meetings they blocked steps by the major powers to implement the Geneva arrangements. Further negotiations with the United States and her allies, especially for initial disarmament steps, came to nought since the Soviet refused to allow international inspection and control. In time, Russia shifted again to a more aggressive policy. Beginning in 1958, a new attempt was undertaken to expand Russian influence and push back the West by "neutralizing" those parts of Berlin which were under Western control. Despite increasing exchanges of scholars, scientists, artists, farmers, and students, and despite an increasing number of tourist visits, a vociferous anti-Western and especially anti-American and anti-German propaganda was carried on.

The 1960's. At the beginning of the 1960's, the Soviet Union stepped up the pace of the Cold War. A reduction in the number of her armed forces was compensated for by an improvement in nuclear and other military strength. A serious deterioration in her relations with the United States occurred in connection with the shooting down of an American spy plane (the U-2 incident) and, following renewed demands for the incorporation of all of Berlin into her orbit, the erection of a wall between the eastern and western sectors of Berlin. The wall was intended to seal off more tightly the Eastern from the Western world and to force the West to retreat further. Super atomic weapons were tested, and by making advances to England or France, no chance was missed to drive a wedge between the nations composing the Western alliance. However, by 1962, the strength of the six European member nations of the Common Market (which was bitterly denounced by the Soviets), the difficulties experienced with the economic integration into the Soviet orbit of growingly independent satellite nations, the determination of the United States (demonstrated through an ultimatum to Cuba for the withdrawal of all aggressive weapons which the Soviets had installed there), and, most of all, growing strain in Russia's relations with China—all these forced another change of policy. The demands for Berlin were suspended, and in 1963 negotiations with the United States regarding a nuclear test ban were allowed to be brought to a successful conclusion. Despite continued denunciations of the United States and Germany, caution was exercised in foreign policies. Revolutionary activity in areas of concern to the Western powers in Africa, Latin America, and even in Asia was not supported by much more than promises, and in various minor practical issues an understanding, especially with the United States, was sought.

RELATIONS WITH THE SOVIET BLOC NATIONS. After Stalin's death, coexistence notwithstanding, the Soviet government persistently refused to discuss the areas of Eastern Europe under its sway, but tried with an iron hand to keep control. For this purpose, it concluded, in 1955, a "Treaty of Friendship" with the various countries involved. Desperate revolts of the East Germans in 1953 against their Communist regime and in 1956 of the Poles and especially the Hungarians against theirs were ruthlessly crushed after a few concessions were made to assuage the oppressed peoples. But all this could not repress the growing national consciousness of the individual Eastern European nations, which reasserted itself the more as living standards failed to match Western standards or even to rise at the expected rate. The appeal which Communist ideology was to have for cooperation lessened rather than increased; and economic cooperation, which the Moscow government because of its predicaments at home was forced to exploit rather than support, remained at a level far below original plans. By the middle 1960's Rumania, Bulgaria, Poland, and Hungary showed a previously unknown independence in political as well as economic and cultural affairs and Yugoslavia continued to pursue her own aims. Extra efforts, initiated by Moscow to counteract nationalist and to a certain extent separatist tendencies among the satellites, were rendered difficult by the sharp tension between Russia and China.

RELATIONS WITH THE ASIAN AND AFRICAN NATIONS. Soviet policy was, at least during the 1950's, more consistently constructive in relation to the East and to Africa. Links with Israel, interrupted earlier, were renewed in 1954, and overtures for closer cooperation were made to Iran and Turkey. The USSR also built a mighty steel work for India. In 1956 a peace treaty was signed with Japan. Large scale financial and technical support was given to China. Aid —diplomatic, military, or economic—was extended to Arab states, Indochina, and other Asiatic and African nations which had recently emancipated themselves from French, English, or Belgian colonial domination, or which were struggling for independence. Difficulties besetting Western nations in their colonial areas were shrewdly exploited. When Israeli, English, and French troops invaded Egypt in 1956, because of Egypt's nationalization of the Suez Canal, vigorous support was extended to Egypt; and when the Belgians had to give up the Congo, attempts were made to spread Soviet influence there. In the 1960's economic and technical aid was also extended to new African nations, to Indonesia, and to the United Arab Republic, and was supported by propaganda and personal diplomacy, which Khrushchev carried on through visits to some of these countries as well as the United Nations headquarters in New York. But more so even than in Europe, relations with eastern nations came to be overshadowed by the Sino-Russian rift, which had by 1960 taken on serious dimensions, leading to bitter mutual denunciations for betraying revolutionary theory and objectives, and had brought about the suspension of Russian technical and other aid to the former Chinese friends. Especially in southeastern Asia, the Soviets had to chart a precarious course between a hard Chinese line supporting Communist revolutions and American endeavors to maintain the existing balance of power. This middle course gave the Soviets a small advantage in connection with neutralist countries, such as India, but it also made it impossible for them to follow a consistent policy in Indonesia when Communism was shaken there in 1965, or to interfere actively in the American war effort in Vietnam, which came to be the major political issue early in 1966.

SOCIAL SCENE

Internally, Stalin's successors followed, as in external affairs, a rather flexible policy. Without renouncing any major Bolshevik objective, they eased considerably the strains that had existed in the last years of Stalin's rule. The influence of the party, though consistently emphasized in all pronouncements, was perhaps somewhat lessened during the following twelve years in favor of that exercised by the more practically minded administrative bureaucracy. In 1956, the Sixth Five-Year Plan was put into effect, but it was replaced in 1957 by more general directives. In 1961, a general twenty-year plan was worked out, but more specific shorter-term planning, for seven years and for two years, went hand in hand with it. All plans, rather than providing for consumer goods, still gave priority to the increase in heavy industry, the promotion of space technology, the training of technicians, and the production of steel, coal, machinery, oil, and electricity. A trend toward decentralization by reducing the number of central agencies and handing some economic controls over to local administrative offices was not consistently followed. Instead, especially after 1965, a course was steered which straddled decentralization and mechanized and bureaucratized direction; the regional peoples' councils under party control, to which under Khrushchev much supervision of the productive process had been confided, were abolished in favor of central ministerial responsibility, as had existed earlier. Ideology was subordinated to practicality.

Economic Conditions.   During the fifteen years after Stalin's death, living standards improved considerably. Industrial production rose, and so did labor productivity. As more consumer goods became available retail prices were lowered. Labor camps were largely abolished, but in the later 1950's considerable pressure was exercised on young people to volunteer for work on great projects, such as developing new agricultural regions in Western Siberia and Kazakhstan.

INDUSTRY.   Relaxation of pressure in the middle 1950's had helped industrial development, but during the last years of Khrushchev's premiership, economic growth was slowed down. A currency reform at the beginning of 1961, whereby ten old rubles were exchanged for one new ruble (which was somewhat higher in value than the US dollar) had little effect. Like earlier currency reforms, it was intended to bring about social as well as economic readjustments. In an attempt to eliminate much criticized inefficiency and waste, experiments were made in reshuffling economic areas. Automation of industry was begun, and in line with this, higher wages were ordered, pensions were increased, and the workday was reduced, in some instances to seven hours. Hydroelectric plants were built and a canal from the Amu Daria to Ashkhabad was completed. Oil production rose to such an extent that large scale exports became possible, partly through newly built pipelines, and steel output in the summer of 1962 came to challenge that of the European Common Market or the United States. But crucial areas of the economy did not fulfill demands. This was especially true of the chemical industry, lumber production, and some of the transportation systems. The scarcity of investment capital made itself sharply felt, and in view of this the planners, often averse to new ideas and great risks, failed to update and redistribute the priorities for the individual industries. On the other hand, they did put a new emphasis on careful, modern accounting methods in factories similar to those followed in capitalistic countries. They insisted on more profit-conscious management and therefore permitted, where needed, an increase in prices, and they helped with more credit. They also encouraged a greater measure of competition between industrial enterprises and attempted a greater flexibility in planning.

AGRICULTURE. Particularly weak was the agricultural sector of the economy. Despite Khrushchev's great efforts to improve cattle raising and expand grain production through bringing vast areas of Kazakhstan under the plow, bad crops there in 1961, followed by further poor harvests in subsequent years, forced the government to increase prices for as fundamental a foodstuff as bread. Such crop failures necessitated partial rationing; the hardships of the house-wife were not over, and, in 1963, wheat had to be imported from Canada and the United States. Under Khrushchev's successors, some of his agricultural experiments were therefore abandoned. Some of the large sovkhoze which had been created under his direction, and many of the kolkhoze which had been greatly ex-tended, were now reduced to more manageable size. Through special allotments, such as assigning fodder for cattle raising, en-couragement was given even to small-scale private enterprises of peasants. As a result, at least the supply of meat, eggs, and vege-tables in the kolkhoz markets increased.

Living Conditions. Population losses owing to war as well as to other political causes had been enormous, and population growth was slower than had been anticipated. Women, who far out-numbered men because of war and purges, continued to play a large part in the Soviet economy. By the end of the 1950's, the total population numbered about 206 million. Thereafter, it was growing at a steady rate, so that after five years, it had increased to more than 225 million. In view of the difficulties in raising agricultural output quickly and in view of the desire of satisfying at least some demands for improvement of living standards, the fact that the population had not increased more rapidly was per-haps rather welcome. Indeed, in 1954 the government withdrew the law prohibiting abortions. Family life was rendered easier through the construction of many apartment houses. At first their quality was unsatisfactory, too little attention being paid to the comforts of the inhabitants, but considerable improvement could be noted by 1965. Great urban and suburban housing projects were completed not only in Moscow and Leningrad, but in Central Asia, Siberia, and the Caucasus as well. Somewhat greater freedom of movement became possible, and discrimination, as for example that against Jews, diminished, though it did not disappear. With about eleven million party members and over twenty million youth group members, the party seemed numerically strong; but, as criticism voiced at party congresses indicated, enthusiasm was lacking among the younger generation. Criminality and hooliganism were widespread.

Cultural Conditions.   Special attention was paid to cultural tasks. In line with Soviet foreign policy, enthusiasm was fostered for all things Russian, and disdain and fear of "Anglo-American" concepts were spread. Soviet patriotism was preached as the road to equality and brotherhood of men; it was described as true internationalism, based on the rule of the working class, and was contrasted with "bourgeois cosmopolitanism," which was said to infringe on the ideals of state and folk and to render impossible national self-determination. Growing nationalism did not prevent, however, the increase of more critical attitudes which had an effect on cultural developments.

Education and Science. During the Second World War, co-education in elementary schools of cities had been to a large extent abolished, because the authorities came to consider the physical growth and intellectual needs of girls and boys as too divergent. This step was not reversed until 1954, and accent was again put on systematic training for practical aims. Strict discipline was maintained in the schools and continued preference given to education in the natural sciences and related fields. In the late 1950's, the government ordered that pupils above the age of fifteen, unless physically unfit, devote part of their school time to practical work in industry and agriculture, but this rule had only a narrow and temporary application.

The number of universities and professional schools was increased in order to offer gifted students opportunities and to provide Russia with the facilities needed for educating the elite of the coming generation. These facilities were open to all; but unless stipends, which were generally available for good students, were provided, a fee had to be paid. Then after completing their training in technical schools, students were often obliged to serve a number of years wherever the state authorities decided their skills could be used best. High standards were maintained and were attractive also to students from abroad—especially from Communist-dominated or former colonial countries. Achievement such as the construction of hydrogen bombs in 1953, the launching of the first earth satellite or *sputnik* in 1957, a manned spaceship in 1961, a walk in space in 1965, and a soft landing of a missile with instruments on the moon in 1966 gave evidence of the standards of Russian scientific training —particularly in the field of space technology. Outstanding work was done likewise in medicine. Other areas, such as archaeology, linguistics, and biology also profited, and men like Lysenko, whose unscientific attitudes had caused grave damage, were removed from places of authority and influence. Altogether, interference from the side of party or bureaucracy in the areas of scientific investigation was, regardless of ideological implications, sharply reduced; natural sciences and mathematics, needed to secure for Russia the immediate advantages of latest discoveries, benefited perhaps more from the change than fields such as history and sociology, which continued to evince the pressure of Marxist doctrinaire rules.

ARTS AND RELIGION. After the infertile years of Stalin's rule a certain revival occurred also in the arts when a "thaw" (symbolized by the title of a book by Ehrenburg after Stalin's death) opened up new possibilities for the creative artist. Along with cosmopolitanism, "idealism" and "romanticism" were still denounced; but the young generation showed an increasingly rebellious spirit. Discussion of artistic forms and aims became more lively and modified the heroic and anti-Western pose of the creations of overzealous followers who clung to the party slogan of "concrete representation of reality in its revolutionary development." Yet, party supervision did not relent, nor did it permit criticism to go beyond narrow limits. Authors, such as Ehrenburg himself and the Nobel Prize winner Pasternak, were compelled to submit to party directives or to remain silent. After Khrushchev's dismissal, official policy became somewhat more vacillating. Authors, and even the party newspapers and journals, occasionally published controversial and quite liberal contributions, and in discussions openness to non-party views was shown; still, action was taken repeatedly against those who voiced opinions or published books not in line with official directives.

The state exercised a similar control over the church. Again and again, the government clearly expressed its belief in scientific instead of metaphysical thinking, renewed from time to time its antireligious campaigns, and demanded the support of the church for its national goals. While it is true that by 1960 the church operated freely within its prescribed limits, monasteries functioned, and seminaries for the training of new clergymen did not lack students, the hold of religious institutions on the young generation had not increased.

NEW PROBLEMS AND NEW GOALS

When the communistic form of government in Russia approached the half-century mark of its existence in 1967, there was a worldwide evaluation of its accomplishments. There were both negative and positive aspects. The latter seemed to come more into focus after Khrushchev had fallen from power at the end of 1964. Certainly, the numerous problems that faced the Soviet Union and its satellites had caused much experimentation on the social, industrial, and even governmental level, and perhaps there was no longer as clear a trend in Russian policy as under Stalin's dictatorship. Externally, the stability and the maintenance of the *status quo* and, internally, the preservation of the system built up by the *apparachiks* (the functionaries and bureaucrats) both constituted the major aim. Experiments had to stay within limits that would not endanger the Soviet governmental structure and its international position—even if revolutionary objectives had to be sacrificed.

Achievements. On the positive side, the most important fact was that, contrary to dire prognoses at its birth, the Soviet Union had not only survived interventions, wars, destruction, hunger, purges, and unrest, but had emerged as one of the two great powers. Industries had been built on a huge scale, agriculture reorganized, vast irrigation and transportation projects carried out, and advances in the most sophisticated areas of science made. The changes carried out along socialist lines in social and cultural policy and the elimination of private property in the means of production and distribution had endured; and, as in capitalistic countries, living standards were greatly improved when compared with conditions of a half century earlier. The government had shown its ability to overcome shocks such as the transfer of power from Lenin to Stalin, to Malenkov, to Khrushchev, and to the collective of Brezhnev and Kosygin. It had expanded the territory of the Soviet Union through conquest, had gained dominant influence in neighboring countries, and had built a powerful military apparatus. Its voice could not be ignored in any part of the world.

Problems. Nevertheless, there were many misgivings. The revolutionary movement had failed to spread to the great capitalist countries and, instead of vaunted unity, there were considerable breaks within the socialist ranks. Nationalism within the Soviet orbit was on the increase, while beyond it labor parties abandoned the Marxist creed. Living standards, though improved, remained far behind those of the West. Five-year planning had not proved as satisfactory a solution for economic development as originally hoped. Money incentives for the individual worker could not be dispensed with nor could private enterprise be entirely eliminated, and wage differentials remained high. In spite of all efforts, agriculture lagged far behind. Intellectuals, writers, and artists proved restive under the standards imposed on them by the rulers, and their creativity was stifled. The Marxist hope of changing man through communism had not come true, and the West had neither been "overtaken" nor "buried."

New Tensions. As the 1960's approached their end, both internal and external tensions increased. Internal tensions were evinced by the fact that, despite self-applause for the changes that had taken place during the first half century, Soviet newspapers were invariably full of criticisms and exhortations to ever new endeavors.

INTERNAL. To be sure, there was progress in many areas of life. More houses and better hospitals were built, additional land was reclaimed for cultivation, and schooling was extended so that by 1968 twice as many Soviet young people finished high school as in 1960. Further great advances were made in the natural sciences, in medicine and biology, as well as in the technology of war materials and missiles, and in perfecting the space sciences. An unmanned flight around the moon was achieved. Opposition to cybernetics was overcome by recognizing that computers and other sophisticated machinery were indispensable, and, with the urgently solicited help of women laborers, industrial production increased perhaps as much as 10 per cent in 1967—a higher rate than in the West. But the living standards of a simultaneously growing population did not improve in proportion, nor were the Soviets spared such new problems connected with technological advance as air and water pollution. If, however, there were expectations of overcoming these difficulties, other problems appeared less easy to solve. Tensions among the various nationalities throughout the Soviet Union persisted, and the government still seemed to be unable to tolerate criticism from a restless intelligentsia. It maintained censorship and muzzled outstanding minds; while scholarship, in history, archaeology, linguistics, and other fields was improving, substantial artistic and literary achievements were not forthcoming. The competitive spirit and the profit system with its incentives for more work, far from disappearing, were steadily enhanced, and the workers of state farms, local soviets, and factories had to be induced with promises of financial gain. Central planning did not prove to be sufficiently flexible. Factories were not used to full capacity, especially when combined (for reasons of rentability) into larger units, and costs and prices were often too high. Raw materials were wasted, stocks piled up in undesirable quantities, luxuries remained out of the reach of the ordinary citizen, and factories paid more attention to the formal filling of quotas than to making salable goods. Therefore, concessions were made to capitalistic modes of accounting and to the idea of "competition" and "profit" for the individual factory; managers were permitted increased control over "investment" and they could charge "interest" on capital—though in disguised form. An entrepreneurial spirit militated against the attitudes of the mere *apparachik*. Perhaps it was significant that when a new marriage code came under discussion in 1967-68, the question of support by fathers of illegitimate children was hotly debated—something doubly inconceivable for a fifty-year-old "communistic" society.

EXTERNAL. Tensions also rapidly increased on the international stage, nurtured by Soviet nationalism and continued newspaper campaigns against the United States, Germany, Israel, and China. A new crisis arose over the status of Berlin when the Soviets demanded rights of interference in the internal affairs of Germany. They gave financial, technological, and military support to the Arab nations, which were seeking redress for their defeat in the short war against Israel in June 1967. In exchange, the Soviet Union was permitted to extend its power into the western Mediterranean and install naval bases there; in December 1967 it acquired new rights in Iraq for the development of oil deposits. The Soviet Union opposed every move toward greater independence by its satellite states. It closely watched all actions in Rumania, and its insistence on domination reached a climax when Czechoslovakia sought to liberalize restrictive Marxist policies. Soviet troops invaded Czechoslovakia in August 1968 and occupied it. Czechoslovakia was compelled to remove its leading figures and revoke its liberal reforms; censorship and travel restrictions were imposed. As a result of these actions, the existing balance of power was altered somewhat. Involved in a war in Vietnam and caught in illusions about a détente, the United States concluded two new treaties with the Soviets—the Consular Exchange Treaty in 1967 and the Non-Proliferation Treaty for Nuclear Arms in 1968, which, despite superficial forms of reciprocity, permitted Russia to strengthen herself militarily far beyond the borders of her allotted sphere of interest. Although Soviet acts of force and suppression had alienated Communist parties in both East and West, there were vast gains in Soviet power; with apprehension, the peoples of the world watched new conflicts shape up.

51

COEXISTENCE AND DÉTENTE

Significant Dates
Treaty with West Germany and Détente . . . 1972
Conference of Helsinki 1975
Twenty-Fifth Party Congress 1976

The dire prospects of the late 1960's changed somewhat in the early 70's. By 1972 aggressive attitudes in the West and East had given way to a desire for strengthening the *status quo*. Internally, the Soviets carried out no major experiments; they promoted industrial growth and gained in military strength but failed to solve their agricultural problems. Externally, they succeeded in consolidating their territorial gains. However, they lost ground because of increasing disenchantment among foreign Socialists and Communists with the practical functioning of the Soviet system and its failure to provide an adequate rising living standard or to guarantee democratic procedures at home and in the satellite countries.

INTERNAL AFFAIRS

The Five-Year Plans adopted in 1971 and 1976 confirmed existing trends. There was the usual emphasis on education, scientific work, maintenance of Marxist-Leninist ideology, military prowess, and party unity and leadership. Both plans again emphasized heavy rather than consumer industries and the need for greater productivity. The Soviet leadership, when adopting the 1976 Plan, claimed that the U.S.S.R. did not experience crises such as beset capitalist countries with inflation, currency disorders, unemployment, energy shortages, and high military expenses; Soviet military spending was even higher, and other equally grave problems existed.

The National Economy. In the first half of the 1970's, industrial production registered an annual growth of perhaps 5 to 8 per cent. The figures for internal as well as foreign trade likewise improved as détente contributed vigorously to an increase in exports and imports. On the other hand, agricultural shortcomings led to sharp criticism at the Twenty-Fifth Party Congress in February, 1976, and to changes in the administration and personnel at the top bureaucracy responsible for the agricultural sector.

INDUSTRIAL PRODUCTION. With pride, the Soviet leadership announced during the Congress that not only in steel but also in oil, cement, coal, and other items such as mineral fertilizers, wool, and tractors Soviet production had surpassed that of the United States. New Siberian resources and especially oil reserves were developed; huge pipelines were built (the largest, connecting Moscow with the Medvezhnye fields, was completed in 1974). The natural gas supply was increased. The oil crisis that troubled the West hardly affected the Soviets; indeed, they could export increasing amounts of oil at higher prices. New railroad lines were constructed to bring natural resources such as copper, ore, and coal to the markets. Foreign plants and multinational corporations were granted licenses to erect factories—for steel, pipes, automobiles, and so on—and plans for cooperation in large-scale projects, especially for Siberia, were made with Japan, the United States, Germany, and England. However, planned developments were limited by the need for foreign capital, foreign technology, and Western know-how. Moreover, high production costs, the poor quality of many of the products produced in large quantities, shortages of machinery for industry and agriculture, mismanagement, and worker absenteeism impeded progress. Too much of what was actually produced was unwanted and unneeded. Ever new efficiency drives had to be undertaken; and experiments with decentralization by giving more power to local farm councils, plant managers, trade-unions, cooperatives, and the 55,000 local Soviets did not bring the desired results. Likewise, experiments with allowing enterprises to retain a larger share of their profits to use for making improvements, establishing training centers for skilled workers and increasing worker incentives were not as successful as had been hoped.

TRADE. Much attention was paid to water and air transport in order to improve internal trade, but land transport developed slowly. The Soviets signed trade pacts with many capitalist countries. Exports now included machinery, metals, and natural gas. Two-thirds of all foreign trade was carried on with socialist states and satellites, and for the first time, detailed plans were drawn up for fusion of these countries' resources, leveling of their living standards, and division of labor among them in order to integrate their economies and strengthen the key position of the Soviet Union.

AGRICULTURE. The unsatisfactory condition of agriculture was due in part to bad weather in 1972, which led to a crop failure and necessitated huge grain purchases abroad. In 1975, a weak harvest of grain, if not of industrial crops, caused further distress. But the roots of the difficulties lay also in fundamental institutional shortcomings. Management of the kolkhozes was poor, investments in agriculture insufficient, fertilizer scarce, and, most of all, the Soviet government failed to provide incentives for workers in the kolkhozes. Small private plots, which were well tended by their owners, continued to exist and had to provide a—proportionately—unduly large share of the food supply for the Soviet people.

Social Conditions.   Like other parts of the world, the Soviet Union witnessed both an improvement in general living standards and an increasing demand for further progress. Differences in status persisted between privileged groups—party officials, managers, sectors of the intelligentsia, athletes, and artists—and other strata of the population. The privileged enjoyed adequate housing and had access to consumer goods (sometimes of foreign origin and sold in special stores) which the others lacked.

LIVING CONDITIONS. By 1976 the population of the Soviet Union was estimated at about 250 million. It increased steadily (the "pill" not being available) but at a decreasing rate, depending upon the region and its degree of industrialization and partly owing to bad housing conditions for the masses. Between 1968 and 1975, real income per family rose considerably, and it continued to rise thereafter. Meat consumption climbed. As a whole, the population felt that the Soviet Union made progress economically and in world status; that progress would continue under the existing system; and that, whatever the shortcomings, change was not feasible for lack of an alternative. But women complained about their double work burden, at home and in factories or offices. The average citizens, exposed to the harsh realities of daily life and the many demands made upon them, were forced to use all kinds of small stratagems in order to circumvent the most pressing regulations. A codification of laws and penal reforms was undertaken; yet, bribery could not be eliminated, and unreliable statistics provided by industries and party organizations that wished to show attractive results often concealed from the government the actual state of their enterprises.

CULTURAL AND SCIENTIFIC AFFAIRS. Because of continued state supervision (exemplified by the treatment of the writer Solzhenitsyn, the biologist Medvedev, and the physicist Sakharov), intellectual unrest continued, though persecutions on the order of earlier ones no longer occurred and a measure of dissent could be voiced provided it did not challenge the basis of the existing system. Western fashions spread. Educational institutions steadily increased in number and served to promote the social as well as the natural sciences, to improve technology, and to strengthen social homogeneity. In 1969 the Soviets sent an unmanned rocket to Venus. They launched the first supersonic aircraft and by 1975 had put such aircraft into regular service. Fights against pollution, against the use of pesticides, and even against the excessive growth of cities were stepped up. A new patriarch of the Orthodox Church, Pimen, could be installed peacefully, and church income rose. Restrictions against the emigration of Jews were eased, though discrimination against them persisted. By 1975 some 150,000 had left the country.

ECONOMIC THOUGHT. While scientific achievements in many areas—biology, space, medicine, chemistry, mathematics—were outstanding, there were other areas in which, because of earlier ideological restraints, Soviet scholars were hard put to catch up with the West. Among them was economics, although a certain variety in economic thinking, reflecting different views among party leaders, was permitted with all its contradictions. Generally, the importance of capital and capital formation and monetary policies was now accepted, but no consensus could be reached as to how far the state should go with central planning and with fixing price levels. The victim was the consumer.

ADMINISTRATION. Even after the Twenty-fifth Party Congress, Brezhnev and his old guard, all advanced in years, retained leadership of Party and country. Brezhnev did not become a personal leader, though, as Stalin or even Khrushchev had been. The government remained in the hands of the Politburo, of one single party and its increasingly complex, cumbersome, and technocratic bureaucracy; and the "building of a Communist society . . . now that socialism had been achieved" had to be further postponed. The collective leadership pursued a cautious path. It played with the thought of rewriting the constitution and dividing the U.S.S.R. into perhaps eighteen large economic districts instead of the existing fourteen national states. This policy reflected Russian nationalism and a potentially serious domestic threat, namely the aggravation of the internal nationality problem. Georgians, Ukrainians, Armenians, Lithuanians, and others resented the domination of the Great Russians and the repression under which many felt they had to live. Formal concessions were made to them from time to time, but these were counteracted by the tightening of economic dependency.

MILITARY AND FOREIGN AFFAIRS

The Soviets perfected their atomic weapons, nuclear submarines, and their attack and defense systems, an advance which led in many respects to equality with the United States and in some even to overtaking the United States. Russian naval bases were established in Antarctica. Simultaneously, the U.S.S.R. made demands for troop reductions in Europe. Embroiled in Vietnam, the United States had to renounce her policy of "containment," to open (in 1972) the road to freer trade, and to compromise in arms talks (SALT) and territorial issues (Berlin). And when the United States was defeated in Vietnam, the policy of containment gave way to one of "détente." Showing firmness in essentials, yet flexibility in detail, the Soviets turned this policy to their own great advantage and reaffirmed it in 1976, contrary statements by United States officials notwithstanding.

Diplomacy toward the West. In 1972 West Germany, which had initiated a conciliatory *Ostpolitik*, signed a treaty on lines long demanded by the Soviets and was forced to recognize the separate existence of East Germany and to renounce the Soviet- and Polish-occupied territories. West Germany also concluded trade agreements with the Soviet Union. In the same year, the President of the United States traveled to Moscow to promote détente. Moreover, the Russians strengthened their ties with Canada, France, and other Western countries and engaged in lively diplomatic intercourse with them. Finally, in July, 1975, they succeeded in arranging an international conference at Helsinki, in which the frontiers of the Soviet Union gained during the Second World War were confirmed and the stability, security, and consolidation demanded by them were achieved. In exchange, more contacts with the West were arranged, although not as many materialized as Western nations had hoped for. The "wall" remained. Yet, the Soviets eased their stand against the recently enlarged European Economic Community. Disarmament made little progress despite great preoccupation on all sides with protection against the increase and spread of nuclear war preparations.

Diplomacy toward Socialist Countries.   Relations with the Eastern bloc countries were handled cautiously. The Soviets somewhat eased their political and ideological demands; they left a country like Rumania rather free to pursue her own limited aims and for the time being reduced pressure on independent Yugoslavia. But the economic integration of the Soviet bloc was accelerated, and Eastern Germany especially was subject to wide-ranging demands. Beyond the Soviet bloc great caution was exercised toward Western Communist parties. Both sides—the Western powers and the Soviet Union—opposed violating existing spheres of influence. When in 1975 Communists were on the verge of taking over the government in Portugal, the U.S.S.R. extended as little help to them as it had to a socialist government that had been established in Chile. Restraint was exercised also toward Communist parties in other Western countries, which increasingly challenged the Marxist-Leninist dogma and Moscow leadership and tended toward the Chinese position, anarchism, or variant anti-capitalist stands. All told, the Communist movement was weakened by the rejection among the leading European Communist parties of the concept of the dictatorship of the proletariat and by their demands for a plurality of parties, for independence of trade-unions, and for religious freedom. They even questioned the usefulness of centralized state planning. Thus, the lever the Soviet Union had previously used for subverting Western countries in order to extend Soviet domination was weakened.

Diplomacy toward Africa and Asia. As opposed to Soviet diplomacy pursued toward the West, political endeavors in Africa and Asia were intensified. Consistent support in arms and technical help was given to socialist-oriented forces of African independence movements. In Angola such support brought success, though it called forth increased Western resistance in other parts of Africa. Less successful was Russian diplomacy in North Africa. Relations with Libya remained close, but the strong position the Soviet Union had gained in Egypt was lost between 1972 and 1976 for lack of continued military support. This, however, was a calculated risk, since Soviet policy, for the time being, aimed not at a solution of the Mid-Eastern problem but at the maintenance of existing tensions through a status of "no peace, no war." Least satisfactory for the Soviet Union were her relations with East Asia. Negotiations with Japan, while propitious in the economic field, were politically disappointing because of Japanese demands for restitution of some of the territories Japan had lost in the Second World War and also because of Japanese cooperation with China. With the latter country, Soviet ideological and political rivalry continued and mutual fears increased. Border clashes had diminished after the conclusion of a one-year trade treaty and the exchange of ambassadors between the two countries in 1970; but when Communist China gained international recognition in 1971, the obstacles to the Soviet Union as leader of the international Communist movement increased and were felt not only in Asia but also in Europe, Africa, and South America. Thus, détente at best compensated for setbacks in the over-all diplomatic position of the U.S.S.R. Yet, the Soviet future depended more upon internal than external developments.

52

CONSOLIDATION AND
NEW TENSIONS

Significant Dates
New Constitution Adopted 1977
Invasion of Afghanistan 1979
Death of Brezhnev 1982

The period from 1977 to 1984 was in the Soviet Union not a time of major events, nor great personalities, nor important developments. In contrast to the progressive policies of Khrushchev, a conservative path was followed during the last six years of Brezhnev's presiding over the Politburo. He died in late 1982. Yet, subtle changes occurred, many unwanted, but forced upon the Soviet Union by economic developments in the West as well as the East, by political events in the United States and the Middle East, by unrest among the satellites as well as the nationalities composing the Union, and by technological changes. The end of the age of the old guard approached. The generation which still remembered the Revolution, and was shaped by the concepts of that period, had tried to cling to the lessons of Lenin and Stalin and avoided departure from the established norms. The death, in 1982, of its last great representative and chief ideologist, Mikhail Suslov, may have augured the beginning of a new stage.

INTERNAL DEVELOPMENTS

Communism, which, though still kept as an ideal, had lost much of its worldwide appeal, was upheld within the Soviet Union. Its basic tenets were consistently preached, and strict control of the economy and, to a large extent, the private lives of the citizens was maintained by State and Party. If hoped-for improvements for the individual were not achieved, the opposition of the capitalist world and the shortcomings of the executive organs of the state and particularly of the middle layers of the bureaucracy were blamed. Human rights continued to be violated, and the outside world demonstrated its concern in many ways. But the Soviet citizen tended to put up with the loss of freedom in exchange for social security and that social equality which the system provided.

Living Conditions.   By 1982, the population of the Soviet Union had increased to about 270 million, two thirds of whom lived in cities, and about 70 million in Siberia. As in the West, the birth rate declined, but life expectancy increased. It approximately equaled that in Western countries. The resulting aging of the population brought problems similar to those in the West, especially with regard to the labor force and productivity. Emigration diminished. Most of the Jews who had desired to leave had departed. Few others were permitted to leave. A critical shortage of housing remained and many of the houses available were poorly provided with modern conveniences, including good plumbing. But electricity, once one of the chief concerns of Lenin, was available. Shortages of consumer goods were hardly relieved and long queues formed to buy necessities continued to be part of normal life. The quality of the goods, for a while improved, had by 1983 once more deteriorated, and household goods looked upon as luxuries (which sometimes included such everyday items as table knives) were still available mainly in special stores at exaggerated prices beyond the reach of the ordinary citizen.

Social Developments.   Among the subtle changes was the steady shift in the ethnic composition of the Soviet people. The previously dominant Russian element had diminished until it no longer comprised a half of the total. Unrest among the other groups increased and demands for greater attention to ethnic desires were acknowledged by the government which allowed some additional nationalities the use of their native languages in their schools. Crime was not eliminated but was, as in the West, increasing despite severe punishments. Exile to Siberian or other labor camps was, however, no longer common. Social services, primarily for health, vacation, early retirement, were maintained. Not much was changed in favor of women. They still furnished, regardless of their household duties, more than one half of the total labor force, and most of them performed jobs paying less than those held by men. However, laws were promulgated prohibiting their work in dangerous job. Women were not discriminated against in education or in pursuing a career in the various professions—especially in medicine. Still, they seldom reached high positions in the political world. None was appointed to be a member of the Politburo.

Economic Change. Economic growth had been vigorous through most of the 70's and was aided by the contributions demanded of the nations within the Soviet orbit. In 1978, output had increased by 4.8 per cent over the previous year. But in 1979, this fell to 3.6 per cent and thereafter dropped still lower. In 1982, it was below the target set in the Five-Year Plan. Shortages persisted in the supply of needed materials in the factories and led to bitter competition among the managers who used all kinds of illegal means (and bribes) to secure them. Antiquated habits remained, and this, combined with lack of funds, prevented modernization, mechanization, robots, and computers from being introduced in industry and made the country rely overly on human labor. This, to be sure, prevented unemployment, but the government was aware of the implied dangers, which would make the Soviet economy fall behind that of Japan and the West. Both the Five-Year Plan of 1981 and a second Twenty-Year Plan, worked out also by 1981 and charting in more general terms the future course, asked for greater mechanization and modern production methods. Mechanization was to be applied also in agriculture, foremost in Siberia. In 1983, Brezhnev's successor, Yuri Andropov, emphasized the need for it in ever more urgent terms. He asked again for greater work discipline, for better performance, and he, too, attacked corruption. He blamed the shortcomings on the bureaucracy and, like Khrushchev, once more advocated some decentralization by giving factory managers more responsibility, greater authority over the budgets of their establishments, and more control over wages and bonuses. But in contrast to

Khrushchev's attempt at quick solutions, the necessary steps were to be taken cautiously and gradually. Central planning and political supervision by party officials were to be maintained. In the meantime, the "second economy" flourished, i.e., that large part of the economy which, though not planned and largely in private hands, supplemented the needs of the population in food, appliances, and equipment. In part, it consisted of secondhand goods, including even automobiles, and it was tolerated by the authorities.

INDUSTRY.   Priority was invariably given to heavy industry and energy production. Altogether, production of goods deemed needed for the military took precedence over those which could bring an improvement in the supply of consumer goods. The vast resources in ores, oil, gas, coal, gold (about 250 to 300 tons were gained yearly), platinum, mercury, and magnesium were exploited regardless of costs. Additional ones were secured by drawing upon the products of allies in Eastern and Central Europe—especially in East Germany and Czechoslovakia. Up to 1982, the economy could profit from high oil prices. Still, the Five-Year Plan of 1981 called, once again, for more parsimonious use of the resources.The need was all the greater as the Western nations, with the Soviet debt to them amounting to billions of dollars, showed increasing reluctance to extend additional credit to them. Nevertheless, a huge gas pipeline project to bring Siberian gas to Central and Western Europe was successfully arranged for in the face of vain opposition by the United States, which sought to have its allies boycott the project.

AGRICULTURE AND TRADE.   Agriculture remained a major problem. An excellent harvest in 1976 was followed by poorer ones; and they diminished further between 1979 and 1983. Not only the weather but poor organization and management, which included the whole kolkhoz system, were to blame. The incentive for greater efforts was still lagging and the expansion of agricultural land in Siberia proceeded unsatisfactorily. Nor did the private plots, still allowed and used especially for growing vegetables for the city markets, serve as well as in former times. Large purchases of grain abroad became necessary. Politics notwithstanding, mainly the United States provided it, but also other countries, such as Argentina. In 1983, the United States even agreed to long-term commitments, supporting thereby Soviet meat production, inasmuch as the cattle depended upon a sufficient grain supply. Under the circumstances, the Soviet government laid considerable accent on fishing. It kept a technically well-advanced fishing fleet. Unfortunately, pollution of much of the water worldwide, a continued decrease of the water level of the Caspian Sea, and international fishing regulations set limits to the increase in food supplies which fishing could provide. Moreover, inadequate improvements in the transportation system hindered efficient distribution. Rail service, on which the economy chiefly depended, was slow; road and truck (or automobile) services were poor; and air transport, while well-developed, could not make up for what was lacking on land. Foreign trade, except with satellite nations and Finland, stayed on the customary low level.

Cultural Activities. Subtle changes extended also to the cultural scene. Although by 1984 cultural exchange programs (especially with the United States) had diminished, Western thought, music, and art were not excluded to the same degree as before. Jazz and rock musicians were heard, contact with foreign visitors became somewhat easier, and talk became more frank. "Samizdat" authors, i.e., those whose writing were not accepted by official publishing agencies but could be distributed privately, were tolerated within limits. Religious beliefs began to appeal again to the young who, whether of the Orthodox faith or other beliefs, frequented the churches somewhat more than before. Discrimination against the clergy was eased, as, e.g., with regard to income taxes. On the other hand, realistic novels and television programs preaching love of the country and depicting its beauty were invariably favored. Films of the quality and worldwide appeal as those once made by Eisenstein no longer came out; Tarkovsky's *Mirror* represented perhaps some of the best of what was produced. As a whole, censorship remained strict. Emigré writers bitterly denounced the Soviet system which, relations notwithstanding, stifled free thought and its expression through literature and the press, as well as through innumerable measures affecting the daily life of the Soviet citizen.

Education. In line with both ideology and practical needs, a thorough foundation in basic knowledge, including the three R's, was invariably required of pupils in all parts of the country. History and the study of Marxism were emphasized in order to stimulate patriotism and devotion to the Soviet system. Teaching of the natural sciences was further stressed. In addition, sports were favored. Their importance was enhanced when, in 1980, the Olympic Games were held in Moscow. In spite of the politically motivated boycott by the United States, the games turned out to be very successful. Higher education was open to all on the basis of qualification and achievement, even though political reliability, ethnic origin, and good connections could not fail to play a role. High standards were maintained in the universities, and especially the Academies of Science stressed fundamental research. But lack of good equipment proved a steady hindrance in many places—particularly in the lesser institutes outside the capitals.

GOVERNMENT AND FOREIGN AFFAIRS

The transition of power from Lenin to Stalin brought about a terrible struggle, lasting for years; that from Stalin to Malenkov and then Khrushchev was still violent yet demanded few victims; that to Brezhnev went fast and implied little conflict. The transition from Brezhnev to Andropov took but two days and went without any complication. Likewise, when Andropov died in February 1984, his successor, Konstantin Chernenko, was quickly named. The system had matured. Yet, questions remained, since those in the highest places were all men of advanced age and a younger generation was waiting.

Government. A new constitution was adopted for the country in 1977. It fully preserved the principles which had governed the system in the past, and provided mainly for administrative adjustments, many of which had in various ways already been put into practice before. The role of the Communist party was reaffirmed. Thus, the pervasiveness of the Party, noticeable in every part of the country, and its control over all activities persisted. Party officials rather than state officials exercised that supervision and provided that cohesion which the regime demanded. They provided the foremost link between the various Union republics and were responsible to the top state authorities. They even checked up on the military establishment. The other arm of the state, the police and the K.G.B., over which Andropov had once presided, retained likewise its enormous powers. But in the early 1980's, it acted far less conspicuously than in former times—and was less needed. Charged also with the fight against corruption, it achieved little there. Perhaps corruption helped to modify the harshness of the system and to make possible certain activities which, while not quite legal, were yet useful.

Foreign Affairs. International relations were conducted with circumspection. Only once between 1976 and 1984 was force applied: in 1979, when Afghanistan was invaded. Thereafter, a military force estimated at up to 85,000 troops had to be maintained there. Elsewhere, even in Poland where a rebellious movement arose, force was avoided. Intervention in favor of nations, groups, or parties was limited to the type of support such as, in this age of nationalism, all great powers were accustomed to extend to their friends and to the potential opponents of their enemies: propaganda, subsidies, military advice, sometimes also arms deliveries. Unrest anywhere in the world was consistently exploited, especially when bad social conditions, political oppression, and poverty, as in Latin America and Africa, offered chances to spread socialist ideas. But the accent was no longer put on these ideas; rather, nationalism, self-determination, and social improvement were the factors used to further Soviet influence all over the world, especially in competition with the United States.

RELATIONS WITH THE WEST. Policies toward the Western nations were dominated by the power struggle between the U.S.S.R. and the United States. Each side tried to keep a firm hold on its allies, and efforts were made by both to break the hold of the other, as by the West through support of Polish unrest and by the East through attempts at splitting up NATO. Accusations were hurled from both sides. Yet, although détente was dead, a new cold war did not begin. Talks between the two sides continued and centered around trade and disarmament. New trade deals were constantly arranged. As to disarmament, a second SALT treaty was negotiated in 1979, but the United States refused to ratify it. Therefore, new disarmament proposals were worked out. They concerned armament in outer space, chemical weapons, and primarily the reduction of military forces and installations in Central Europe. But even by the beginning of 1984, after long negotiations, they had come to little. Rather, both sides made preparations to install new weapon systems there. One of the problems was how to weigh the relative strength of the very different types of armament and how to arrange for supervision so that treaty conditions would be respected.

RELATIONS WITH SATELLITE COUNTRIES. For the Soviet Union, the major problem arising in Europe was its relationship to one of the satellite countries, Poland. Inefficiency and nationalism there, enhanced by religious factors, had led to deterioration in the country's economic situation and to deep dissatisfaction among the Polish workers. They tried in 1980 to form unions and secure thereby an improvement in their working conditions. This brought them into conflict with their Soviet-backed government and altogether threatened the Communist regime. Unlike in Afghanistan, the Soviet Union was, however, careful not to intervene directly. Instead, it acted through the Polish Party and patiently helped the Polish government reduce resistance and reestablish its hold on the population. Significantly, unrest in Poland did not spread. But caution had to be shown also in relation to other dependent nations in the Soviet orbit. Nor was interference risked in Yugoslavia when its ruler, Marshall Tito, died in 1980 and his successors, beleaguered by adverse economic conditions and nationalistic ambitions among the various peoples composing the Yugoslav state, sought to retain their status of non-alignment toward both sides—the U.S.S.R. and the United States.

RELATIONS WITH NON-EUROPEAN COUNTRIES. Significantly, non-European countries moved, as in the United States and elsewhere, increasingly into the foreground of Soviet attention. The Soviet Union maintained friendly relations with Vietnam as a counterweight to China; with India, which was supported with weaponry; and with Turkey. It aided faraway friends, Angola and Cuba, through deliveries of weapons and other goods, through subsidies, and through technical and military advice. It concluded new trade or friendship pacts with Brazil and Argentina, with Zimbabwe, Libya, and Algeria, and in 1983 reestablished relations with Egypt, which had been interrupted in 1977. A rapprochement was sought with China; and negotiations, started in 1979, reduced tension between the two nations. In 1982, a new trade treaty was concluded with Afghanistan. In the wake of the overthrow of the Shah of Iran in 1979 and the threat of American intervention there, Soviet troops had occupied Afghanistan with the consent of a government long friendly to the Soviets, who thereby gained greater safety for their southern frontier. The invasion was denounced by most nations of the world. Fighting against local resistance went on for years, but in the meantime the Soviets introduced a number of reforms in the country. In Latin America, the Soviet Union—either directly or through Cuba—supported, wherever it could, native revolutionaries seeking social and political changes, as in El Salvador. It sided with Argentina when England made war on her in 1982 after Argentina's seizure of the Falkland Islands, but it did not participate in any war operations.

RELATIONS WITH THE MIDDLE EAST.   The Soviets' main non-European problem remained, as for the whole world, the situation in the Middle East. They bitterly denounced Israel's policies with regard to the Palestinians and other Arab neighbors, but they were simultaneously cautious in their relations with the Arabs. Treaties were made with Saudi Arabia and others, but closer cooperation was established only with Syria. This country received loans and arms—which in combat with the better armed Israeli forces proved of little value. The Middle East was perceived as the most dangerous powder keg threatening the peace of the world, and the Soviet Union, realizing that confrontation of the two superpowers there could lead to an atomic war, essentially refrained from interfering in American diplomacy in the region and likewise from the struggles inside Lebanon, which followed an Israeli invasion in 1983.

The Military.   Fearful of each other and worried about the lack of progress toward a resolution of conflicts through diplomatic means, both sides, East and West, prepared for the possibility of war. The Soviet Union had the advantage in "conventional" weapons, including tanks and short-range missiles fit for land warfare on the European continent. But the real issue was the danger of atomic war affecting directly both the United States and the U.S.S.R. An incident which aroused anger and fear worldwide was the destruction of a South Korean passenger airliner, shot down in September, 1983, by Soviet pilots. There were no survivors. The subsequent mutual denunciations increased further a month later when the United States invaded Grenada. Such events indicated the precariousness of the international situation—the more so as East and West were now equally aware of the difficulty of preventing errors or decisions which might bring about hasty retaliation and war. Thus, while they carried on negotiations for new disarmament pacts providing "nuclear parity" and reduction of missile installations along the wall separating them in the middle of Europe, both sides stepped up production of armaments. This involved new missile systems, bombers, submarines and other naval vessels, military spacecraft, surveillance satellites, nuclear arms for spacecraft, and possibly other weapons, such as chemicals. The Soviet Union sustained the largest body of armed forces in the world—a burden the more worrisome to it inasmuch as it affected its up-to-then successfully balanced budget and interfered with the costly effort to create the type of society at home to which Communism was pledged. Nor was it clear whether or not the quality of the weapons would equal that of possible adversaries. Even in a world where national power and, possibly, expansion were still accepted as desirable aims, the desire for peace thus remained a genuine factor in military matters and in international relations.

CHRONOLOGICAL TABLE

ca. 1500 B.C.—Bronze Culture in Eastern Europe.
ca. 900 B.C.—Cimmerians in Eastern Europe.
ca. 700 B.C.—Scythians in Eastern Europe.
ca. 200 B.C.—Sarmatians in Eastern Europe.
ca. 1 A.D.—Alans in Eastern Europe.
ca. 150 A.D.—Goths in Ukraine and Crimea.
325—Council of Nicea: Christianity recognized in the Roman Empire.
375—Hun Invasion; Beginning of the Great Migration of Peoples.
476—End of the Roman Empire.
485—Foundation of Frankish kingdom.
***ca.* 550—Avars in Russia.**
***ca.* 620—Origins of Khazar State.**
***ca.* 700—Northmen in Volga Region.**
711—Mohammedans invade Spain.
768–814—Reign of Charlemagne.
***ca.* 855–885—Cyril and Methodius convert Slavic tribes.**
862—Rurik, ruler of Novgorod.
907—Oleg's expedition against Constantinople.
936–973—Otto the Great, German Emperor.
967–971—Sviatoslav's expedition against Byzantine Empire.
988—Christianity adopted by Vladimir I.
1015—Death of Vladimir I.
1017—Church of St. Sophia begun in Kiev.
1019–1054—Reign of Yaroslav the Wise.
1037—Kiev becomes metropolitan see.
1043—Last expedition against Byzantium.
1054—Catholic-Orthodox schism.
1066—Battle of Hastings: Norman invasion of England.
1073–1085—Pope Gregory VII.
1099—First Crusade: Jerusalem taken by Christians.
1113–1125—Reign of Vladimir II.
1139–1174—Reign of Andrew Bogolubsky.
***ca.* 1147—Founding of Moscow.**
1158—Swedes begin occupation of Finland; Germans and Danes settle
in Livonia and Estonia.

1215—Magna Charta issued.
1216—Death of Pope Innocent III.
1223?—Battle of the River Kalka.
1226—Death of St. Francis.
1236—Second Tartar invasion.
1240—Battle of the Neva: defeat of Swedes.
1240—Kiev taken by Tartars.
1242—Battle of Lake Peipus: defeat of Teutonic Knights.
1252–1263—Reign of Alexander Nevsky in Muscovy.
1274—Death of Thomas Aquinas.
1295—Model Parliament in England.
1320—Kiev falls under Lithuanian Rule.
1321—Death of Dante.
1325–1341—Reign of Ivan I Kalita.
1325—Moscow becomes metropolitan see.
1339–1453—Hundred Years' War between England and France.
1348—Black death in Europe.
1359–1389—Reign of Dimitri Donskoy.
1380—Battle of the Don.
1386—Union of Poland and Lithuania.
fl. **1400—Andrew Rublev.**
1408—Re-establishment of Tartar rule over Russia.
1438–1439—Council of Ferrara-Florence: attempts to unify Catholics and Orthodox.
ca. 1450—Printing press with movable type invented in Germany.
1453—Fall of Constantinople to the Turks.
1462–1505—Reign of Ivan III the Great.
1471–1494—Conquest of Novgorod and its destruction as trading center.
1480—Battle of the Oka River: end of Tartar rule.
1485—Incorporation of Tver.
1492—Discovery of America.
1492—End of Mohammedan rule in Spain.
1505–1533—Reign of Basil III.
ca. 1510—Climax of Renaissance in Italy and Germany.
1510—Conquest of Pskov.
1514—Conquest of Smolensk.
1517—Beginning of Reformation (Luther).
1519–1522—First voyage around world (Magellan).
1532—Machiavelli, *The Prince.*
1533–1584—Reign of Ivan IV the Terrible.
1534—Break between England and Rome (Henry VIII).
1552—Conquest of Kazan.
1553—Discovery of North Cape route to Russia.

1554–1556—Conquest of Astrakhan.
1556—Abdication of Emperor Charles V.
1558–1603—Reign of Queen Elizabeth in England.
1558—Beginning of Livonian War.
1565—Oprichnina founded.
1568—Beginning of Netherlands' War of Independence.
1581—Yermak's first expedition into Siberia.
1582—Peace of Yam Zapolie.
1584–1598—Reign of Feodor I, last Tsar of Rurik family.
1588—Defeat of Spanish Armada.
1589—Moscow becomes a patriarchate.
1595—Establishment of "Uniate church" in Ukraine.
1597—Law against fugitive peasants.
1598–1605—Reign of Boris Godunov.
1604—Appearance of "False Dimitri." Beginning of Time of Troubles.
1604–1608—Cossack revolts in Ukraine against Poland.
1605–1606—Dimitri as Tsar.
1605—Gunpowder Plot in England.
1606–1610—Reign of Basil IV Shuisky.
1607—English colony established at Jamestown, Virginia.
1608—Appearance of "Second False Dimitri."
1611–1612—The Poles in Moscow.
1613—Election of Romanov family to the throne.
1613–1645—Reign of Michael I.
1616—Death of Shakespeare.
1618–1648—Thirty Years' War.
1618—Russians reach upper Yenisei River in Siberia.
1619–1633—Philaret, Patriarch of Moscow.
1620—Landing of Pilgrims at Plymouth, New England.
1625–1649—New Cossack revolts in Ukraine against Poland.
1632—Russians reach Lena River in Siberia.
1637—A "Siberian Department" established in Moscow.
1643–1715—Reign of Louis XIV in France.
1645—Russians reach Pacific Coast of Siberia.
1645–1676—Reign of Alexis I.
1648—Peace of Westphalia.
1649—Charles I beheaded: Puritan Commonwealth established in England.
1649—Publication of new Russian law code.
1652—Nikon becomes Patriarch of Moscow.
1653—Convening of last Zemsky Sobor.
1654–1656—Church council in Moscow for sake of reform: beginning of the Schism.

1660—Restoration of Stuarts in England.

1661—Peace of Cardis with Sweden.

1667–1671—Revolt of Stenka Razin.

1676–1682—Reign of Feodor II.

1681—Pennsylvania granted to William Penn.

1682–1725—Reign of Peter I the Great.

1682–1689—Regency of Sophia.

1683—Vienna besieged by Turks.

1687—Newton, *Principia.*

1688—"Glorious Revolution" in England: Bill of Rights.

1689—Russo-Chinese Treaty of Nerchinsk.

1689—Peter seizes government.

1690—Locke, *Essay concerning Human Understanding.*

1696—Capture of Azov.

1697—Kamchatka reached by Russian explorers.

1697–1698—Peter's trip through Europe; suppression of Streltsi.

1700—New calendar introduced.

1700–1721—Great Northern War.

1700—Defeat at Narva.

1703—Founding of St. Petersburg.

1709—Battle of Poltava.

1710–1711—Russo-Turkish War: loss of Azov.

1713—St. Petersburg becomes capital of Russia.

1713—Peace of Utrecht: end of Louis XIV's wars of aggression.

1716—Invasion of southern Sweden.

1718—Death of Alexis, son of Peter.

1721—Peace of Nystad.

**1721—Patriarchate abolished in Moscow; Holy Synod estab-
lished.**

1722–1723—War against Persia.

1725—Academy of Science founded in St. Petersburg.

1725–1727—Reign of Catherine I.

1727—Russo-Chinese Treaty of Kyakhta.

1727–1730—Reign of Peter II.

1730–1740—Reign of Anna I.

1731—Ladoga Canal completed.

1733–1735—War of Polish Succession (Stanislaw Leszcyński).

1737—Charting of northern Siberian coast line.

1738—Russian ballet school founded.

1738- 1739—War with Turkey.

1739—Treaty of Belgrade: coast on Black Sea gained.

1740–1741—Reign of Ivan VI; regency of Anna Leopoldovna.

1740–1786—Reign of Frederick the Great of Prussia.

1741–1762—Reign of Elizabeth.
1741—Discovery of Bering Straits.
1743—Ostermann exiled.
1743—Peace of Abo: Sweden cedes Viborg.
1745—Capture of Louisburg (King George's War).
1755—Moscow University founded.
1755—Lomonosov, *Russian Grammar*.
1755—Lisbon earthquake.
1756–1763—Seven Years' War (French and Indian War).
1757–1762—Russian participation in Seven Years' War.
1758—Academy of Fine Arts founded.
1762—Reign of Peter III.
1762—Nobility freed from compulsory service.
1762–1796—Reign of Catherine II the Great.
1762—Rousseau, *Le Contrat Social*.
1763—Peace of Paris: British gain French colonies in America and India.
1764—Secularization of church lands and property.
1765—Death of Lomonosov.
1767–1774—Commission for the Study of Reforms.
1768—Outbreak of war with Turkey.
1772—First Partition of Poland.
1772–1774—Pugachev Revolt.
1774—Treaty of Kuchuk Kainardji.
1775—End of Cossack autonomy in the Ukraine.
1776—Declaration of Independence of United States.
1776—Adam Smith, *Wealth of Nations*.
1778—Death of Voltaire.
1780—Armed Neutrality against England during American Revolution.
1781—British surrender at Yorktown.
1781—Kant, *Critique of Pure Reason*.
1783—Annexation of Crimea.
1785—Charter for Russian nobility and merchants.
1787—Adoption of American Constitution.
1787–1790—Russo-Swedish War.
1787–1792—Russo-Turkish War: campaigns of Suvorov.
1789—Outbreak of French Revolution.
1792—Treaty of Jassy.
1793—Second Partition of Poland.
1793—Execution of Louis XVI; beginning of Reign of Terror in France.
1795—Third Partition of Poland.
1796—Odessa founded.
1796—Napoleon's first campaign in Italy.

1796–1801—Reign of Paul I.
1799—Suvorov's Italian and Swiss campaigns (War of Second Coalition).
1801—Russian suzerainty formally recognized by Georgia.
1801–1825—Reign of Alexander I.
1801–1809—Thomas Jefferson, President of United States.
1802—Philharmonic Society founded.
1803—Expedition around world.
1804–1815—Napoleon I, Emperor of France.
1805—Defeat at Austerlitz.
1806—Napoleon's Continental System begun.
1806—Outbreak of war with Turkey.
1807—Defeat at Friedland.
1807—Treaty of Tilsit: alliance with France.
1807—First steamboat service (Fulton on the Hudson River).
1808—Congress of Erfurt.
1808–1809—Russo-Swedish war.
1808–1809—Constitutional reforms proposed by Speransky.
1809—Treaty of Frederikshavn with Sweden: acquisition of Finland.
1809—Opening of official relations with United States.
1812–1814—War of 1812 (United States and Great Britain).
1812—Peace with Turkey at Bucharest: acquisition of Bessarabia.
1812—Napoleon's invasion of Russia.
1813–1815—Wars of liberation of the Germanies.
1813—Battle of the Nations at Leipzig.
1813—Persia cedes Baku; incorporation of Georgia.
1814—Occupation of Paris.
1815—Congress of Vienna; Holy Alliance founded.
1816–1819—Emancipation of peasants in Baltic provinces.
1818—Constitution for Poland.
1819—Colombia first independent South American republic.
1820—Missouri Compromise.
1821—Outbreak of Greek War of Independence.
1822—Congress of Verona.
1823—Monroe Doctrine.
1825–1855—Reign of Nicholas I.
1825—Dekabrist Rising.
1826–1828—War against Persia; expansion in Caucasus region.
1826—Death of Karamzin.
1827—Battle of Navarino.
1828—Outbreak of war with Turkey.
1829—Peace of Adrianople.

1829–1837—Andrew Jackson, President of United States.
1830—Railroad with locomotives opened from Manchester to Liverpool.
1830—July Revolution in France; revolution in Belgium.
1830–1832—Revolution in Poland.
1831—Death of Hegel.
1832—Completion of *Faust;* death of Goethe.
1832—First Reform Bill in England.
1832—First commercial treaty with United States.
1833—Treaty of Unkiar Skelessi.
1837—Death of Pushkin.
1837–1901—Reign of Queen Victoria in England.
1840–1842—British Opium War against China.
1841–1844—Emerson's *Essays.*
1846–1848—Mexican War.
1848—Gold Rush to California.
1848—Marx and Engels, *Communist Manifesto.*
1848—February Revolution in France; revolutions in Germanies, Austria, Italy, Hungary.
1848—Death of Belinsky.
1849—Suppression of Hungarian revolution.
1851—St. Petersburg-Moscow railroad opened.
1852—Louis Napoleon (Napoleon III), French Emperor.
1853—Occupation of Sakhalin and Korea.
1854–1856—Crimean War.
1855–1881—Reign of Alexander II.
1855—Fall of Sevastopol.
1856—Peace of Paris.
1856—Death of Glinka.
1857–1867—Herzen, *The Bell.*
1857—Indian Mutiny against Britain.
1859—J. S. Mill, *On Liberty.*
1860—Founding of Vladivostok; Treaty of Peking.
1861—Italy becomes kingdom; death of Cavour.
1861–1865—United States Civil War.
1861—Emancipation of serfs.
1862—Financial reform.
1863—Educational reform.
1863—Secession from Academy of Fine Arts.
1863—United States Emancipation Proclamation.
1863–1864—Revolt in Poland.
1864—Judicial reform; introduction of Zemstvos.
1865—Assassination of Lincoln.
1865—Capture of Tashkent.
1866—Attempted assassination of Alexander II.

1867—Reduction of protective tariffs.
1867—Sale of Alaska to United States.
1868—Capture of Samarkand.
1869—Karl Marx, *Das Kapital* (Vol. I).
1869—Opening of Suez Canal.
1870—Outbreak of Franco-Prussian War; German victory at Sedan.
1870—Abrogation of Black Sea clauses of Treaty of Paris.
1870—Municipal reform.
1871—German empire proclaimed (Bismarck, Chancellor).
1871—Communist uprisings in Paris (*La Commune*).
1872—Three Emperors' League (Germany, Austria, Russia).
1873—Conquest of Khiva.
1874—Introduction of universal military service.
1875—Southern Sakhalin ceded to Japan; western Kuril Islands
          acquired.
1875–1876—New uprisings in Balkans.
1876—Death of Bakunin.
1876—Annexation of Kokand.
1877—Reintroduction of protective tariffs.
1877–1878—War against Turkey.
1878—Treaty of San Stephano.
1878—Congress of Berlin.
1878–1881—Second British war against Afghanistan.
1878–1881—Terrorist activities.
1878–1884—Populist movement.
1881—Assassination of Alexander II.
1881—Death of Mussorgsky.
1881—Death of Dostoyevsky.
1881–1894—Reign of Alexander III.
1882–1886—Payments and burdens of emancipated serfs re-
          duced.
1882–1890—Social legislation (child labor, working hours, fac-
          tory inspection).
1883—Triple Alliance formed (Germany, Austria, Italy).
1883—United States Civil Service Act.
1884—Merv taken.
1885—Revolution in Bulgaria.
1887—Reinsurance Treaty with Germany.
1890—Resignation of Bismarck.
1890—Anti-Jewish legislation enforced.
1891–1892—Franco-Russian alliance: French loans for Russia.
1891–1903—Trans-Siberian railroad constructed.
1894–1895—Sino-Japanese War.
1894–1917—Reign of Nicholas II.

1896—Treaty with China regarding trans-Siberian railroad in Manchuria.

1896–1897—Strike movement.

1898—Hawaii annexed by United States.

1898—Social Democratic party founded.

1898—Spanish-American War: Philippines acquired by United States.

1898—Port Arthur leased.

1898—United States Open-Door Policy proclaimed.

1899—Hague Peace Conference.

1899—Finnish legislature abolished.

1899–1902—British Boer War.

1900—Boxer Rebellion.

1901–1909—Theodore Roosevelt, President of United States.

1901—Russo-Persian treaty.

1902—Anglo-Japanese Alliance.

1903—Menshevist-Bolshevist split in Social Democratic party.

1903—Abolition of joint-tax liability of peasants.

1903—Pogroms in Kishinev, Gomel.

1903—German-Turkish agreement regarding Bagdad railroad.

1904—Anglo-French Entente Cordiale.

1904–1905—Russo-Japanese War.

1904—Assassination of Plehwe.

1905—Fall of Port Arthur; naval Battle of Tsushima.

1905—Demonstration under Father Gapon: Bloody Sunday.

1905—Peace of Portsmouth.

1905—Meeting of Tsar Nicholas with Emperor Wilhelm II of Germany.

1905—First Moroccan crisis.

1905—Union of Sweden and Norway dissolved.

1905—October Revolution.

1906—First Duma.

1906—Stolypin's agrarian reform; dissolution of mir.

1907—Second Duma.

1907—Second Hague Peace Conference.

1907—Anglo-Russian convention: foundation for Triple Entente.

1907—Russo-Japanese convention.

1907–1912—Third Duma.

1908—Convention with Austria at Buchlau.

1910—Potsdam agreement with Germany regarding Bagdad railroad.

1910—Russo-Japanese treaty.

1910—Death of Tolstoy.

1911—Turko-Italian war.

1912—Outbreak of Balkan wars.

1912–1917—Fourth Duma.

1913–1921—Woodrow Wilson, President of United States.

1914—Assassination of Archduke Francis Ferdinand at Sarajevo.

1914–1918—World War I.

1914—Defeat at Tannenberg.

1914—First Battle of Marne.

1915—Defeat in Galicia.

1915—Fall of Warsaw.

1916—Brusilov offensive.

1916—Assassination of Rasputin.

1917—February Revolution; abdication of Nicholas II; Provisional Government.

1917—United States enters World War I.

1917—Kerensky offensive.

1917—July uprising of Soviets.

1917—Russia becomes a republic; renewal of patriarchate.

1917—Bolshevist October Revolution (Lenin, Trotsky, Stalin); Kerensky government overthrown.

1917—Armistice with Central Powers.

1918—Constituent Assembly dispersed.

1918—Brest-Litovsk Peace Treaty with Central Powers.

1918—Outbreak of civil war; Allied intervention in Russia begins.

1918—Red Army created.

1918—Death of Nicholas II.

1918—First Soviet Constitution (Fundamental Law); creation of Federation of Soviet National Republics.

1918—End of World War I; revolution in Germany.

1919—Treaty of Versailles; League of Nations founded.

1919—Third International (Comintern) established.

1919—Foreign trade monopoly established.

1920—Recognition of Soviets by Estonia.

1920—End of Allied intervention.

1920—End of civil war; death of Kolchak; withdrawal of Denikin and Wrangel.

1920–1921—War against Poland.

1920–1922—Famine.

1921—Washington Disarmament Conference.

1921—Peace of Riga; cession of White Russian lands to Poland.

1921—Institution of N.E.P.

1921—Friendship treaties with Turkey, Persia, Afghanistan.

1922—Conference at Genoa; Treaty of Rapallo with Germany.

1922—End of Far Eastern Republic.

1922—Fascist regime established in Italy (Mussolini).

1922—Arrest of Patriarch Tikhon; dissolution of Synod.

1922—Stalin becomes secretary of Communist party.

1922—Union of Soviet Socialist Republics (U.S.S.R.) created.

1923—French invasion of Ruhr.

1923—Revised Fundamental Law published.

1924—Death of Lenin.

1924—Treaty with China.

1924—Recognition of U.S.S.R. by England, Italy, France.

1924—Incident of Zinoviev letter.

1924—Trotsky stripped of power.

1925—Locarno Pact.

1925—Recognition of U.S.S.R. by Japan.

1925—Fourteenth Party congress: announcement of industrialization plan.

1926—Pilsudski dictatorship established in Poland.

1926—Trotsky expelled from Politburo.

1927—Raid on Soviet trade headquarters in London; relations with England broken.

1927—Tenth Jubilee of Revolution.

1928—First Five-Year Plan inaugurated.

1928—Briand-Kellogg Peace Pact.

1929–1933—Herbert Hoover, President of United States.

1929—New York stock market crash; beginning of Depression.

1929—East Protocol signed.

1929—Resumption of relations with England.

1929—Trotsky expelled from U.S.S.R.

1929—Raid on Soviet consulate in Harbin; Treaty of Nikolsk Ussuriisk.

1930—Turksib railroad opened.

1930—Liquidation of kulaks.

1931—Mukden incident; Japanese invasion of Manchuria.

1931—Trial of Industrialist party.

1932—Dnieprostroy Dam opened.

1932–1937—Second Five-Year Plan.

1933—Hitler becomes German Chancellor.

1933–1945—Franklin D. Roosevelt, President of United States.

1933—Recognition of U.S.S.R. by United States.

1934—Russia joins League of Nations.

1934–1938—Party purges: execution of Zinoviev, Kamenev, Bukharin, Rykov, Tukhachevsky.

1935—Italy invades Ethiopia.

1935—Sale of Chinese Eastern railway.

1935—Franco-Russian alliance.
1936—Outbreak of Spanish civil war.
1936—Stakhanov Year.
1936—Stalin Constitution: revision of Fundamental Law.
1936—Death of Gorky.
1936—German-Japanese Anticomintern Pact.
1937—Outbreak of Sino-Japanese war.
1937—Italy joins Anticomintern Pact.
1938—Third Five-Year Plan started.
1938—Germany annexes Austria.
1938—German-French-English agreement at Munich concerning Czechoslovakia.
1939—Annexation of Czechoslovakia by Germany.
1939—Collapse of English and French military negotiations with U.S.S.R.
1939—Nonaggression pact with Germany.
1939—Outbreak of World War II.
1939—Annexation of eastern Poland.
1939—Mutual assistance pacts with Estonia, Latvia, Lithuania.
1939–1940—War against Finland.
1939—Expulsion of U.S.S.R. from League of Nations.
1940—Incorporation of Baltic republics into U.S.S.R.
1940—Collapse of France.
1941—Stalin becomes Premier.
1941—Russo-Japanese neutrality pact.
1941—Nazi invasion of Russia.
1941—U.S.S.R. accepts Atlantic Charter.
1941—United States declares war against Japan, Germany.
1942—United Nations Declaration signed.
1942—Siege of Moscow raised.
1942—Fall of Sevastopol.
1942—Twenty-year alliance with Great Britain.
1943—Re-establishment of patriarchate.
1943—Siege of Stalingrad raised.
1943—Capitulation of Italy.
1943—Anglo-Russian-United States conference in Moscow.
1943—Teheran Conference.
1944—Siege of Leningrad raised.
1944—Bretton Woods Conference.
1944—Allied invasion of Normandy.
1944—Alliance with France.
1944—Armistice with Rumania, Bulgaria, Finland.
1945—Yalta Conference (United States, England, Russia).
1945—San Francisco Conference.
1945—Berlin taken.

1945—Potsdam Conference.
1945—Atomic bomb destroys Hiroshima.
1945—Russian declaration of war against Japan.
1945—Surrender of Japan: end of World War II.
1946—Discord in United Nations over Iran and Greece.
1946—Proposals in United Nations for atomic energy control.
1947—Peace treaties signed with Finland, Italy, Bulgaria, Rumania, Hungary.
1947—Marshall Plan for economic rehabilitation of Europe.
1947—Currency reform.
1948—Establishment of a communistic government in Czechoslovakia.
1948–1949—Berlin blockade.
1949—Excommunication of Communists by the Pope.
1949—Defeat of Nationalist China by the Chinese Communists.
1949–1955—Interruption of political relations with Yugoslavia.
1950–1953—Korean War.
1951—Fifth Five-Year Plan initiated.
1952—General Party Congress.
1953—Death of Stalin; Malenkov becomes Premier.
1953—Anti-Communist rising in Berlin.
1954—Establishment of a Communist regime in Northern Indochina.
1955—Malenkov resigns; Rise of Khrushchev.
1955—Conclusion of Austrian Peace Treaty.
1955—Germany enters NATO.
1956—Risings in Poland and Hungary.
1957—Launching of *sputnik*.
1958—Khrushchev becomes Premier.
1960—Failure of Geneva and Disarmament conferences.
1961—Currency Reform.
1961—Launching of man into orbit in space.
1961–1962—Berlin Crisis.
1962—Cuba crisis.
1963—Widening gulf between Russia and China.
1963—Atomic Test Ban negotiated.
1964—Ouster of Khrushchev.
1967—Arab-Israeli War.
1968—Soviets invade Czechoslovakia.
1971—New Five-Year Plan. Increased decentralization.
1971—Berlin Agreement with Western powers.
1971—People's Republic of China enters United Nations.
1972—Treaty with West Germany.
1972—U.S. President visits Moscow.
1974—End of Vietnam War.
1975—Conference of Helsinki.

1977—**New constitution adopted**
1979—Overthrow of Shah in Iran (Khomeni)
    —**Invasion of Afghanistan**
1980—Moscow Olympic Games
    —Unrest in Poland
1982—**Death of Brezhnev**
1983—War in Lebanon
1984—Death of Andropov

BIBLIOGRAPHY

The following bibliography has been compiled with four aims in view: (a) to include only such books on Russia as are easily accessible; (b) to provide a comparatively wide choice of such books as long as they are written in English; (c) to cover all periods and phases of Russian life; (d) to lead to material containing further detailed bibliographical material for the interested student.

BIBLIOGRAPHIES
Horecky, Paul L., ed. *Russia and the Soviet Union: A Bibliographic Guide to Western-Language Publications* (Chicago: University of Chicago Press, 1965).

Todd, Albert C., *et al. American Bibliography of Russian and East European Studies*, 3 vols. (Bloomington, Ind.: Indiana University Press, 1963–66).

ENCYCLOPEDIA
The Modern Encyclopedia of Russian and Soviet History (Gulf Breeze, Fla.: Academic International Press, 1976–). In progress.

PERIODICALS
Canadian American Slavic Studies
Current Digest of the Soviet Press
Jahrbücher für Geschichte Osteuropas
Russian Review
Slavic and East European Journal
Slavic Review
Slavonic and East European Review

GENERAL HISTORIES
Carr, Edward H. *History of Soviet Russia*, 7 vols. (New York: Macmillan, 1951–60).

Clarkson, Jesse D. *A History of Russia*, 2nd ed. (New York: Random House, 1969).

Florinsky, Michael T. *Russia: A History and Interpretation*, 2 vols. (New York: Macmillan, 1953).

Pipes, Richard. *Russia under the Old Regime* (London: Weidenfeld & Nicolson, 1974).

Pokrovsky, M. N. *Brief History of Russia*, 2 vols. (Orono, Me.: University Reprints, 1933).

Portal, Roger. *The Slavs* (London: Weidenfeld & Nicolson, 1969).

Walsh, Warren B., ed. *Readings in Russian History*, 4th ed., 3 vols. (Syracuse, N.Y.: Syracuse University Press, 1963).

Walsh, Warren B. *Russia and the Soviet Union: A Modern History*, rev. ed. (Ann Arbor, Mich.: University of Michigan Press, 1968).

SPECIAL HISTORIES

Blum, Jerome. *Lord and Peasant in Russia from the Ninth to the Nineteenth Century* (Princeton, N.J.: Princeton University Press, 1961).

Crummey, Robert. *The Old Believers and the World of Anti-Christ* (Madison: University of Wisconsin Press, 1970).

Evans, Allan S. *Russia: Tsars and Commissars*. (Toronto: McGraw-Hill, 1971).

McNeill, William. *Europe's Steppe Frontier, 1500–1800* (Chicago: University of Chicago Press, 1964).

Mirsky, D. S. *Russia: A Social History, 1931–1952*, 2nd ed. (Chester Springs, Pa.: Dufour Editions).

Vucinich, Alexander S. *Science in Russian Culture, 1700–1917*, 2 vols. (Stanford, Calif.: Stanford University Press, 1963, 1970).

HISTORIES BY PERIODS

Adams, Arthur E., ed. *Imperial Russia After 1861* (Boston: D. C. Heath, 1965).

Berdyaev, Nicolas. *The Origins of Russian Communism* (Ann Arbor, Mich.: University of Michigan Press, 1960).

Dmytryshyn, Basil, ed. *Imperial Russia: A Source Book, 1700–1917*, 2nd ed. (New York: Holt, Rinehart and Winston, 1974).

———. *The Modernization of Russia under Peter I and Catherine II* (New York: Wiley, 1974).

Garrard, John G., ed. *The Eighteenth Century in Russia* (Oxford: Clarendon Press, 1973).

Mazour, A. G. *The Rise and Fall of the Romanovs* (New York: Van Nostrand, 1960).

Presniakov, Alexandr E. *Formation of the Great Russian State: A Study of Russian History in the Thirteenth to Fifteenth Centuries* (New York: Quadrangle Books, 1970).

Raeff, Marc. *Imperial Russia, 1682–1825* (New York: Knopf, 1970).

Riha, Thomas, ed. *Russia Before Peter the Great, 900–1700 (Readings in Russian Civilization*, Vol. 1) (Chicago: University of Chicago Press, 1964).

Seton-Watson, Hugh. *The Russian Empire 1801–1917* (New York: Oxford University Press, 1967).

Smith, David. *Russia of the Tsars 1796–1917* (London: Benn, 1971).

Thaden, Edward C. *Russia since 1801* (New York: Wiley, 1971).

Treadgold, Donald W. *Twentieth Century Russia*, 3rd ed. (Chicago: Rand McNally, 1964).

Vernadsky, George. *Ancient Russia; Kievan Russia; The Mongols and Russia; Russia at the Dawn of the Modern Age; The Tsardom of Russia*, 5 vols. (New Haven: Yale University Press, 1943–69).

RUSSIA AND THE EAST

Fourst, Clifford M. *Muscovite and Mandarin: Russia's Trade with China and Its Setting* (Chapel Hill: University of North Carolina Press, 1969).

Golder, Frank A. *Russian Expansion on the Pacific: 1641–1850* (Gloucester, Mass.: Peter Smith, 1914).

Lensen, George A. *Russia's Eastward Expansion* (Englewood Cliffs, N.J.: Prentice-Hall, 1964).

Lobanov-Rostovsky, Andrei. *Russia and Asia* (Ann Arbor, Mich.: George Wahr, 1951).

Treadgold, Donald. *The West in Russia and China: Vol. 1, Russia, 1462–1917* (New York: Cambridge University Press, 1973).

Vucinich, Wayne S., ed. *Russia and Asia: Essays on the Influence of Russia on the Asian People* (Stanford, Calif.: Hoover Institution Press, 1972).

ECONOMIC HISTORY

Blackwell, William. *The Beginnings of Russian Industrialization* (Princeton, N.J.: Princeton University Press, 1968).

———. *Russian Economic Development from Peter the Great to Stalin*. (New York: New Viewpoints, 1974).

Kirchner, Walther. *Studies in Russian American Commerce 1820–1860* (Leyden: Brill, 1975).

Letiche, John M. ed. *A History of Russian Economic Thought: Ninth through Eighteenth Centuries* (Berkeley: University of California Press, 1964).

Von Laue, Theodor. *Sergei Witte and the Industrialization of Russia* (New York: Columbia University Press, 1963).

BIOGRAPHIES

Bain, Robert N. *The First Romanovs, 1613–1725* (New York: Russell and Russell, 1905).

Deutscher, Isaac. *Stalin: A Political Biography*, 2nd ed. (New York: Oxford University Press, 1967).

————. *The Prophet Armed: Trotsky, 1879–1921; The Prophet Unarmed: Trotsky, 1921–1929*, 2 vols. (New York: Oxford University Press, 1954, 1959).

Fülöp-Miller, René. *Rasputin: The Holy Devil* (New York: Frederick Ungar, 1962).

Graham, Stephen. *Tsar of Freedom: The Life and Reign of Alexander II* (Hamden, Conn.: Shoe String Press, 1935).

Grey, Ian. *Boris Godunov* (London: Hodder and Stoughton, 1973).

Kurbsky, Prince A. M. *History of Ivan IV*, trans. by J. K. I. Fennell (New York: Cambridge University Press, 1965).

Massie, Robert K. *Nicholas and Alexandra* (New York: Atheneum, 1967).

Oliva, Lawrence Jay. *Russia in the Era of Peter the Great* (Englewood Cliffs, N.J.: Prentice-Hall, 1969).

Palmer, Alan W. *Alexander I* (London: Weidenfeld & Nicolson, 1974).

Payne, Robert, and Nikita Romanoff. *Ivan the Terrible* (New York: Crowell, 1975).

Presniakov, Aleksandr E. *Emperor Nicholas I of Russia* (Gulf Breeze, Fla.: Academic International Press, 1974).

Schuyler, Eugene. *Peter the Great, Emperor of Russia*, 2 vols. (New York: Russell and Russell, 1884).

Shub, Daniel. *Lenin: A Biography* (New York: Penguin Books, 1966).

Trotsky, Leon. *My Life* (Gloucester, Mass.: Peter Smith).

Tucker, Robert C. *Stalin as Revolutionary 1879–1929* (New York: Norton, 1973).

REVOLUTIONARY MOVEMENTS

Berdyaev, Nicolas. *The Russian Idea* (Boston: Beacon Press, 1962).

Kropotkin, Peter. *Memoirs of a Revolutionist*, ed. by J. A. Rogers (Gloucester, Mass.: Peter Smith).

Mazour, A. G. *The First Russian Revolution, 1825* (Stanford, Calif.: Stanford University Press, 1937).

Riasanovsky, Nicholas V. *Russia and the West in the Teaching of the Slavophiles* (Gloucester, Mass.: Peter Smith, 1952).

Schwarz, Solomon M. *Russian Revolution of 1905*, trans. by G. Vakar (Chicago: University of Chicago Press, 1966).

Tucker, Robert C., ed. *The Lenin Anthology* (New York: Norton, 1975).

Venturi, Franco. *Roots of Revolution* (New York: Grosset & Dunlap, 1966).

RUSSIAN REVOLUTION

Bunyan, James, and H. H. Fisher. *The Bolshevik Revolution, 1917–1918* (Stanford, Calif.: Stanford University Press, 1934).

Daniels, Robert C. *Red October* (New York: Scribner, 1967).

Florinsky, Michael. *The End of the Russian Empire* (New York: Macmillan [Collier]).

Golder, Frank A. *Documents of Russian History, 1914–1917* (Gloucester, Mass.: Peter Smith, 1964).

Kennan, George F. *Decision to Intervene* (Princeton, N.J.: Princeton University Press, 1958).

———. *Russia Leaves the War* (Princeton, N.J.: Princeton University Press, 1956).

Rabinowitch, Alexander. *Prelude to Revolution: The Petrograd Bolsheviks and the July Uprising of 1917* (Bloomington, Ind.: Indiana University Press, 1968).

Reed, John. *Ten Days That Shook the World* (New York: Modern Library, 1919).

Moorehead, Alan. *Russian Revolution* (New York: Harper and Row, 1958).

Trotsky, Leon. *History of the Russian Revolution*, trans. by Max Eastman (Ann Arbor, Mich.: University of Michigan Press, 1957).

Wolfe, Bertram D. *Three Who Made a Revolution*, 4th ed. (New York: Dial Press, 1964).

SOVIET PERIOD

Hoetzsch, Otto. *Evolution of Russia* (New York: Harcourt, Brace and World, 1967).

Kohn, Hans, ed. *Mind of Modern Russia* (New York: Harper and Row, 1962).

Matthews, Merwyn. *Class and Society in Soviet Russia* (New York: Walker & Co., 1972).

Rauch, Georg von. *A History of Soviet Russia*, 6th ed. (New York: Praeger, 1972).

Tucker, Robert. *The Soviet Political Mind* (New York: Praeger, 1963).

Ulam, Adam B. *The Bolsheviks* (New York: Macmillan [Collier], 1965).

ECONOMICS

Bergson, Abram. *Economics of Soviet Planning* (New Haven: Yale University Press, 1964).

Bornstein, Morris, and Daniel R. Fusfeld, eds. *Soviet Economy: A Book of Readings*, rev. ed. (Homewood, Ill.: Richard D. Irwin, 1966).

Conyngham, William J. *Industrial Management in the Soviet Union* (Stanford, Calif.: Hoover Institution Press, 1973).

Lewin, Moshe. *Russian Peasants and Soviet Power* (London: Allen & Unwin, 1968).

Nove, Alec. *An Economic History of the U.S.S.R.* (London: Allen Lane, 1969).

POLITICS

Adams, Arthur. *Stalin and His Times* (New York: Holt, Rinehart and Winston, 1972).

Barghoorn, Frederick C. *Politics in the U.S.S.R.*, 2nd ed. (Boston: Little, Brown, 1972).

Conquest, Robert. *The Great Terror: Stalin's Purge of the Thirties*, rev. ed. (New York: Macmillan, 1973).

Crankshaw, Edward. *Khrushchev* (New York: Viking Press, 1966).

Fainsod, Merle. *How Russia Is Ruled*, rev. ed. (New York: Random House, 1963).

Hazard, John W. *Soviet System of Government*, 4th ed. (Chicago: University of Chicago Press, 1968).

Schapiro, Leonard. *The Communist Party of the Soviet Union*, rev. ed. (New York: Random House, 1971).

Shaffer, Harry G., ed. *Soviet System in Theory and Practice* (New York: Appleton-Century-Crofts, 1965).

Werth, Alexander. *Russia Under Khrushchev* (New York: Hill and Wang, 1962).

FOREIGN RELATIONS

Bailey, Thomas A. *America Faces Russia* (Gloucester, Mass.: Peter Smith, 1964).

Brzezinski, Zbigniew K. *Soviet Bloc: Unity and Conflict*, rev. ed. (Cambridge, Mass.: Harvard University Press, 1967).

Fleming, Denna F. *The Cold War and Its Origins, 1917–1960*, 2 vols. (New York: Doubleday, 1961).

Goldwin, Robert A., and Marion Zetterbaum, eds. *Readings in Russian Foreign Policy* (New York: Oxford University Press, 1959).

Kennan, George F. *Russia and the West Under Lenin and Stalin* (Boston: Little, Brown, 1961).

––––––. *Soviet Foreign Policy, 1917–1941* (New York: Van Nostrand, 1960).

Lederer, Ivo, ed. *Russian Foreign Policy* (New Haven: Yale University Press, 1962).

Rubinstein, Alvin, ed. *The Foreign Policy of the Soviet Union*, 3rd ed. (New York: Random House, 1972).

Shulman, Marshall. *Stalin's Foreign Policy Reappraised* (Cambridge, Mass.: Harvard University Press, 1965).

CULTURE

Blakeley, Thomas J. *Soviet Philosophy: A General Introduction to Contemporary Soviet Thought* (New York: Humanities Press, 1964).

Johnson, Priscilla. *Khrushchev and the Arts*, ed. by Leopold Labedz (Cambridge, Mass.: M.I.T. Press).

Lindstrom, Thaïs. *Concise History of Russian Literature* (New York: New York University Press, 1966).

Miliukov, Paul. *Outlines of Russian Culture*, 3 vols. (Gloucester, Mass.: Peter Smith, 1942).

Saunders, George, ed. *Samizdat: Voices of the Soviet Opposition* (New York: Monad Press, 1974).

Spector, Ivar. *Golden Age of Russian Literature*, rev. ed. (Caldwell, Id.: Caxton, 1952).

Swayze, Harold. *Political Control of Literature in the USSR, 1946–1959* (Cambridge, Mass.: Harvard University Press, 1962).

Wiener, Leo, ed. *Anthology of Russian Literature*, 2 vols. (New York: Benjamin Blom, 1902–3).

Zenkovsky, V. V. *History of Russian Philosophy*, trans. by G. L. Kline, 2 vols. (New York: Columbia University Press, 1953).

INDEX